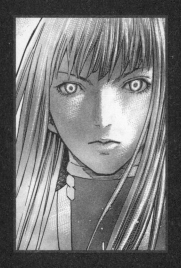

Norihiro Yagi won the 32nd Akatsuka Award for his debut work, *UNDEADMAN*, which appeared in *Monthly Shonen Jump* magazine and produced two sequels. His first serialized manga was his comedy *Angel Densetsu* (Angel Legend), which appeared in *Monthly Shonen Jump* from 1992 to 2000. His epic saga, *Claymore*, is running in *Monthly Jump Square* magazine.

In his spare time, Yagi enjoys things like the Japanese comedic duo Downtown, martial arts, games, driving, and hard rock music, but he doesn't consider these actual hobbies.

CLAYMORE VOL. 18
SHONEN JUMP ADVANCED Manga Edition

STORY AND ART BY
NORIHIRO YAGI

English Adaptation & Translation/Arashi Productions
Touch-up Art & Lettering/Sabrina Heep
Design/Amy Martin
Editor/Megan Bates

Printed in the U.S.A.

Published by VIZ Media, LLC
P.O. Box 77010
San Francisco, CA 94107

10 9 8 7 6 5 4 3 2 1
First printing, June 2011

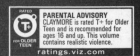

PARENTAL ADVISORY
CLAYMORE is rated T+ for Older
Teen and is recommended for
ages 16 and up. This volume
contains realistic violence.
ratings.viz.com

THE WORLD'S MOST
CUTTING-EDGE MANGA

SHONEN JUMP
ADVANCED
www.shonenjump.com

www.viz.com

SHONEN JUMP ADVANCED Manga Edition

Claymore

クレイモア

Vol. 18
The Ashes of Lautrec

Story and Art by **Norihiro Yagi**

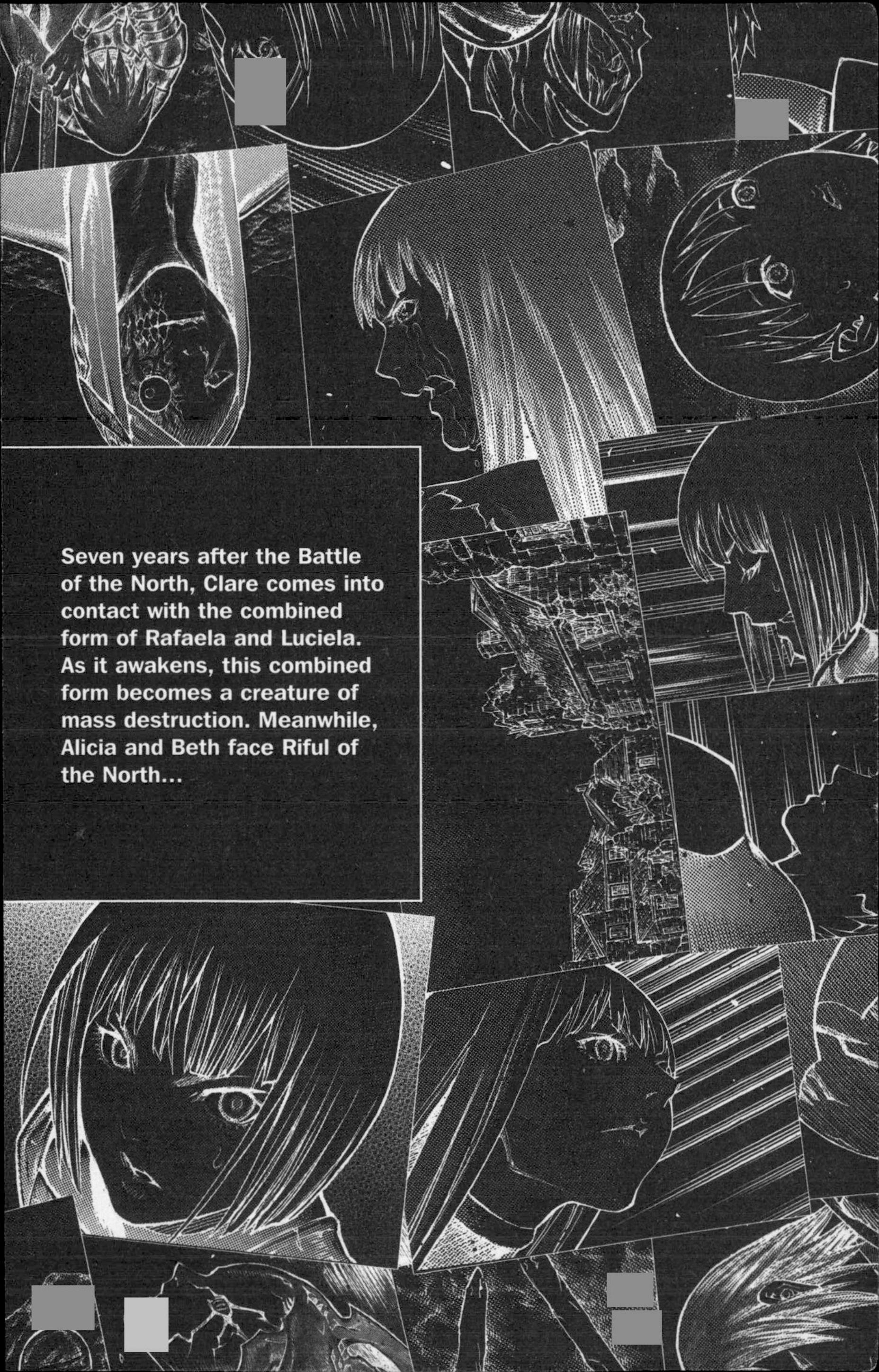

Seven years after the Battle of the North, Clare comes into contact with the combined form of Rafaela and Luciela. As it awakens, this combined form becomes a creature of mass destruction. Meanwhile, Alicia and Beth face Riful of the North...

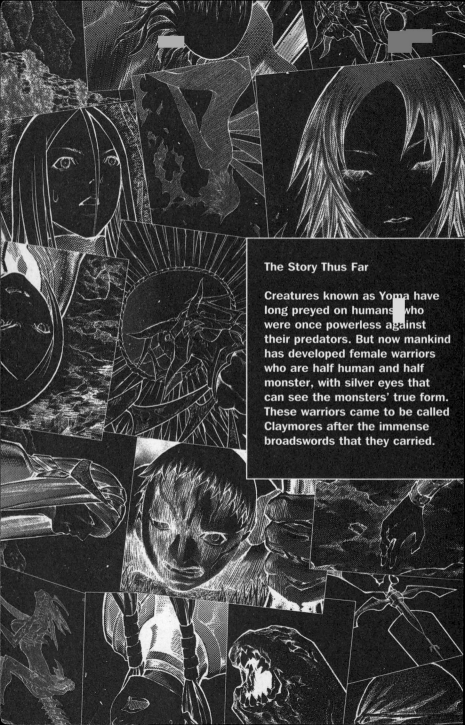

The Story Thus Far

Creatures known as Yoma have long preyed on humans who were once powerless against their predators. But now mankind has developed female warriors who are half human and half monster, with silver eyes that can see the monsters' true form. These warriors came to be called Claymores after the immense broadswords that they carried.

Claymore
クレイモア

Vol. 18

CONTENTS

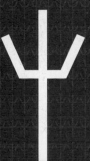

Scene 96: The Ashes of Lautrec, Part 1

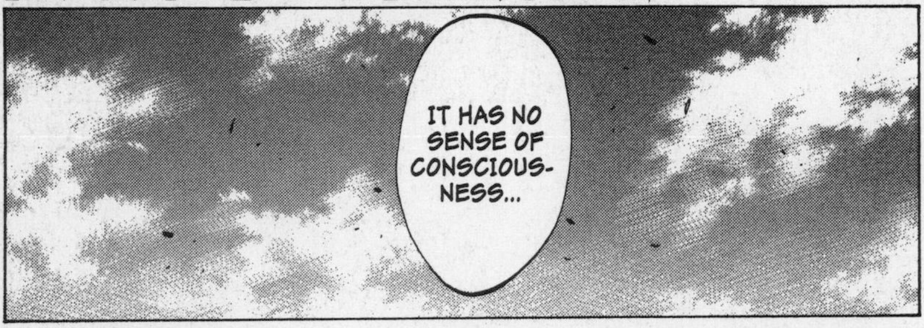
IT HAS NO SENSE OF CONSCIOUS- NESS...

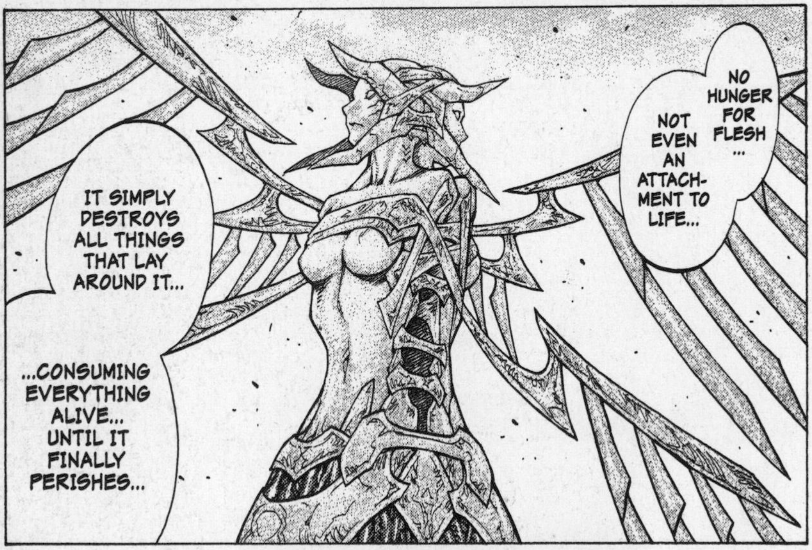
NO HUNGER FOR FLESH ...
NOT EVEN AN ATTACH- MENT TO LIFE...
IT SIMPLY DESTROYS ALL THINGS THAT LAY AROUND IT...
...CONSUMING EVERYTHING ALIVE... UNTIL IT FINALLY PERISHES...

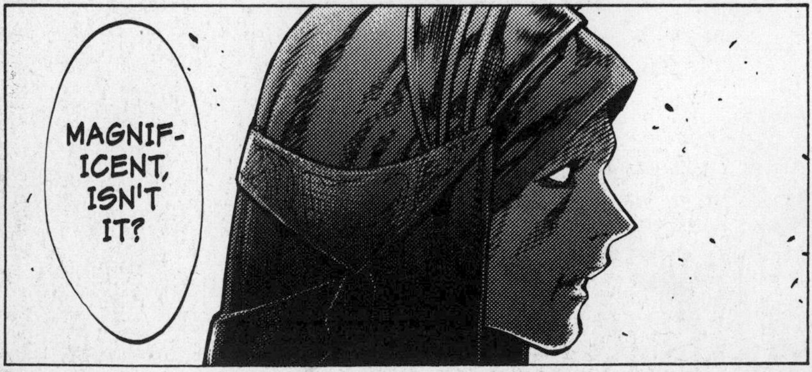
MAGNIF- ICENT, ISN'T IT?

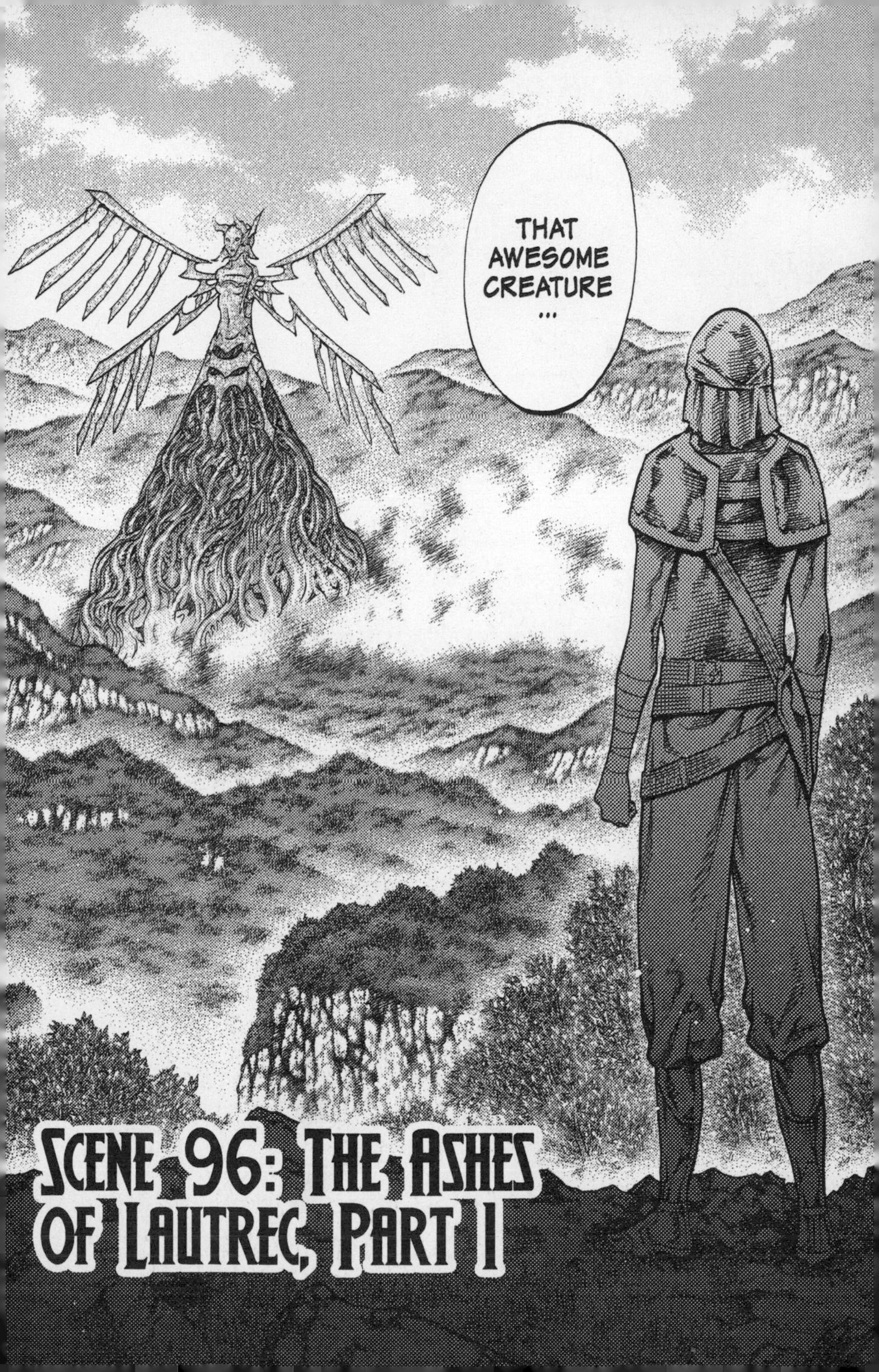
THAT AWESOME CREATURE ...

SCENE 96: THE ASHES OF LAUTREC, PART 1

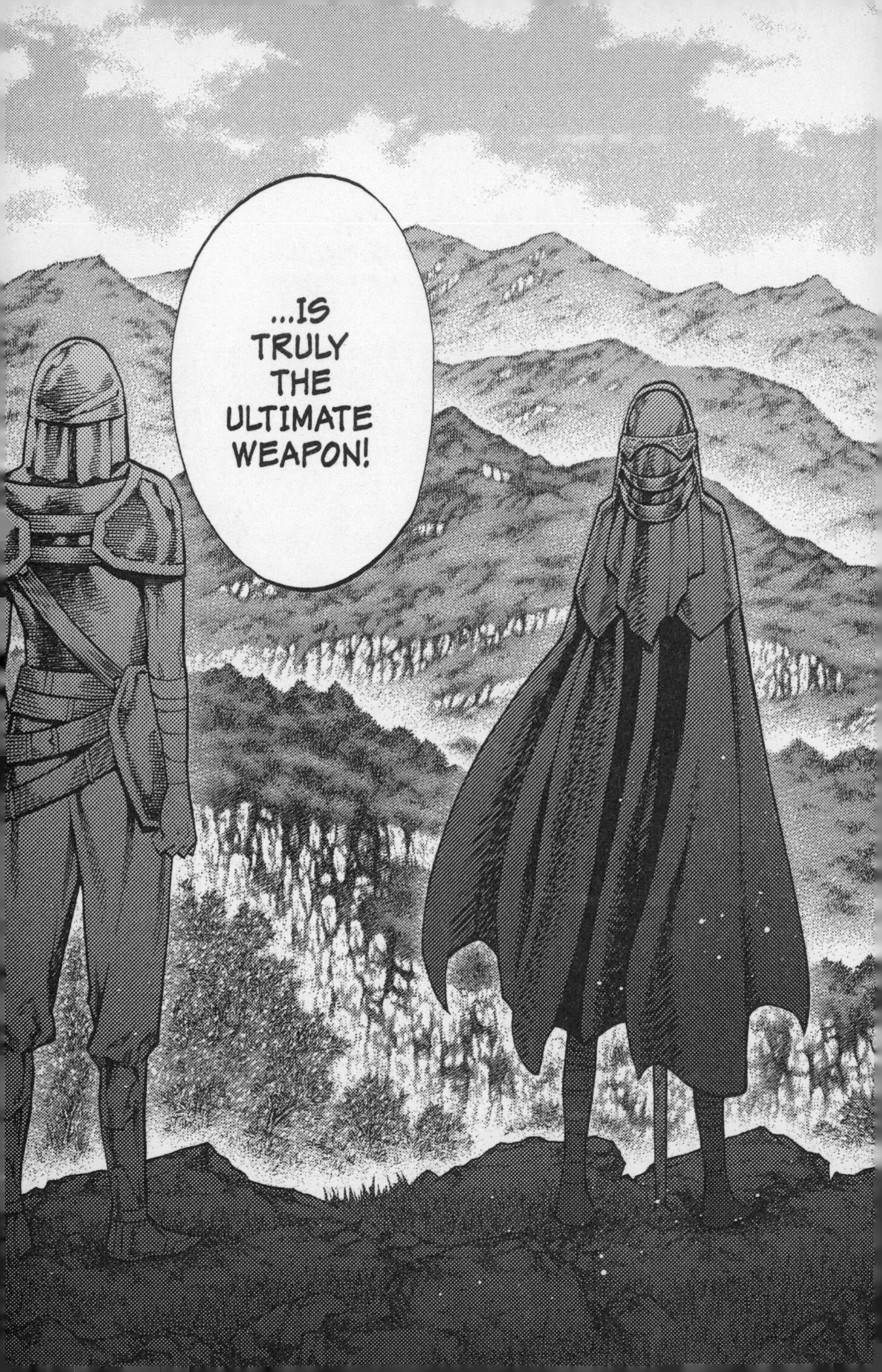
...IS TRULY THE ULTIMATE WEAPON!

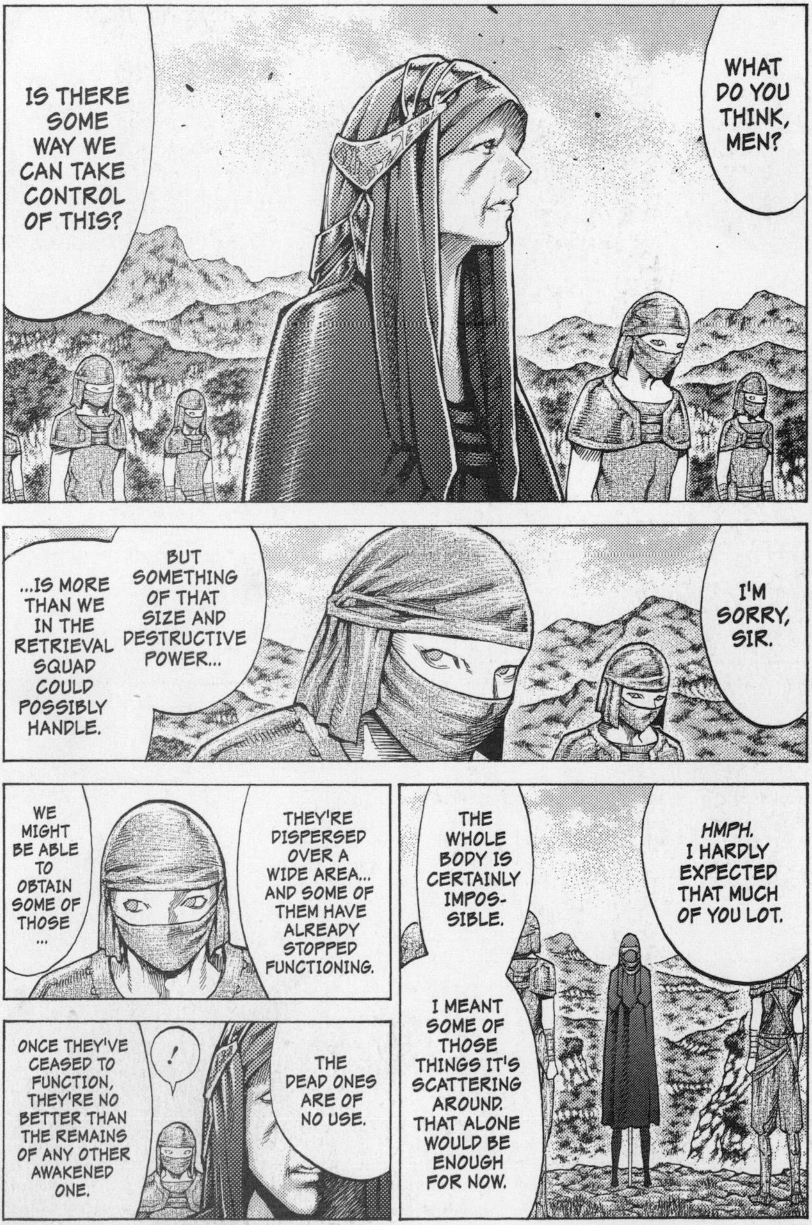
WHAT DO YOU THINK, MEN?
IS THERE SOME WAY WE CAN TAKE CONTROL OF THIS?
I'M SORRY, SIR.
BUT SOMETHING OF THAT SIZE AND DESTRUCTIVE POWER...
...IS MORE THAN WE IN THE RETRIEVAL SQUAD COULD POSSIBLY HANDLE.
HMPH. I HARDLY EXPECTED THAT MUCH OF YOU LOT.
THE WHOLE BODY IS CERTAINLY IMPOS-SIBLE.
I MEANT SOME OF THOSE THINGS IT'S SCATTERING AROUND. THAT ALONE WOULD BE ENOUGH FOR NOW.
THEY'RE DISPERSED OVER A WIDE AREA... AND SOME OF THEM HAVE ALREADY STOPPED FUNCTIONING.
WE MIGHT BE ABLE TO OBTAIN SOME OF THOSE ...
THE DEAD ONES ARE OF NO USE.
!
ONCE THEY'VE CEASED TO FUNCTION, THEY'RE NO BETTER THAN THE REMAINS OF ANY OTHER AWAKENED ONE.

READ THIS WAY

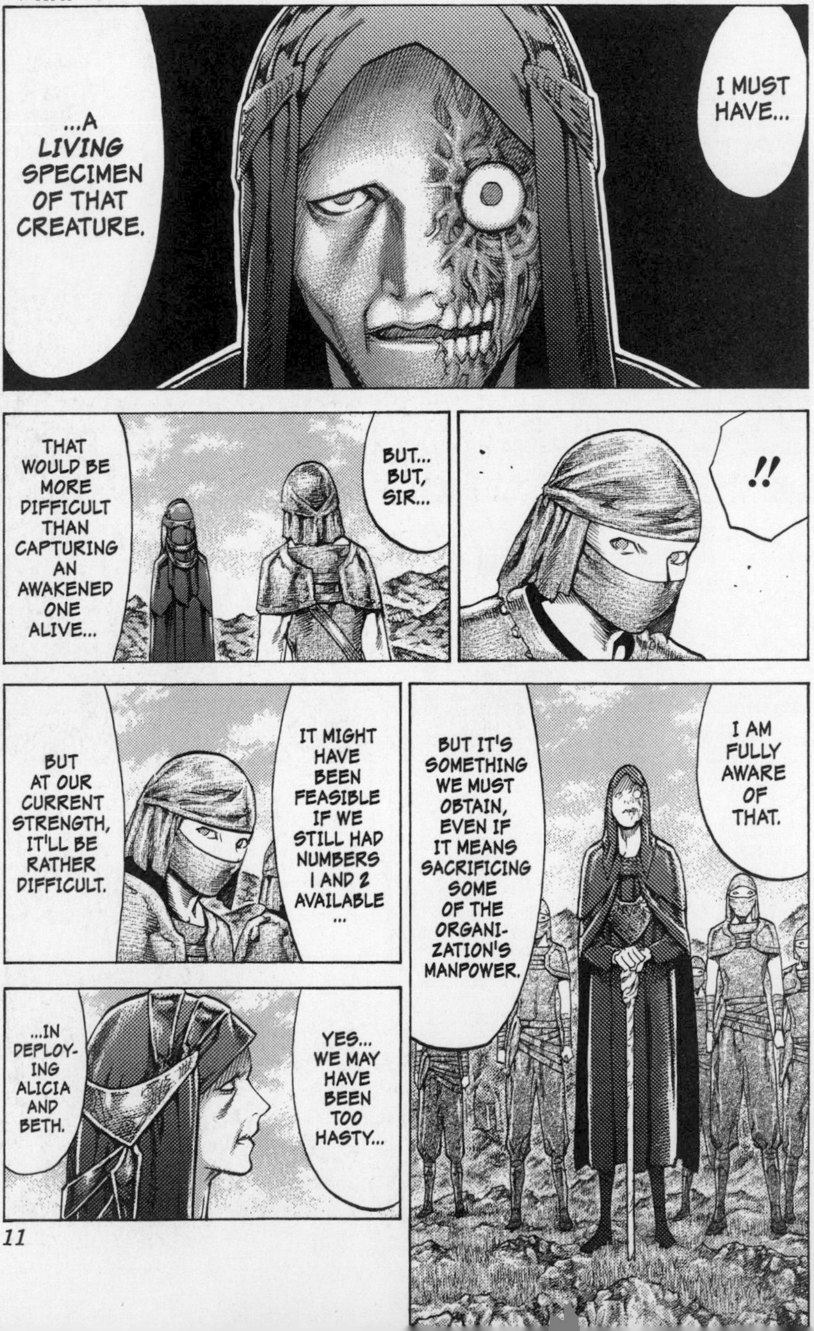
I MUST HAVE...
...A LIVING SPECIMEN OF THAT CREATURE.
!!
BUT... BUT, SIR...
THAT WOULD BE MORE DIFFICULT THAN CAPTURING AN AWAKENED ONE ALIVE...
I AM FULLY AWARE OF THAT.
BUT IT'S SOMETHING WE MUST OBTAIN, EVEN IF IT MEANS SACRIFICING SOME OF THE ORGANIZATION'S MANPOWER.
IT MIGHT HAVE BEEN FEASIBLE IF WE STILL HAD NUMBERS 1 AND 2 AVAILABLE...
BUT AT OUR CURRENT STRENGTH, IT'LL BE RATHER DIFFICULT.
YES... WE MAY HAVE BEEN TOO HASTY...
...IN DEPLOYING ALICIA AND BETH.

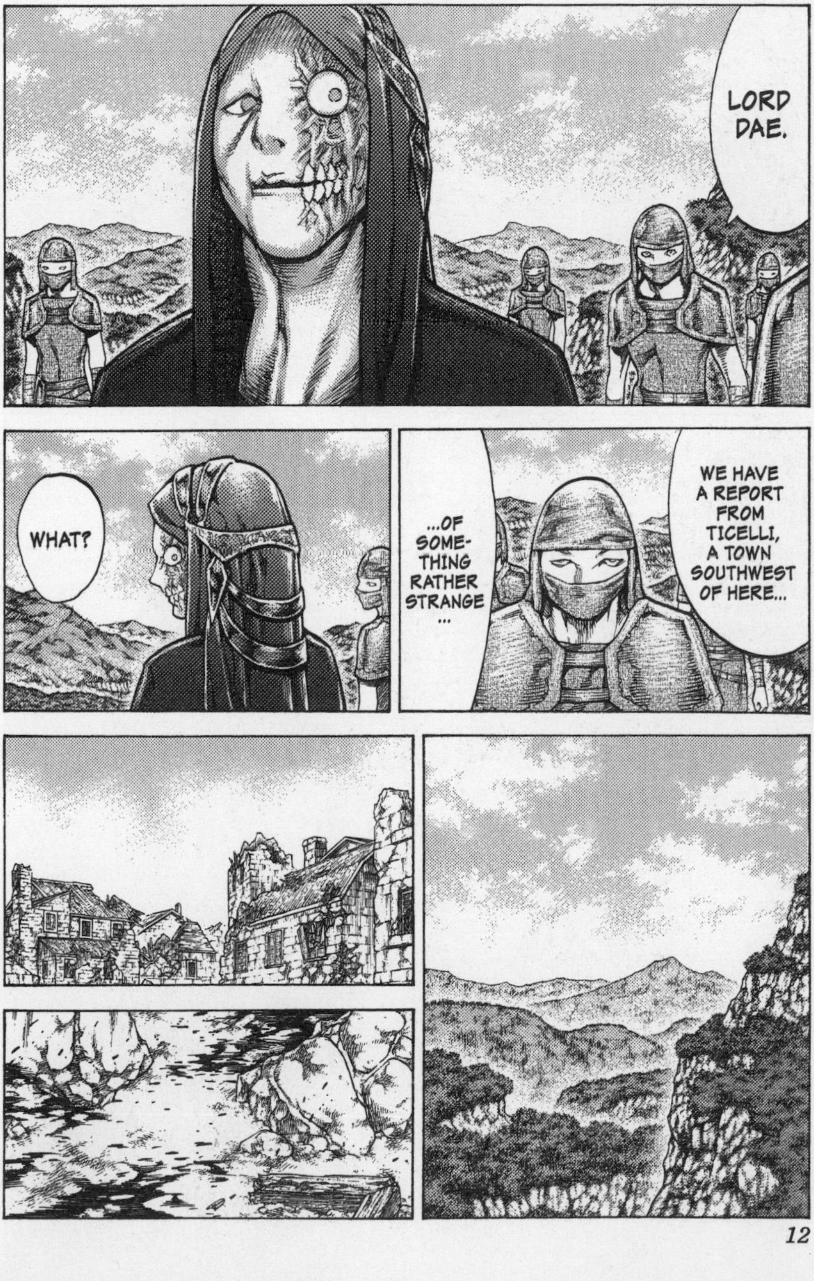
LORD DAE.
WE HAVE A REPORT FROM TICELLI, A TOWN SOUTHWEST OF HERE...
...OF SOME-THING RATHER STRANGE...
WHAT?

READ THIS WAY

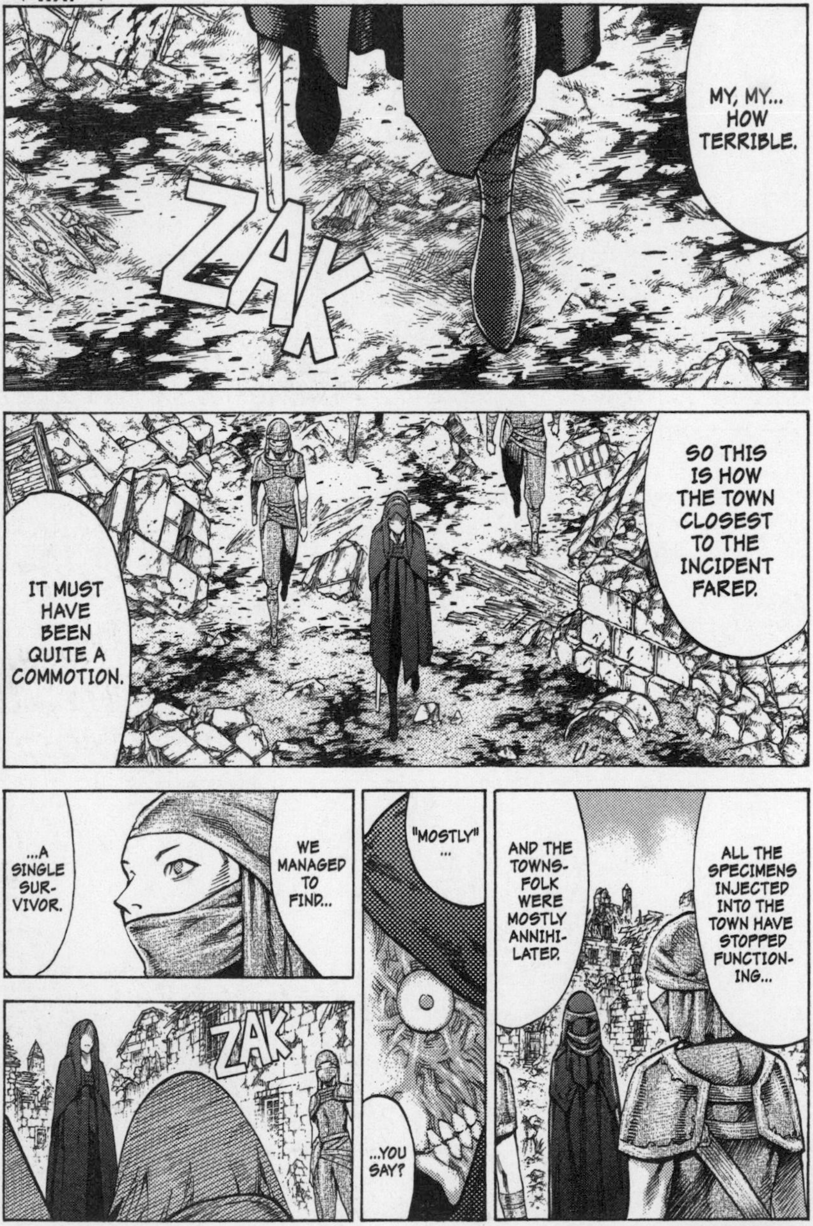
MY, MY... HOW TERRIBLE.
ZAK
SO THIS IS HOW THE TOWN CLOSEST TO THE INCIDENT FARED.
IT MUST HAVE BEEN QUITE A COMMOTION.
ALL THE SPECIMENS INJECTED INTO THE TOWN HAVE STOPPED FUNCTION-ING...
AND THE TOWNS-FOLK WERE MOSTLY ANNIHI-LATED.
"MOSTLY" ...
...YOU SAY?
WE MANAGED TO FIND...
...A SINGLE SUR-VIVOR.
ZAK

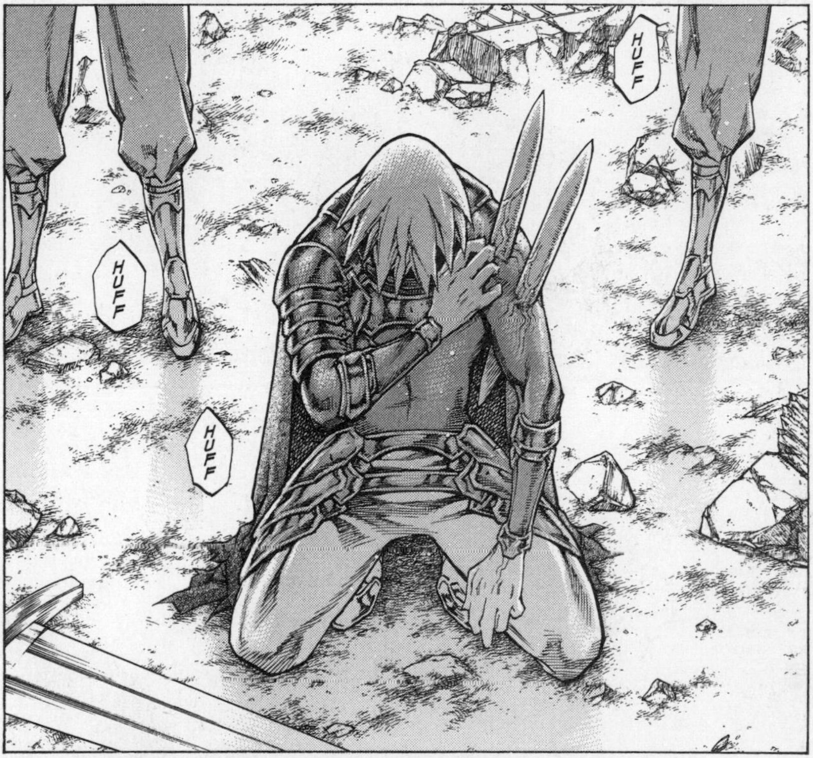
HUFF
HUFF
HUFF

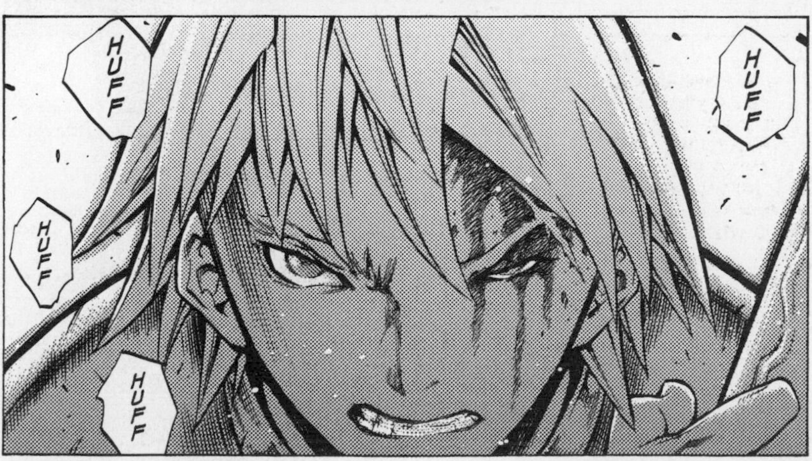
HUFF
HUFF
HUFF
HUFF

READ THIS WAY

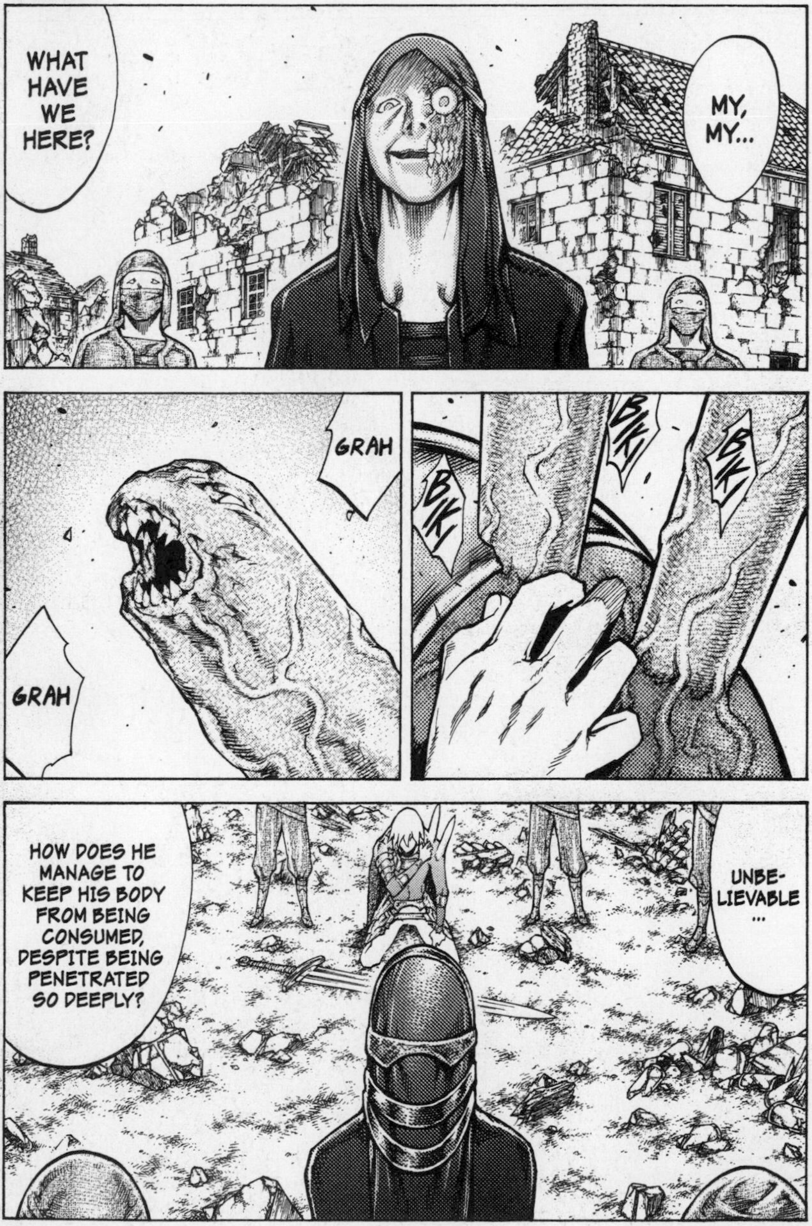

MY, MY...
WHAT HAVE WE HERE?
BIKI
BIKI
BIKI
GRAH
GRAH
UNBE-LIEVABLE...
HOW DOES HE MANAGE TO KEEP HIS BODY FROM BEING CONSUMED, DESPITE BEING PENETRATED SO DEEPLY?

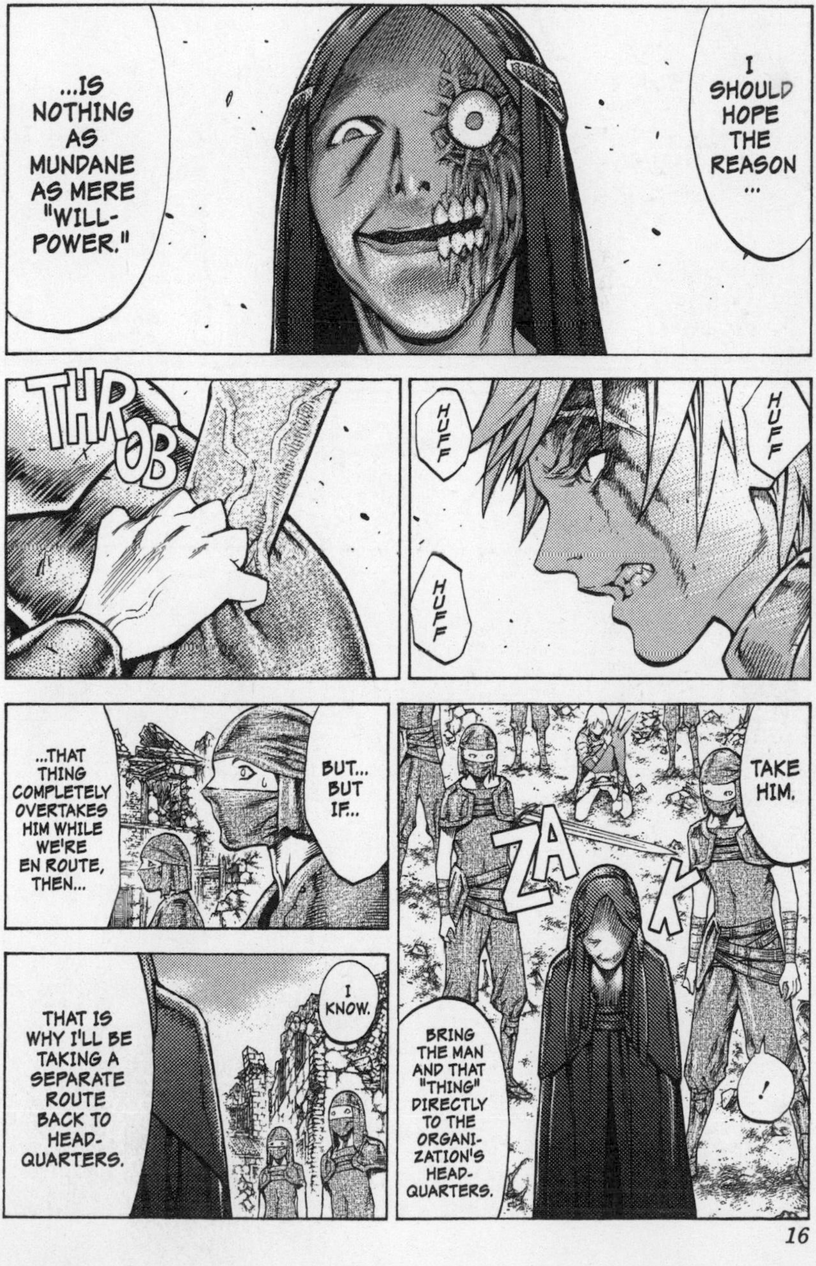
I SHOULD HOPE THE REASON ...
...IS NOTHING AS MUNDANE AS MERE "WILL-POWER."
HUFF
HUFF
HUFF
THROB
TAKE HIM.
ZAK
!
BRING THE MAN AND THAT "THING" DIRECTLY TO THE ORGANIZATION'S HEADQUARTERS.
BUT... BUT IF...
...THAT THING COMPLETELY OVERTAKES HIM WHILE WE'RE EN ROUTE, THEN...
I KNOW.
THAT IS WHY I'LL BE TAKING A SEPARATE ROUTE BACK TO HEADQUARTERS.

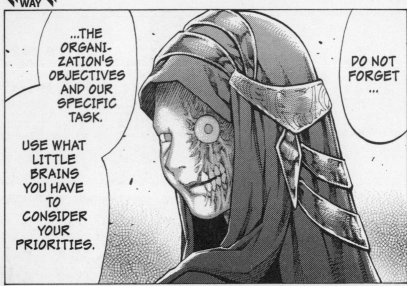

...THE ORGANIZATION'S OBJECTIVES AND OUR SPECIFIC TASK.

USE WHAT LITTLE BRAINS YOU HAVE TO CONSIDER YOUR PRIORITIES.

DO NOT FORGET...

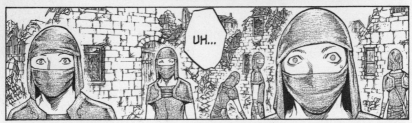

UH...

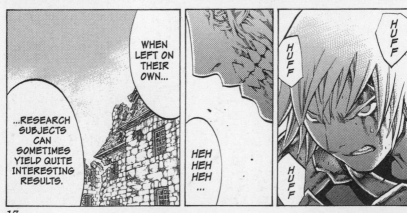

WHEN LEFT ON THEIR OWN...

...RESEARCH SUBJECTS CAN SOMETIMES YIELD QUITE INTERESTING RESULTS.

HEH HEH HEH ...

HUFF

HUFF

HUFF

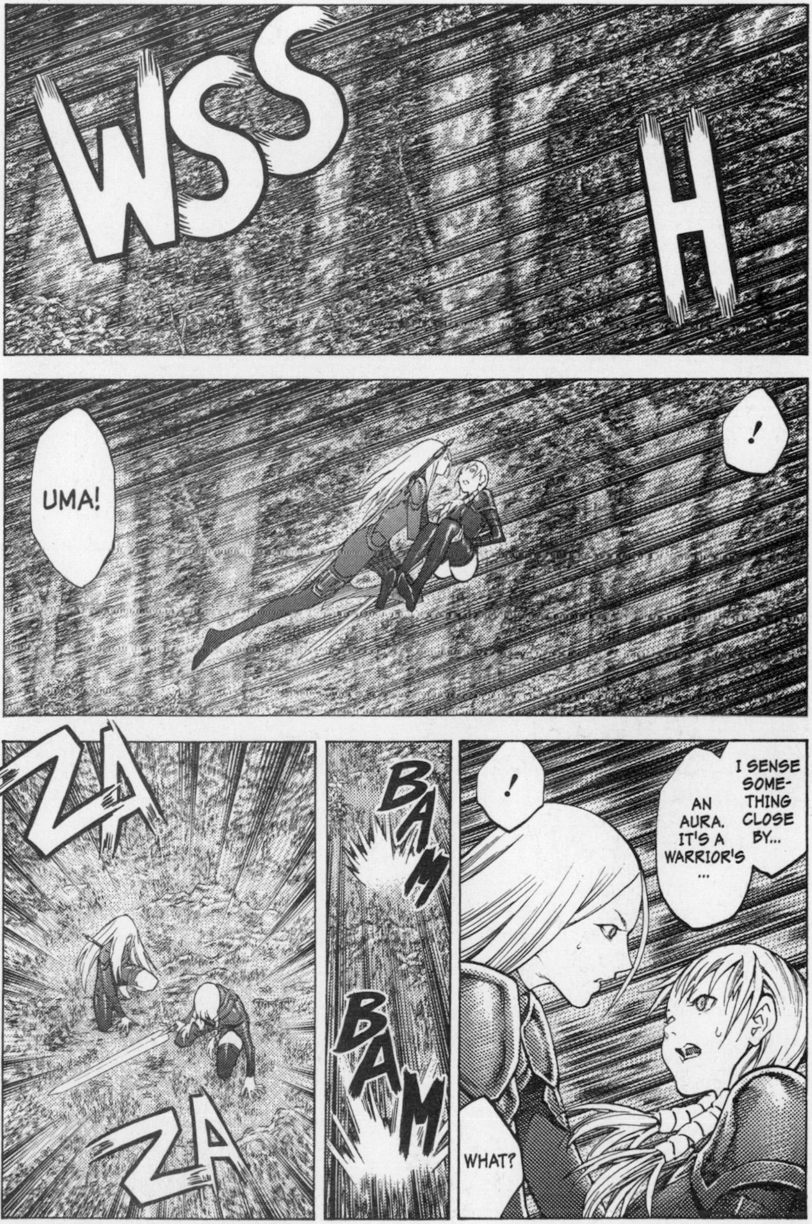
WSSH
!
UMA!
!
I SENSE SOME-THING CLOSE BY...
AN AURA. IT'S A WARRIOR'S ...
WHAT?
BAM BAM
BAM BAM
ZA
ZA

READ THIS WAY

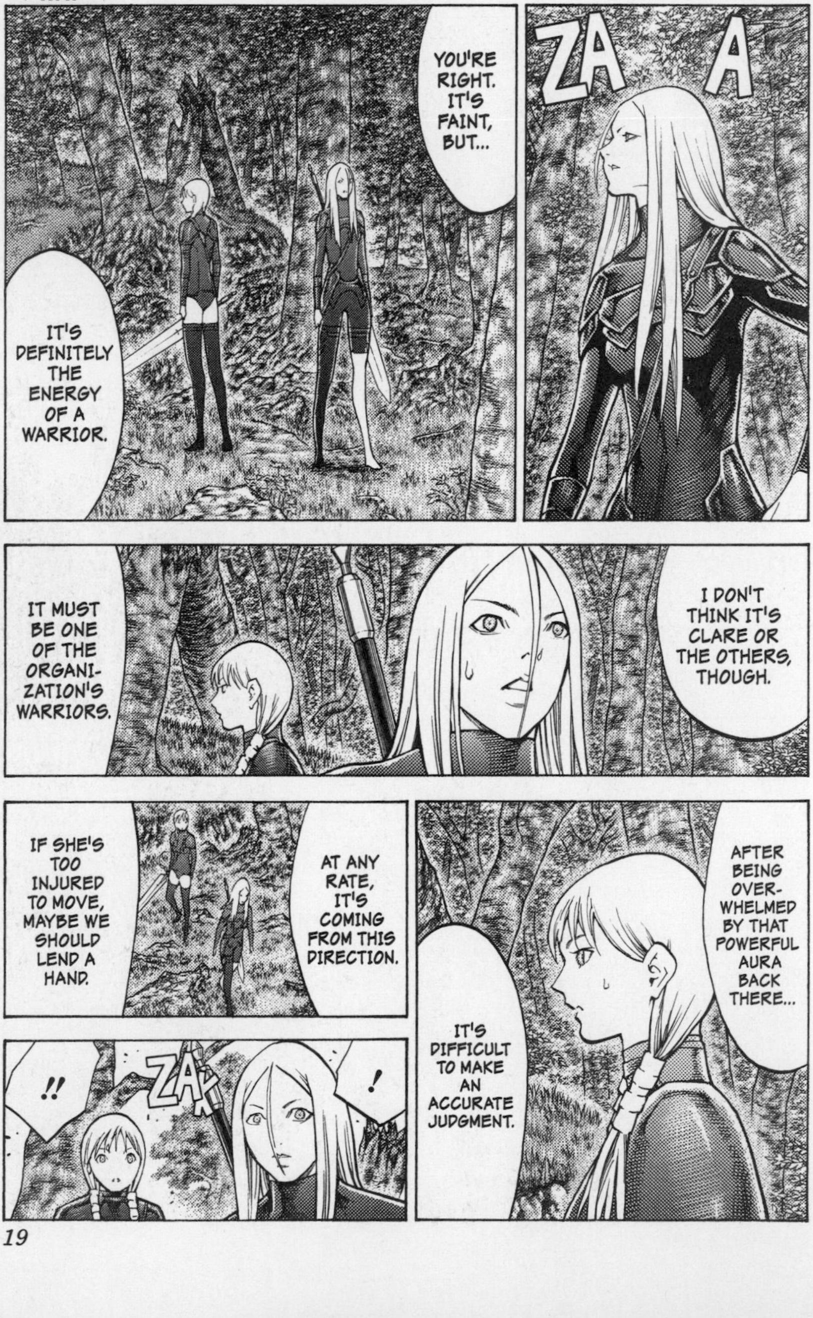
ZA A
YOU'RE RIGHT. IT'S FAINT, BUT...
IT'S DEFINITELY THE ENERGY OF A WARRIOR.
I DON'T THINK IT'S CLARE OR THE OTHERS, THOUGH.
IT MUST BE ONE OF THE ORGANI-ZATION'S WARRIORS.
AFTER BEING OVER-WHELMED BY THAT POWERFUL AURA BACK THERE...
IT'S DIFFICULT TO MAKE AN ACCURATE JUDGMENT.
AT ANY RATE, IT'S COMING FROM THIS DIRECTION.
IF SHE'S TOO INJURED TO MOVE, MAYBE WE SHOULD LEND A HAND.
!
ZA
!!

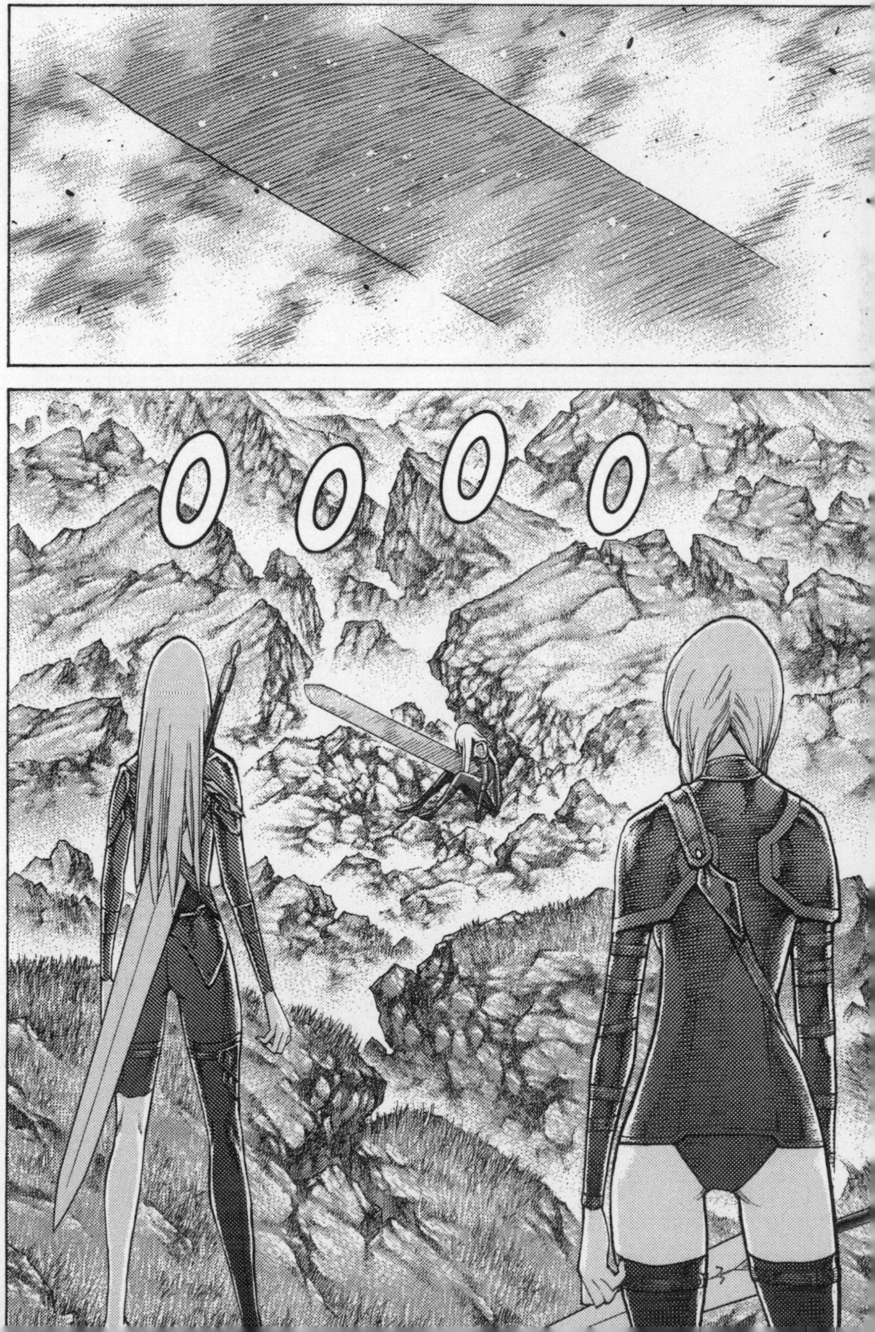
OOOO

READ THIS WAY

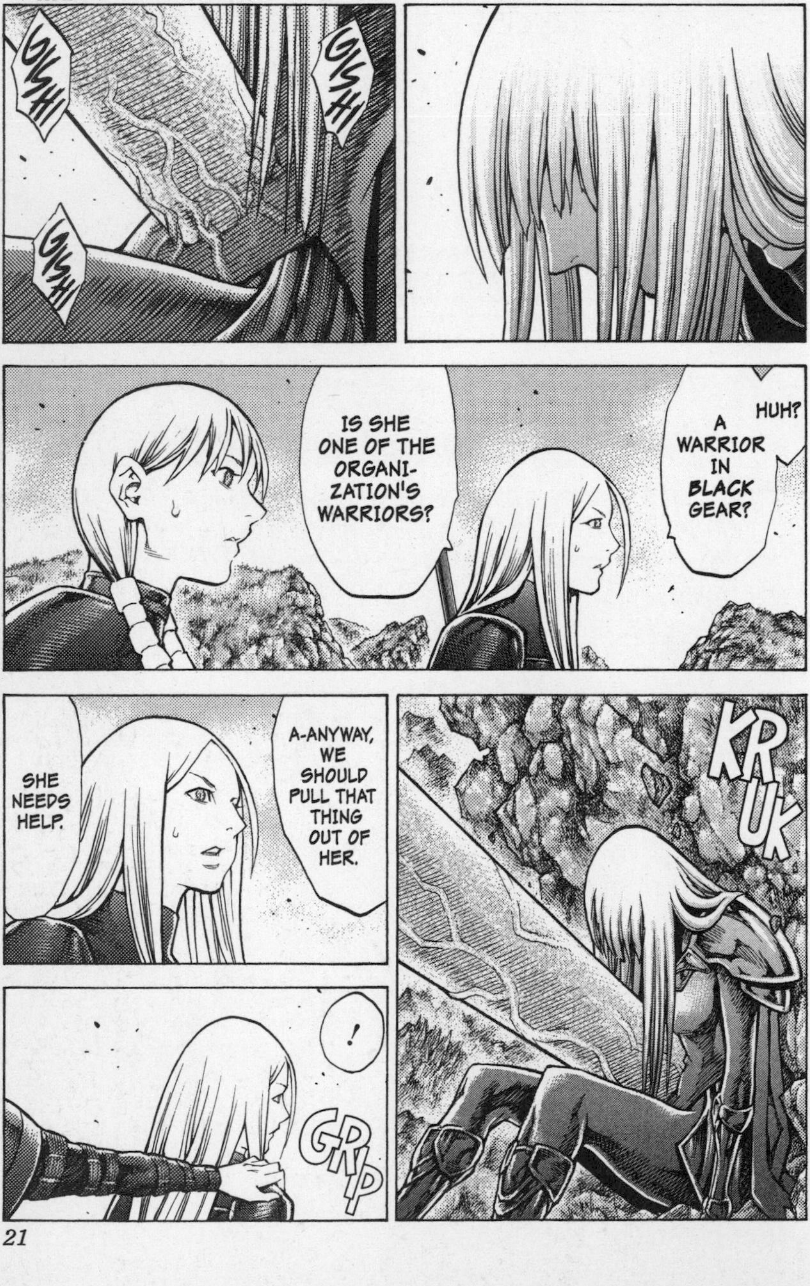
GISHI
GISHI
GISHI
HUH?
A WARRIOR IN BLACK GEAR?
IS SHE ONE OF THE ORGANIZATION'S WARRIORS?
KRUK
A-ANYWAY, WE SHOULD PULL THAT THING OUT OF HER.
SHE NEEDS HELP.
!
GRIP

N-NO... NO, DON'T.
UMA...
WE'RE ...
WE'RE TOO LATE...
WHAT?
CYNTHIA?
BIKU
GRIP
KRUK
BAKI
BAKI
ZU ZU
ZU
ZU ZU ZU

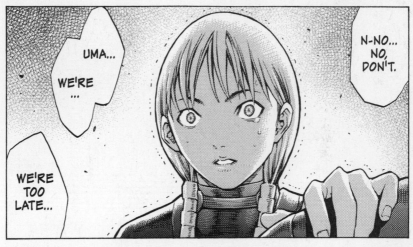

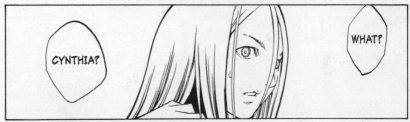

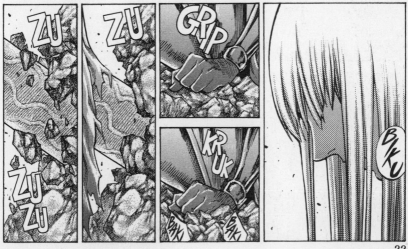

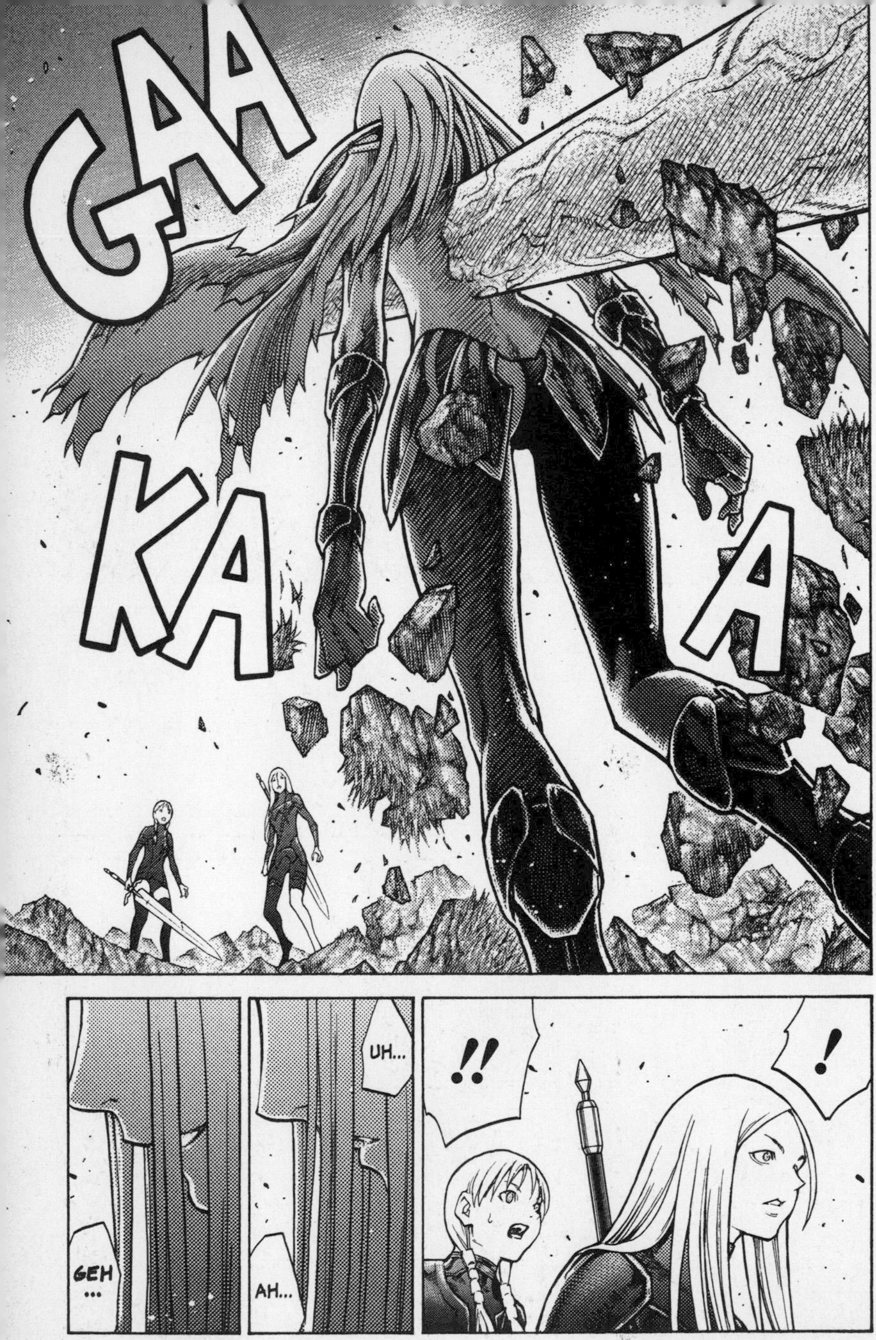
GAA
KA
A
!
!!
UH...
AH...
GEH
...

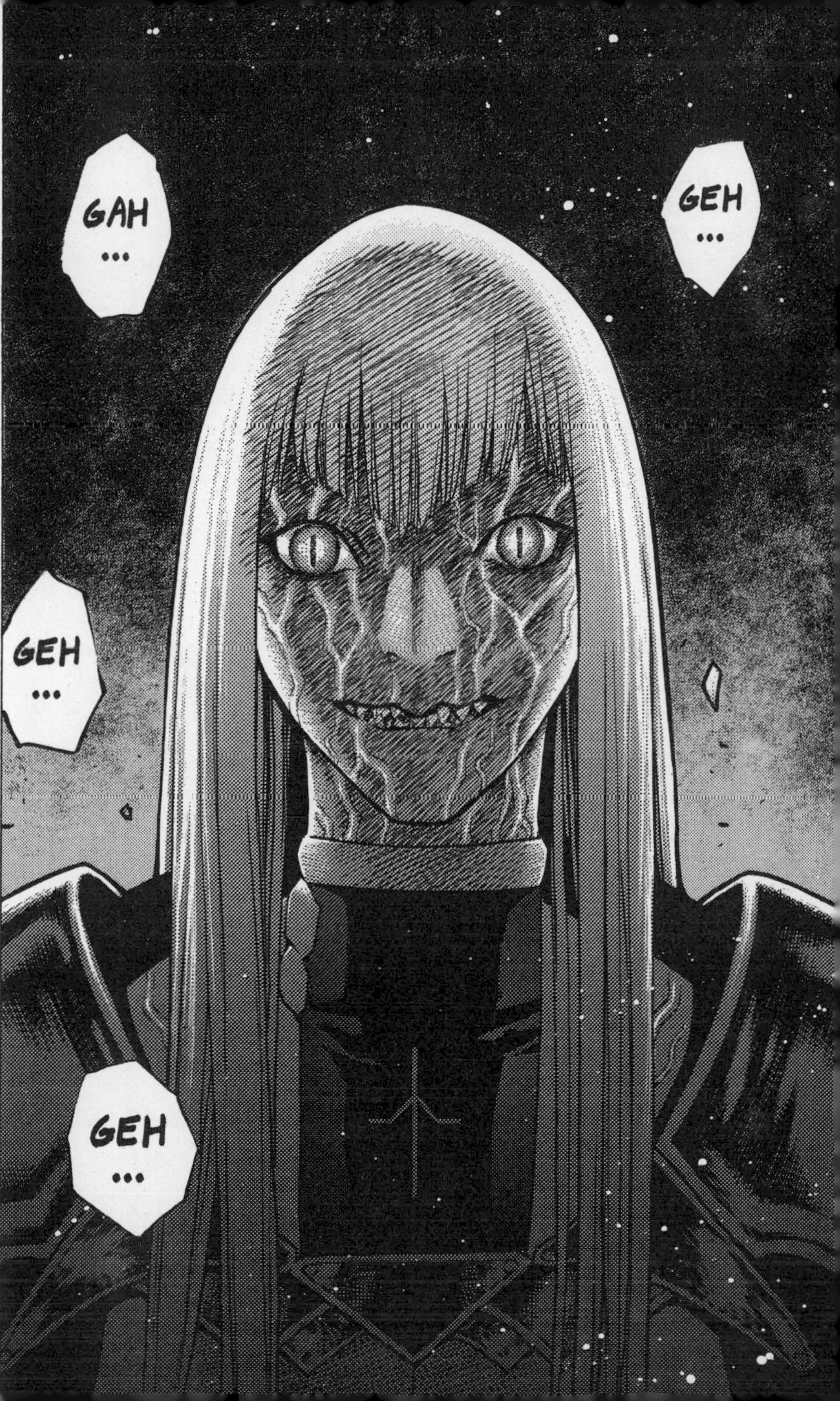
GEH ...
GAH ...
GEH ...
GEH ...

READ THIS WAY

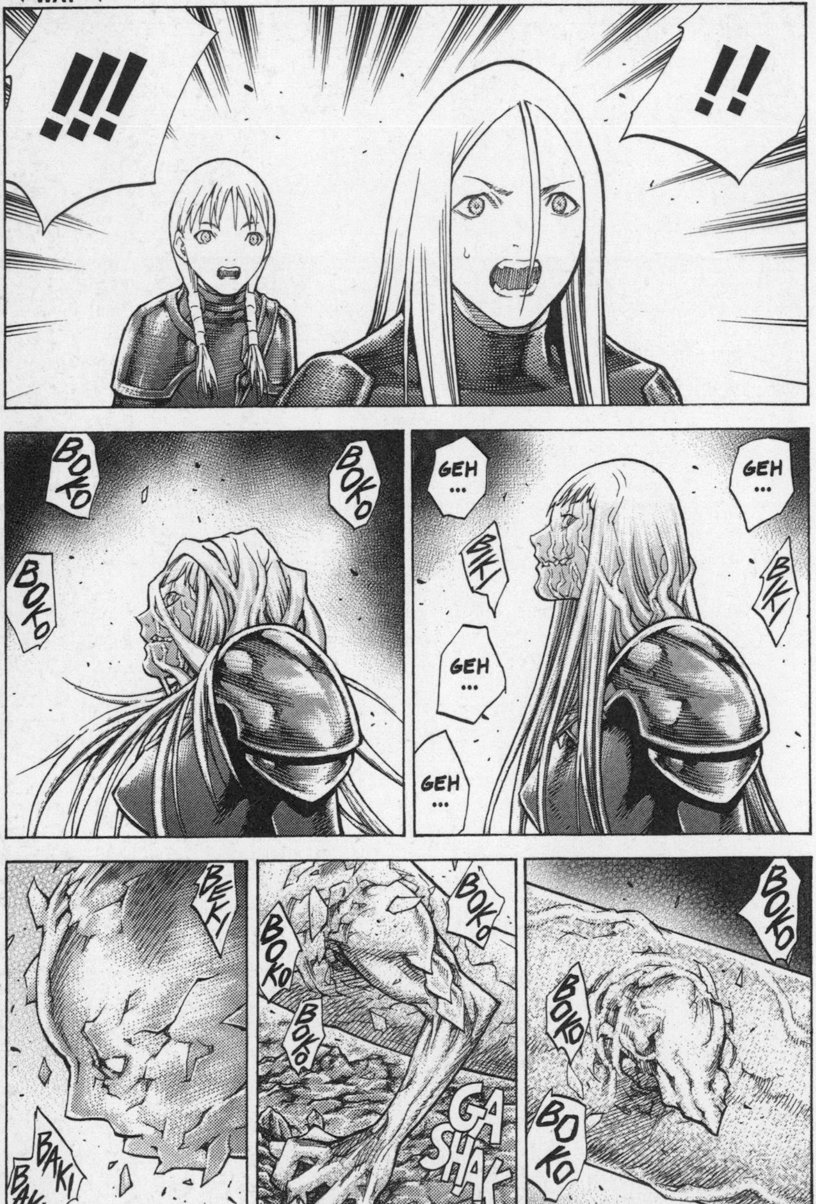
!!
!!!
GEH...
BIKI
GEH...
BIKI
GEH...
GEH...
BOKO
BOKO
BOKO
BOKO
BOKO
BOKO
BOKO
BOKO
BOKO
GASHAK
BEKI
BAKI BAKI

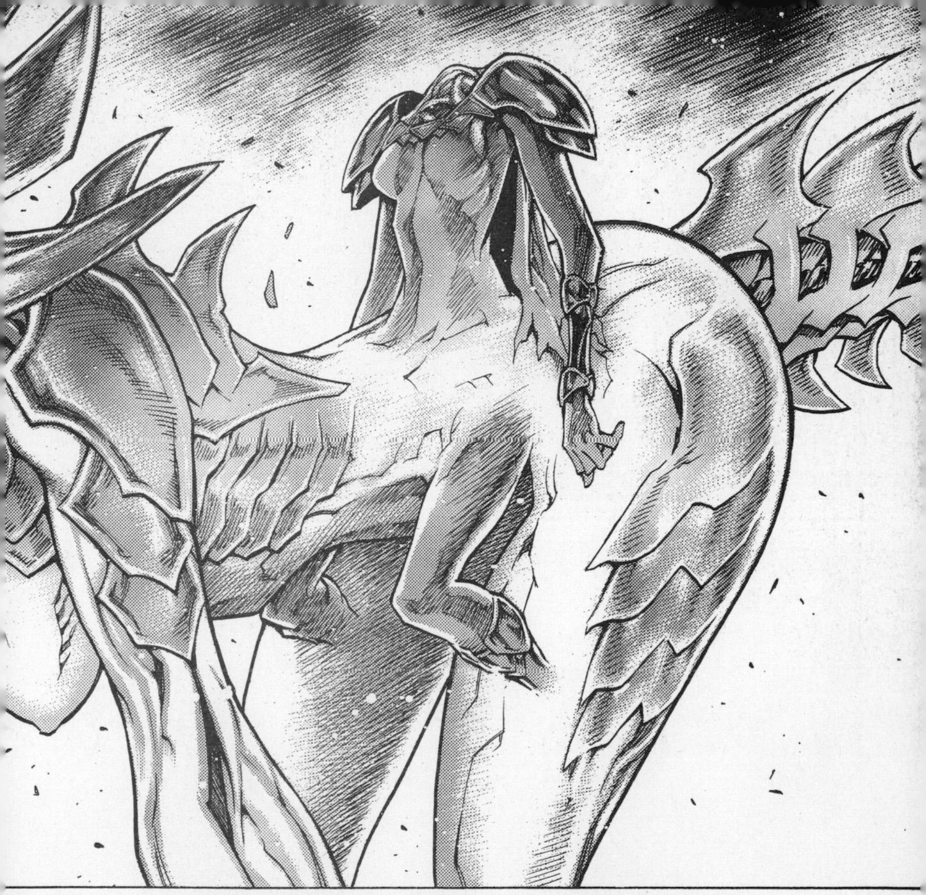
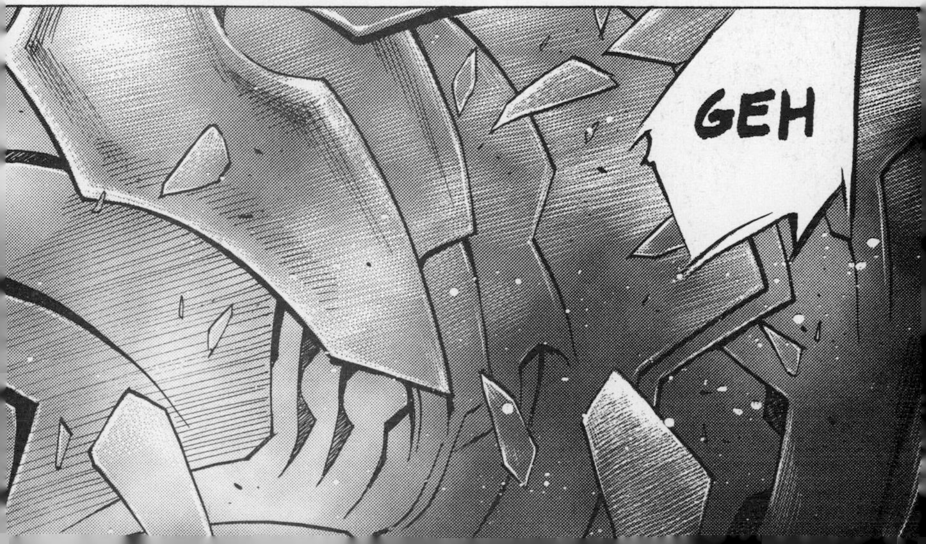
GEH

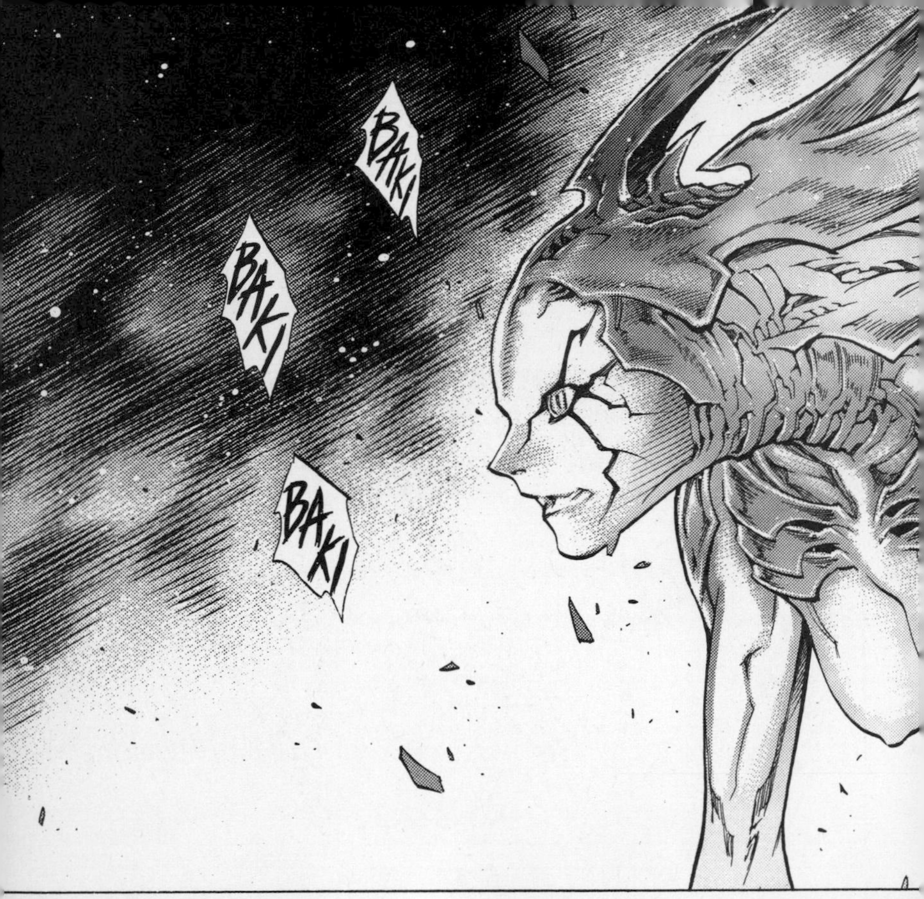
BAKI
BAKI
BAKI
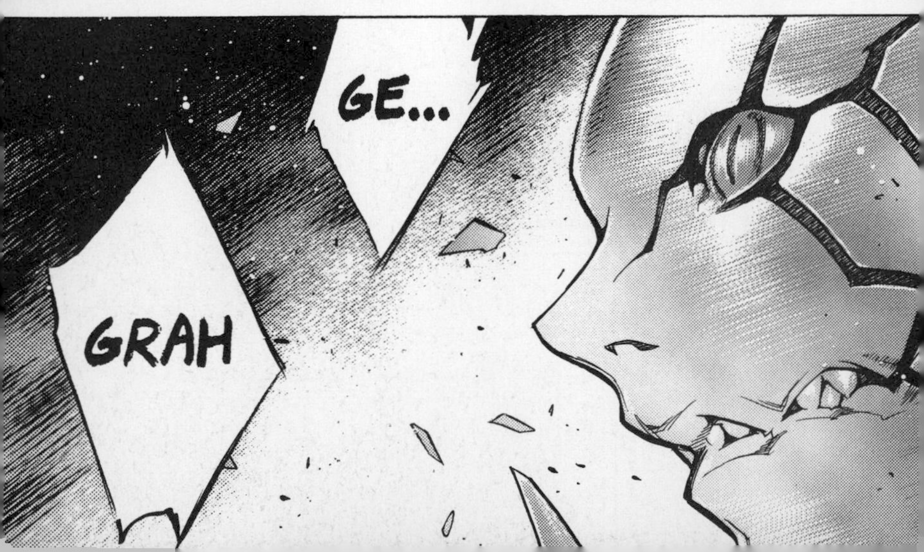
GE...
GRAH

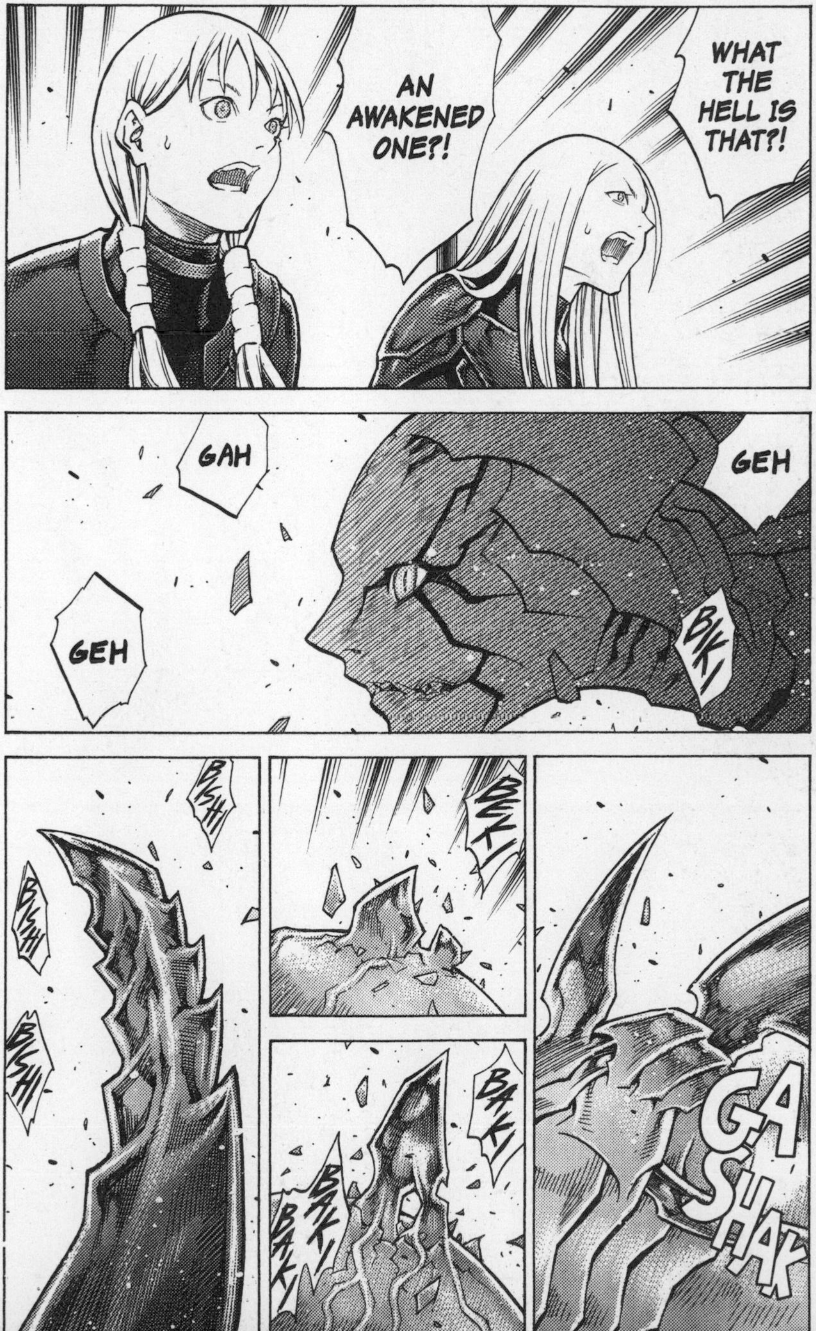
WHAT THE HELL IS THAT?!
AN AWAKENED ONE?!
GEH
BIKI
GAH
GEH
GASHAK
BEKI
BAKI
BAKI
BAKI
BISHI
BISHI
BISHI

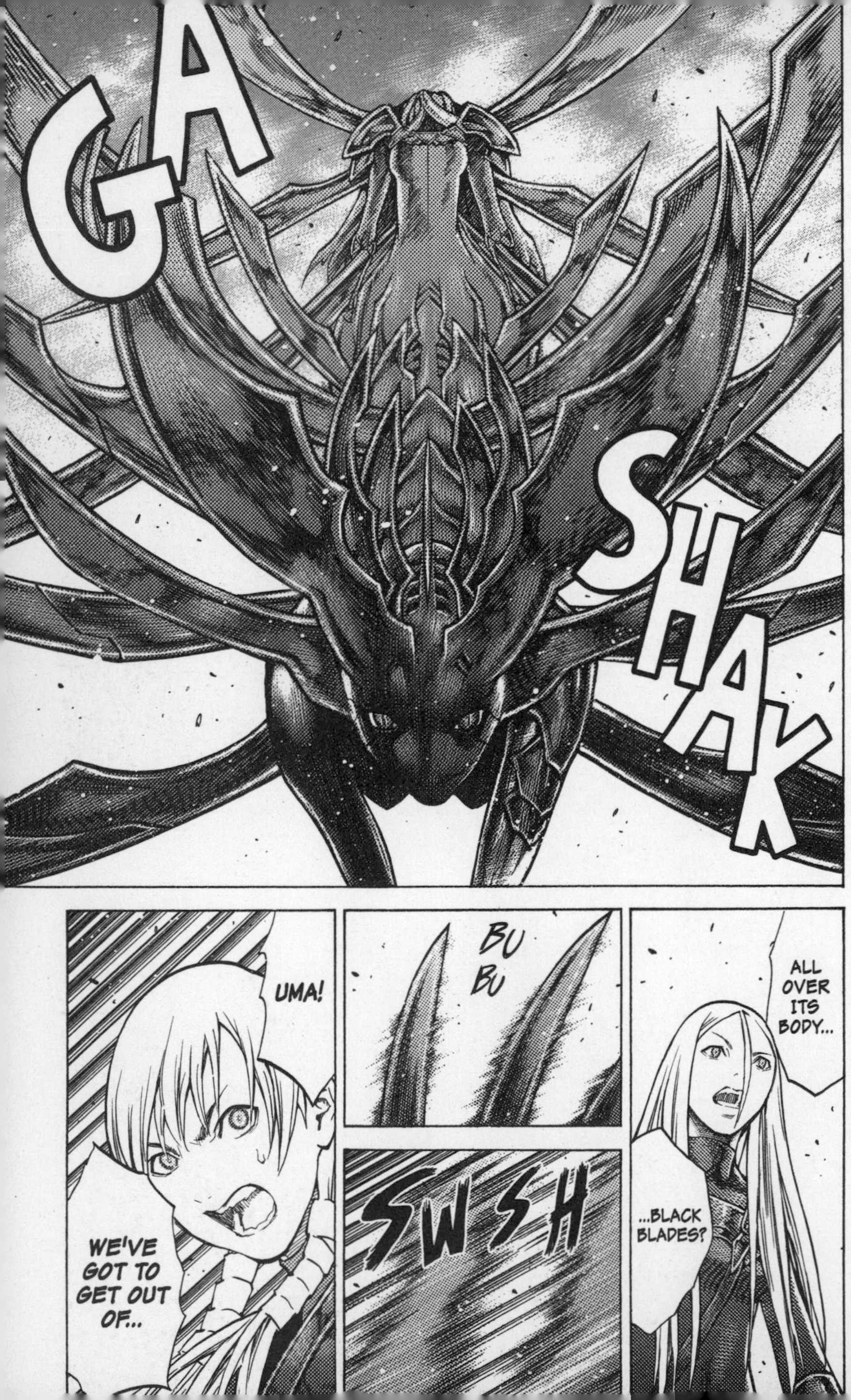
GA
SHAK
ALL OVER ITS BODY...
...BLACK BLADES?
BU BU
SWSH
UMA!
WE'VE GOT TO GET OUT OF...

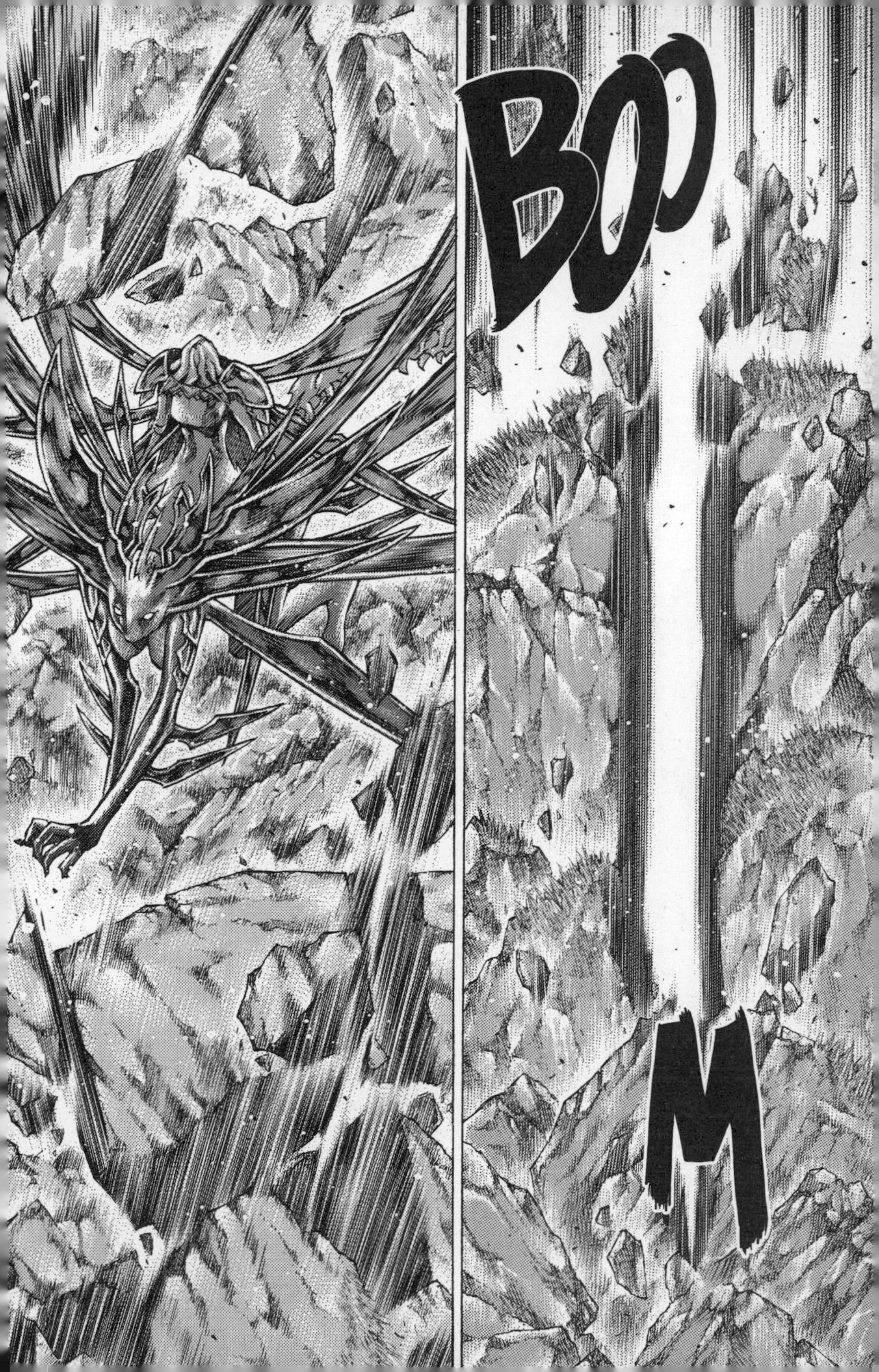
BOOOM

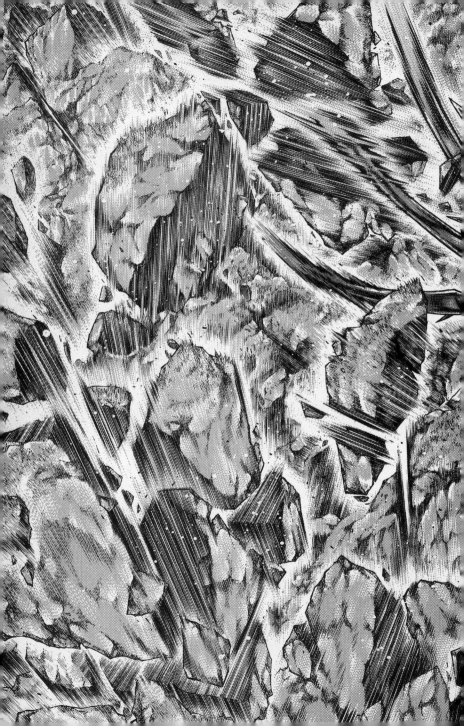

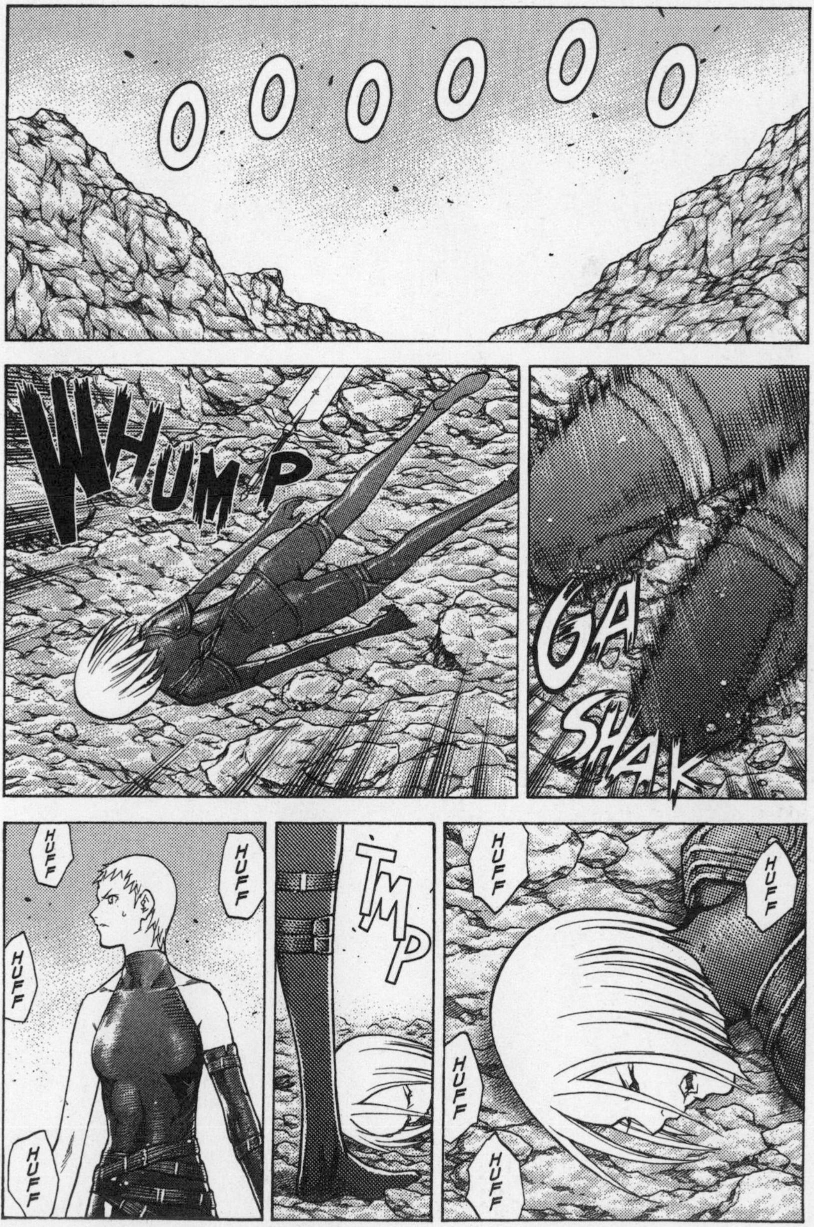
OOOOOO
GA SHAK
WHUMP
HUFF
HUFF
HUFF
HUFF
TMP
HUFF
HUFF
HUFF
HUFF

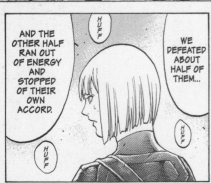

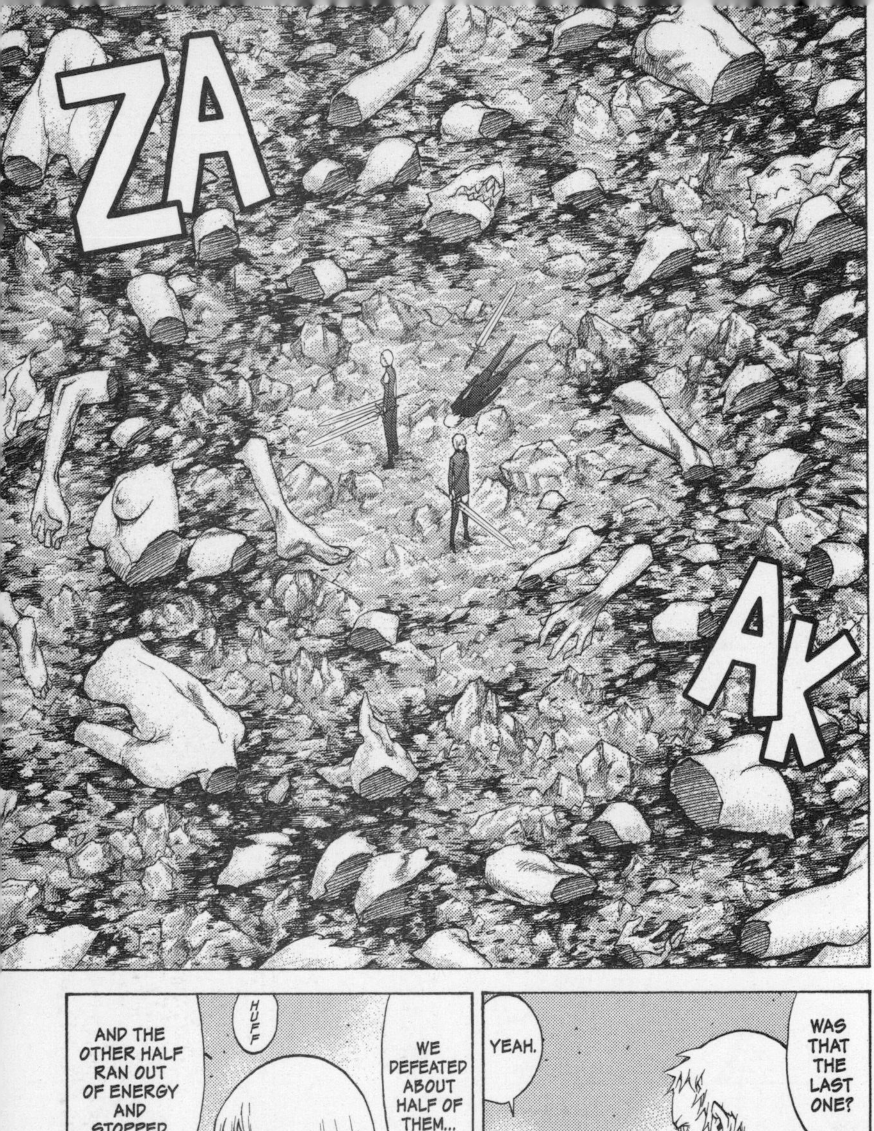
ZA
AK
WAS THAT THE LAST ONE?
YEAH.
HUFF
WE DEFEATED ABOUT HALF OF THEM...
AND THE OTHER HALF RAN OUT OF ENERGY AND STOPPED OF THEIR OWN ACCORD.
HUFF
HUFF

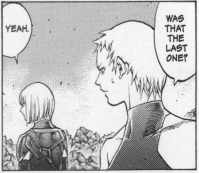

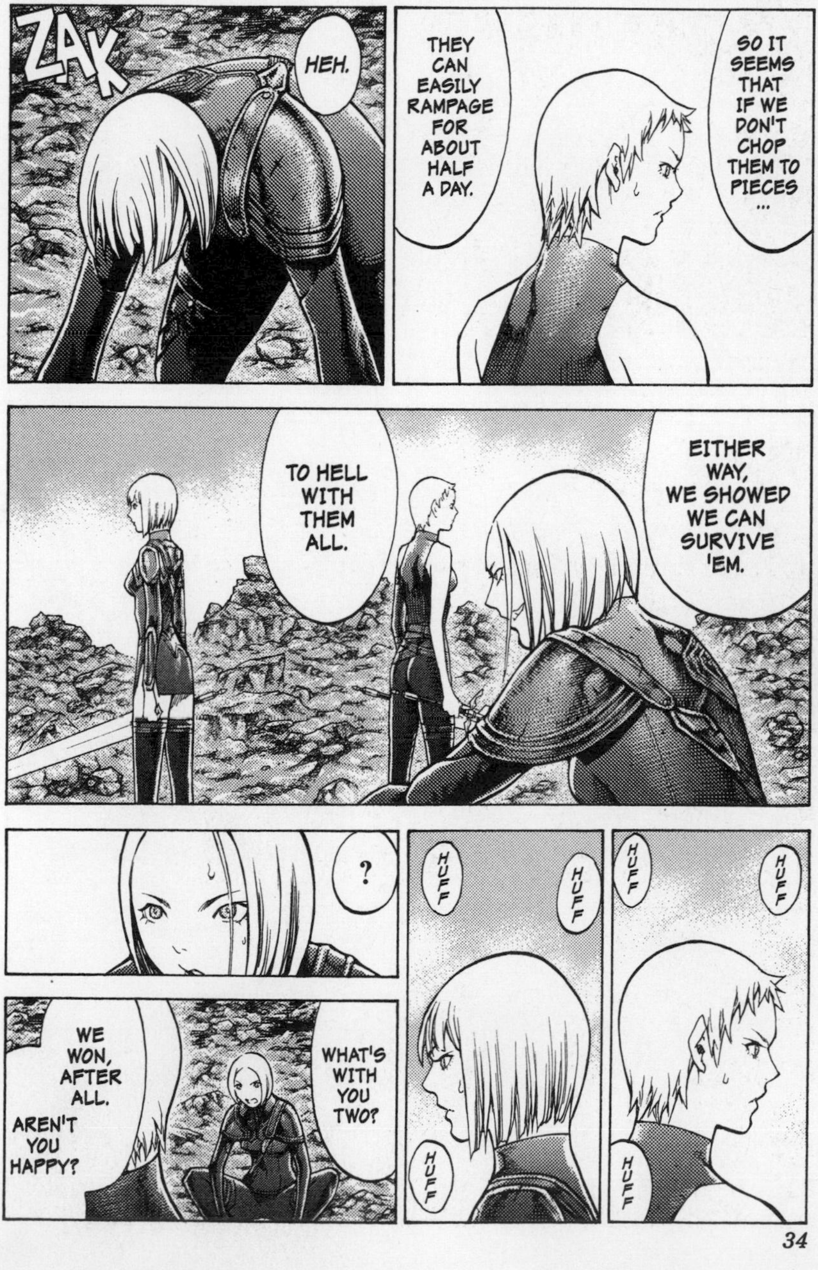
SO IT SEEMS THAT IF WE DON'T CHOP THEM TO PIECES ...
THEY CAN EASILY RAMPAGE FOR ABOUT HALF A DAY.
ZAK
HEH.
EITHER WAY, WE SHOWED WE CAN SURVIVE 'EM.
TO HELL WITH THEM ALL.
HUFF
HUFF
HUFF
HUFF
HUFF
HUFF
?
WHAT'S WITH YOU TWO?
WE WON, AFTER ALL.
AREN'T YOU HAPPY?

READ THIS WAY

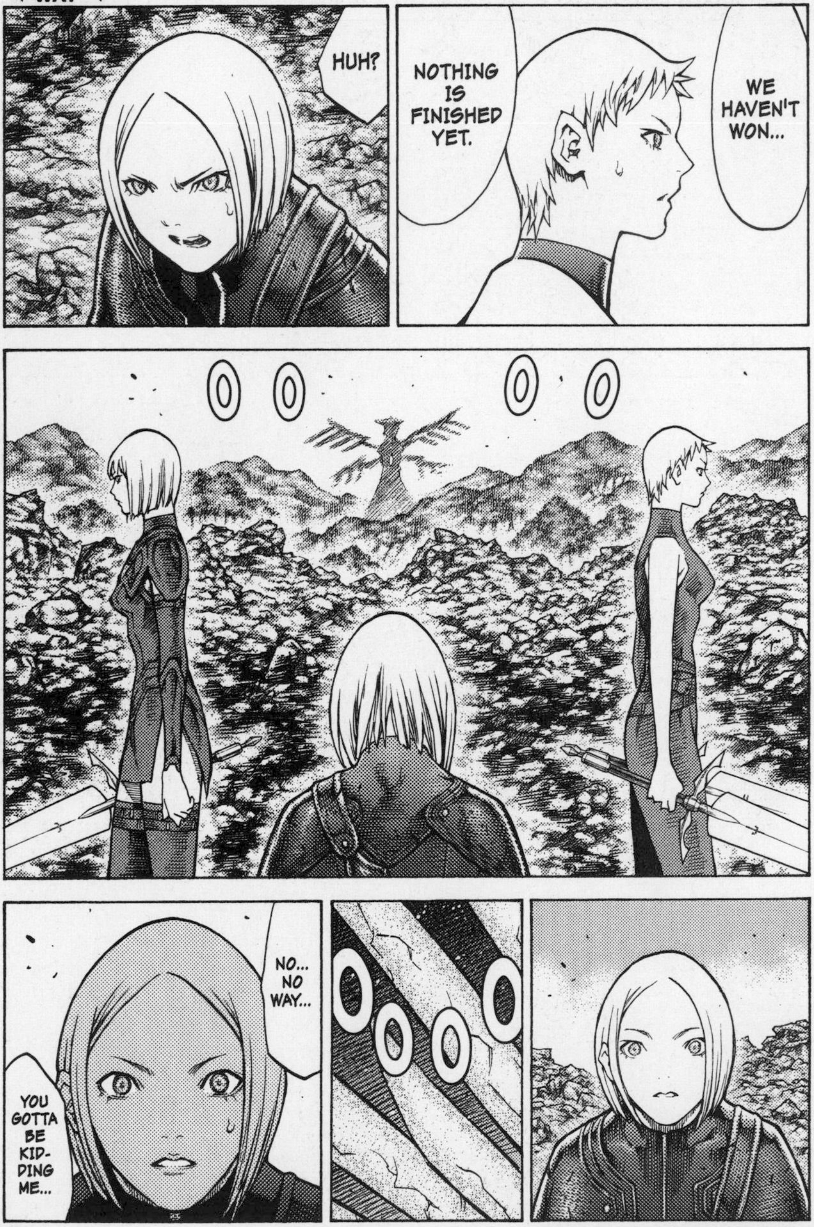

WE HAVEN'T WON...
NOTHING IS FINISHED YET.
HUH?
NO... NO WAY...
YOU GOTTA BE KID-DING ME...

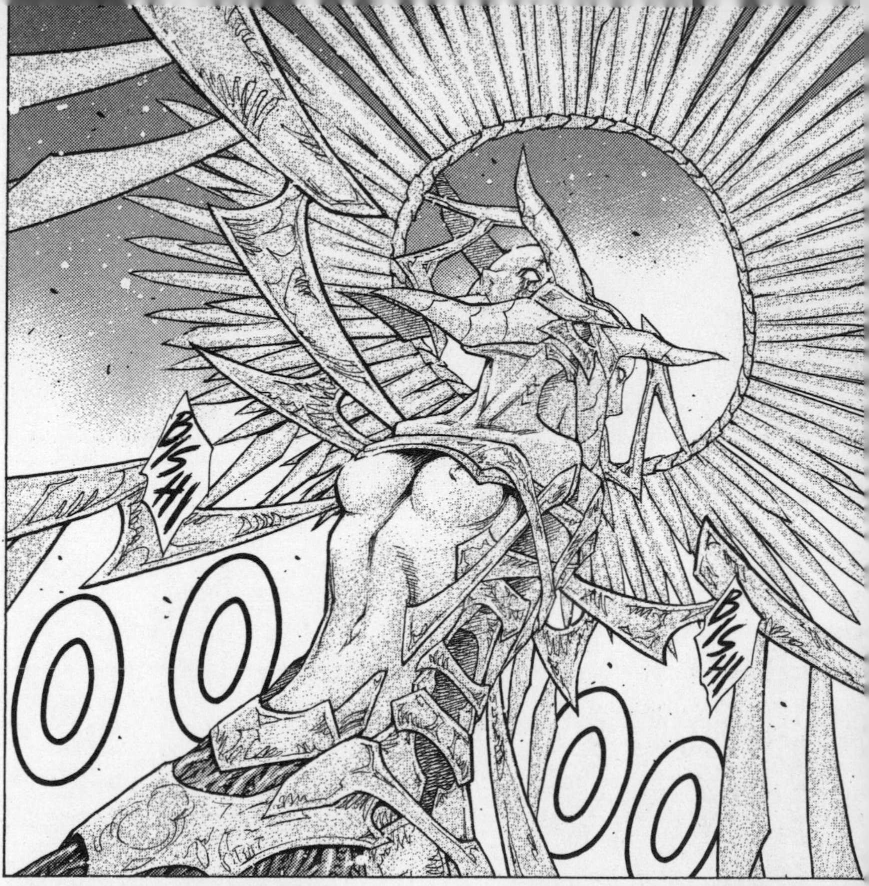
BISHI
OO
BISHI
OO
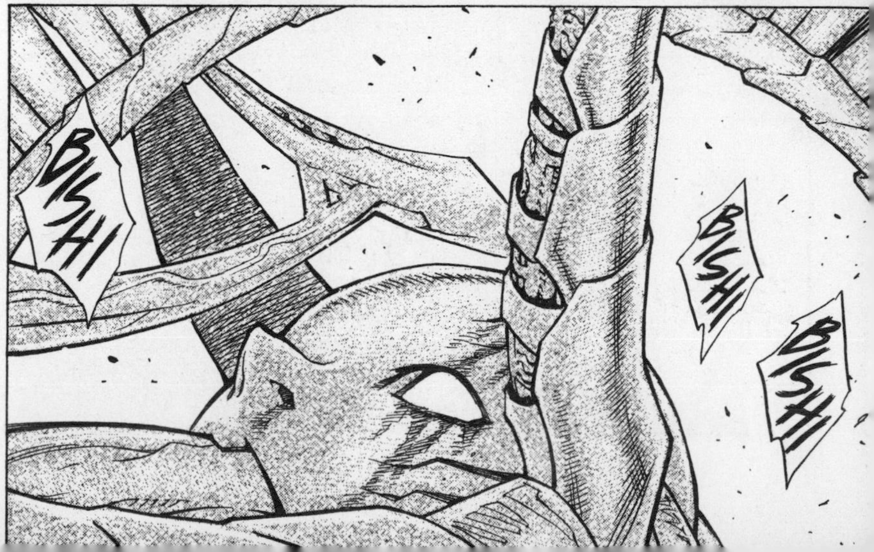
BISHI
BISHI
BISHI

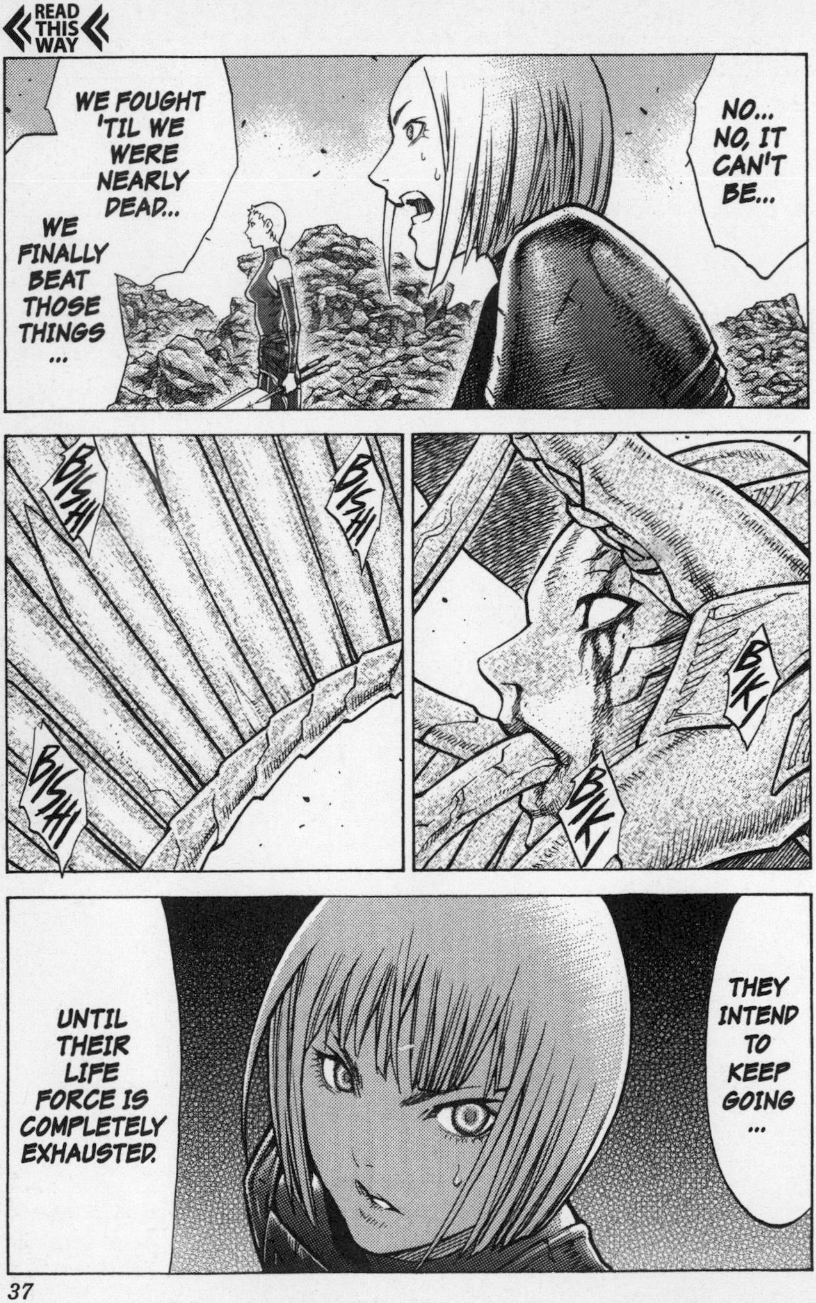
READ THIS WAY
NO... NO, IT CAN'T BE...
WE FOUGHT 'TIL WE WERE NEARLY DEAD...
WE FINALLY BEAT THOSE THINGS...
BISHI
BISHI
BISHI
BIKI
BIKI
THEY INTEND TO KEEP GOING...
UNTIL THEIR LIFE FORCE IS COMPLETELY EXHAUSTED.

Claymore
クレイモア

Scene 97: The Ashes of Lautrec, Part 2

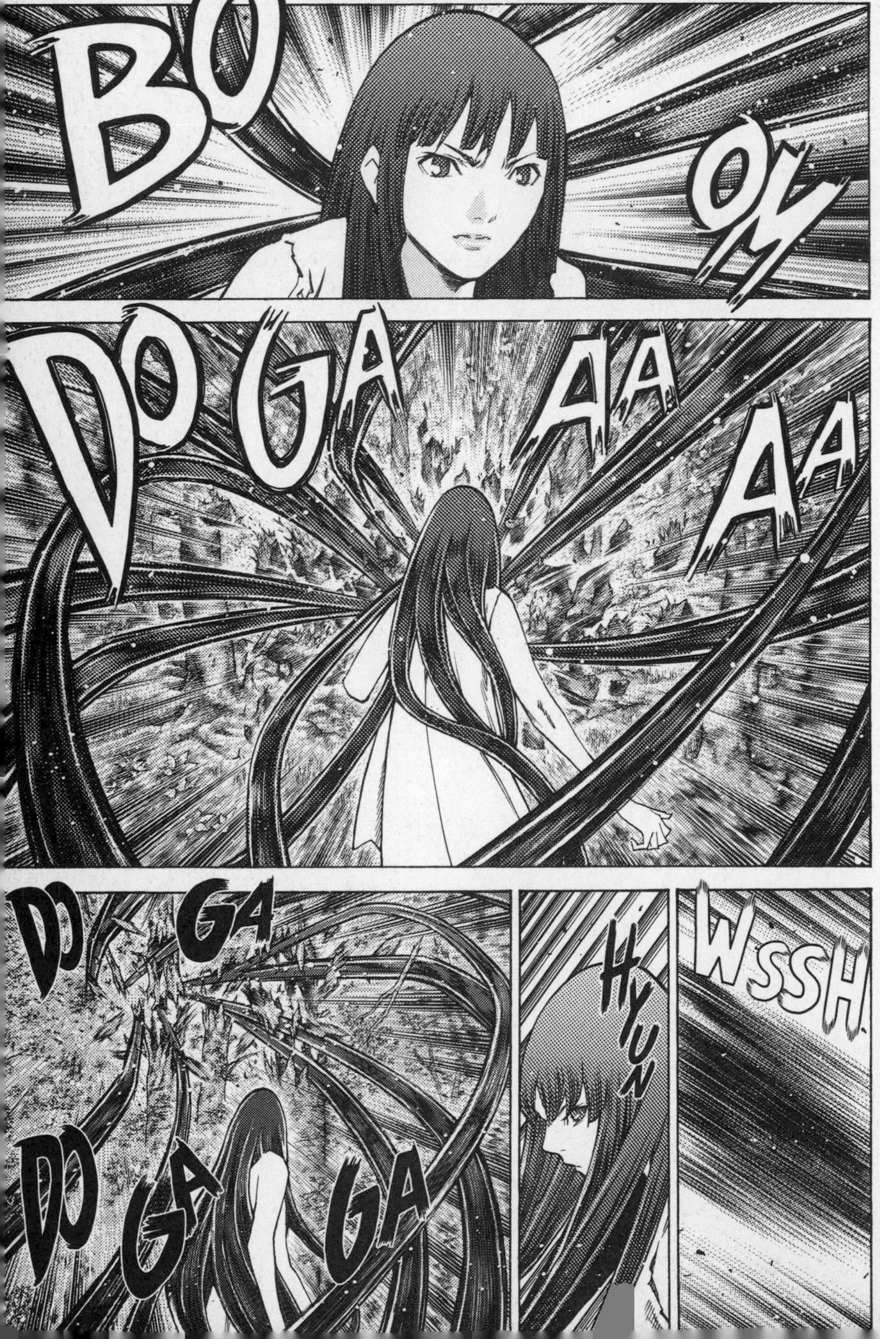
BO
OM
DOGAAAAA
WSSH
HYUN
DOGA
DOGAGA

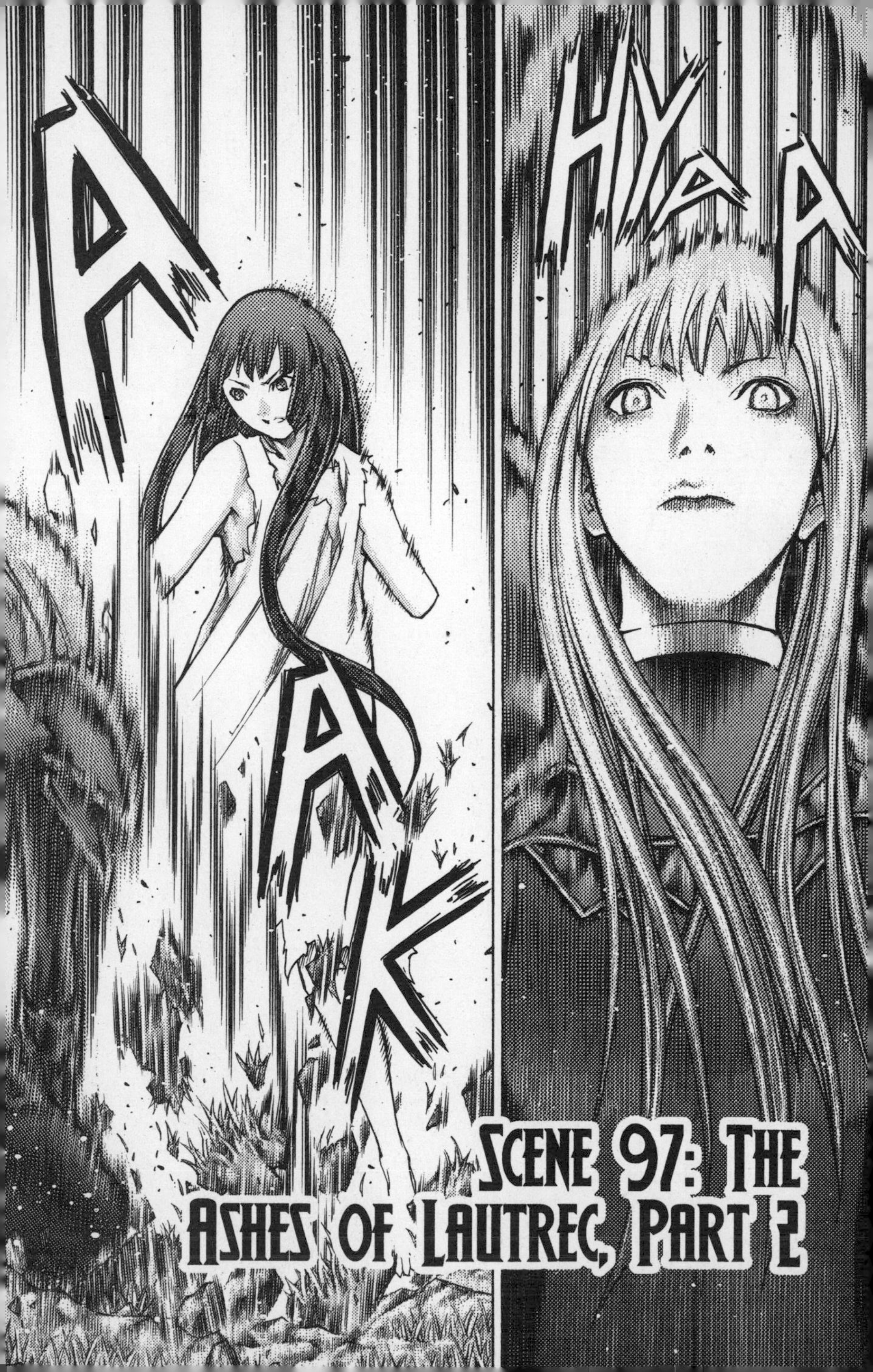
HYAAA
AAAK
SCENE 97: THE ASHES OF LAUTREC, PART 2

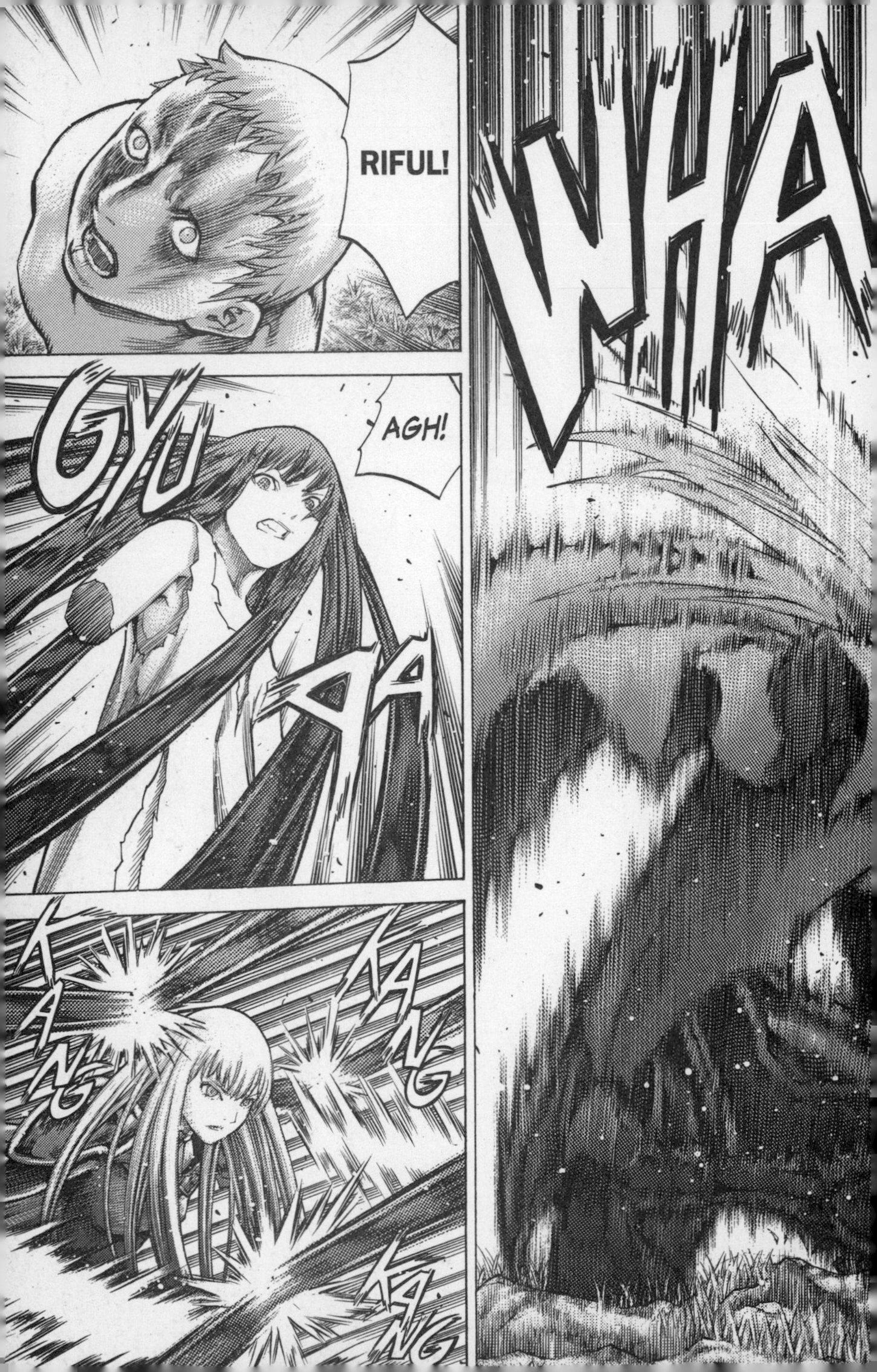
WHA
RIFUL!
GYU
AGH!
AA
KANG
KANG
KANG
KANG

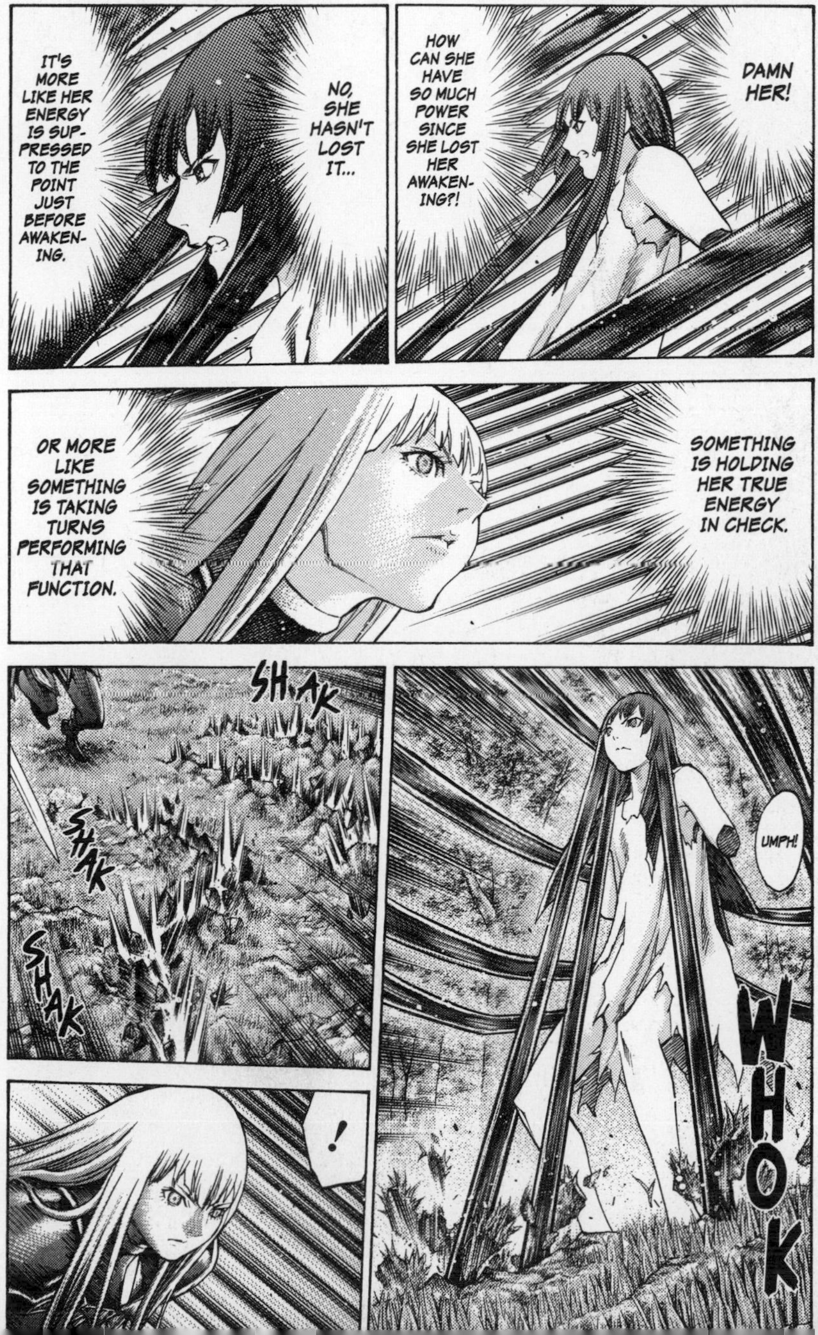
DAMN HER!
HOW CAN SHE HAVE SO MUCH POWER SINCE SHE LOST HER AWAKEN-ING?!
NO, SHE HASN'T LOST IT...
IT'S MORE LIKE HER ENERGY IS SUP-PRESSED TO THE POINT JUST BEFORE AWAKEN-ING.
SOMETHING IS HOLDING HER TRUE ENERGY IN CHECK.
OR MORE LIKE SOMETHING IS TAKING TURNS PERFORMING THAT FUNCTION.
UMPH!
WHOK
SHAK
SHAK
SHAK
!

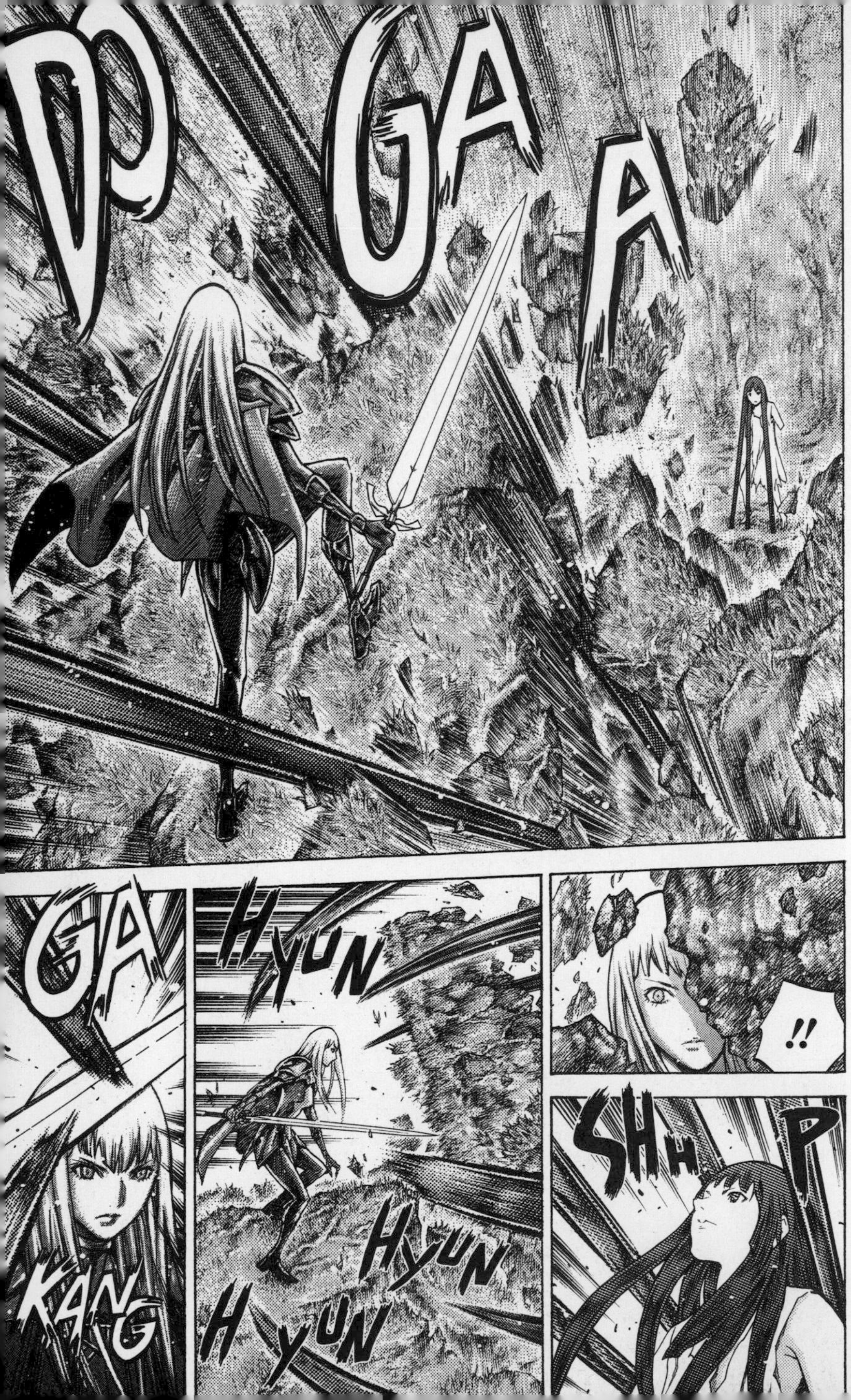
DOGAA
!!
SHHP
HYUN
HYUN
HYUN
GA
KANG

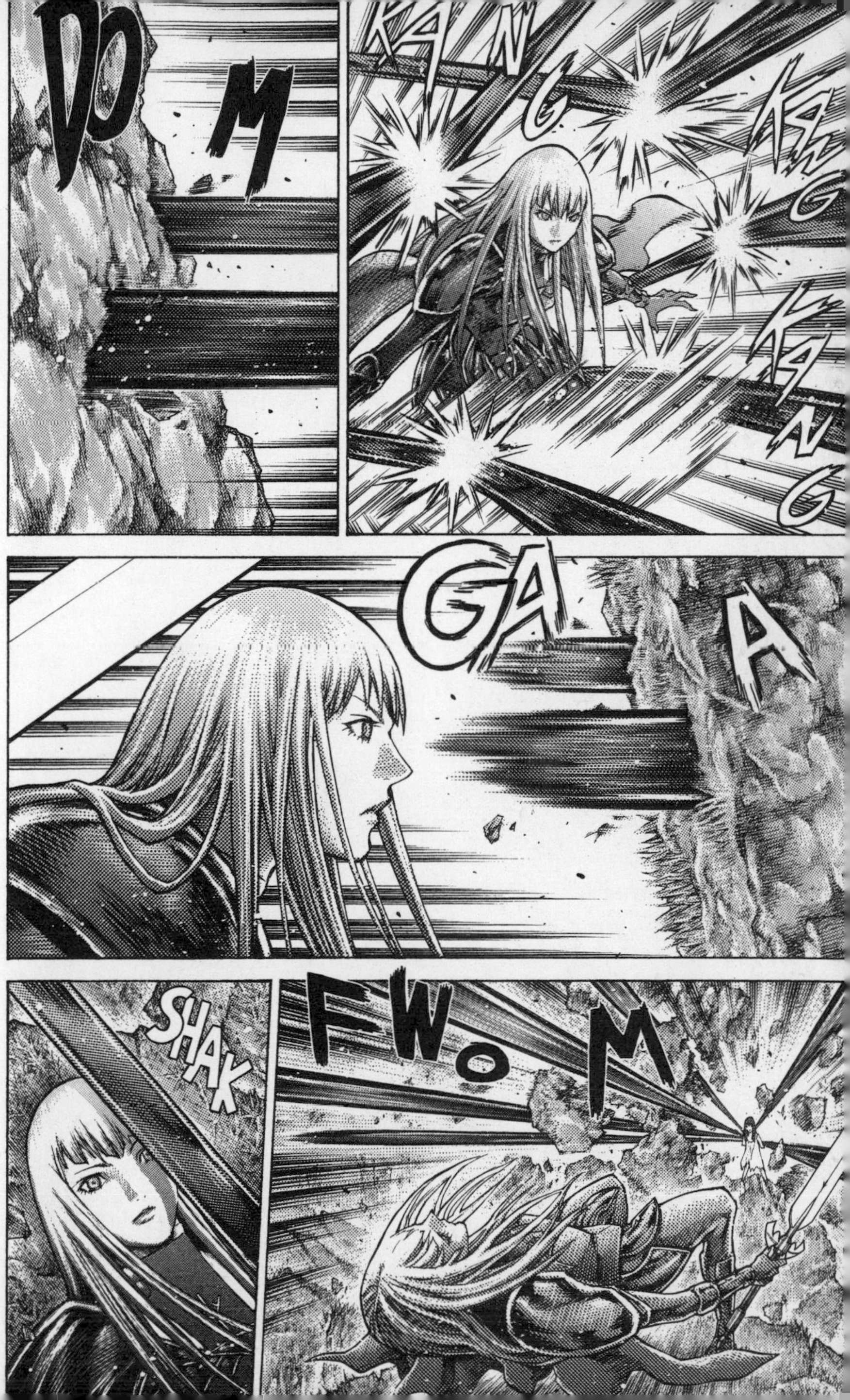
KANG
KANG
KANG
DOM
GAA
FWOM
SHAK

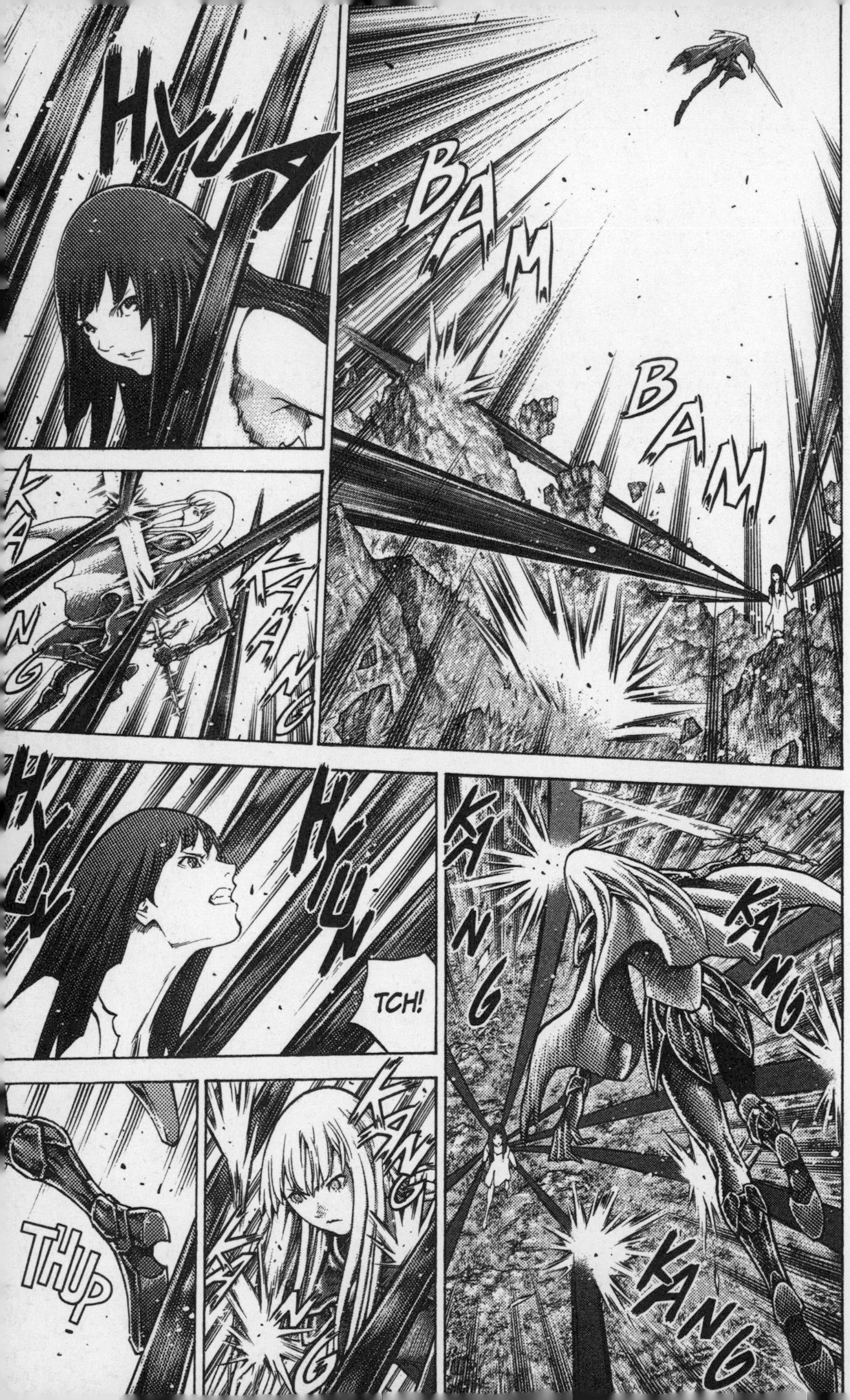
BAM
BAM
HYUA
KANG
KANG
KANG
HYUN
HYUN
TCH!
KANG
KANG
KANG
KANG
KANG
KANG
THUP!

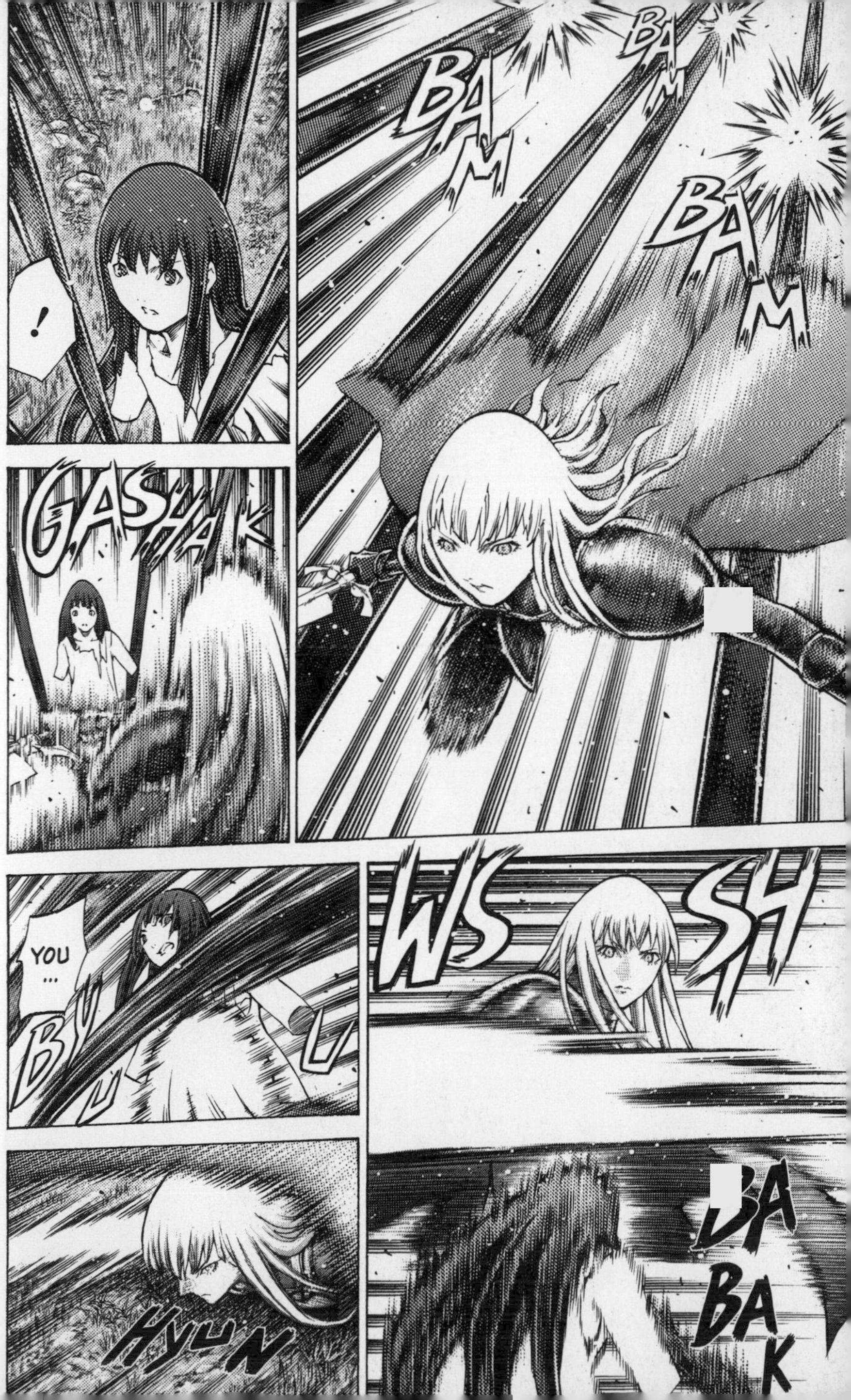
BAM
BAM
BAM
!
GASHAK
WSSH
YOU ...
BYUUL
BABAK
HYUN

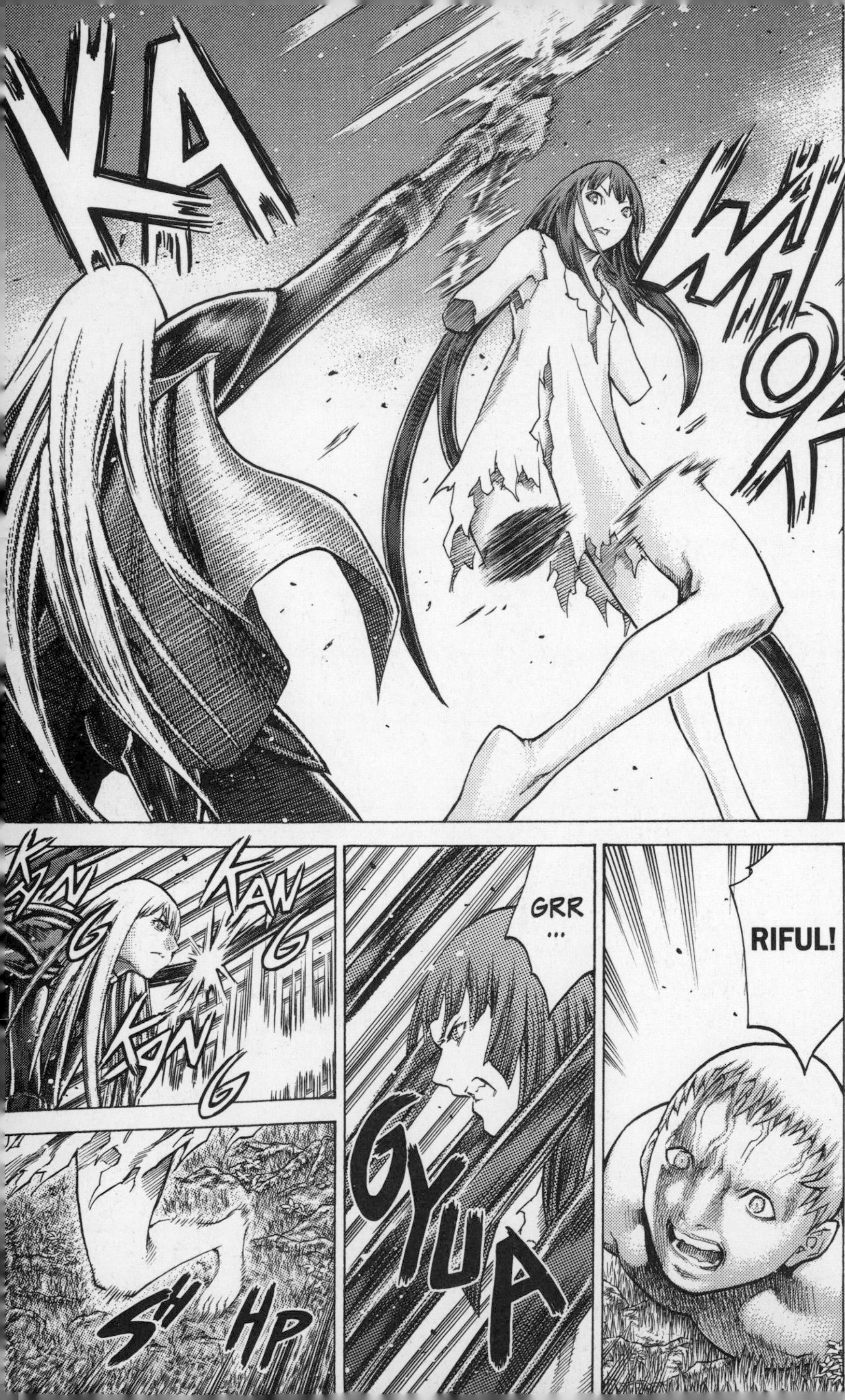
WHOK
KA
RIFUL!
GRR
...
GYUA
KANG
KANG
KANG
SHHP

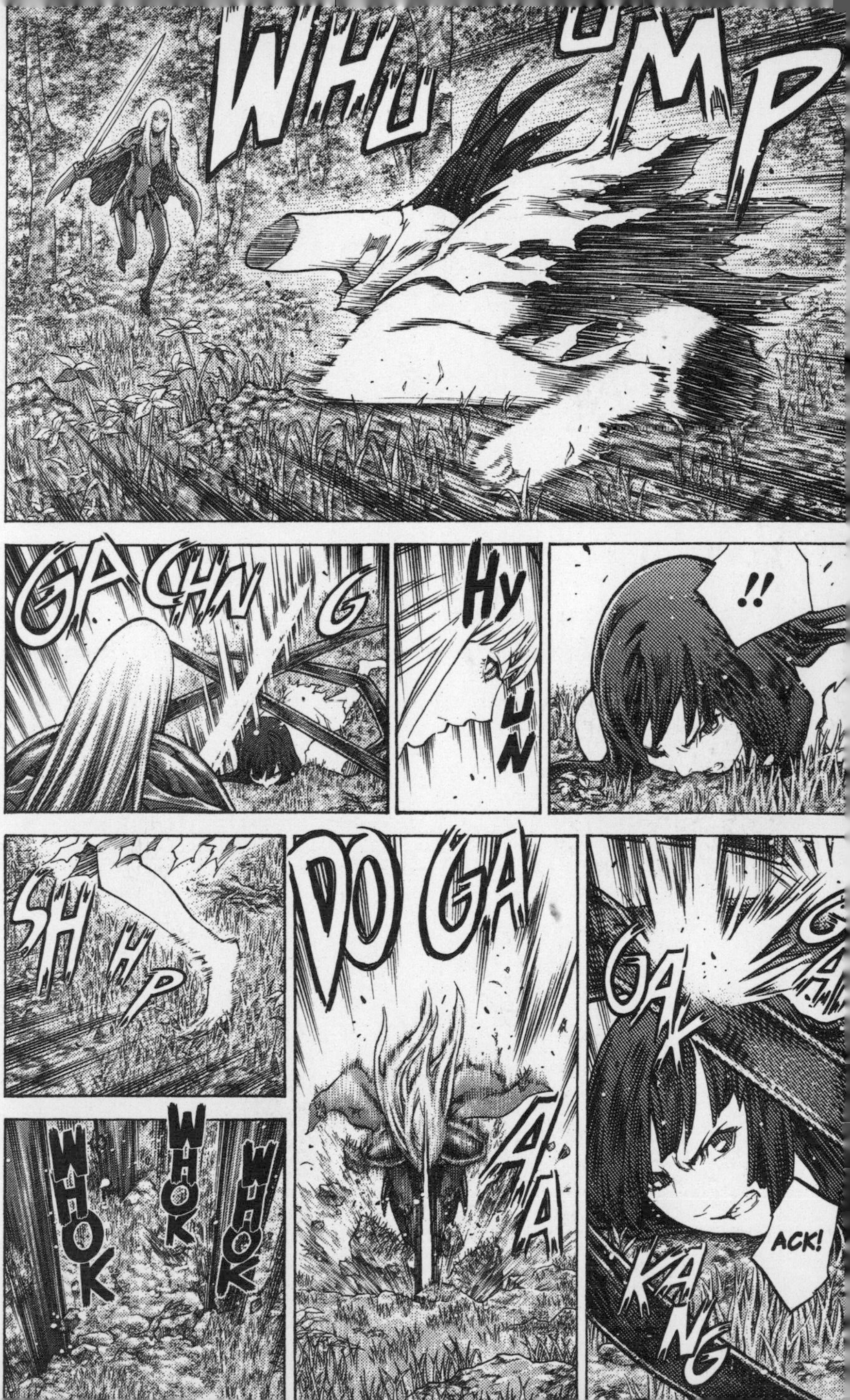
WHUUMP
!!
HYUNN
GACHNG
GAK KANG
GA
ACK!
DOGAAAA
SHHP
WHOK
WHOK
WHOK

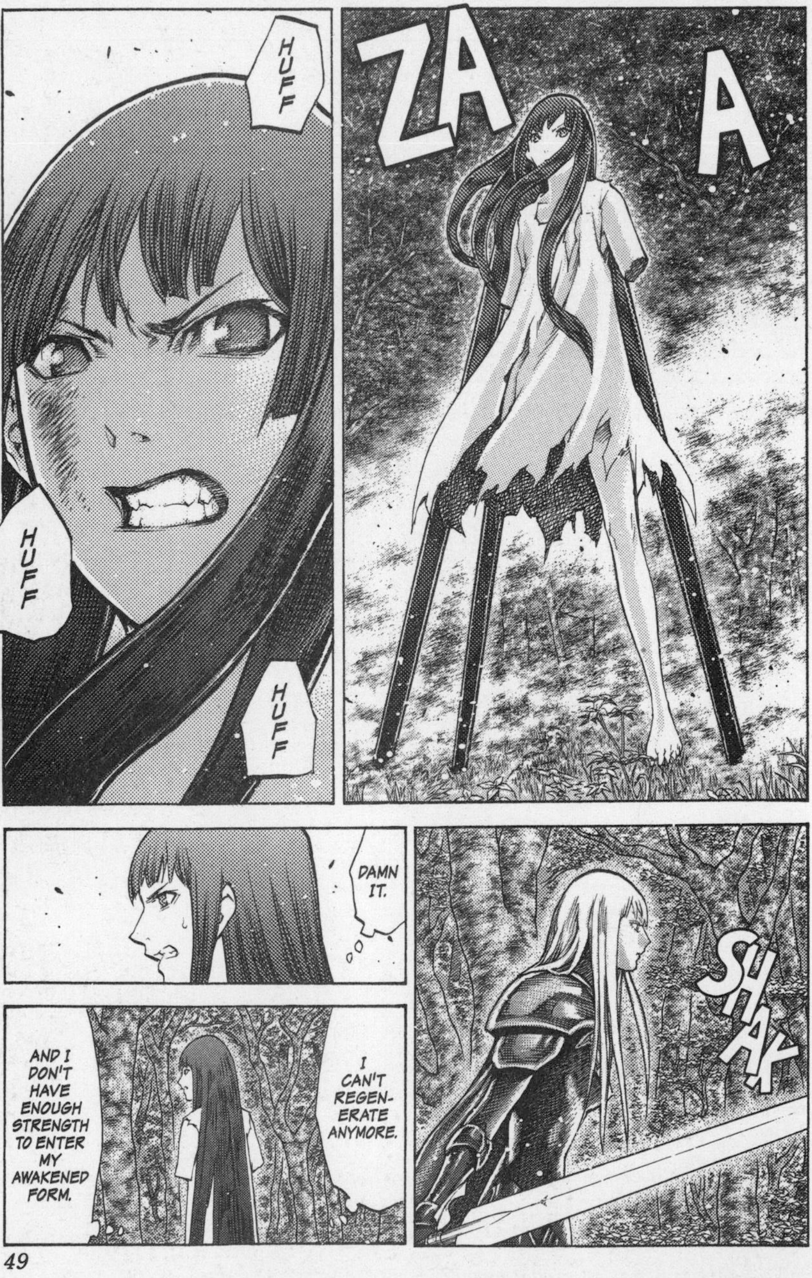
ZAA A
HUFF
HUFF
HUFF
SHAK
DAMN IT.
I CAN'T REGENERATE ANYMORE.
AND I DON'T HAVE ENOUGH STRENGTH TO ENTER MY AWAKENED FORM.

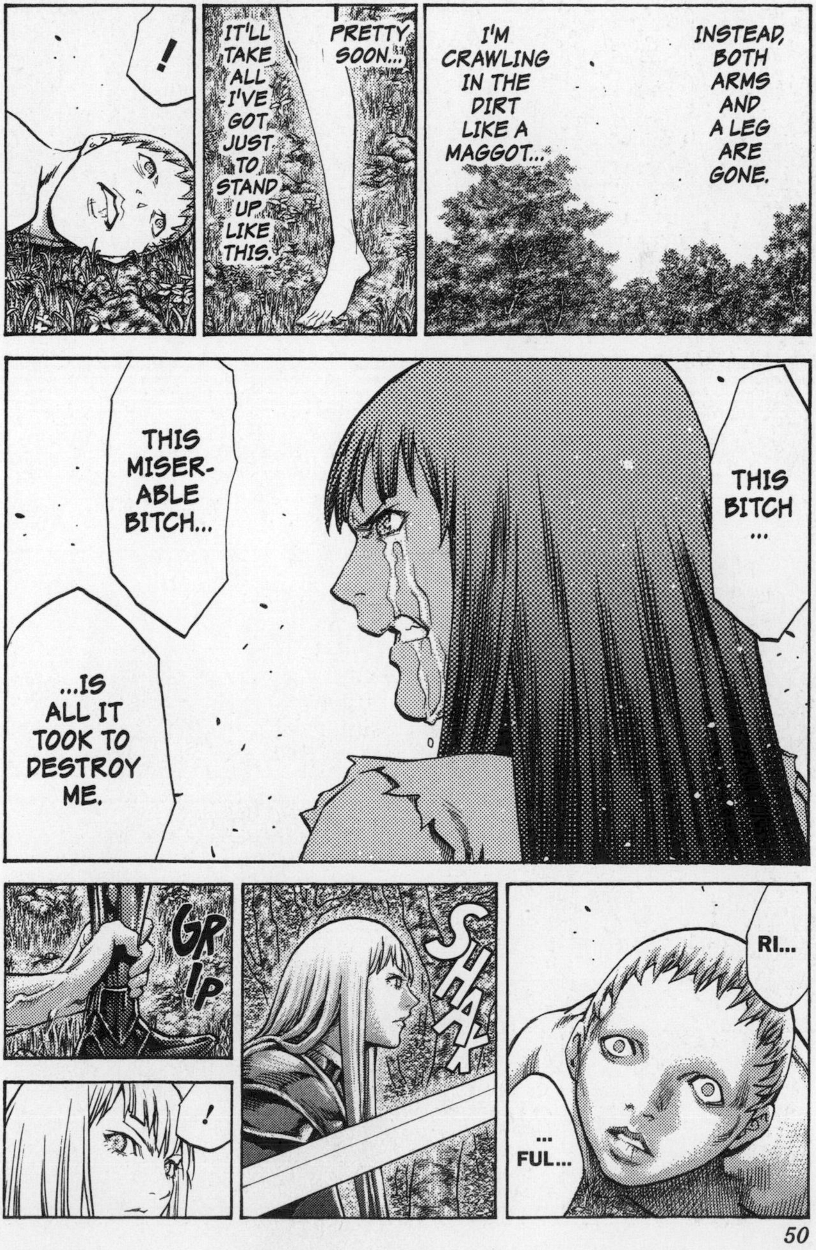
INSTEAD, BOTH ARMS AND A LEG ARE GONE.
I'M CRAWLING IN THE DIRT LIKE A MAGGOT...
PRETTY SOON...
IT'LL TAKE ALL I'VE GOT JUST TO STAND UP LIKE THIS.
!
THIS BITCH ...
THIS MISER-ABLE BITCH...
...IS ALL IT TOOK TO DESTROY ME.
RI...
... FUL...
SHAK
GRIP
!

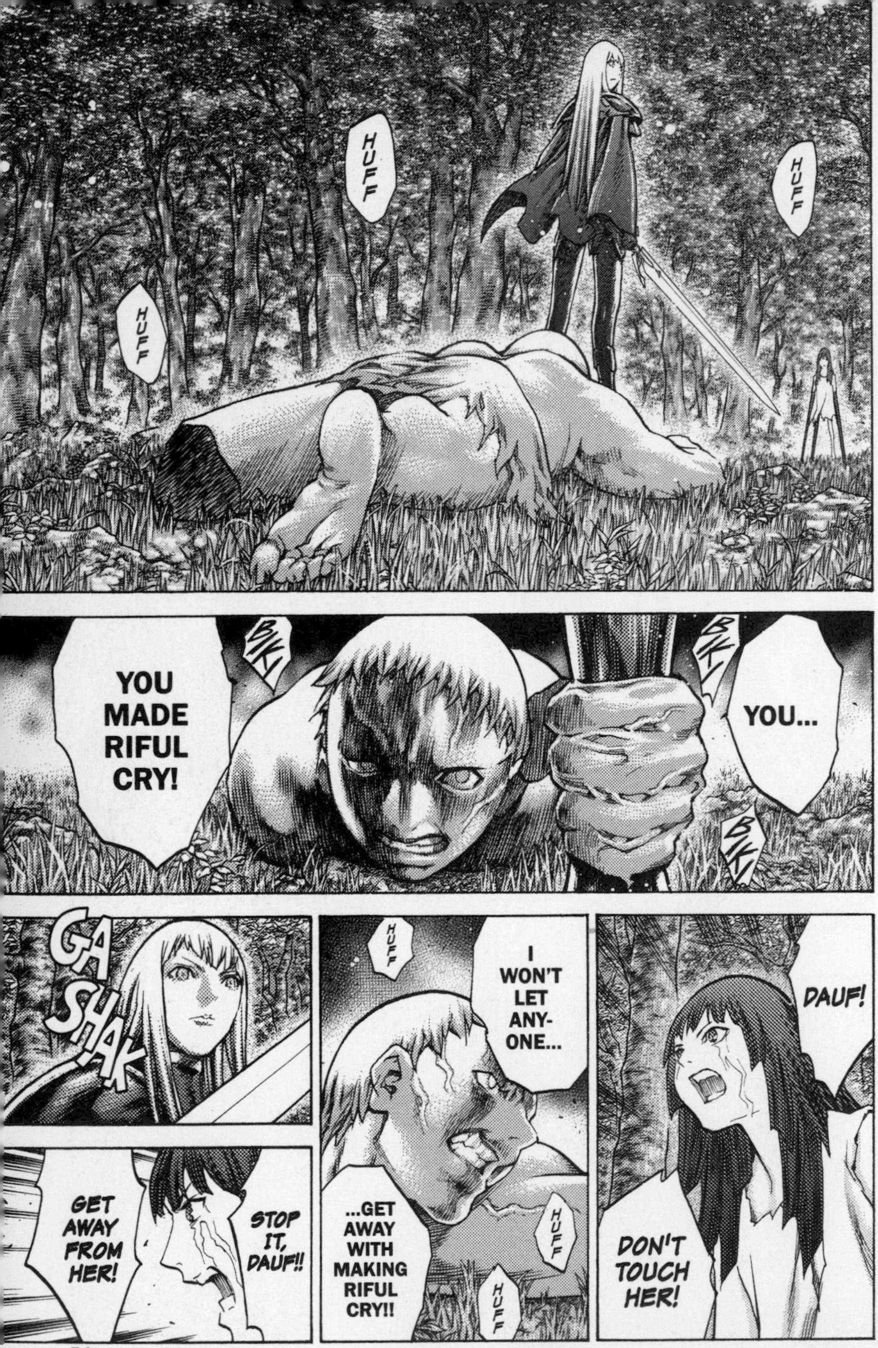
HUFF
HUFF
HUFF
BIKI
YOU...
BIKI
BIKI
YOU MADE RIFUL CRY!
DAUF!
DON'T TOUCH HER!
HUFF
I WON'T LET ANY-ONE...
...GET AWAY WITH MAKING RIFUL CRY!!
HUFF
HUFF
GA SHAK
STOP IT, DAUF!!
GET AWAY FROM HER!

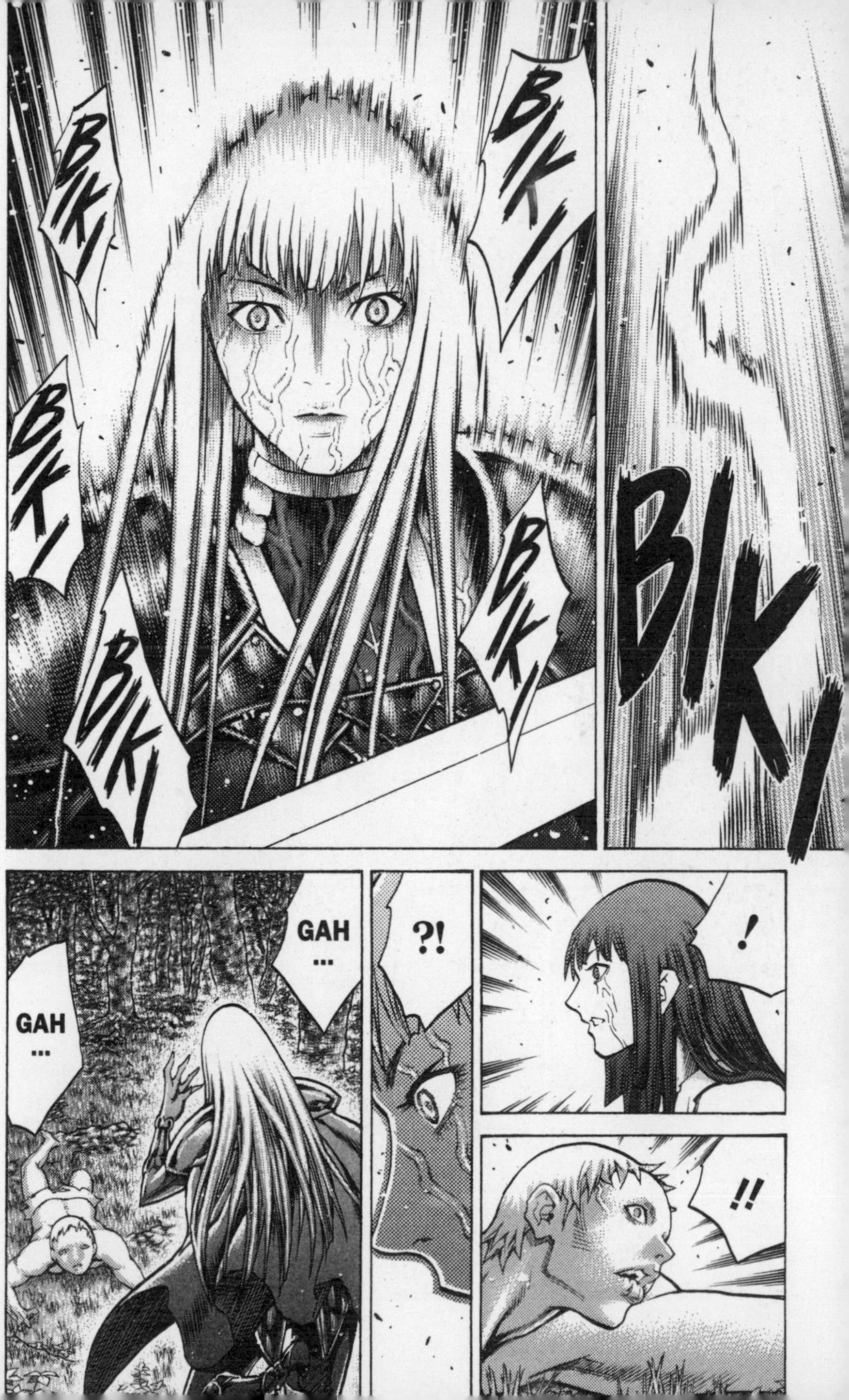
BIKI
BIKI
BIKI
BOKI
BOKI
BOKI
!
!!
?!
GAH ...
GAH ...

READ THIS WAY

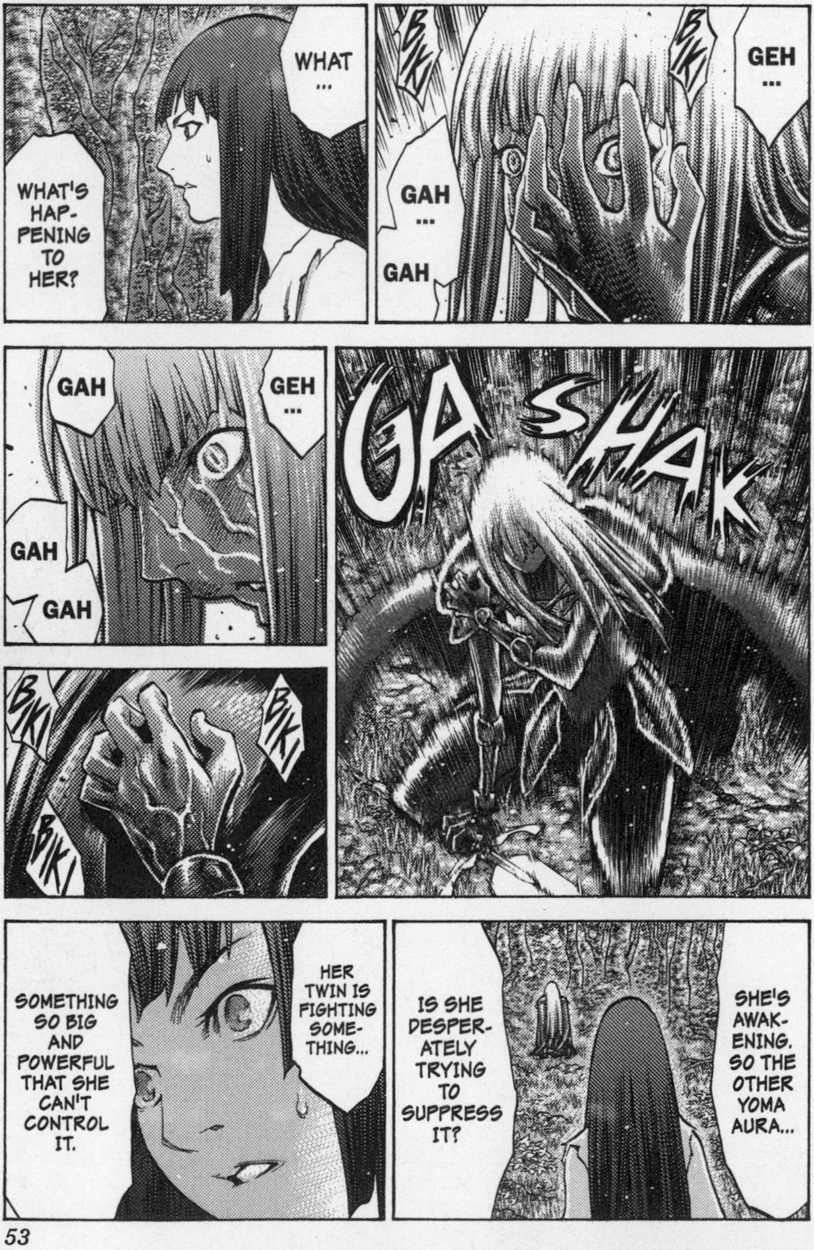
BIKI
BIKI
GEH...
GAH... GAH
WHAT...
WHAT'S HAPPENING TO HER?
GASHAK
GEH...
GAH
GAH
GAH
BIKI
BIKI
BIKI
SHE'S AWAKENING. SO THE OTHER YOMA AURA...
IS SHE DESPERATELY TRYING TO SUPPRESS IT?
HER TWIN IS FIGHTING SOMETHING...
SOMETHING SO BIG AND POWERFUL THAT SHE CAN'T CONTROL IT.

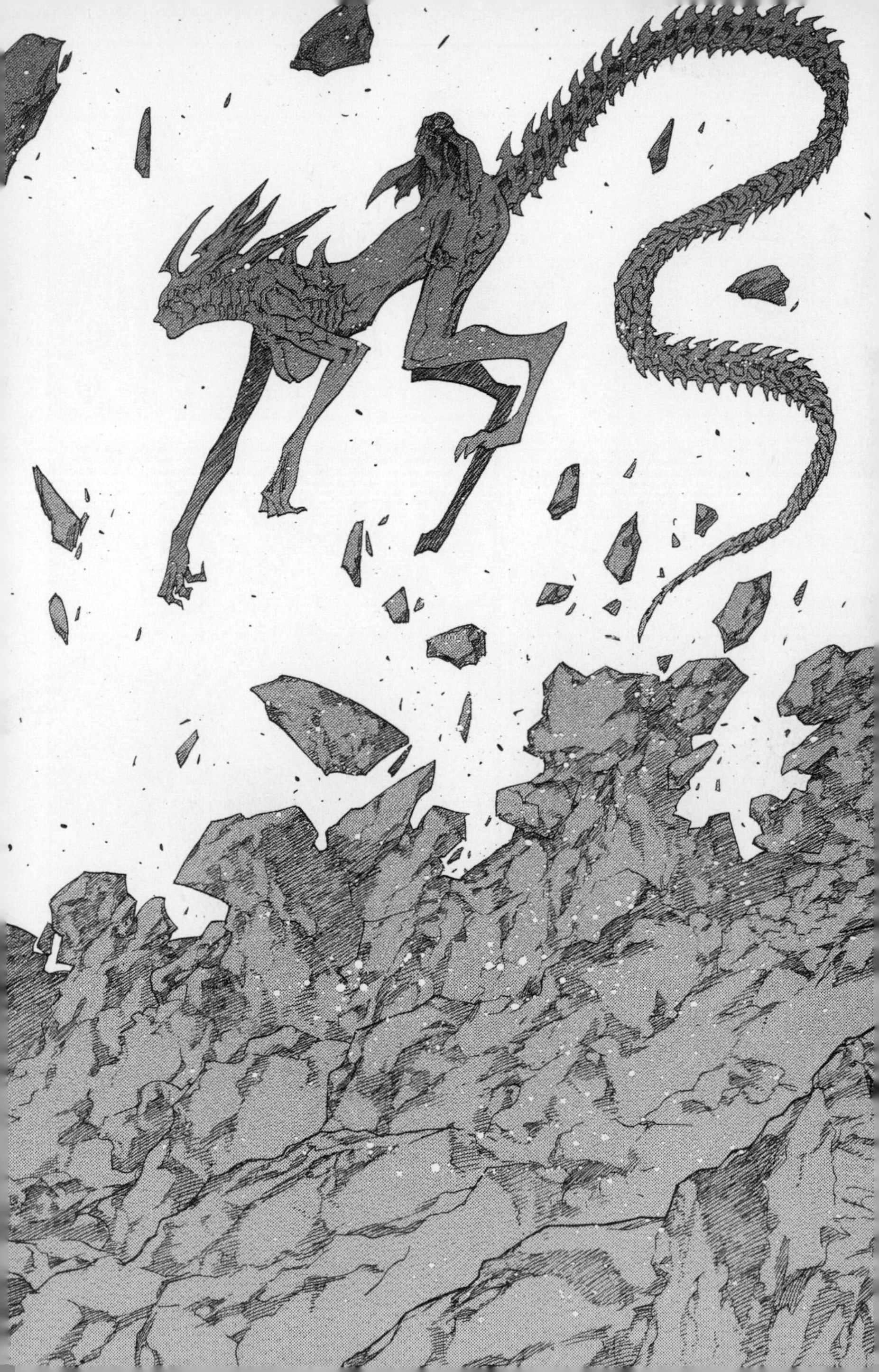

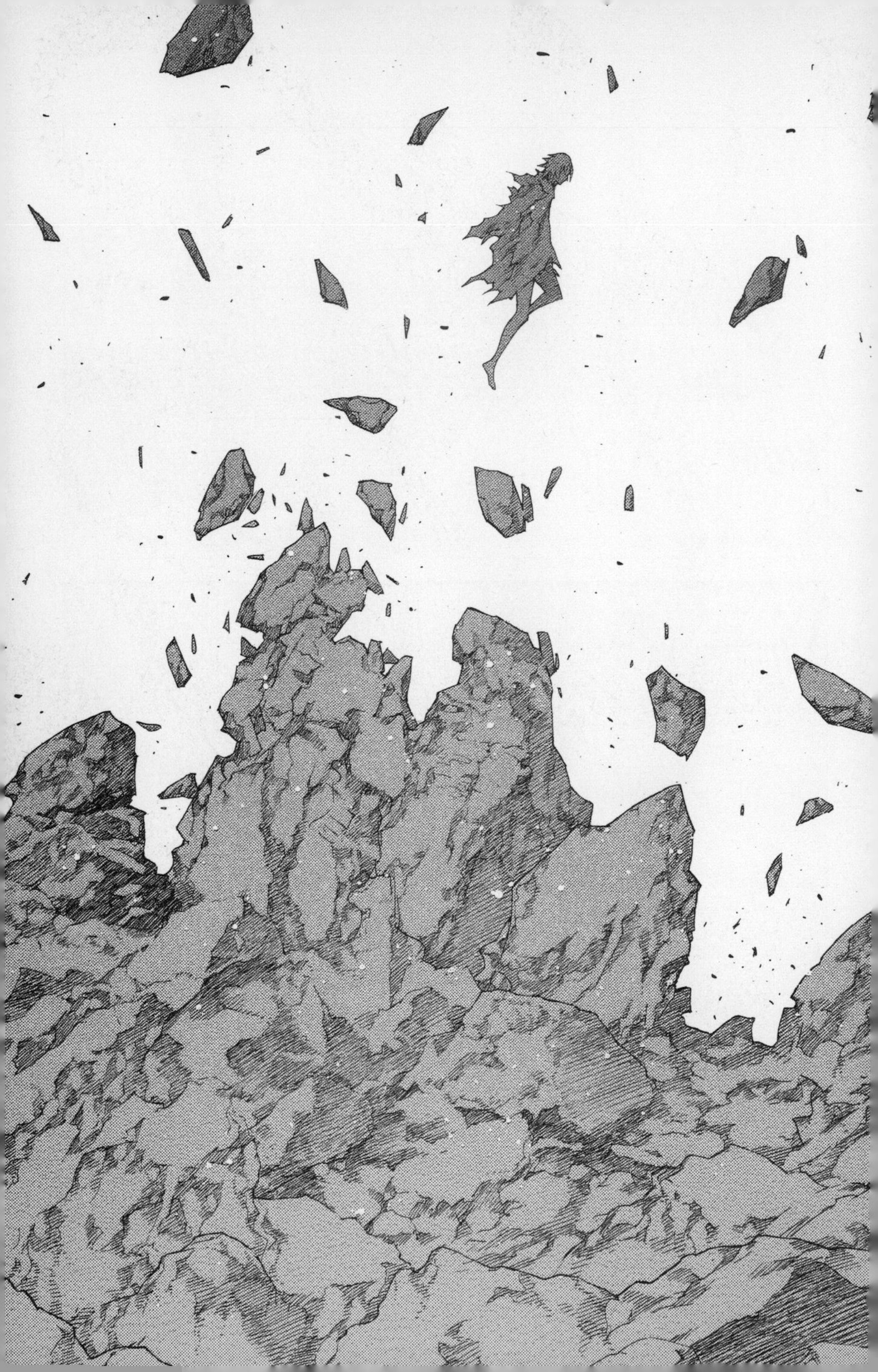

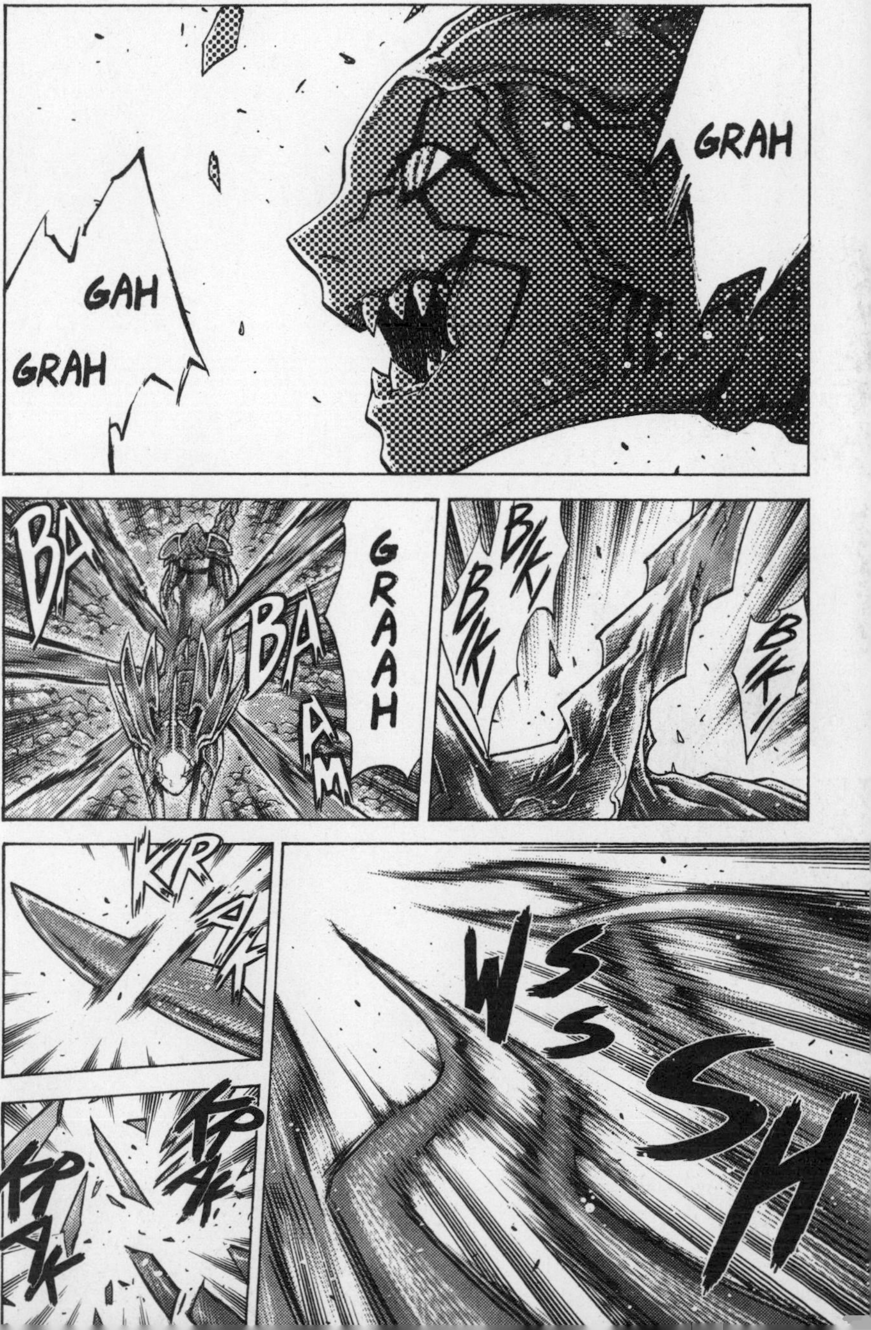
GRAH
GAH
GRAH
BIKI
BIKI
BIKI
GRAAAH
BA
BAAM
WSSSH
KRAK
KRAK
KRAK

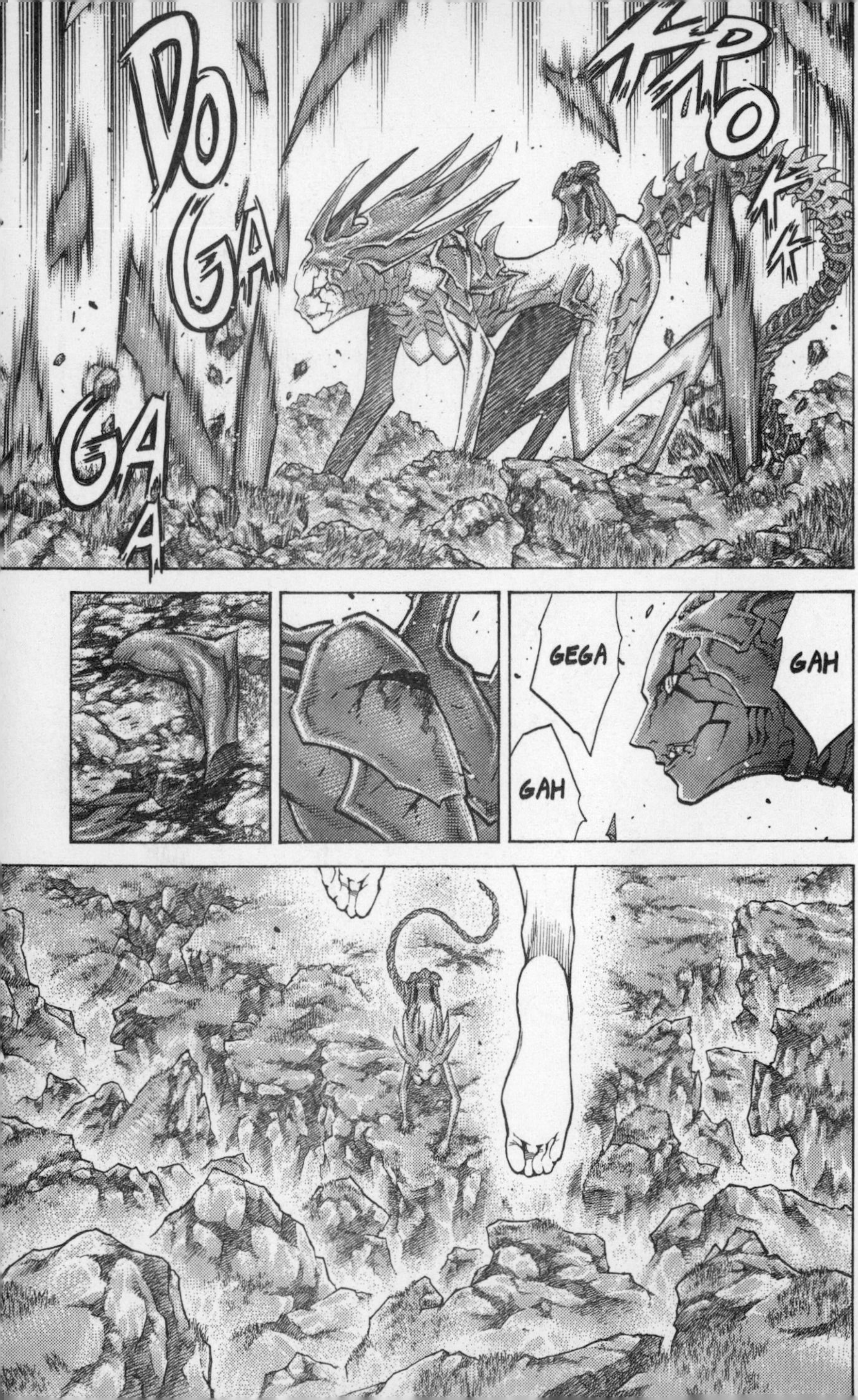
KROKK
DOGA
GAGA
GEGA
GAH
GAH

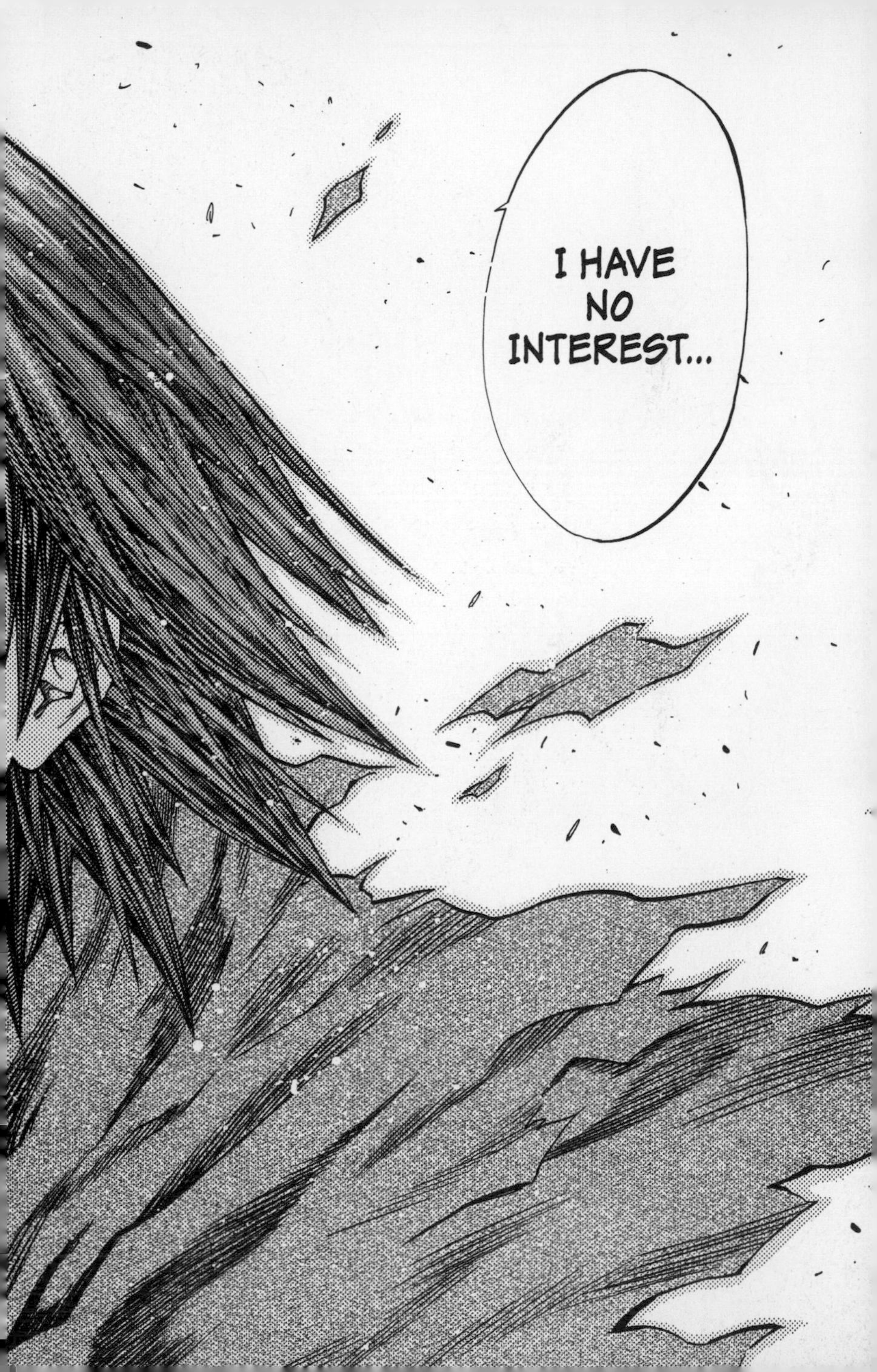
I HAVE NO INTEREST...

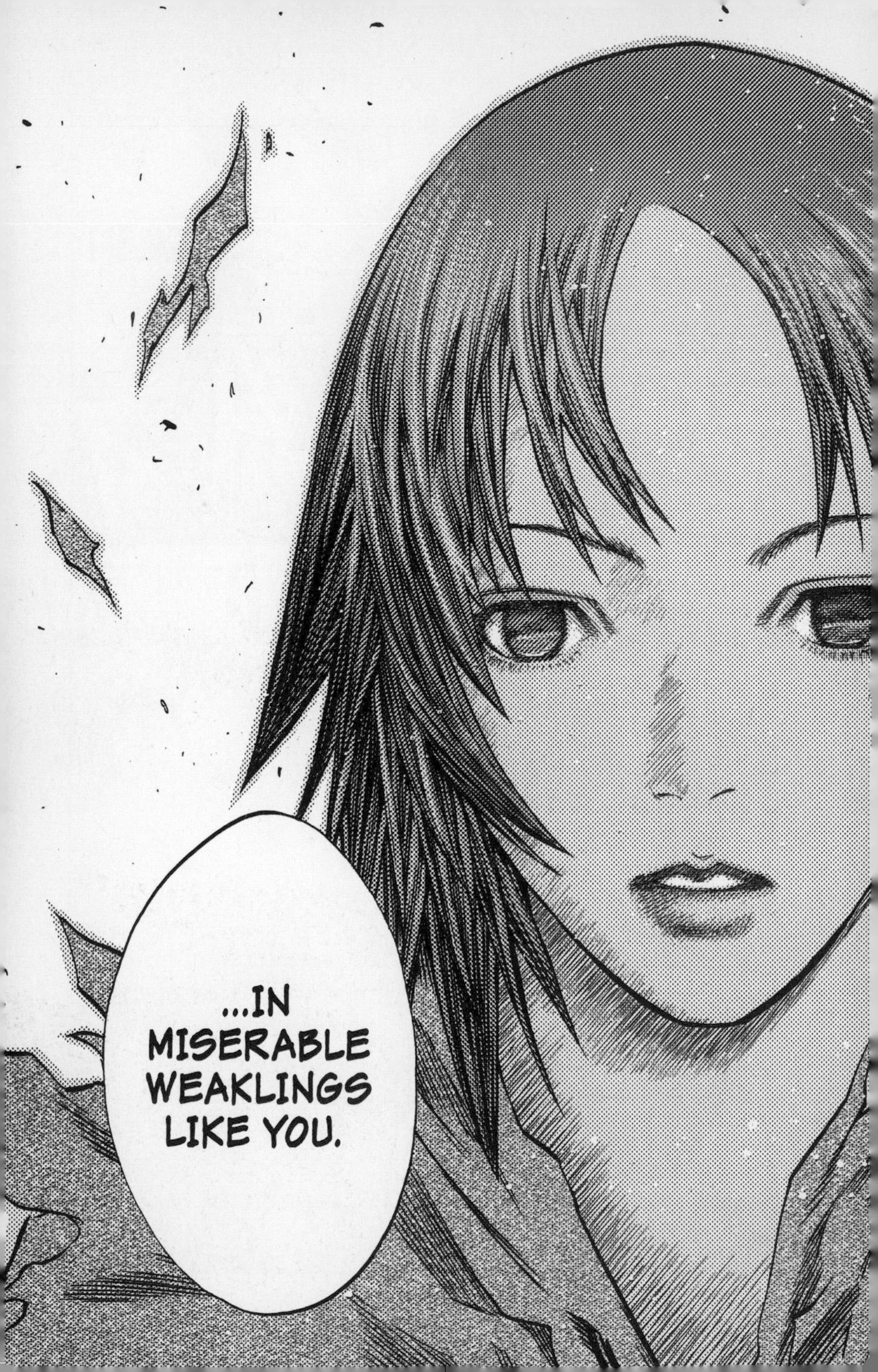
...IN MISERABLE WEAKLINGS LIKE YOU.

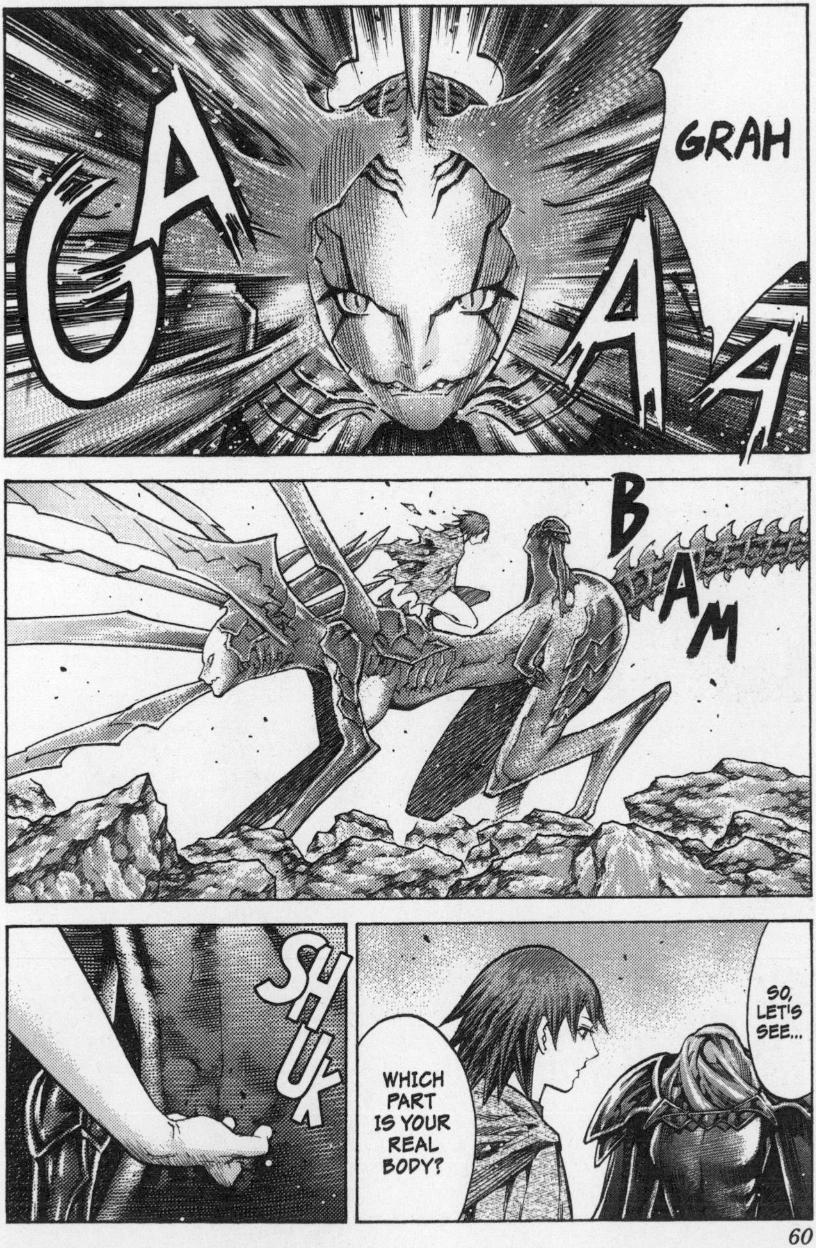
GRAH
GAAA
BAM
SO, LET'S SEE...
WHICH PART IS YOUR REAL BODY?
SHUK

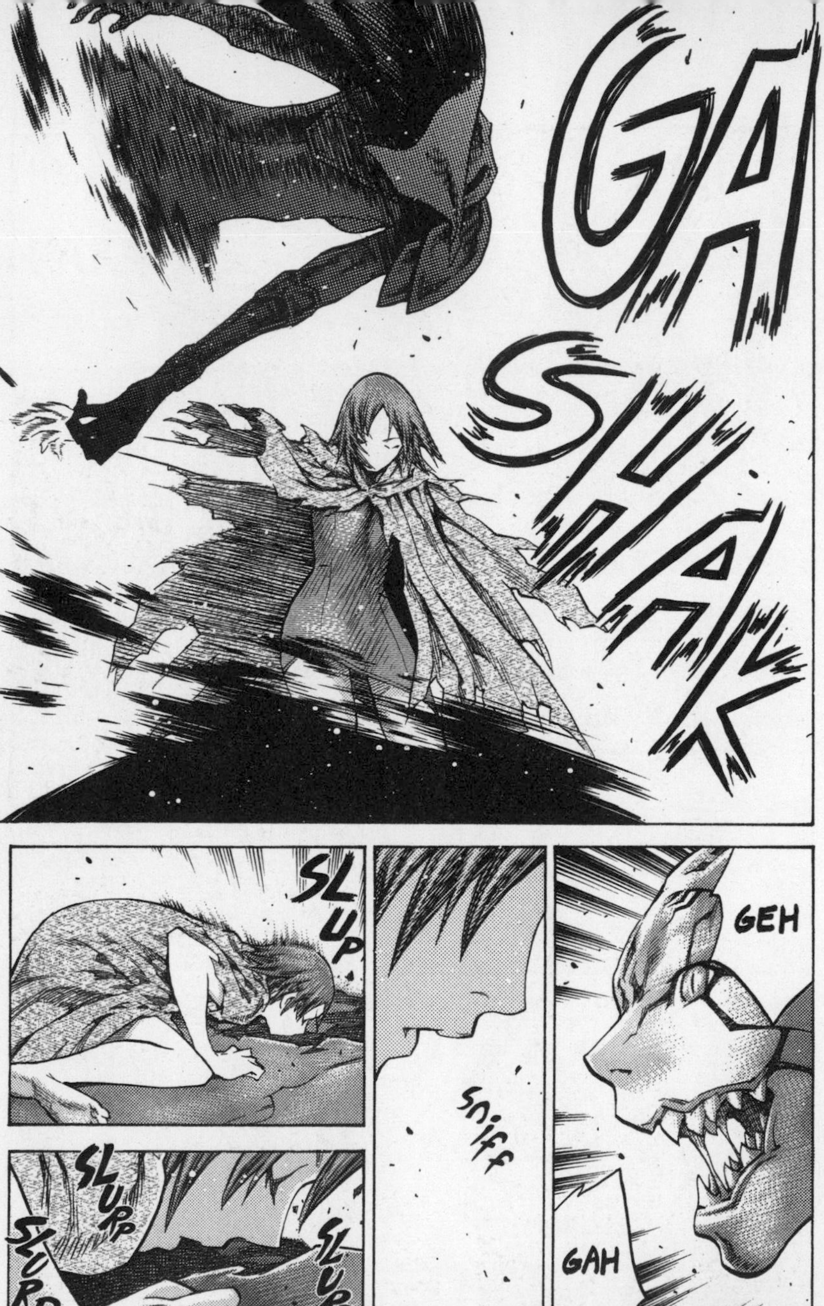
GASHAK
GEH
GAH
sniff
SLUP
SLURP
SLURP
SLURP

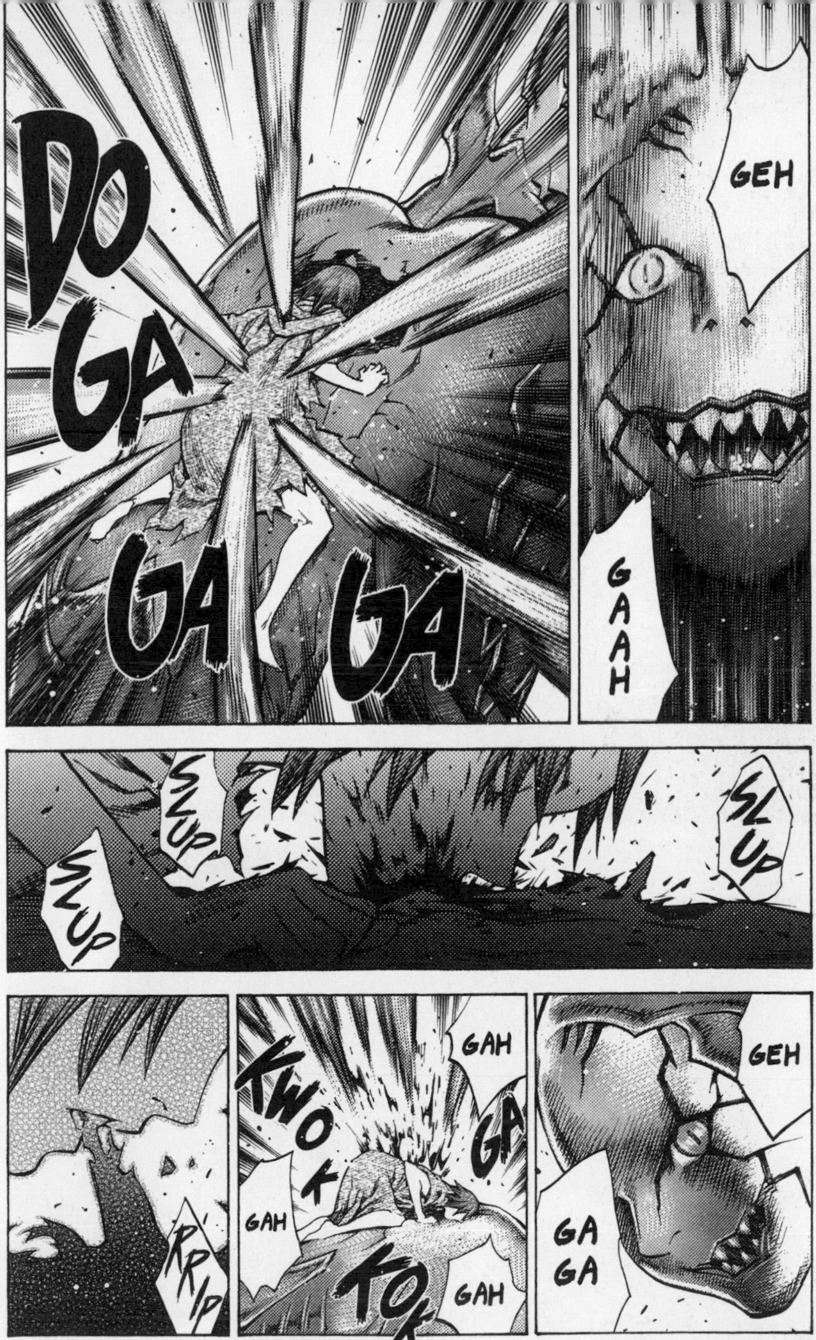
GEH
GAAAH
DO GA
GA GA
SLUP
SLUP
SLUP
GEH
GA GA
GAH
GA
KWOK
GAH
KOK
GAH
RRIP

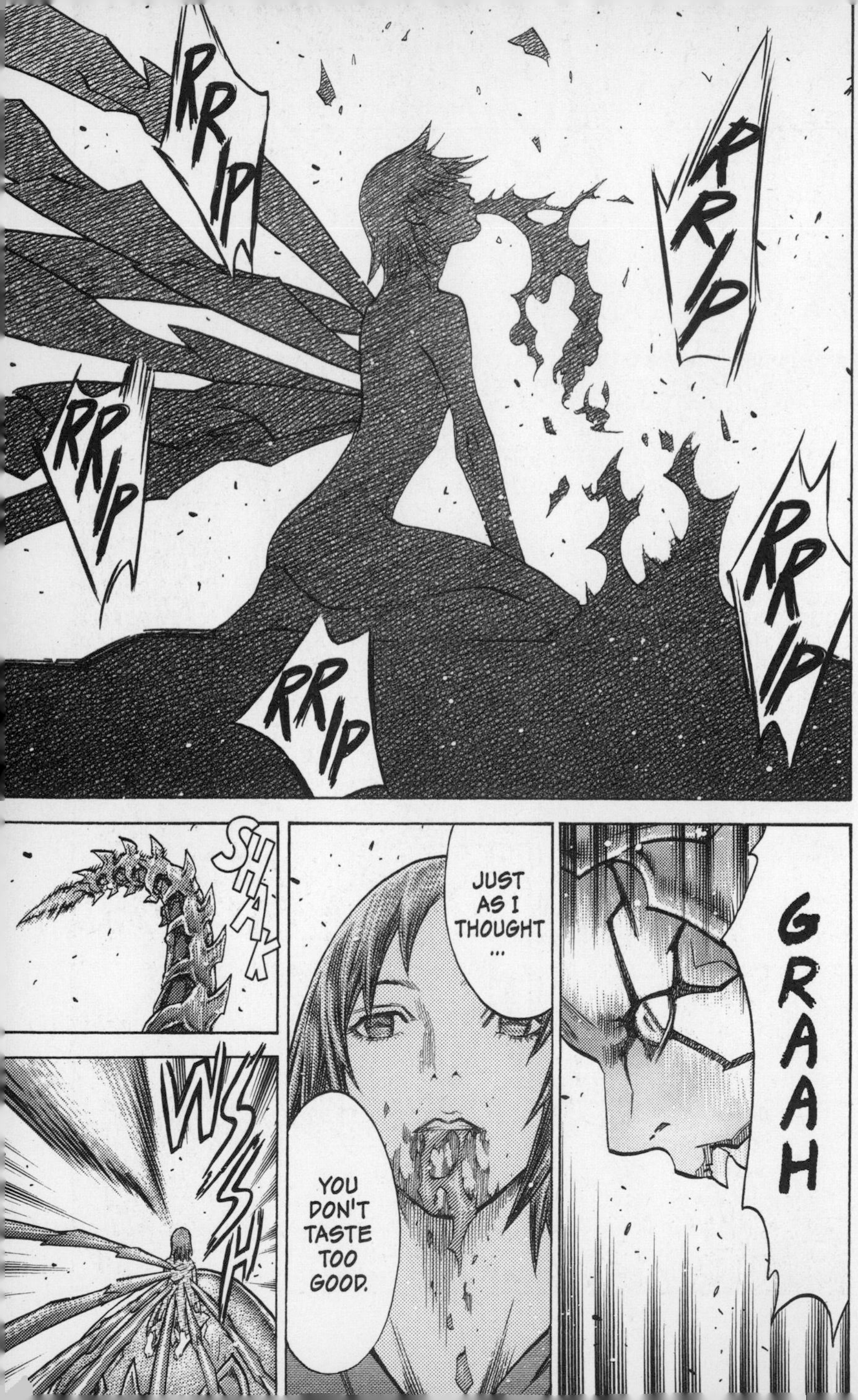
RRIP
RRIP
RRIP
RRIP
RRIP
GRAAH
JUST AS I THOUGHT ...
YOU DON'T TASTE TOO GOOD.
SHAK
WSSH

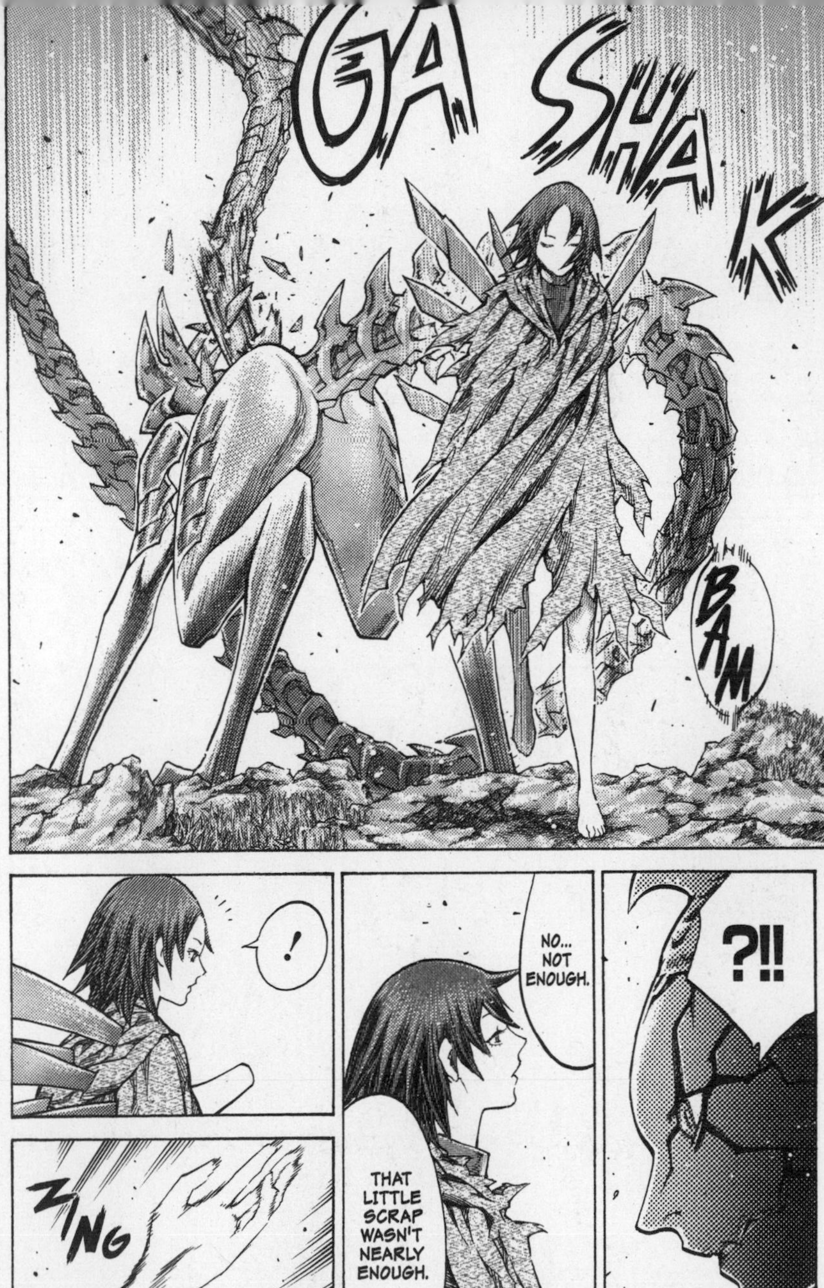
GA SHAK
BAM
?!!
NO... NOT ENOUGH.
THAT LITTLE SCRAP WASN'T NEARLY ENOUGH.
!
ZING

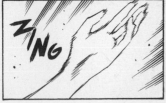

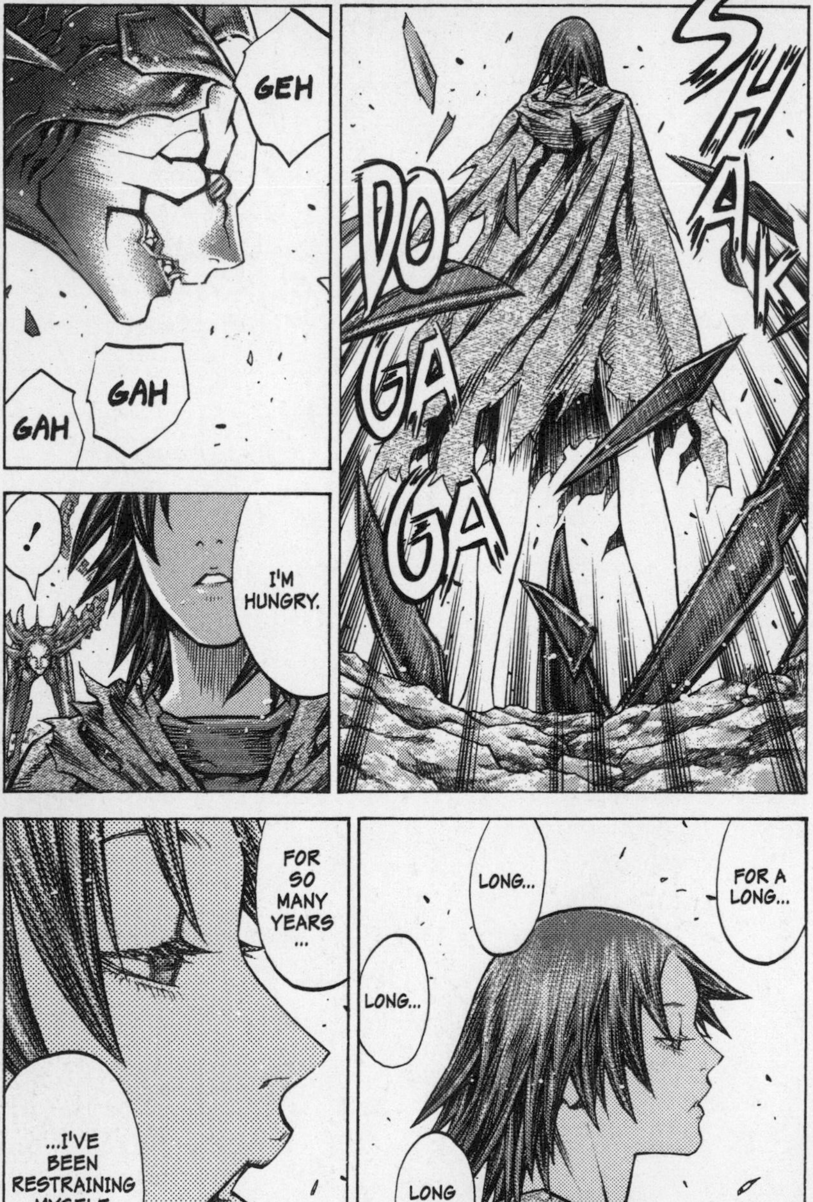
SHAK
DOGAGA
GEH
GAH
GAH
!
I'M HUNGRY.
FOR A LONG...
LONG...
LONG...
LONG TIME...
FOR SO MANY YEARS...
...I'VE BEEN RESTRAINING MYSELF.

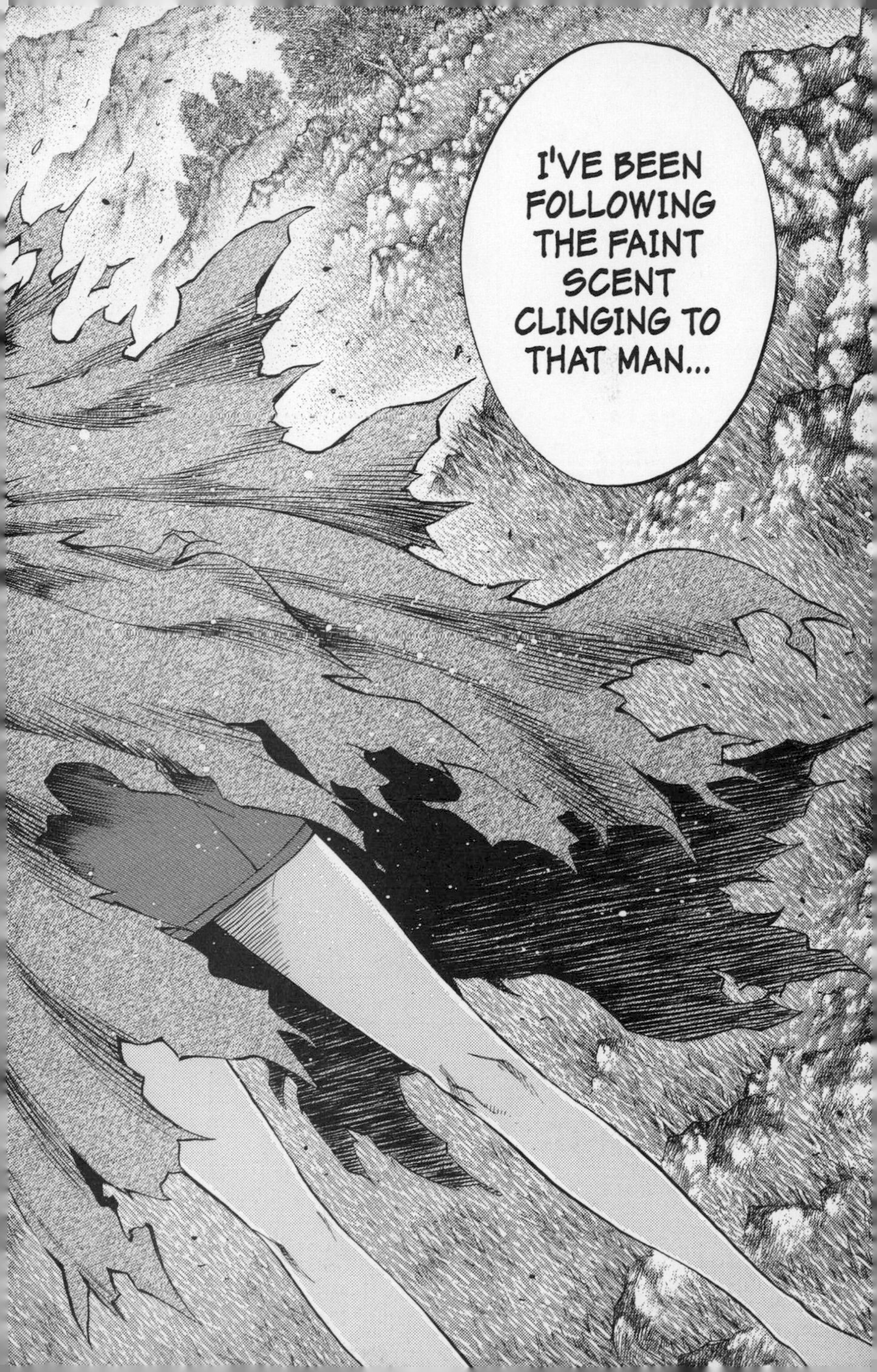
I'VE BEEN FOLLOWING THE FAINT SCENT CLINGING TO THAT MAN...

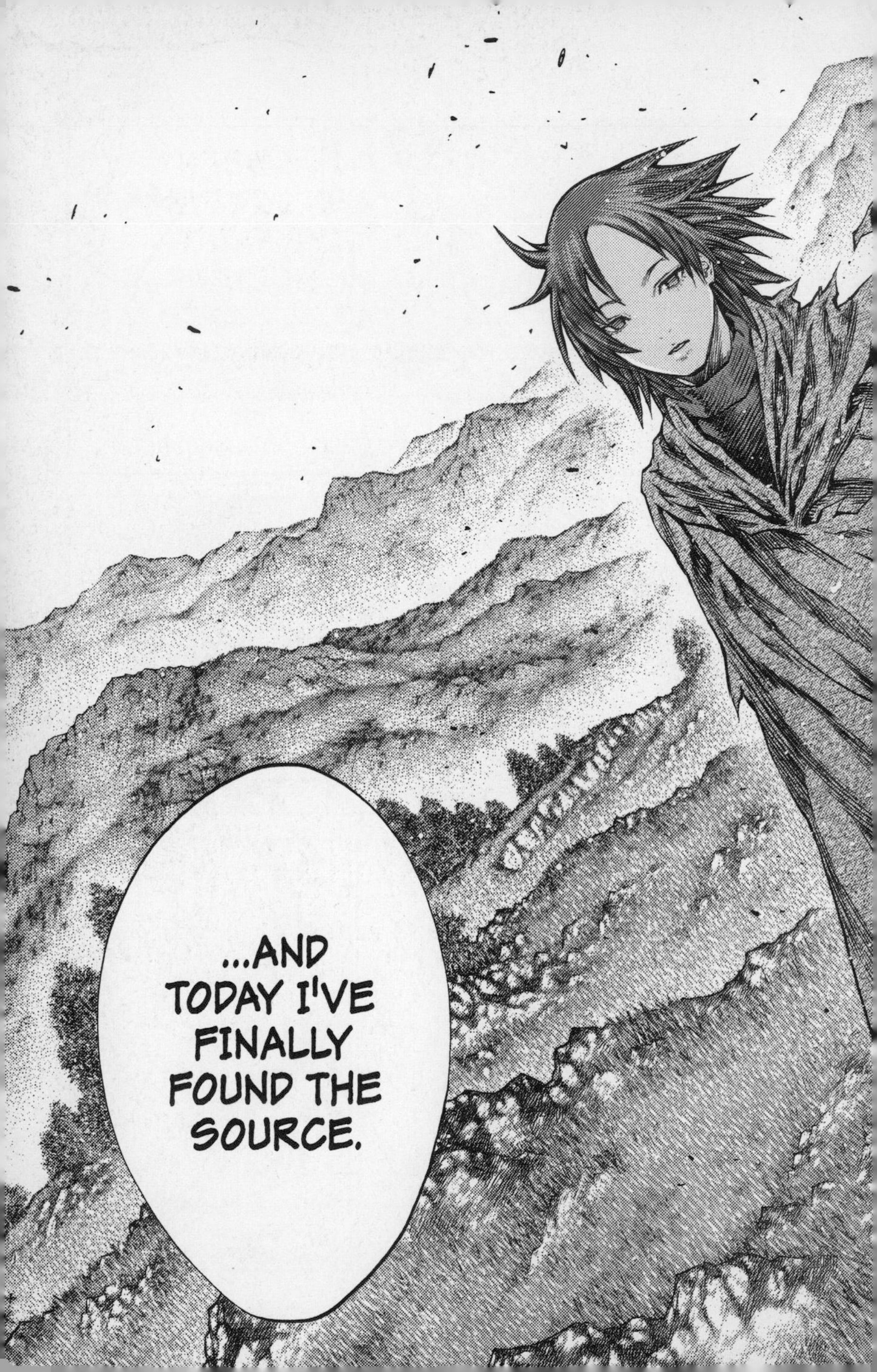
...AND TODAY I'VE FINALLY FOUND THE SOURCE.

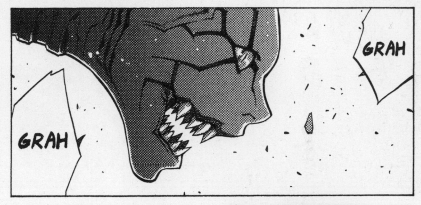

GRAH

GRAH

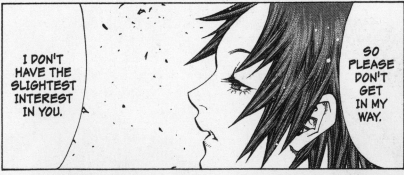

I DON'T HAVE THE SLIGHTEST INTEREST IN YOU.

SO PLEASE DON'T GET IN MY WAY.

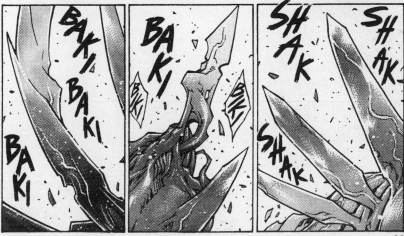

BAKI

BAKI

BAKI

BAKI

BIKI

BIKI

SHAK

SHAK

SHAK

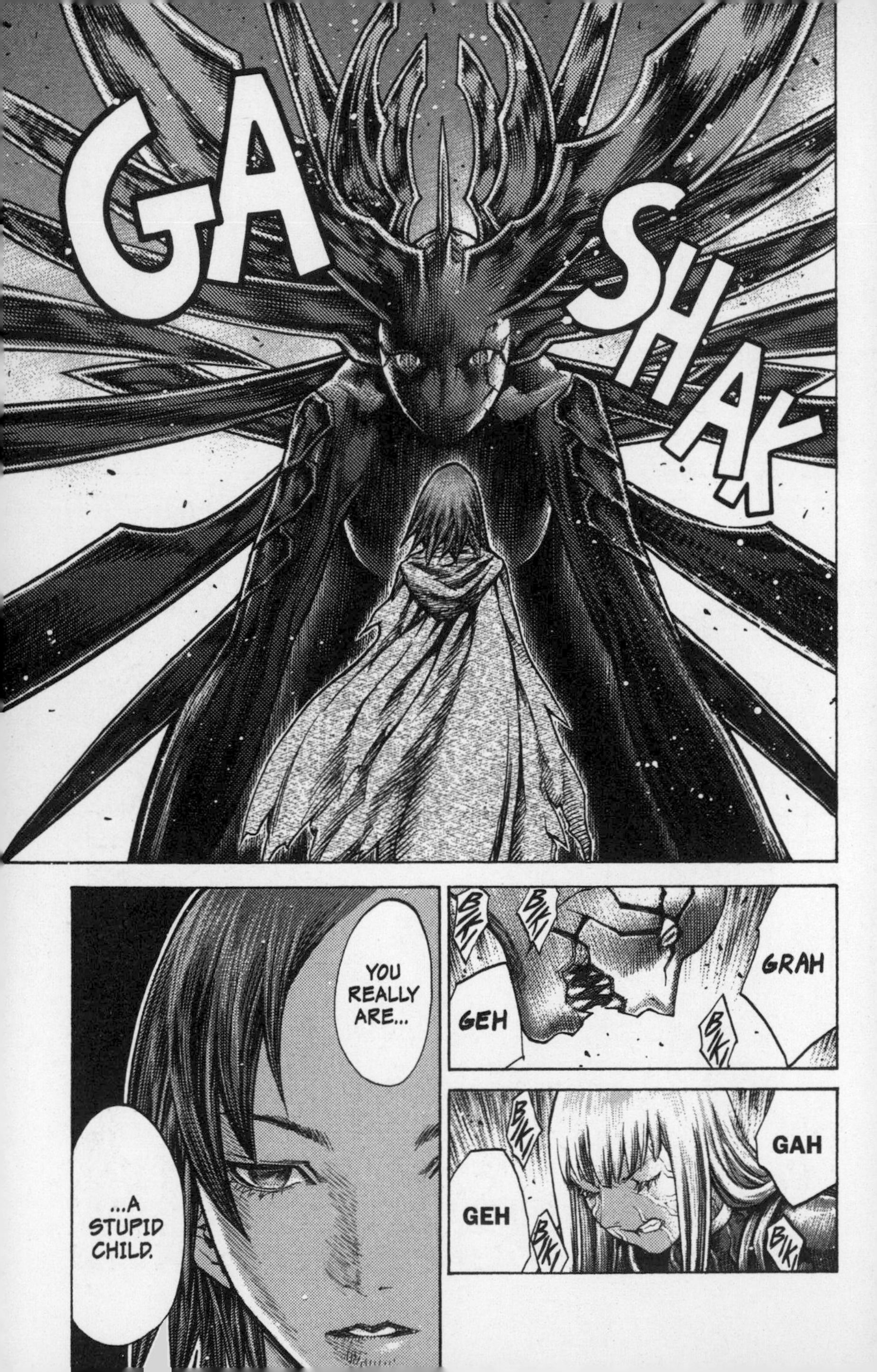
GA SHAK
GRAH
BIKI
BIKI
BIKI
GEH
GAH
BIKI
BIKI
BIKI
GEH
YOU REALLY ARE...
...A STUPID CHILD.

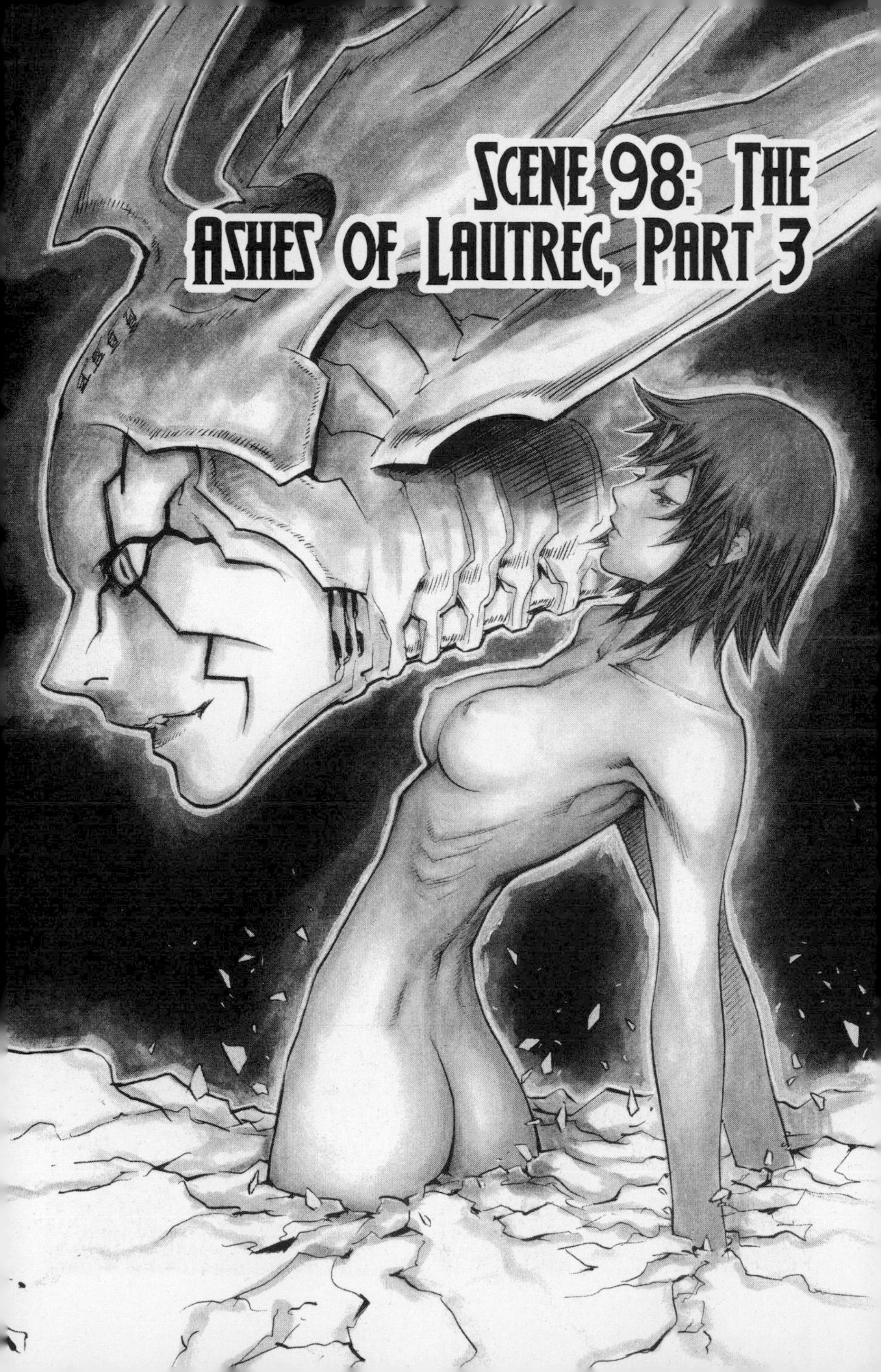
SCENE 98: THE ASHES OF LAUTREC, PART 3

READ THIS WAY

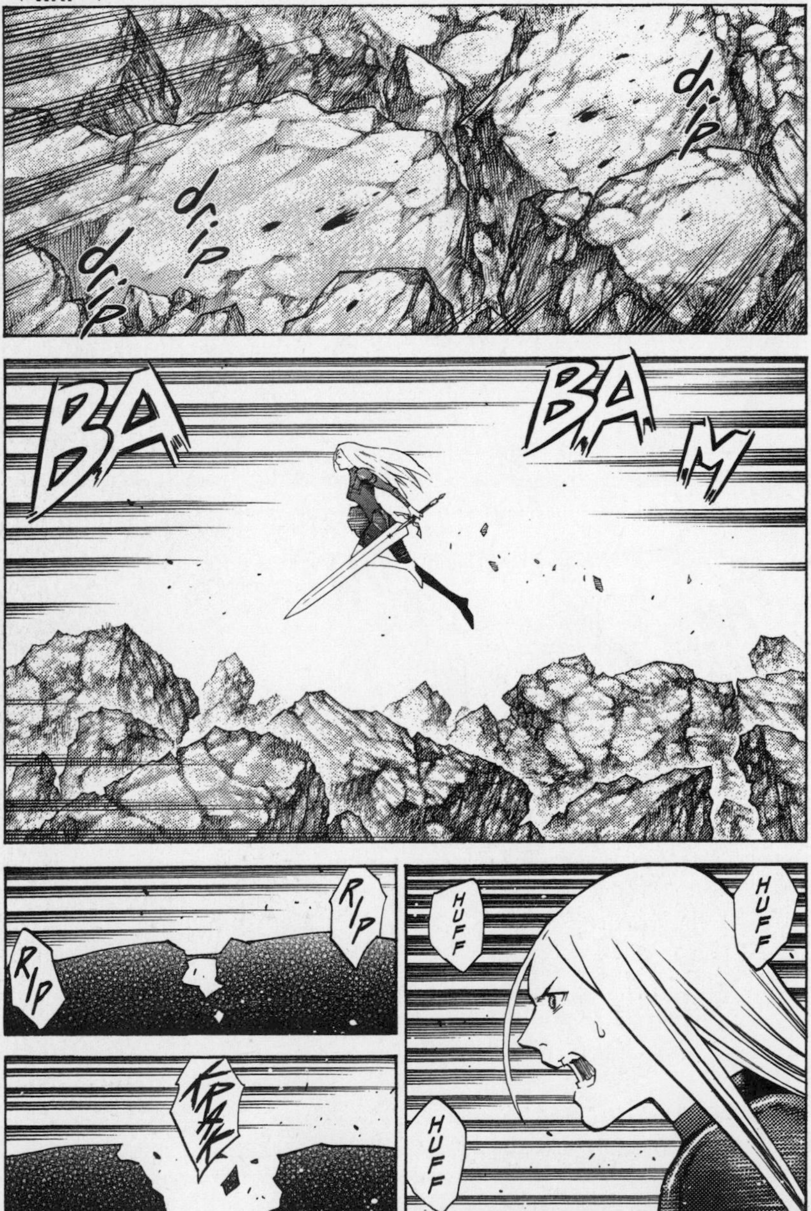
drip
drip
drip
BA
BAM
HUFF
HUFF
HUFF
RIP
RIP
KRAK

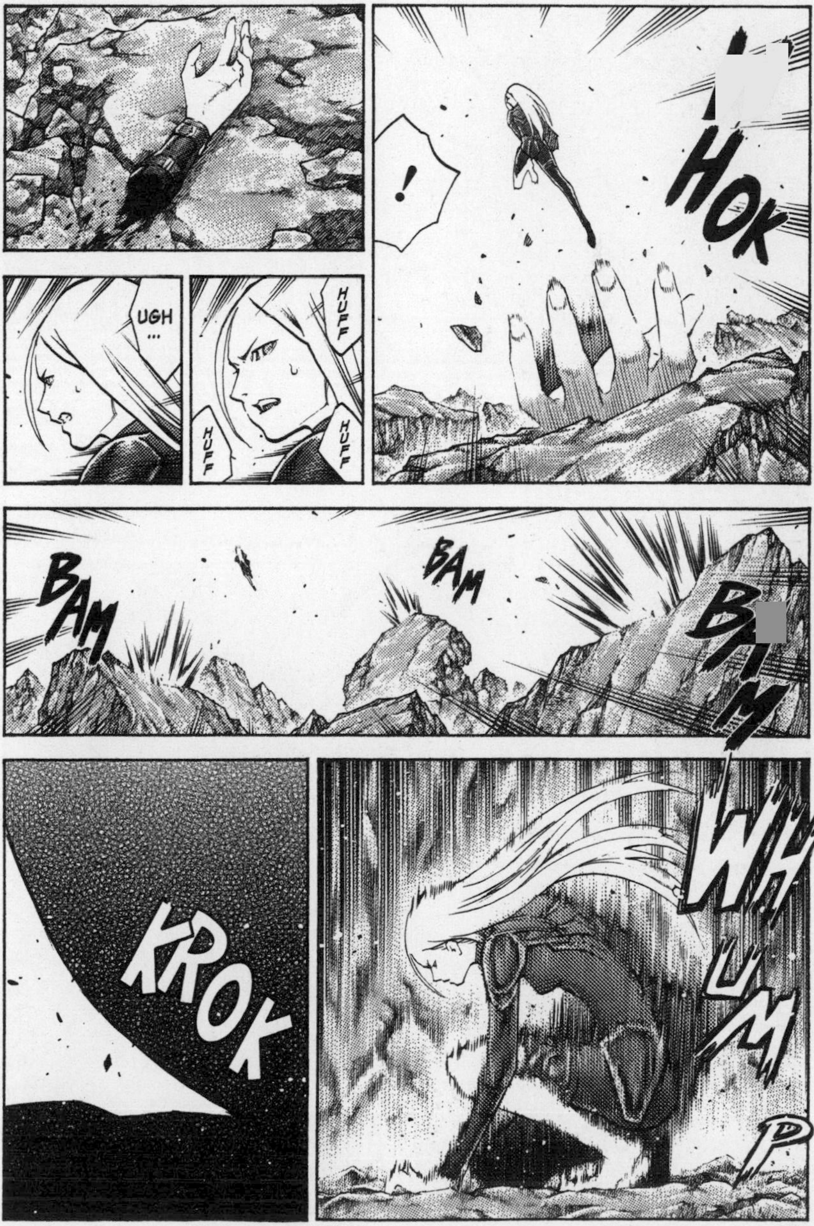
!
HOK
HUFF
HUFF
HUFF
UGH ...
BAM
BAM
WHUMP
KROK

READ THIS WAY

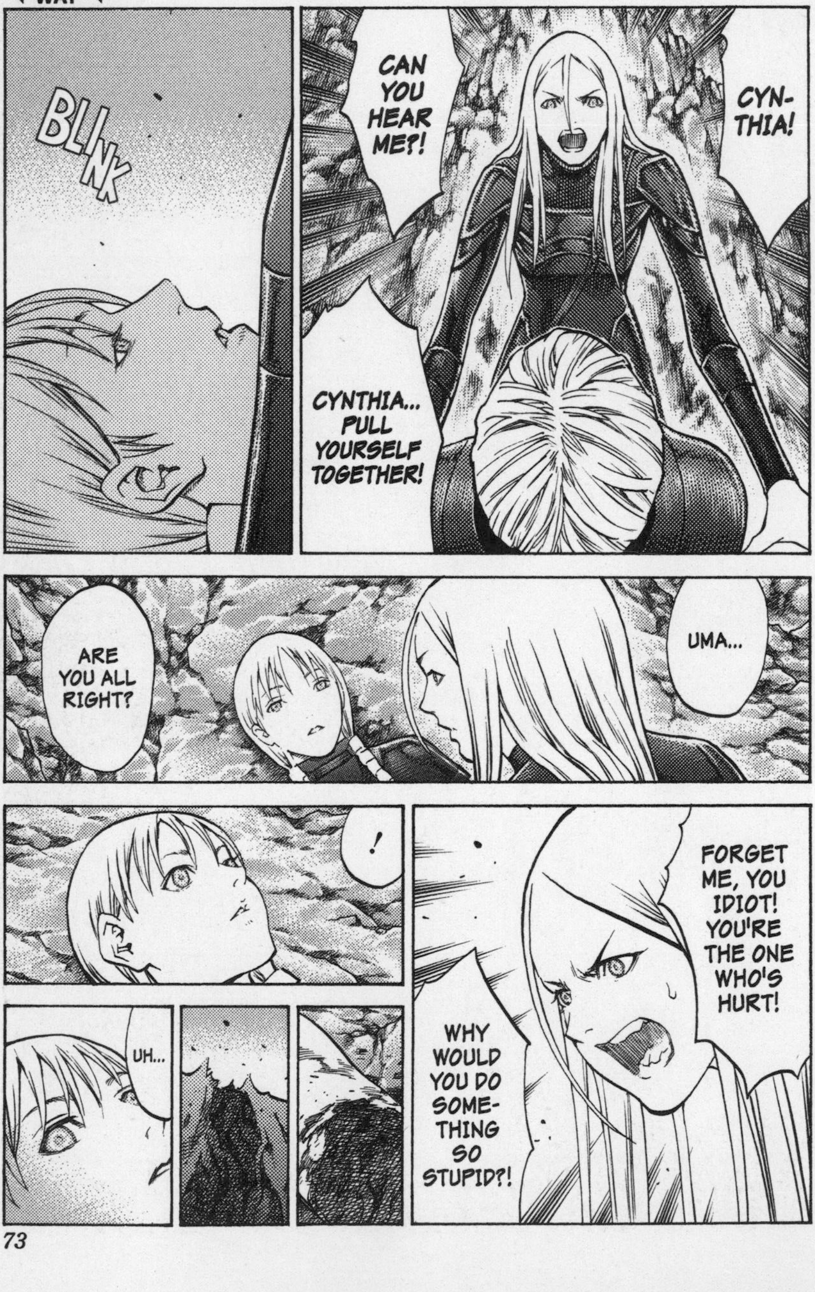
CYN-THIA!
CAN YOU HEAR ME?!
CYNTHIA... PULL YOURSELF TOGETHER!
BLINK
UMA...
ARE YOU ALL RIGHT?
FORGET ME, YOU IDIOT! YOU'RE THE ONE WHO'S HURT!
WHY WOULD YOU DO SOME-THING SO STUPID?!
!
UH...

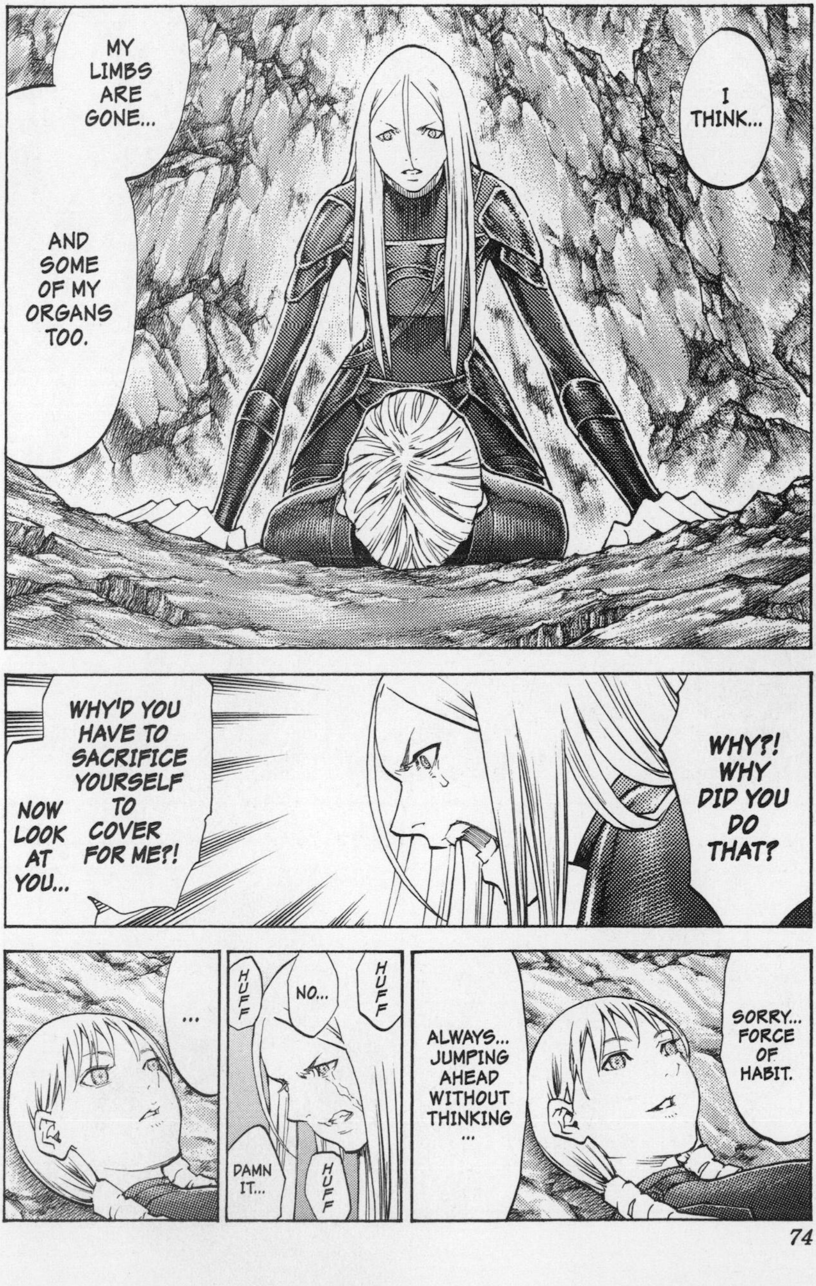
I THINK...
MY LIMBS ARE GONE...
AND SOME OF MY ORGANS TOO.
WHY?! WHY DID YOU DO THAT?
WHY'D YOU HAVE TO SACRIFICE YOURSELF TO COVER FOR ME?!
NOW LOOK AT YOU...
SORRY... FORCE OF HABIT.
ALWAYS... JUMPING AHEAD WITHOUT THINKING ...
HUFF
NO...
HUFF
HUFF
DAMN IT...
...

READ THIS WAY

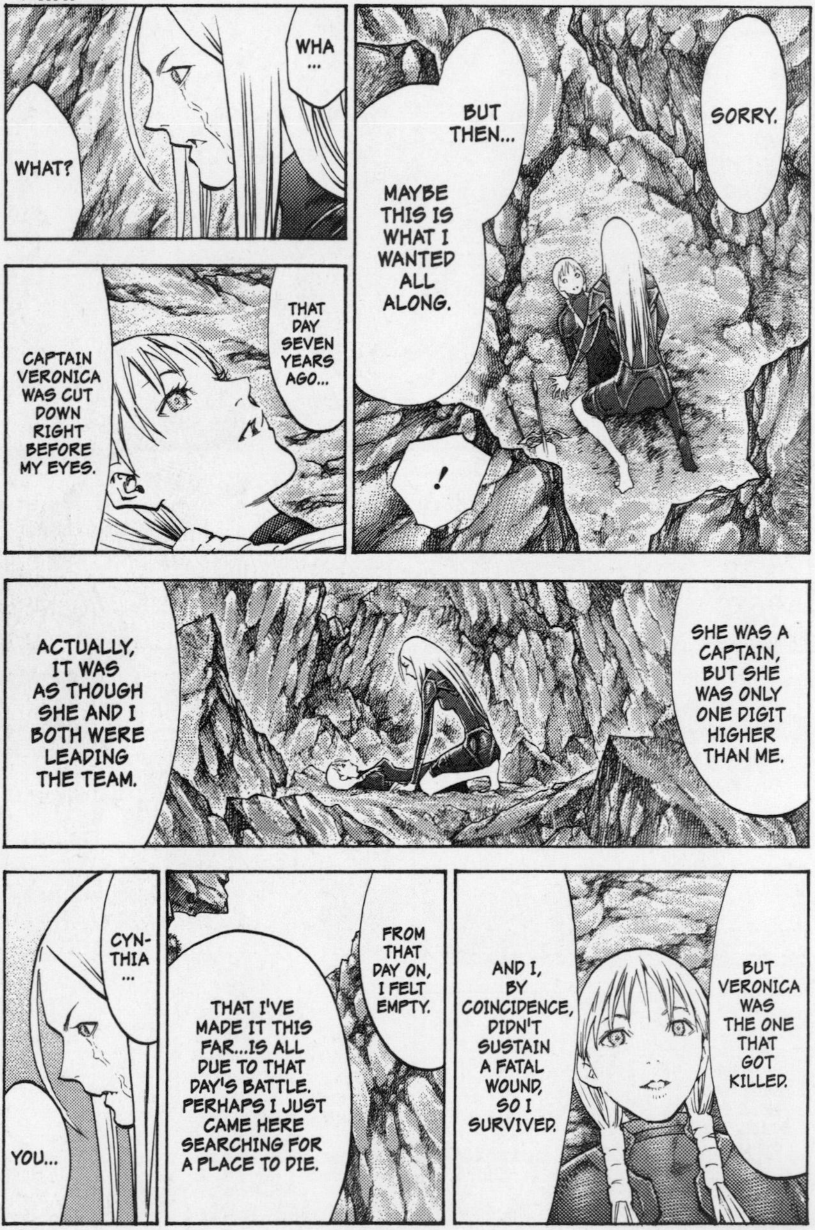
SORRY.
BUT THEN...
MAYBE THIS IS WHAT I WANTED ALL ALONG.
!
WHA ...
WHAT?
THAT DAY SEVEN YEARS AGO...
CAPTAIN VERONICA WAS CUT DOWN RIGHT BEFORE MY EYES.
SHE WAS A CAPTAIN, BUT SHE WAS ONLY ONE DIGIT HIGHER THAN ME.
ACTUALLY, IT WAS AS THOUGH SHE AND I BOTH WERE LEADING THE TEAM.
BUT VERONICA WAS THE ONE THAT GOT KILLED.
AND I, BY COINCIDENCE, DIDN'T SUSTAIN A FATAL WOUND, SO I SURVIVED.
FROM THAT DAY ON, I FELT EMPTY.
THAT I'VE MADE IT THIS FAR...IS ALL DUE TO THAT DAY'S BATTLE. PERHAPS I JUST CAME HERE SEARCHING FOR A PLACE TO DIE.
CYN-THIA ...
YOU...

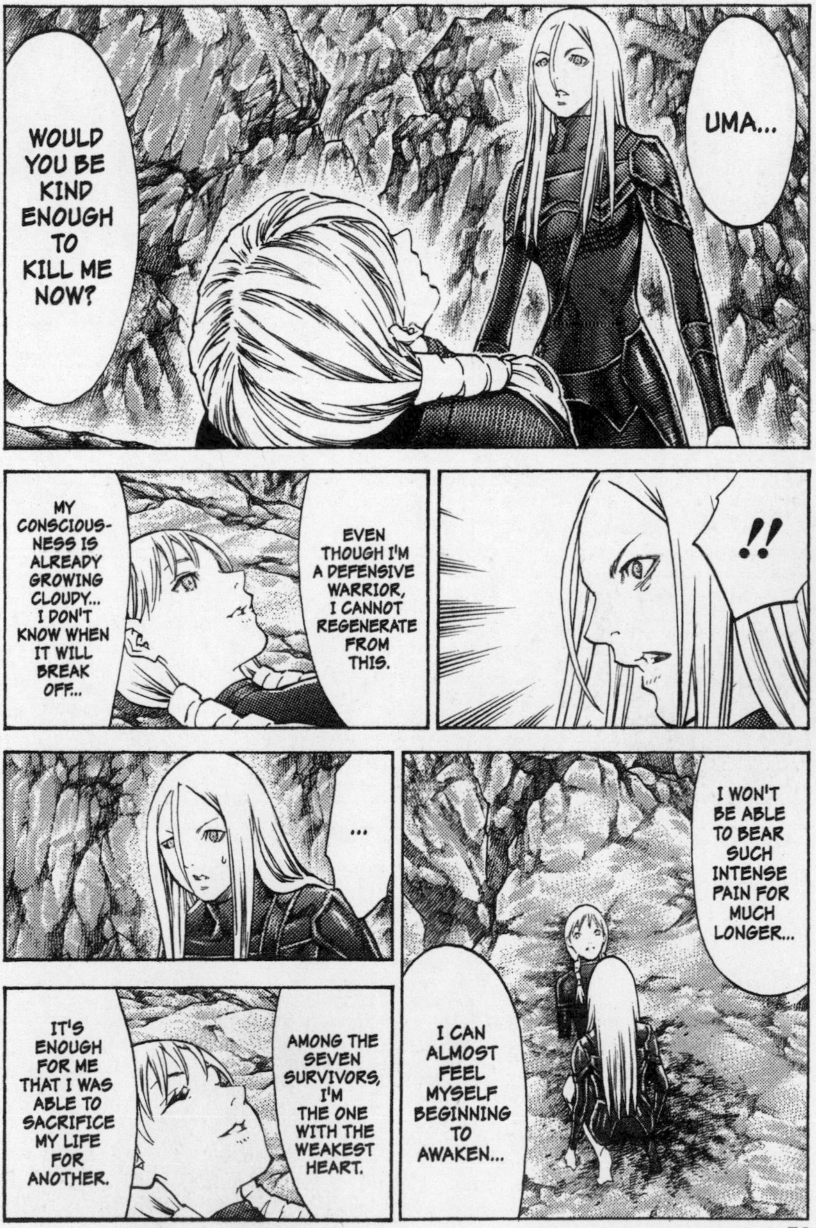
UMA...
WOULD YOU BE KIND ENOUGH TO KILL ME NOW?
!!
EVEN THOUGH I'M A DEFENSIVE WARRIOR, I CANNOT REGENERATE FROM THIS.
MY CONSCIOUSNESS IS ALREADY GROWING CLOUDY... I DON'T KNOW WHEN IT WILL BREAK OFF...
I WON'T BE ABLE TO BEAR SUCH INTENSE PAIN FOR MUCH LONGER...
I CAN ALMOST FEEL MYSELF BEGINNING TO AWAKEN...
...
AMONG THE SEVEN SURVIVORS, I'M THE ONE WITH THE WEAKEST HEART.
IT'S ENOUGH FOR ME THAT I WAS ABLE TO SACRIFICE MY LIFE FOR ANOTHER.

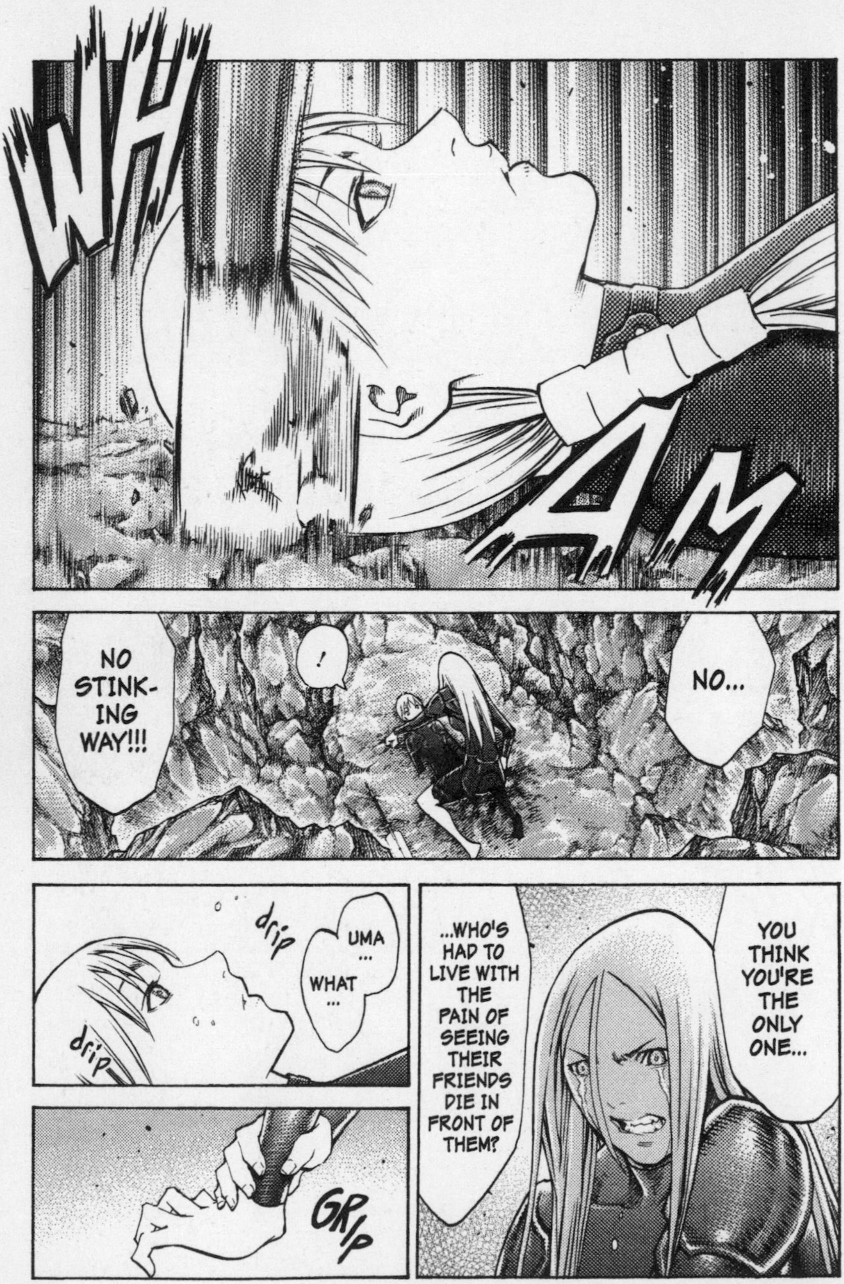
WH
AM
NO...
!
NO STINKING WAY!!!
YOU THINK YOU'RE THE ONLY ONE...
...WHO'S HAD TO LIVE WITH THE PAIN OF SEEING THEIR FRIENDS DIE IN FRONT OF THEM?
drip
UMA ... WHAT ...
drip
GRIP

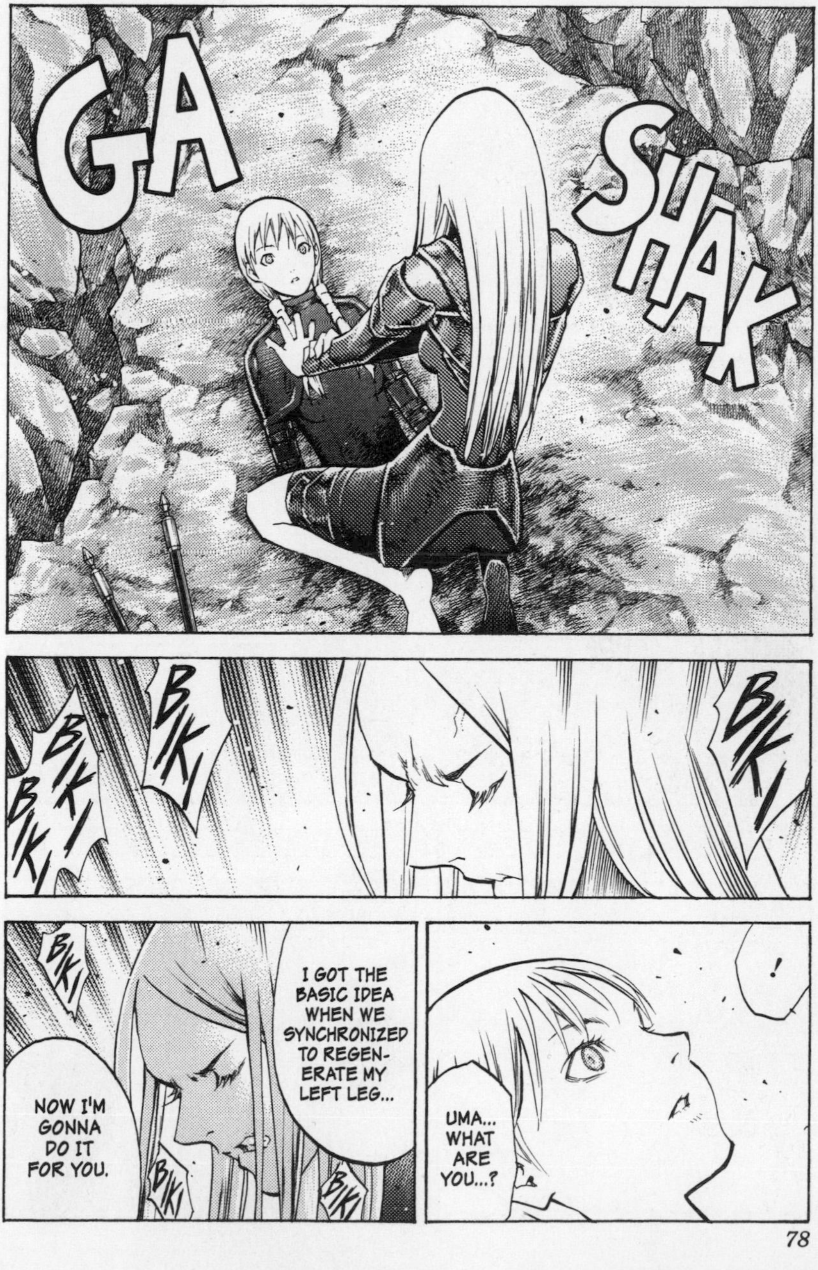
GA
SHAK
BIKI
BIKI
BIKI
BIKI
!
UMA... WHAT ARE YOU...?
BIKI
I GOT THE BASIC IDEA WHEN WE SYNCHRONIZED TO REGEN-ERATE MY LEFT LEG...
NOW I'M GONNA DO IT FOR YOU.
BIKI
BIKI

READ THIS WAY

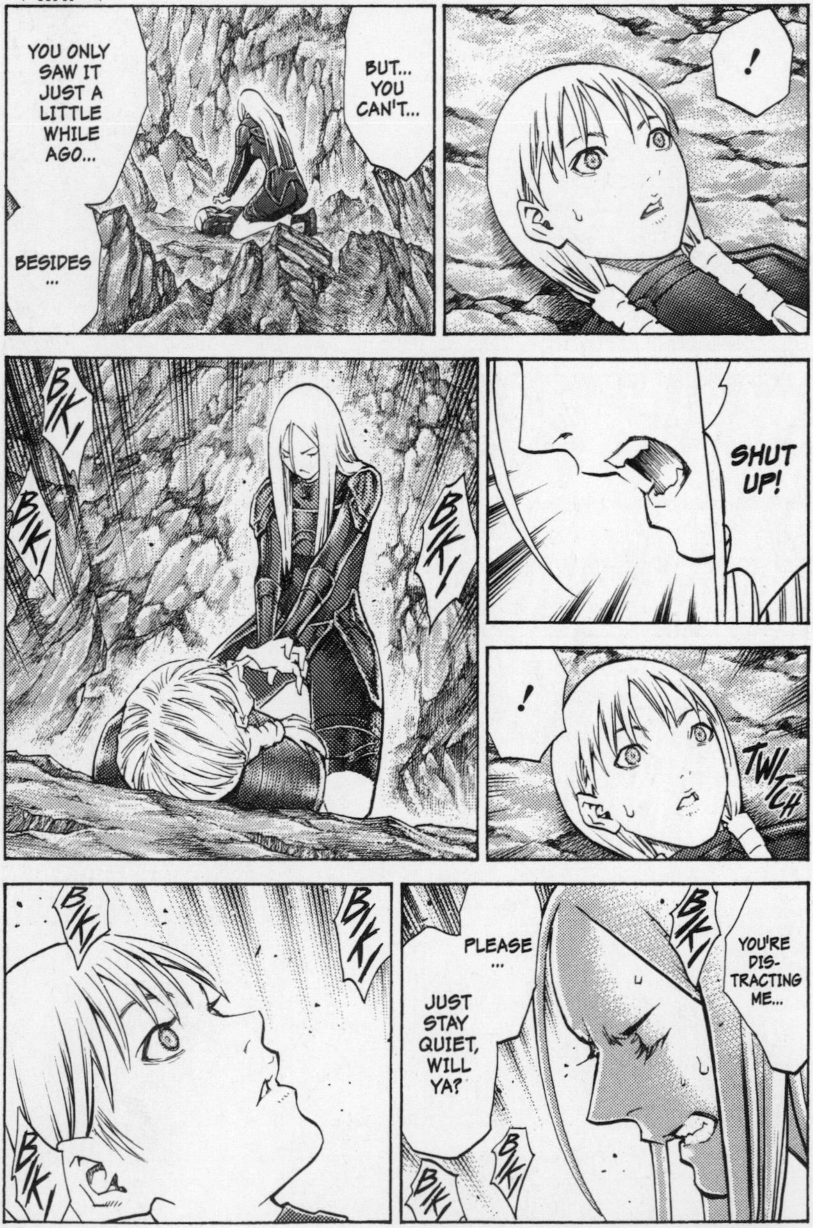
!
BUT... YOU CAN'T...
YOU ONLY SAW IT JUST A LITTLE WHILE AGO...
BESIDES ...
SHUT UP!
TWITCH
!
BIKI
BIKI
BIKI
YOU'RE DIS-TRACTING ME...
BIKI
PLEASE ...
JUST STAY QUIET, WILL YA?
BIKI
BIKI
BIKI
BIKI
BIKI

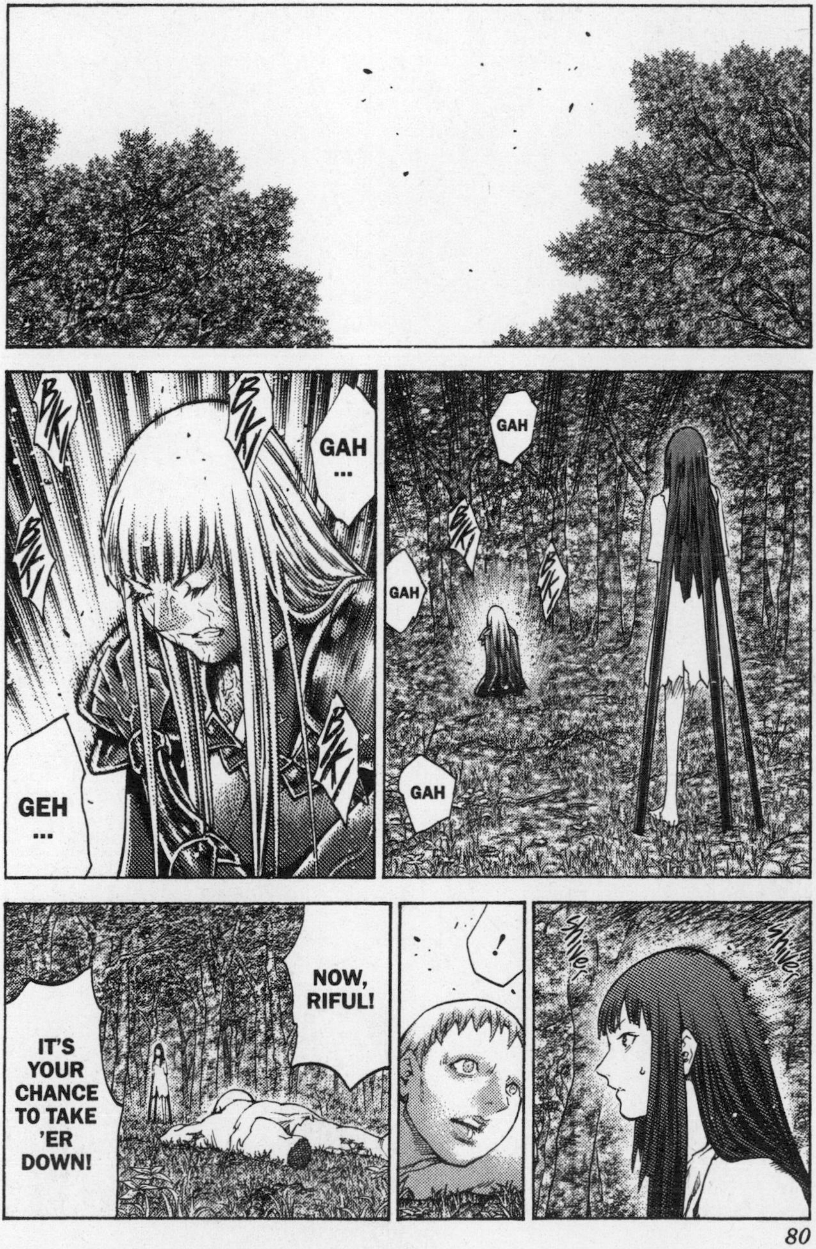
GAH
BIKI
GAH
BIKI
GAH
BIKI
GAH ...
BIKI
BIKI
BIKI
GEH ...
shiver
shiver
!
NOW, RIFUL!
IT'S YOUR CHANCE TO TAKE 'ER DOWN!

READ THIS WAY

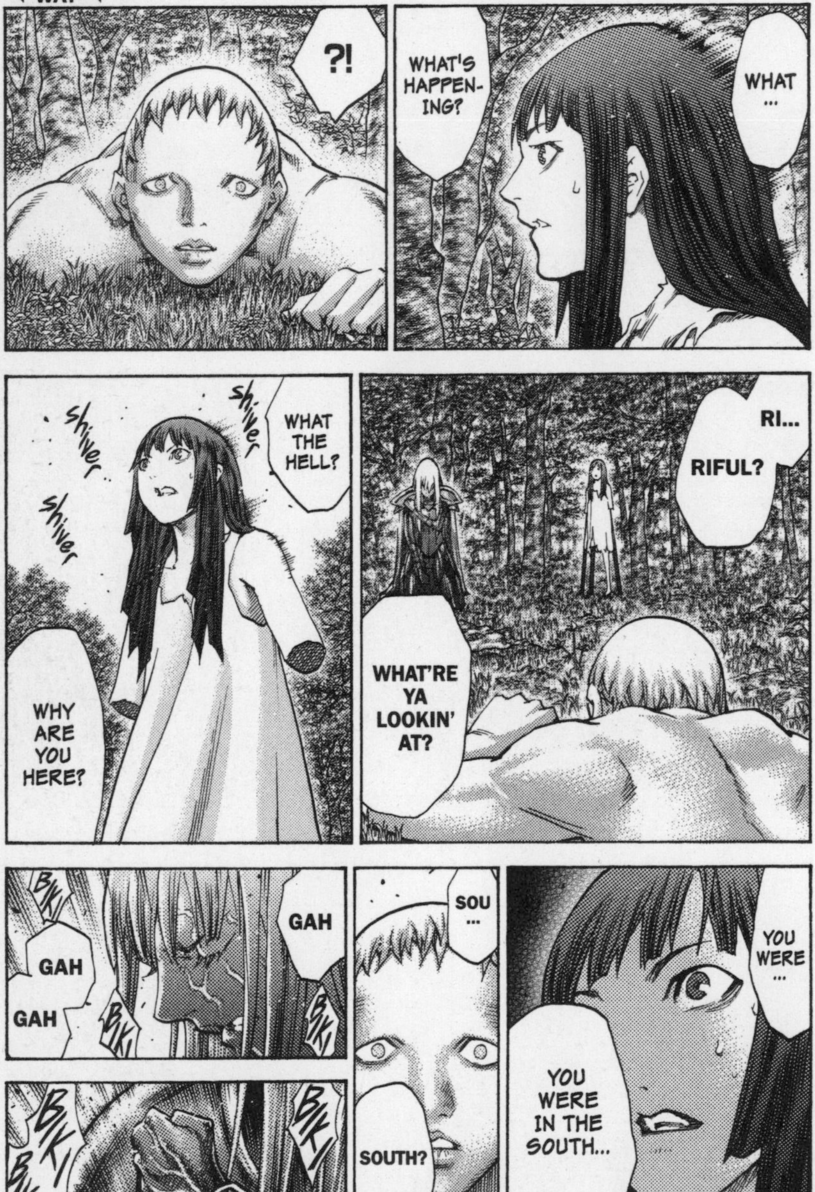
WHAT ...
WHAT'S HAPPEN-ING?
?!
RI...
RIFUL?
WHAT'RE YA LOOKIN' AT?
shiver
WHAT THE HELL?
shiver...
shiver
WHY ARE YOU HERE?
YOU WERE ...
YOU WERE IN THE SOUTH...
SOU ...
SOUTH?
GAH
BIKI
GAH
GAH
BIKI
BIKI
BIKI
BIKI
BIKI

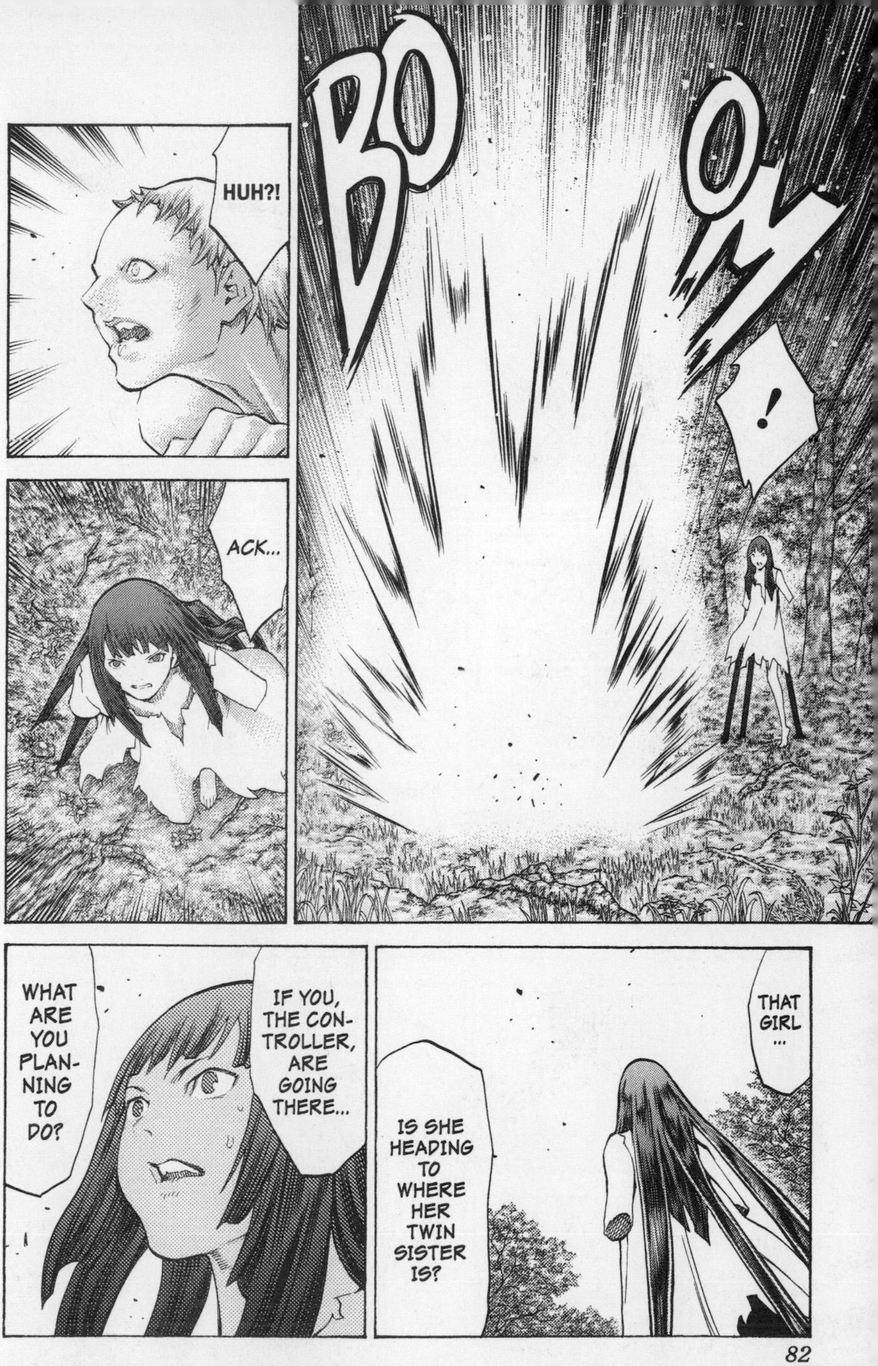
BOOM
!
HUH?!
ACK...
THAT GIRL...
IS SHE HEADING TO WHERE HER TWIN SISTER IS?
IF YOU, THE CONTROLLER, ARE GOING THERE...
WHAT ARE YOU PLANNING TO DO?

READ THIS WAY

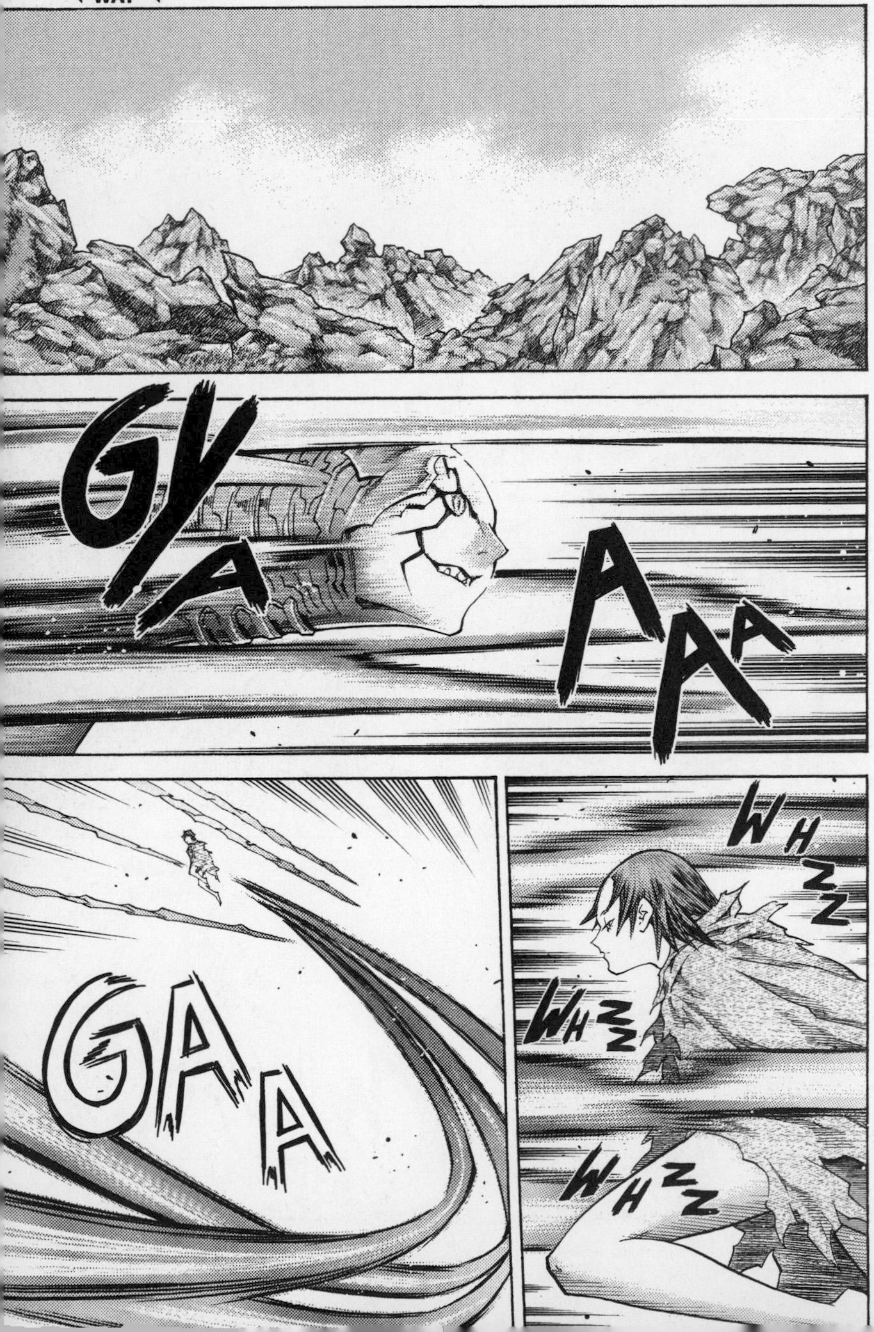
GYAAAAA
WHZZ
WHZZ
WHZZ
GAAA

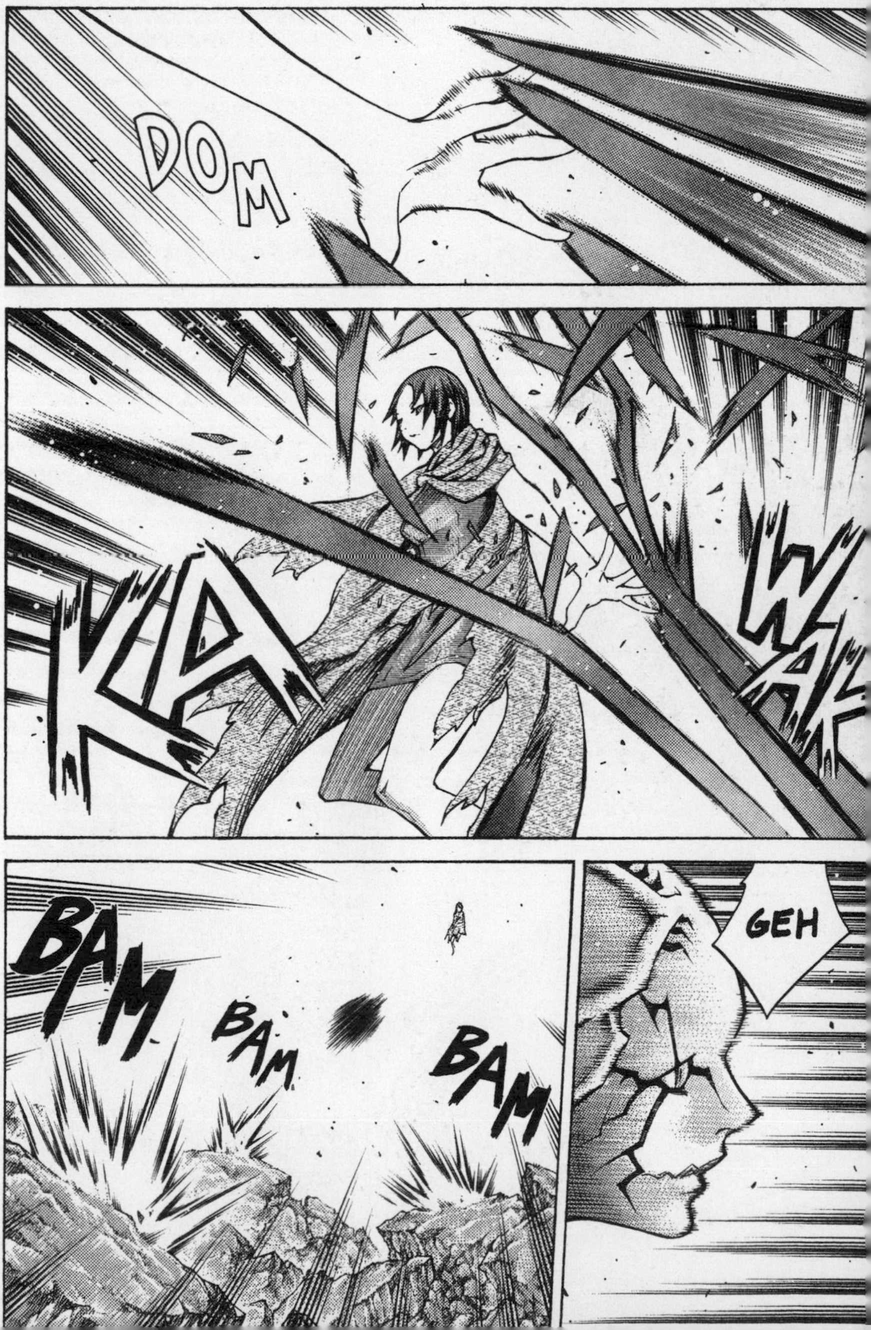
DOM
WAK
KA
GEH
BAM
BAM
BAM

READ THIS WAY

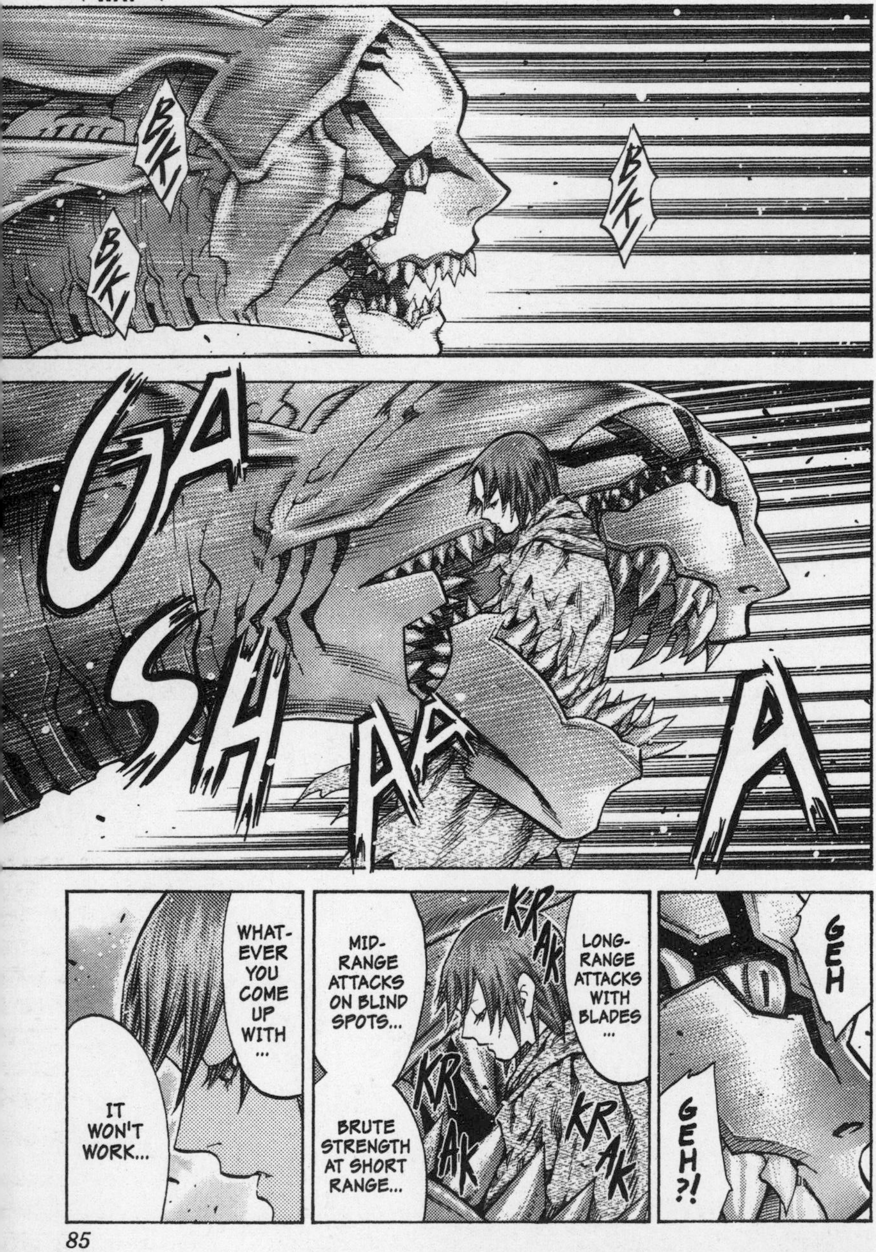
BKK
BKK
BKK
GASHAAA
GEH
GEH?!
LONG-RANGE ATTACKS WITH BLADES...
KRAK
MID-RANGE ATTACKS ON BLIND SPOTS...
KRAK
KRAK
BRUTE STRENGTH AT SHORT RANGE...
WHATEVER YOU COME UP WITH...
IT WON'T WORK...

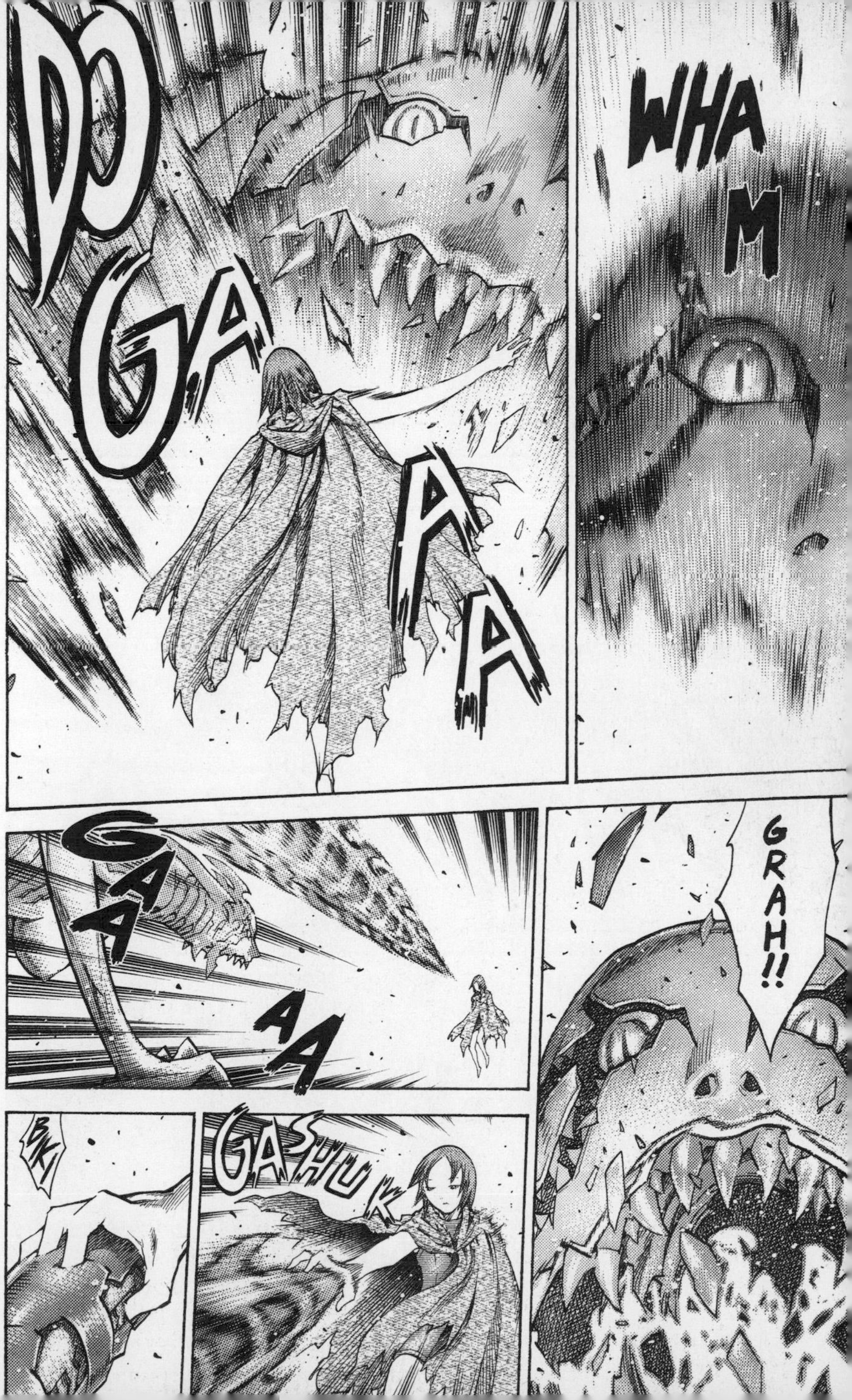
WHAM
DOGAAA
GRAH!!
GAAAA
GASHUK
BAKI

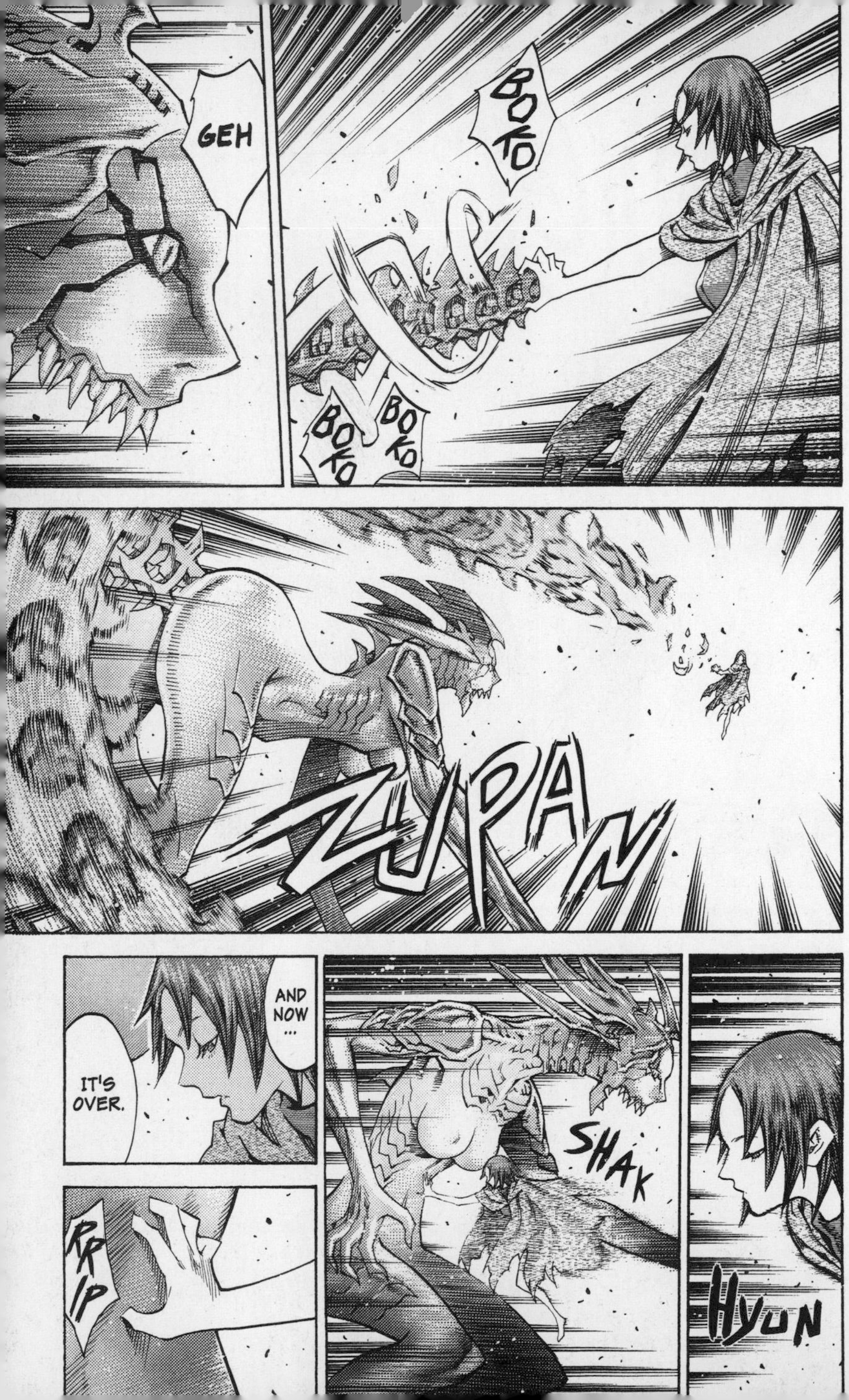
BOKO
BOKO
BOKO
GEH
ZUPAN
HYUN
SHAK
AND NOW ...
IT'S OVER.
RRIP

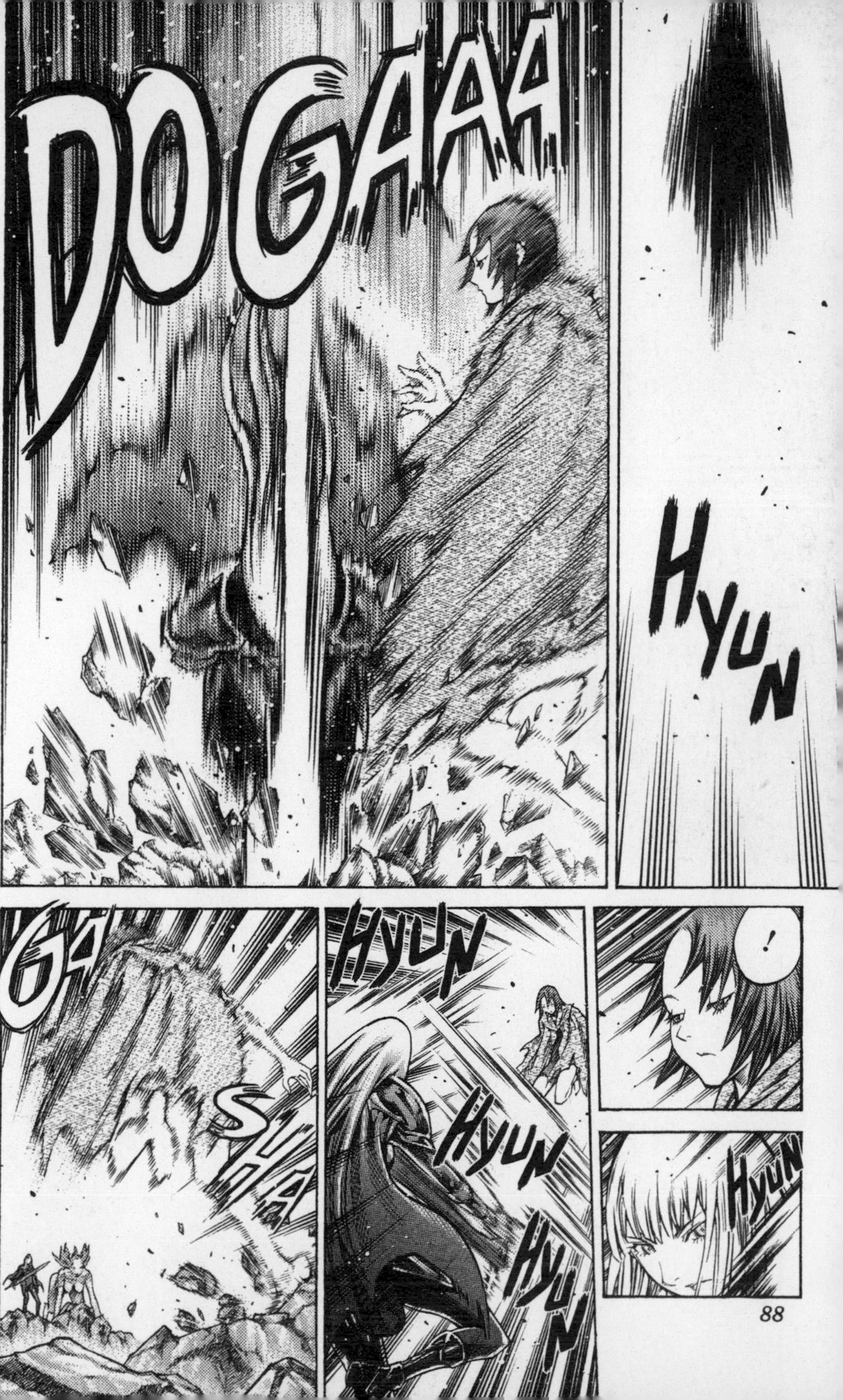
HYUN
DOGAAA
!
HYUN
HYUN
HYUN
HYUN
GA
SHA

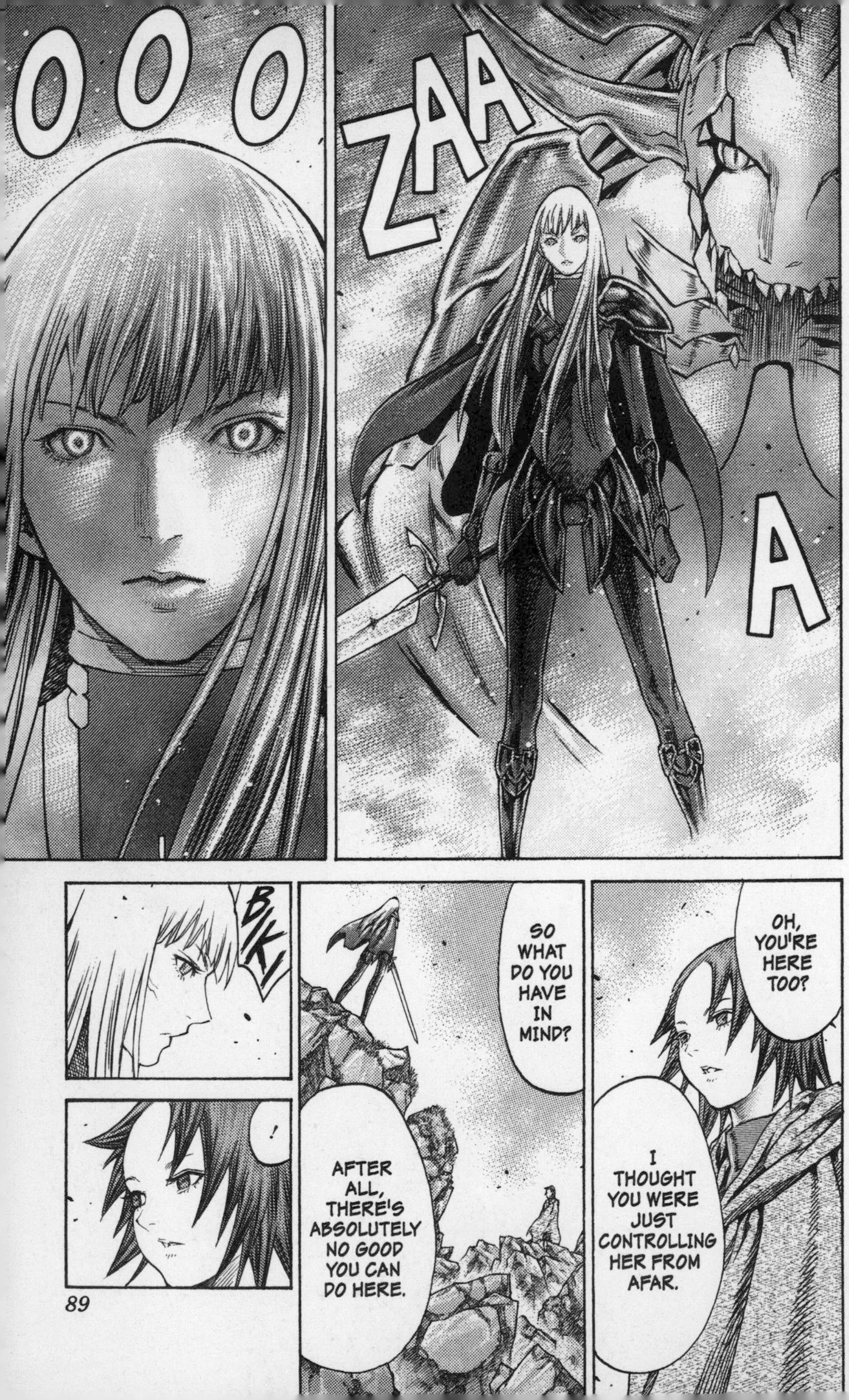
ZAA
A
OOO
OH, YOU'RE HERE TOO?
I THOUGHT YOU WERE JUST CONTROLLING HER FROM AFAR.
SO WHAT DO YOU HAVE IN MIND?
AFTER ALL, THERE'S ABSOLUTELY NO GOOD YOU CAN DO HERE.
BIKI
!

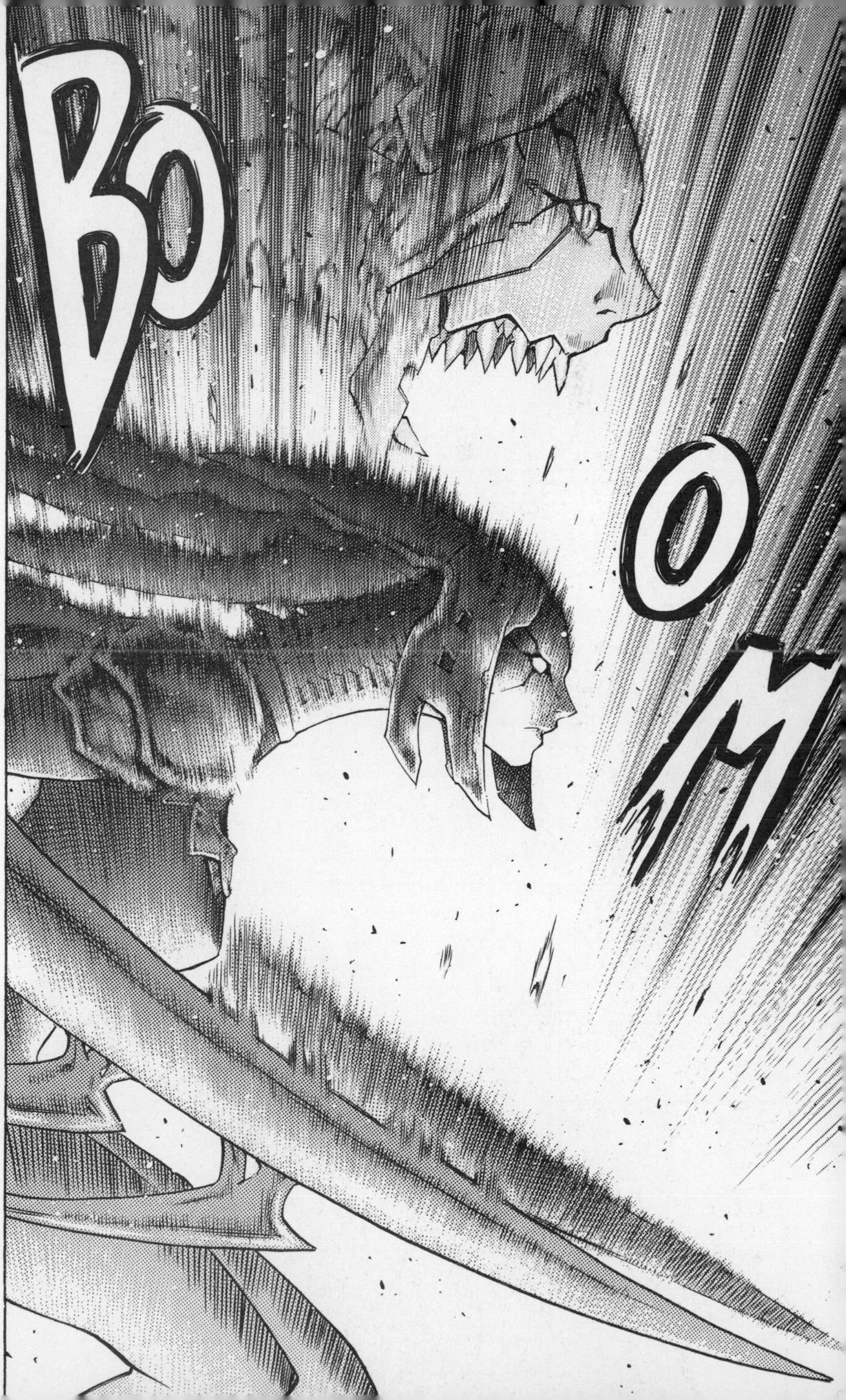
BOOM

READ THIS WAY

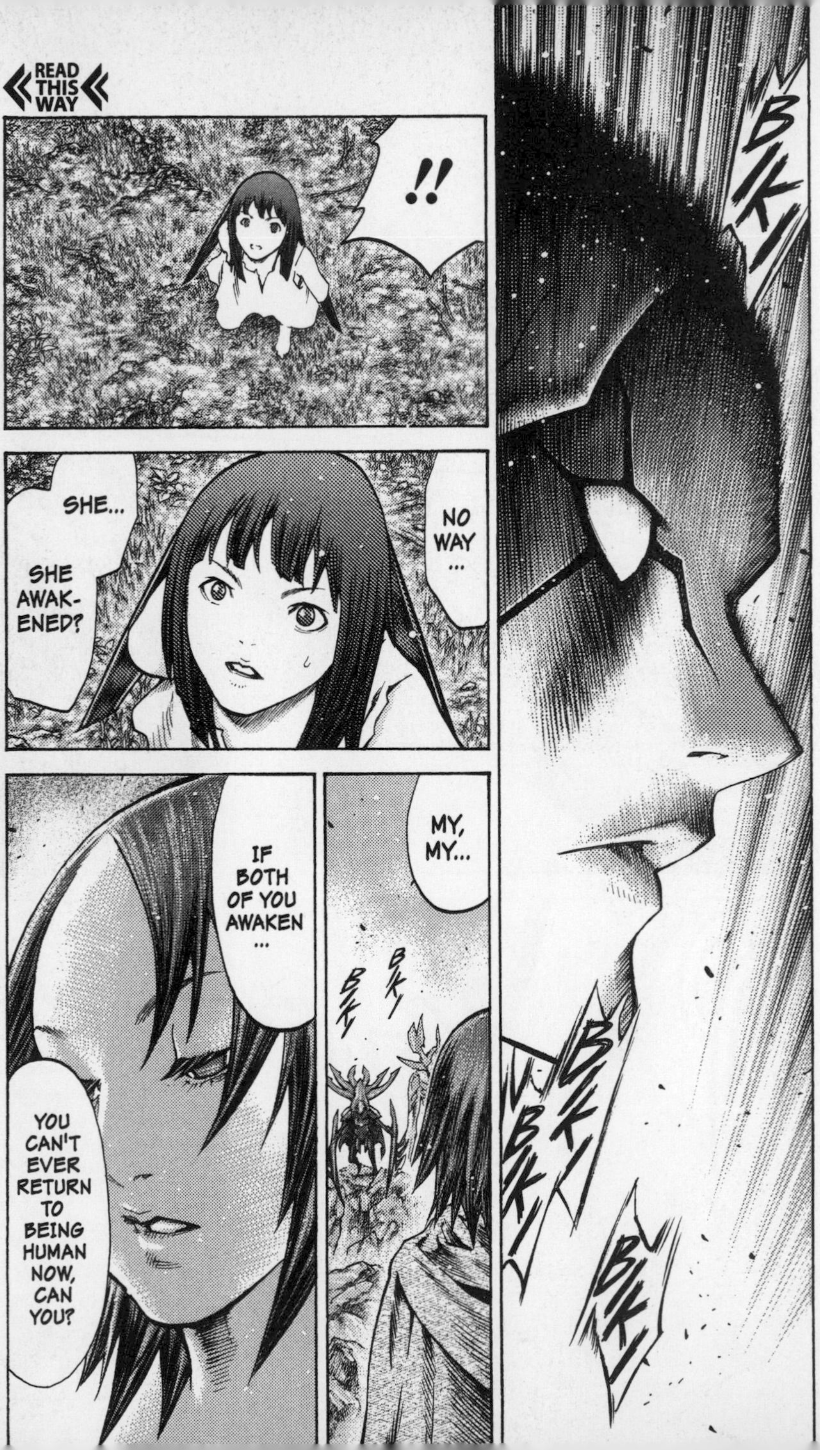
BIKI
BIKI
BIKI
BIKI
!!
NO WAY...
SHE...
SHE AWAKENED?
MY, MY...
BIKI
BIKI
IF BOTH OF YOU AWAKEN...
YOU CAN'T EVER RETURN TO BEING HUMAN NOW, CAN YOU?

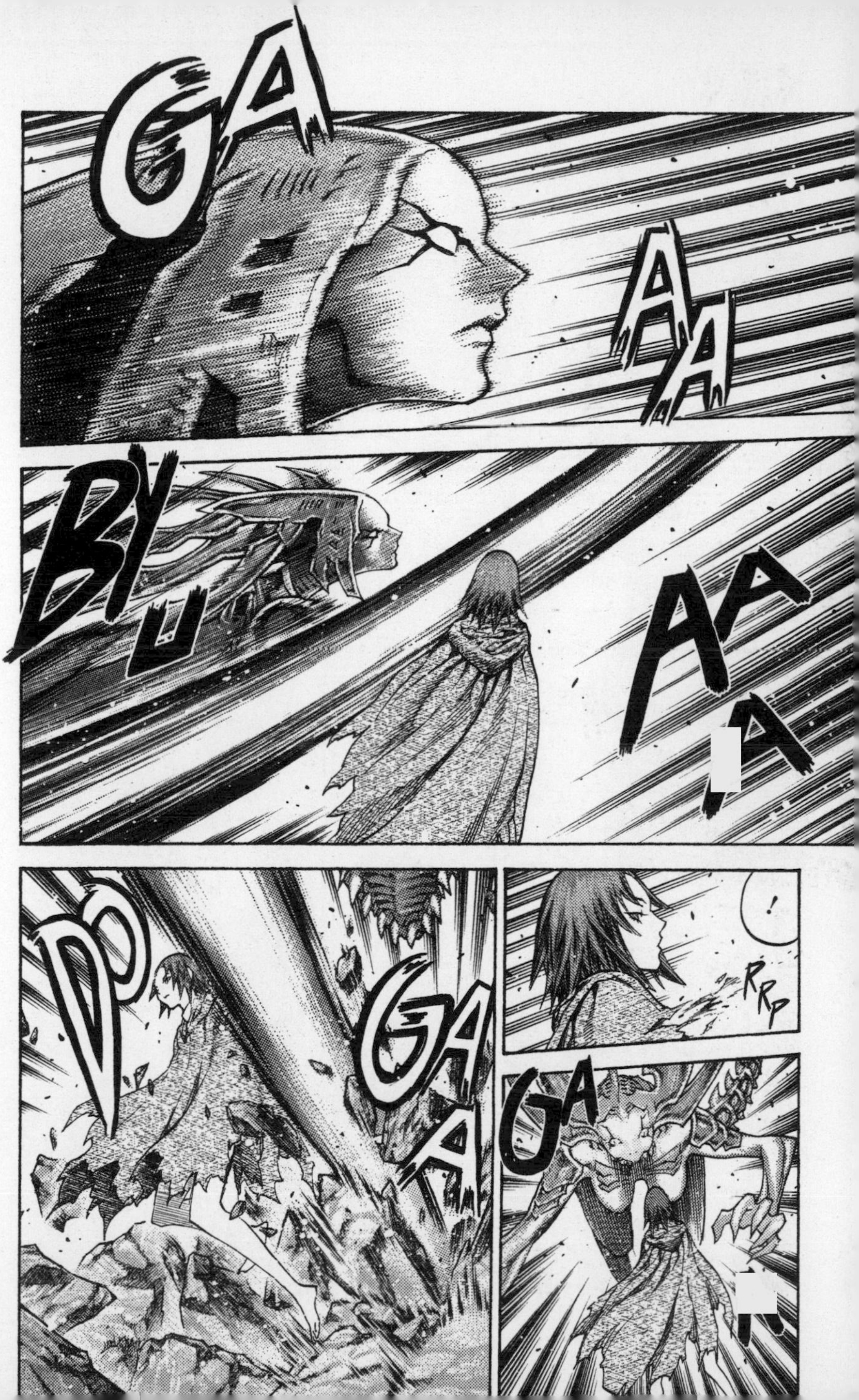
GA
AAA
BYU
AAAA
!
RRP
GA
DO
GA
A

READ THIS WAY

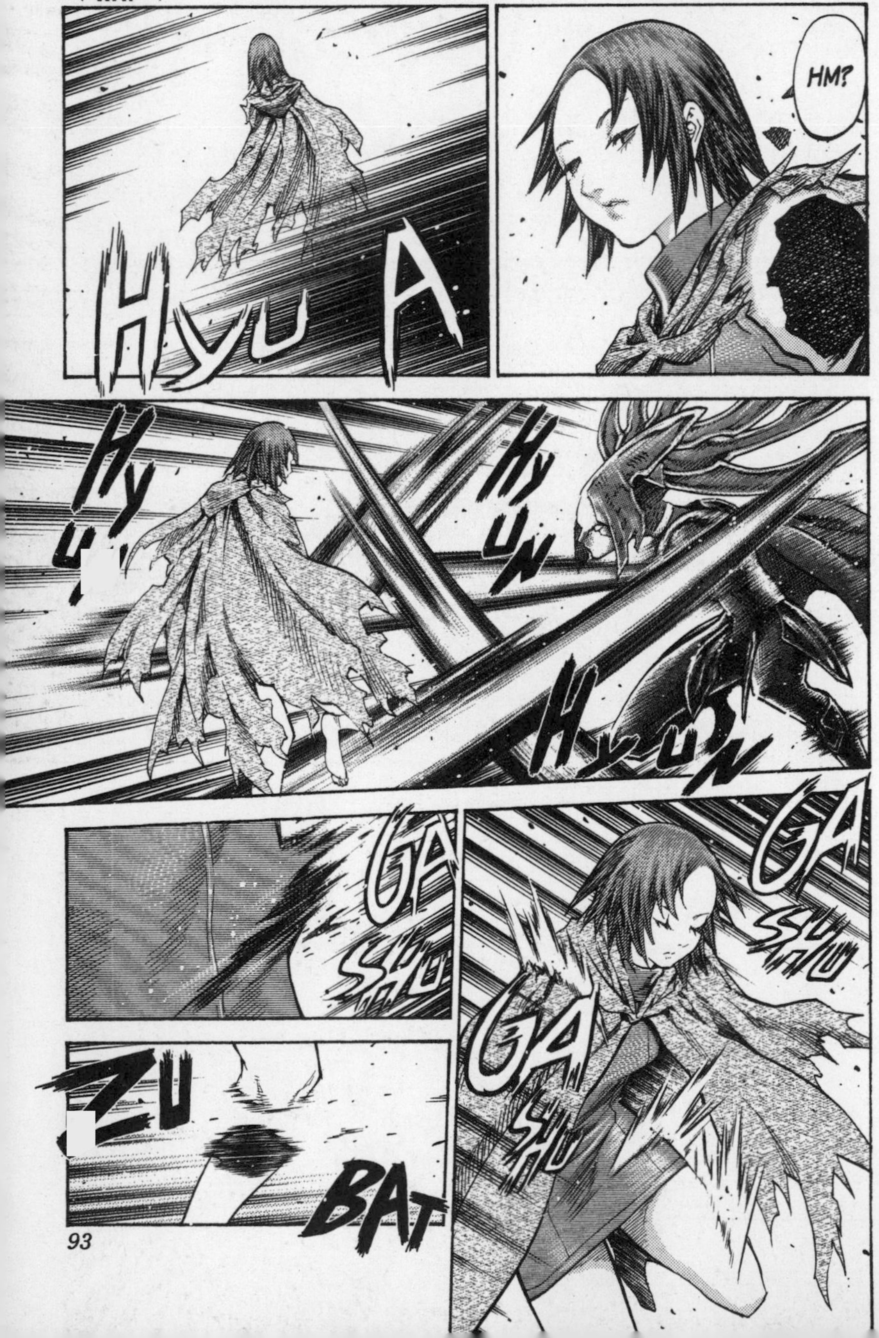
HM?
HYU A
HYUN
HYUN
HYU
GA SSHU
GA SHU
GA SSHU
ZU
BAT

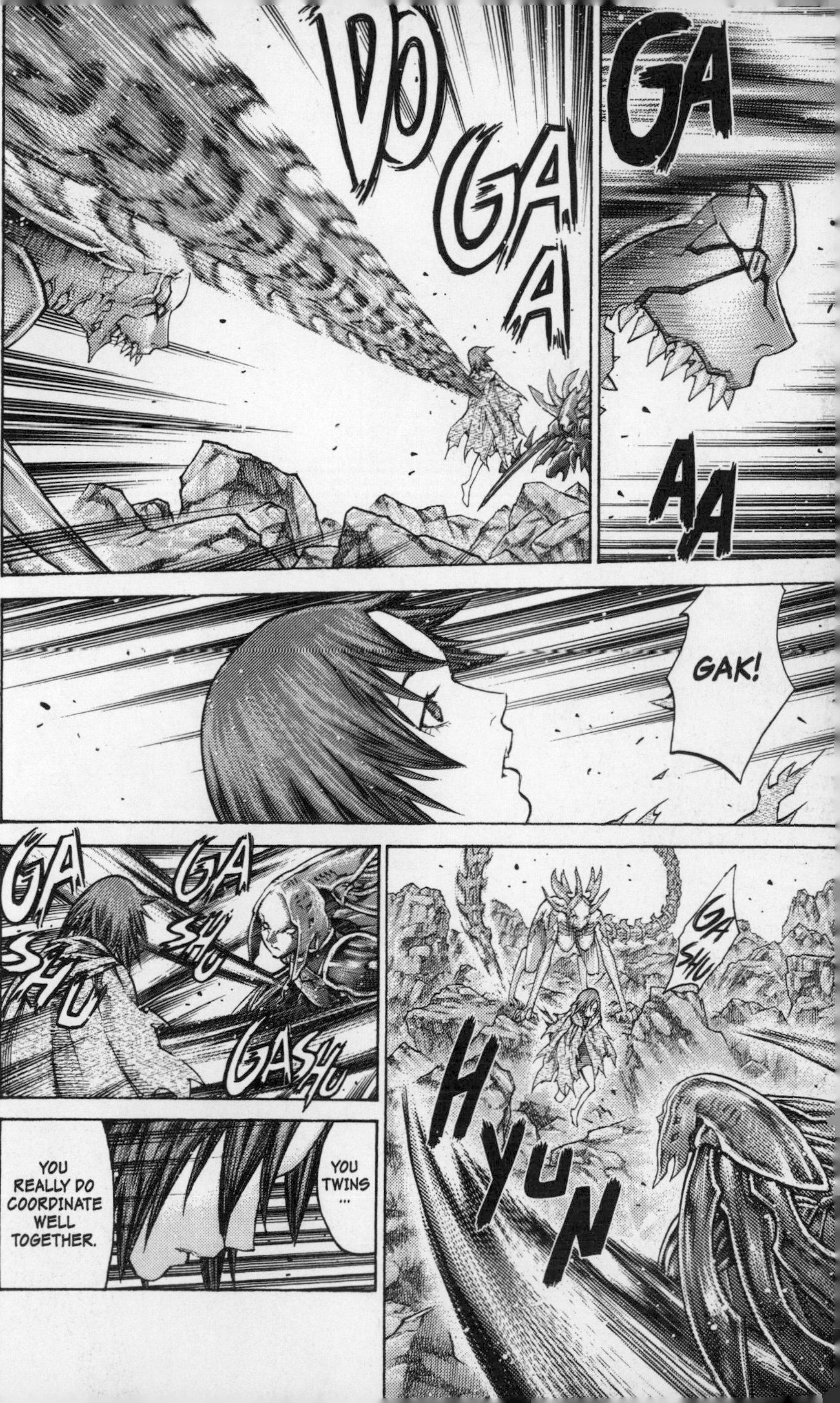
GA
AA
DO
GA
GA
A
GAK!
GASHU
HYUN
GASHU
GASHU
GASHU
YOU TWINS...
YOU REALLY DO COORDINATE WELL TOGETHER.

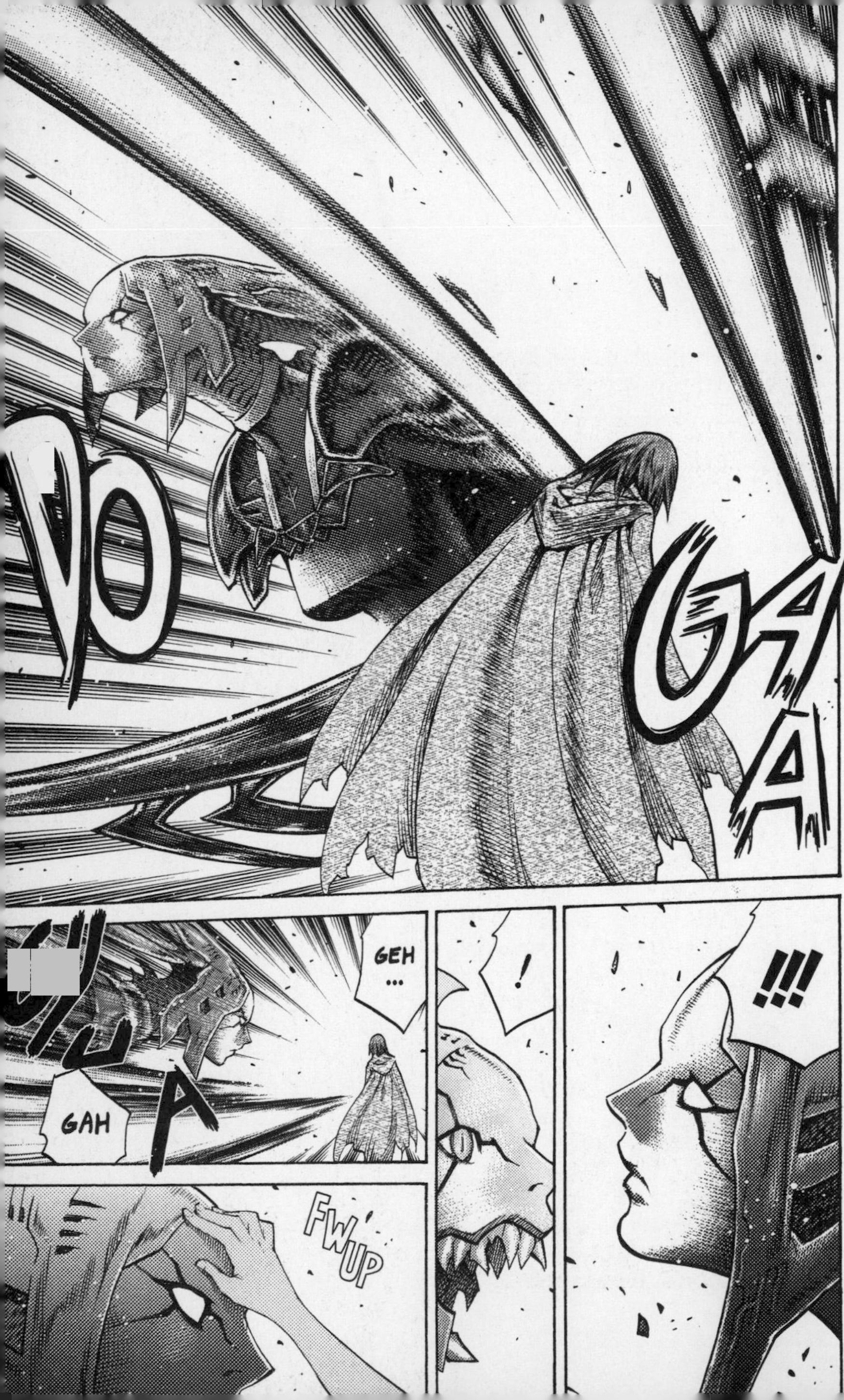

GAA
DO
!!!
!
GEH ...
GAH
FWUP

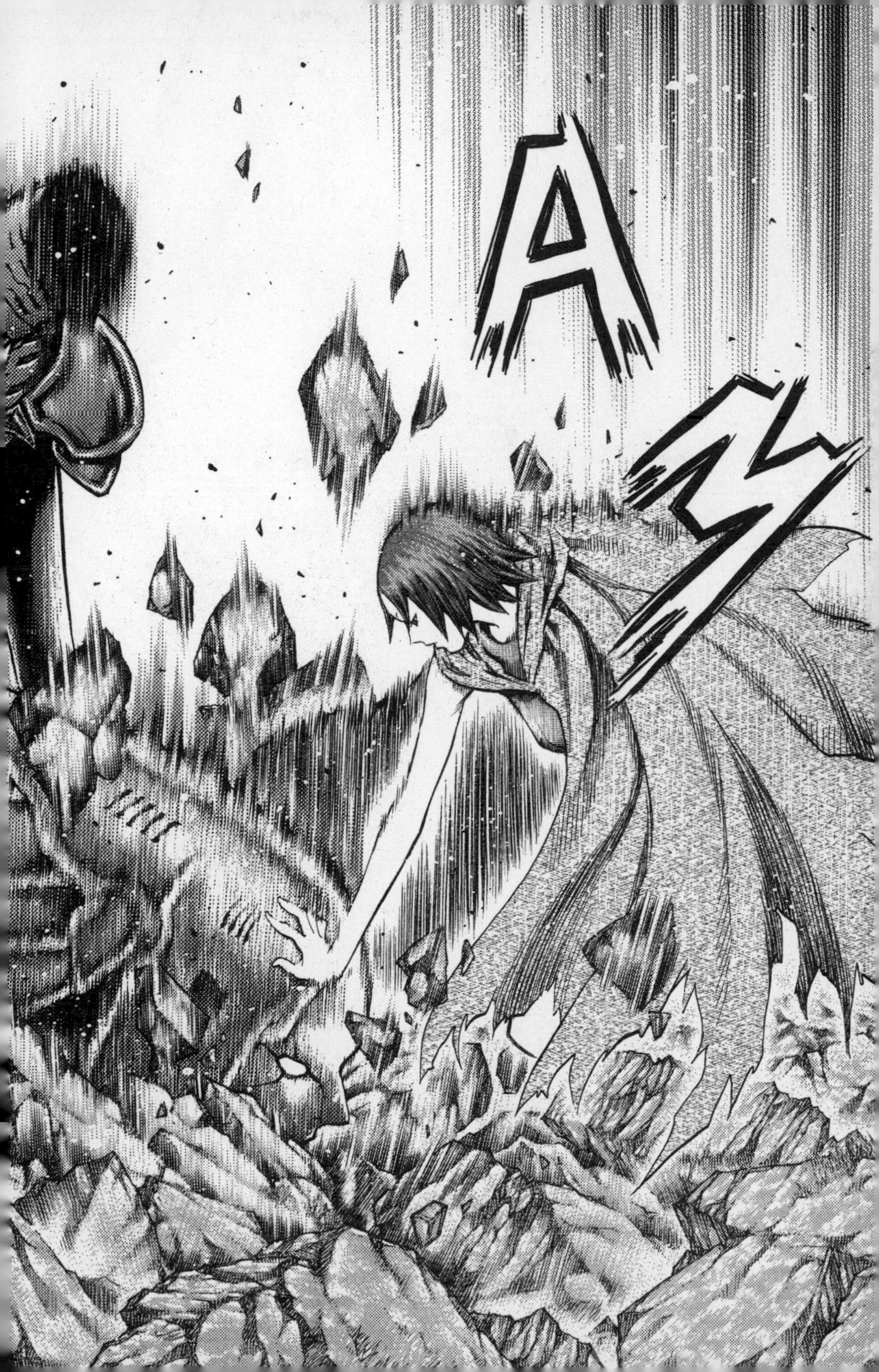
AM

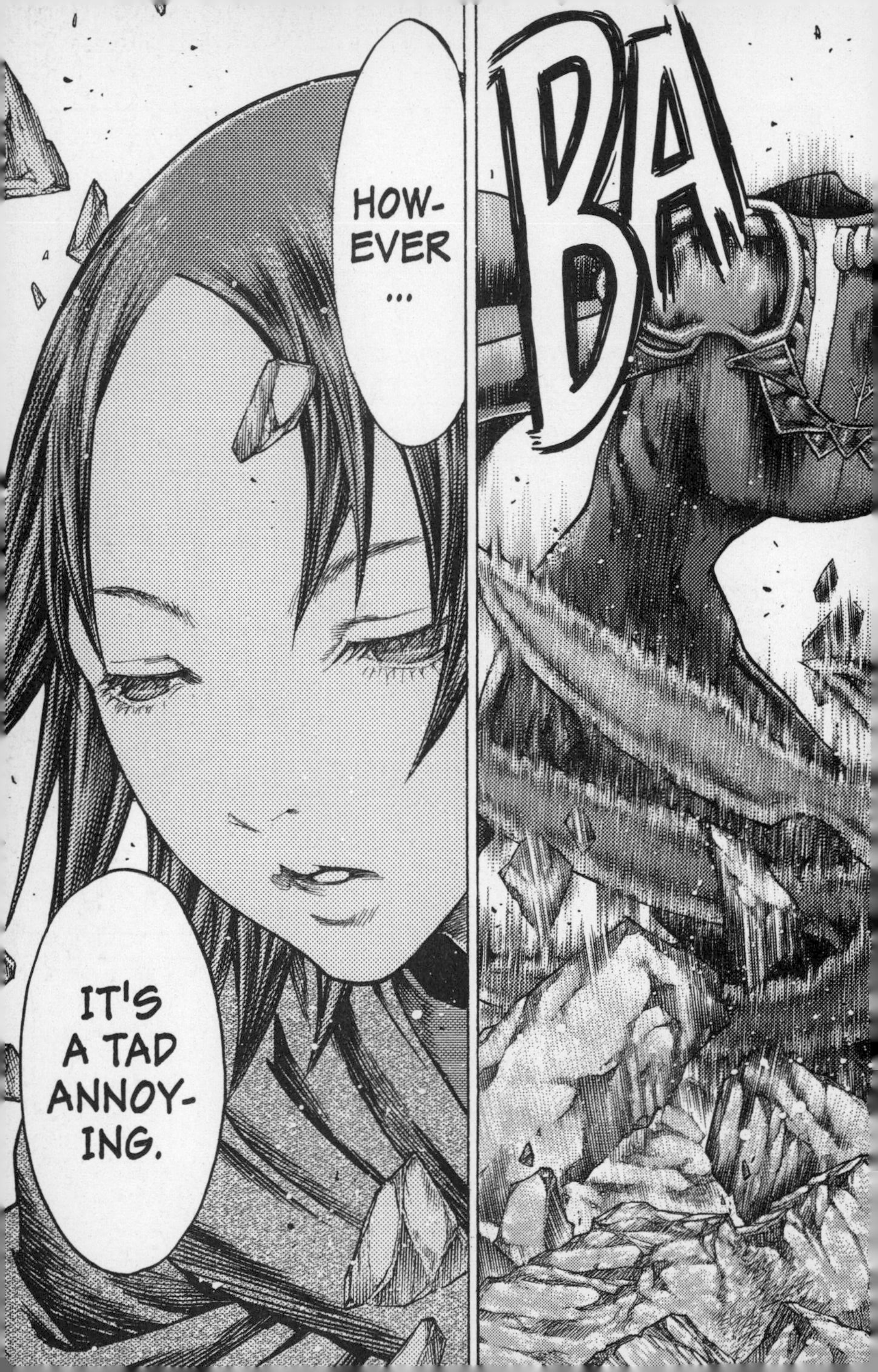
BADA
HOW-EVER ...
IT'S A TAD ANNOY-ING.

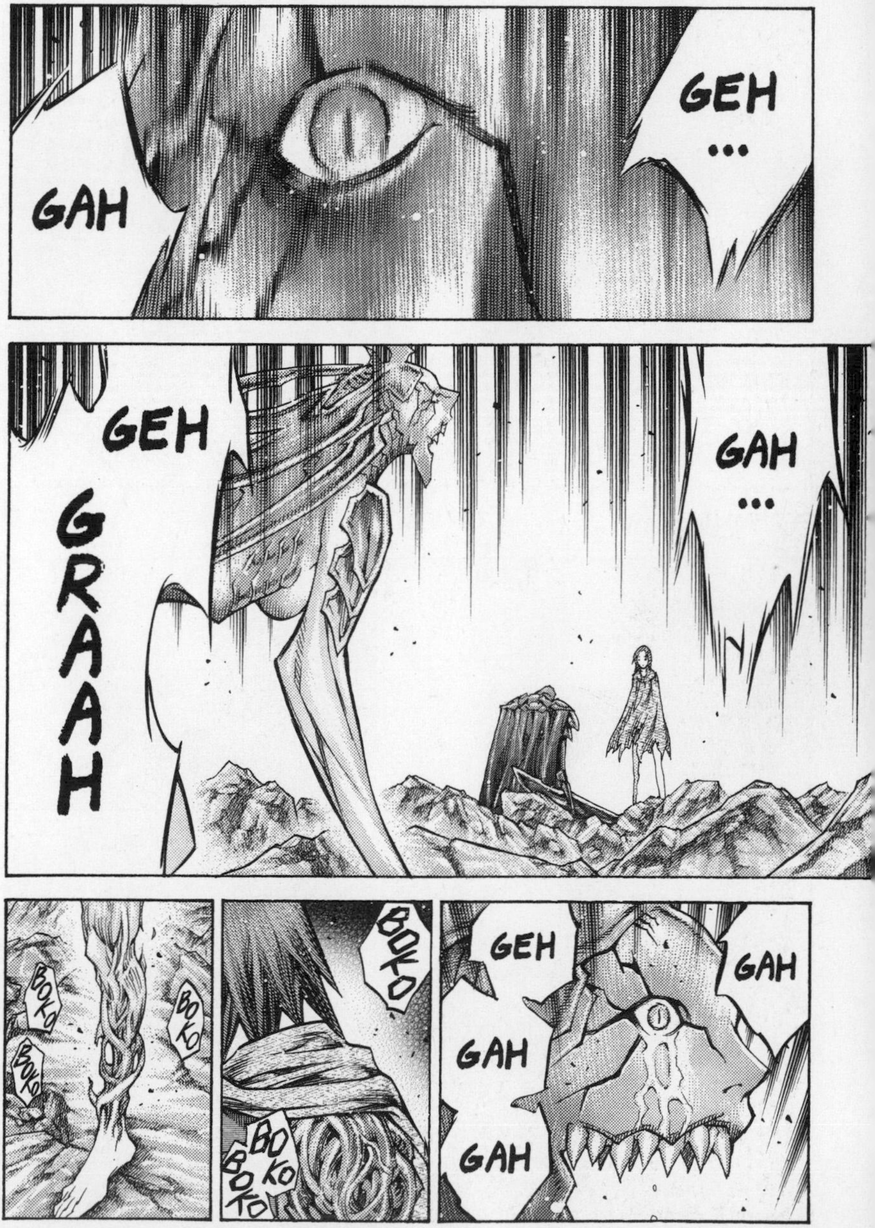
GEH ...
GAH
GAH ...
GEH
GRAAAH
GAH
GEH
GAH
GAH
BOKO
BOKO
BOKO
BOKO
BOKO
BOKO
BOKO

READ THIS WAY

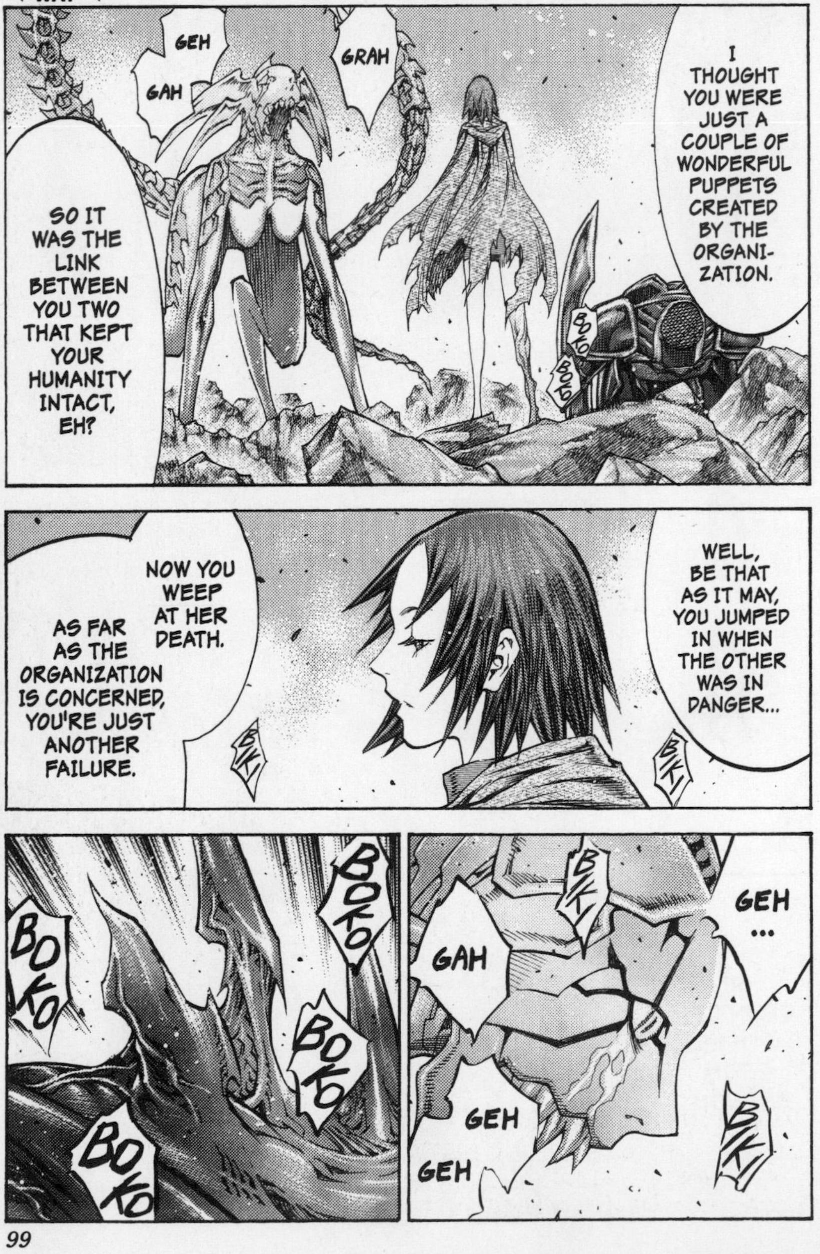
I THOUGHT YOU WERE JUST A COUPLE OF WONDERFUL PUPPETS CREATED BY THE ORGANI-ZATION.
GRAH
GEH
GAH
BOKO
BOKO
SO IT WAS THE LINK BETWEEN YOU TWO THAT KEPT YOUR HUMANITY INTACT, EH?
WELL, BE THAT AS IT MAY, YOU JUMPED IN WHEN THE OTHER WAS IN DANGER...
BIKI
NOW YOU WEEP AT HER DEATH.
AS FAR AS THE ORGANIZATION IS CONCERNED, YOU'RE JUST ANOTHER FAILURE.
BIKI
GEH ...
BIKI
GAH
BIKI
GEH
GEH
BOKO
BOKO
BOKO
BOKO

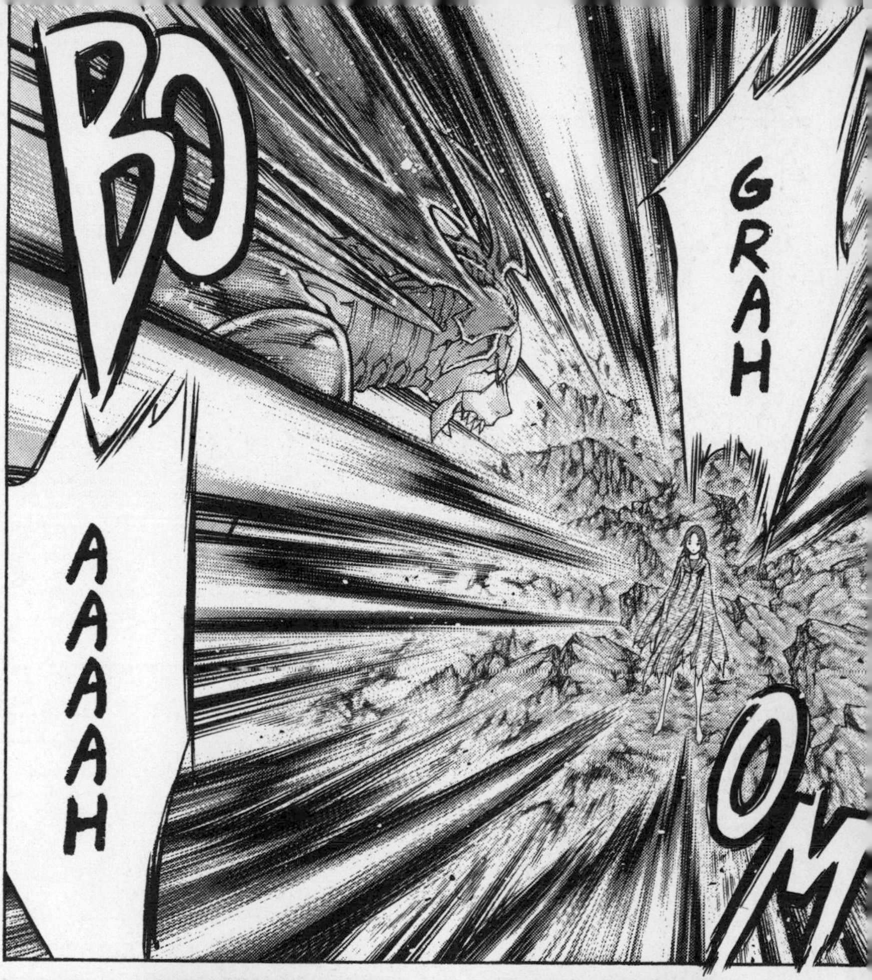
GRAH
OM
BO
AAAAAH

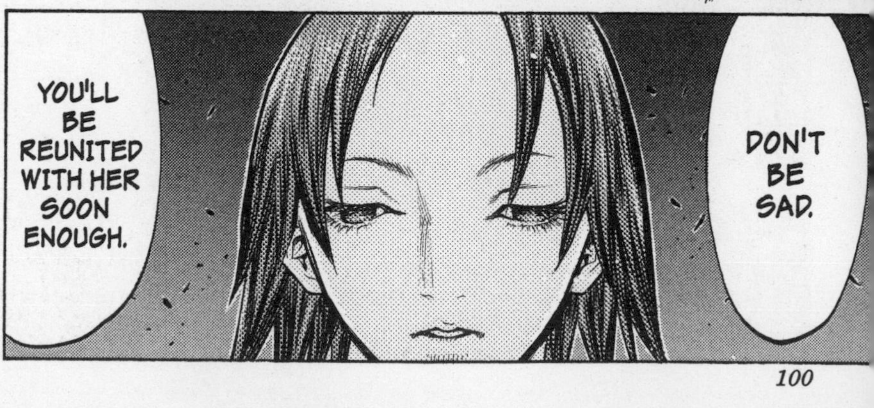
DON'T BE SAD.
YOU'LL BE REUNITED WITH HER SOON ENOUGH.

READ THIS WAY

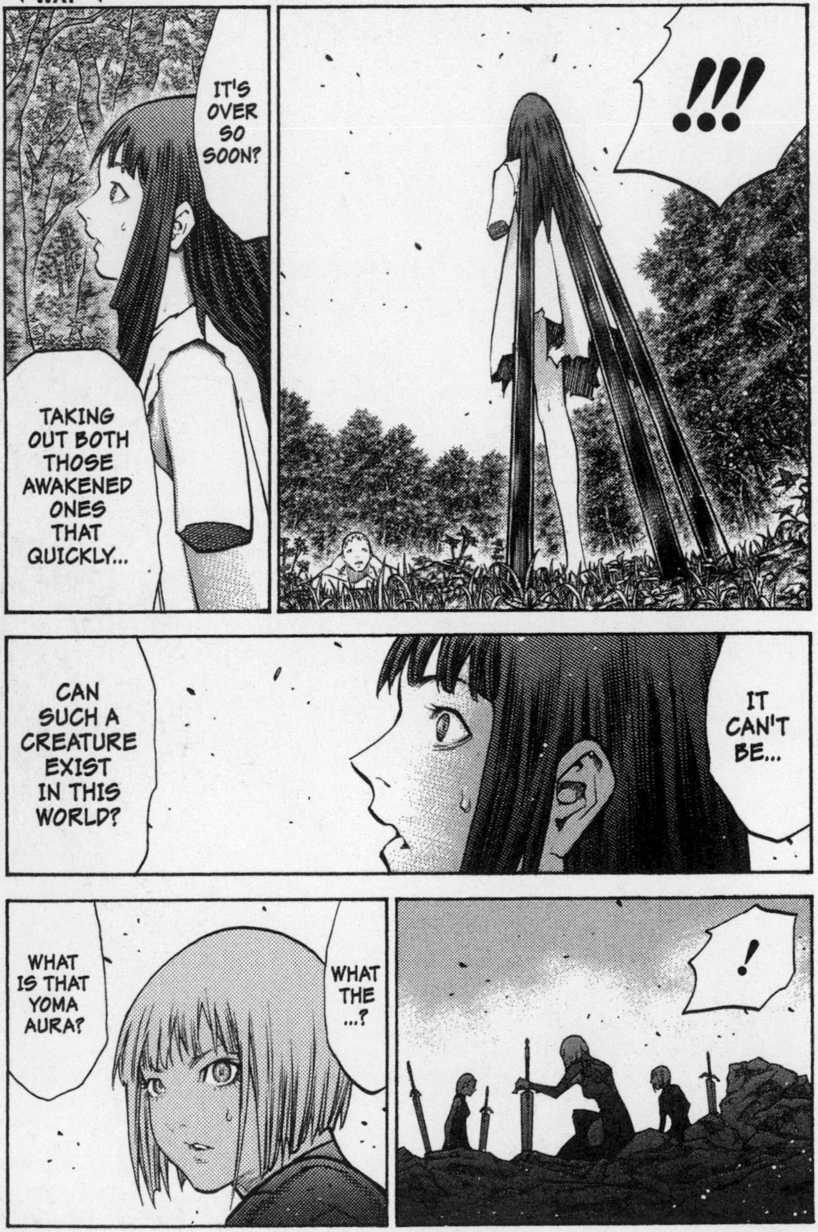
!!!
IT'S OVER SO SOON?
TAKING OUT BOTH THOSE AWAKENED ONES THAT QUICKLY...
IT CAN'T BE...
CAN SUCH A CREATURE EXIST IN THIS WORLD?
!
WHAT THE ...?
WHAT IS THAT YOMA AURA?

クレイモア
Claymore

Scene 99: The Ashes of Lautrec, Part 4

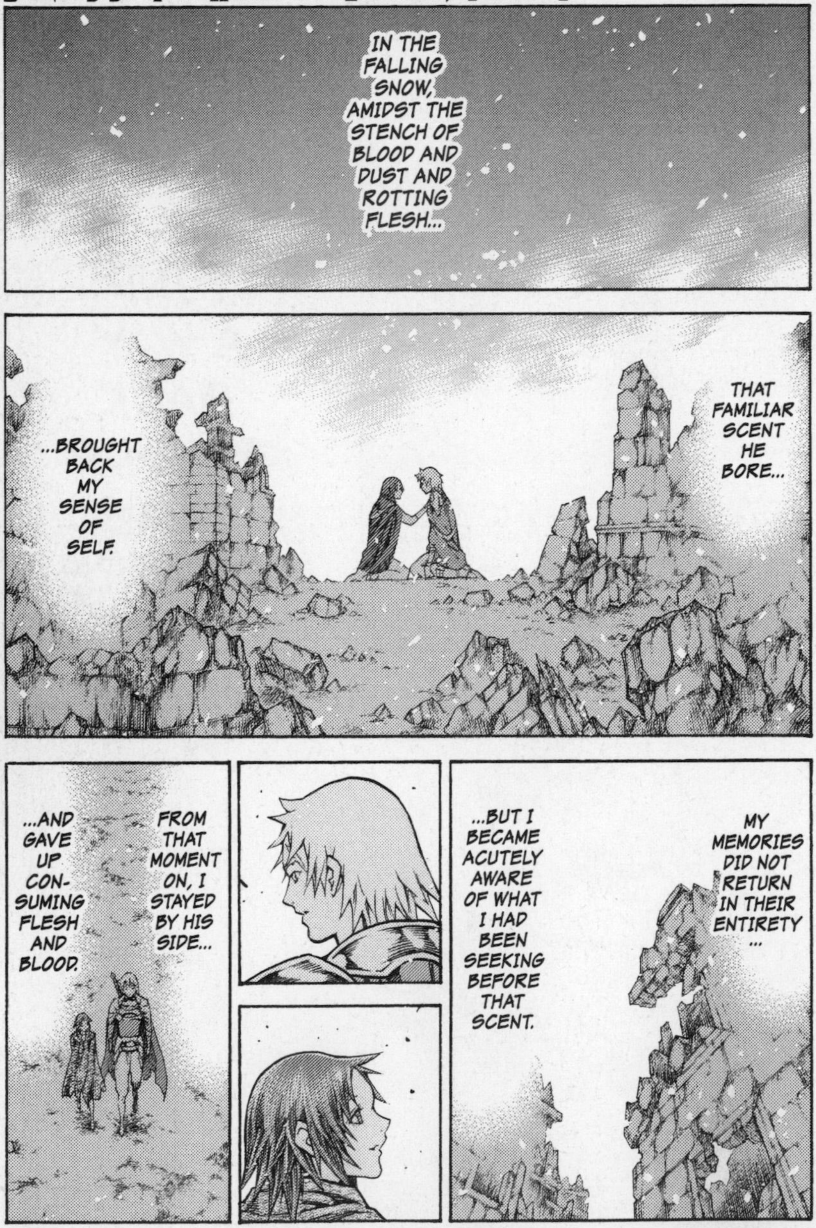
IN THE FALLING SNOW, AMIDST THE STENCH OF BLOOD AND DUST AND ROTTING FLESH...
THAT FAMILIAR SCENT HE BORE...
...BROUGHT BACK MY SENSE OF SELF.
MY MEMORIES DID NOT RETURN IN THEIR ENTIRETY ...
...BUT I BECAME ACUTELY AWARE OF WHAT I HAD BEEN SEEKING BEFORE THAT SCENT.
FROM THAT MOMENT ON, I STAYED BY HIS SIDE...
...AND GAVE UP CON-SUMING FLESH AND BLOOD.

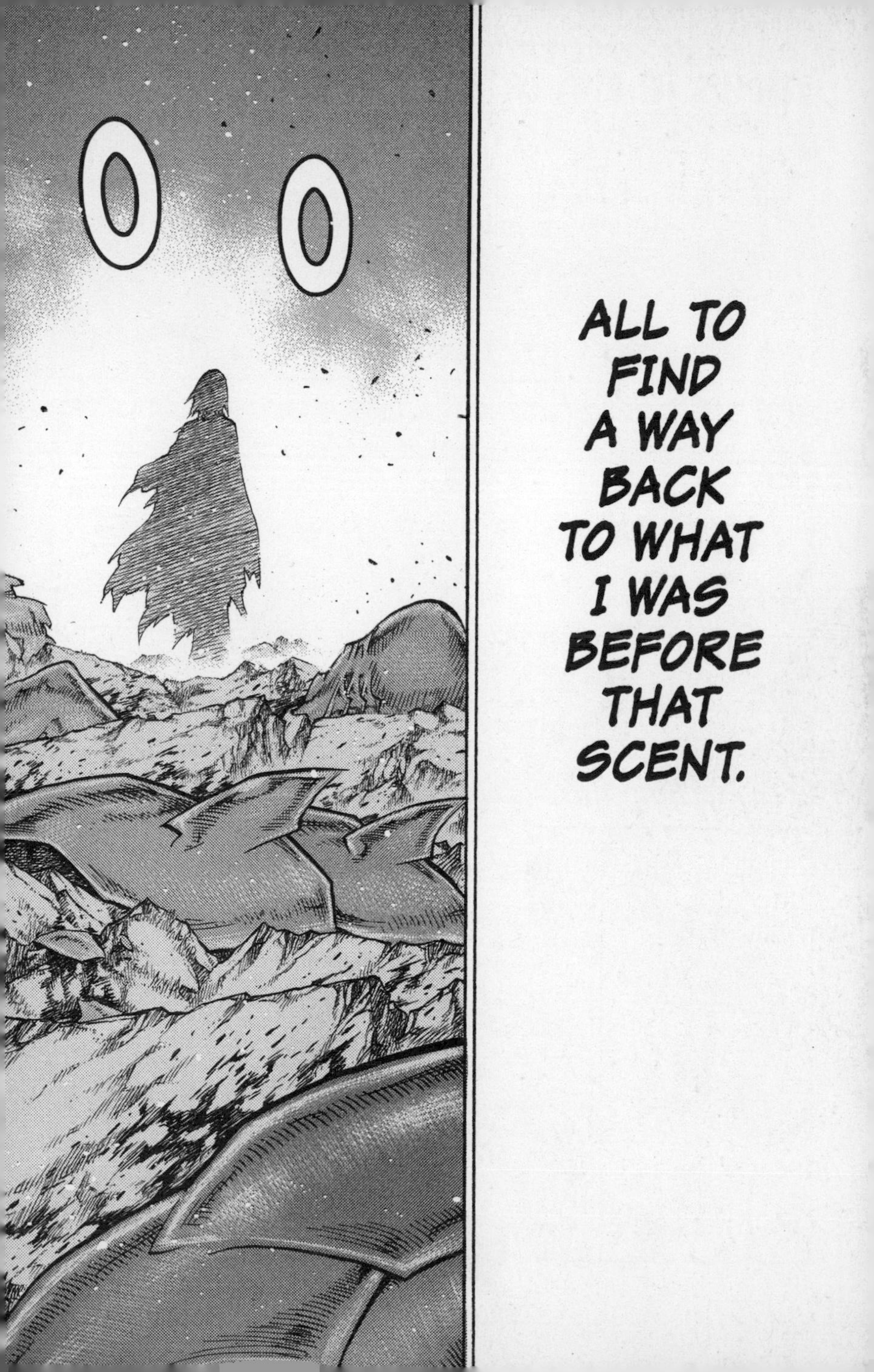
ALL TO FIND A WAY BACK TO WHAT I WAS BEFORE THAT SCENT.

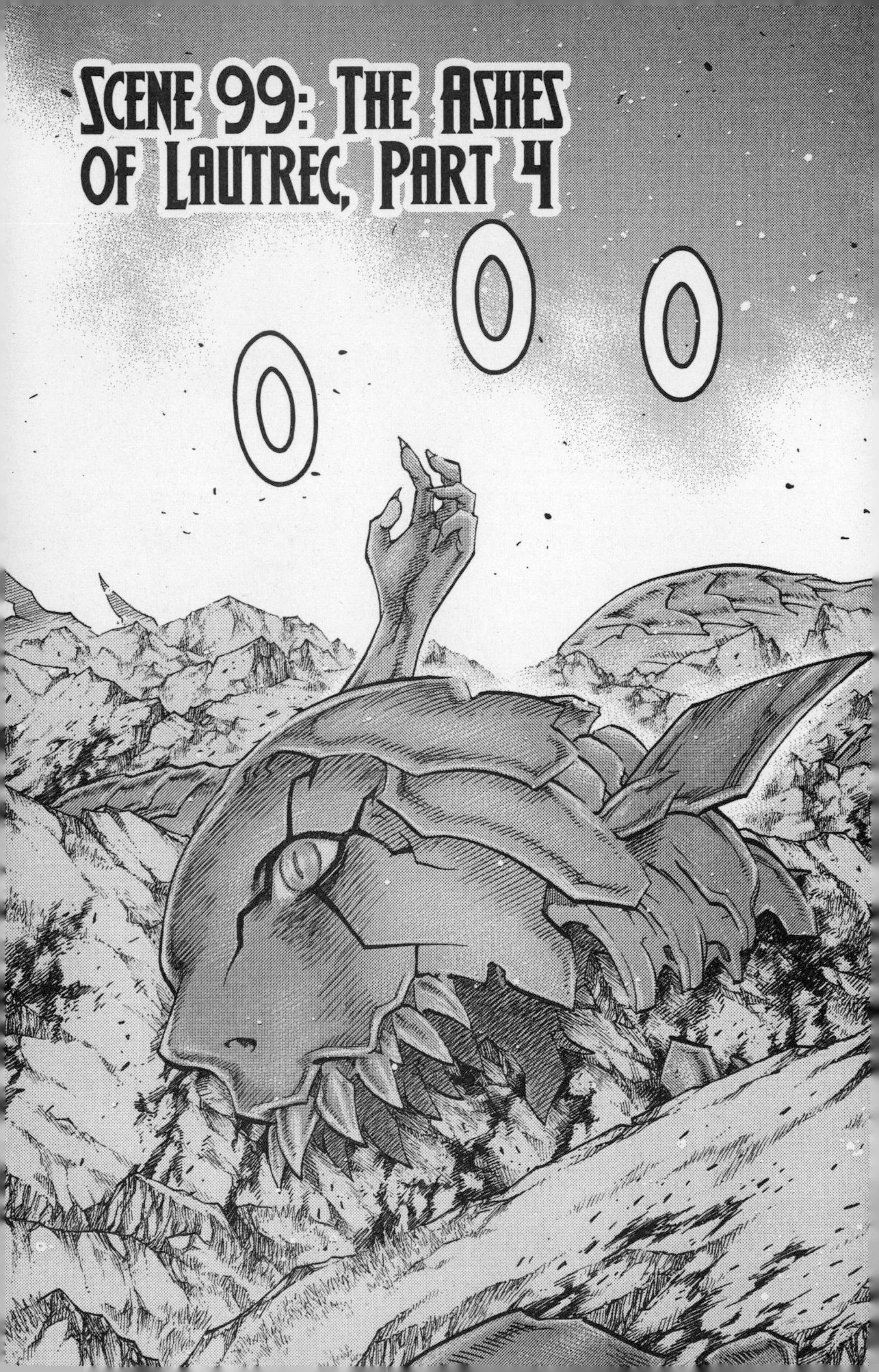
Scene 99: The Ashes of Lautrec, Part 4

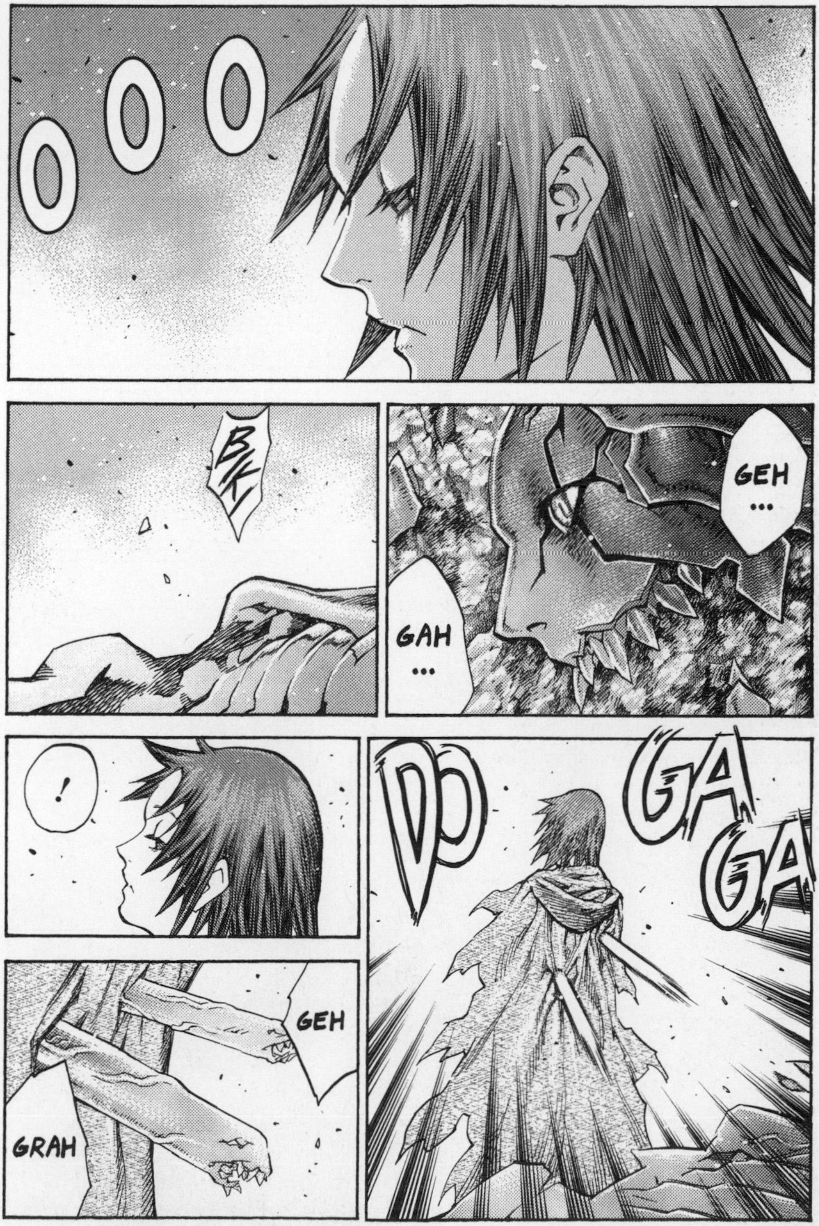
OOO
GEH...
GAH...
BIKI
DO
GA
GA
!
GEH
GRAH

READ THIS WAY

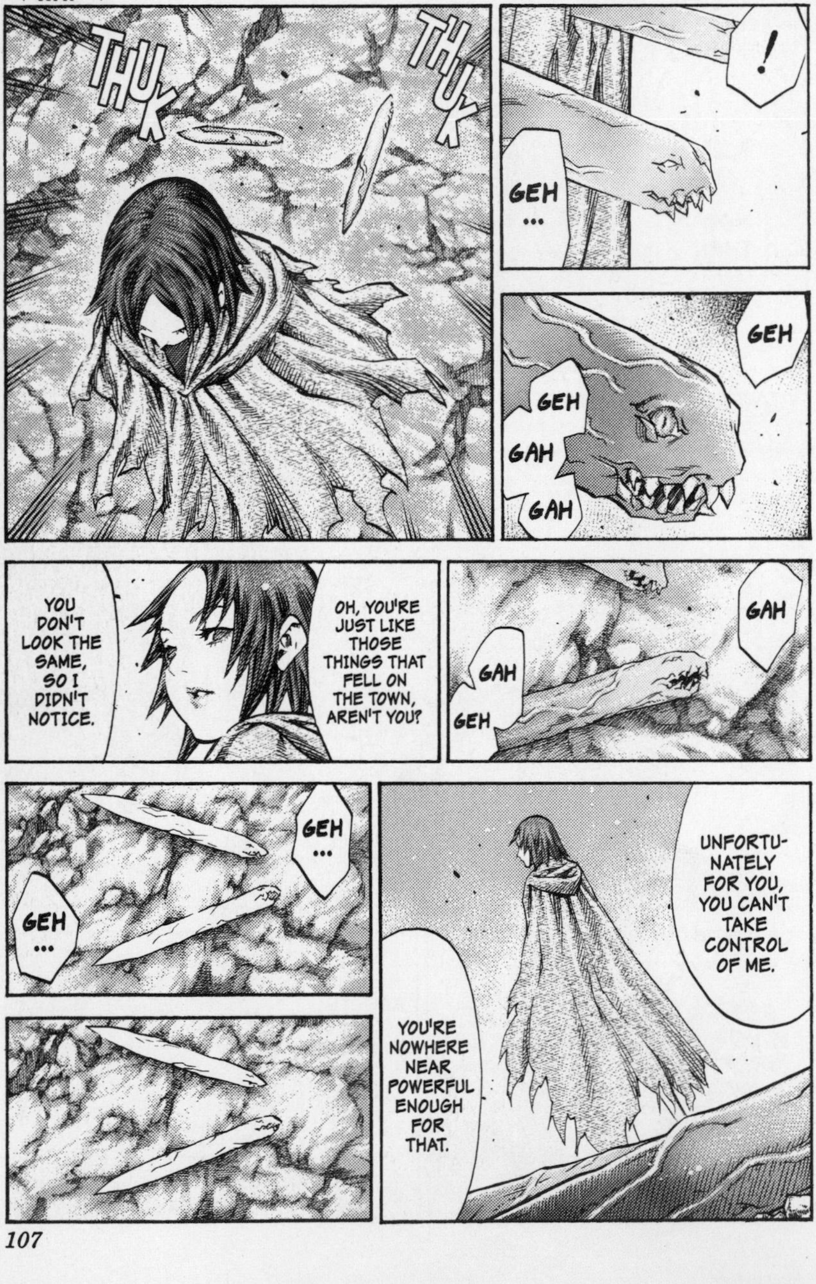
!
GEH ...
GEH
GEH
GAH
GAH
THUK
THUK
GAH
GAH
GEH
OH, YOU'RE JUST LIKE THOSE THINGS THAT FELL ON THE TOWN, AREN'T YOU?
YOU DON'T LOOK THE SAME, SO I DIDN'T NOTICE.
UNFORTUNATELY FOR YOU, YOU CAN'T TAKE CONTROL OF ME.
YOU'RE NOWHERE NEAR POWERFUL ENOUGH FOR THAT.
GEH ...
GEH ...

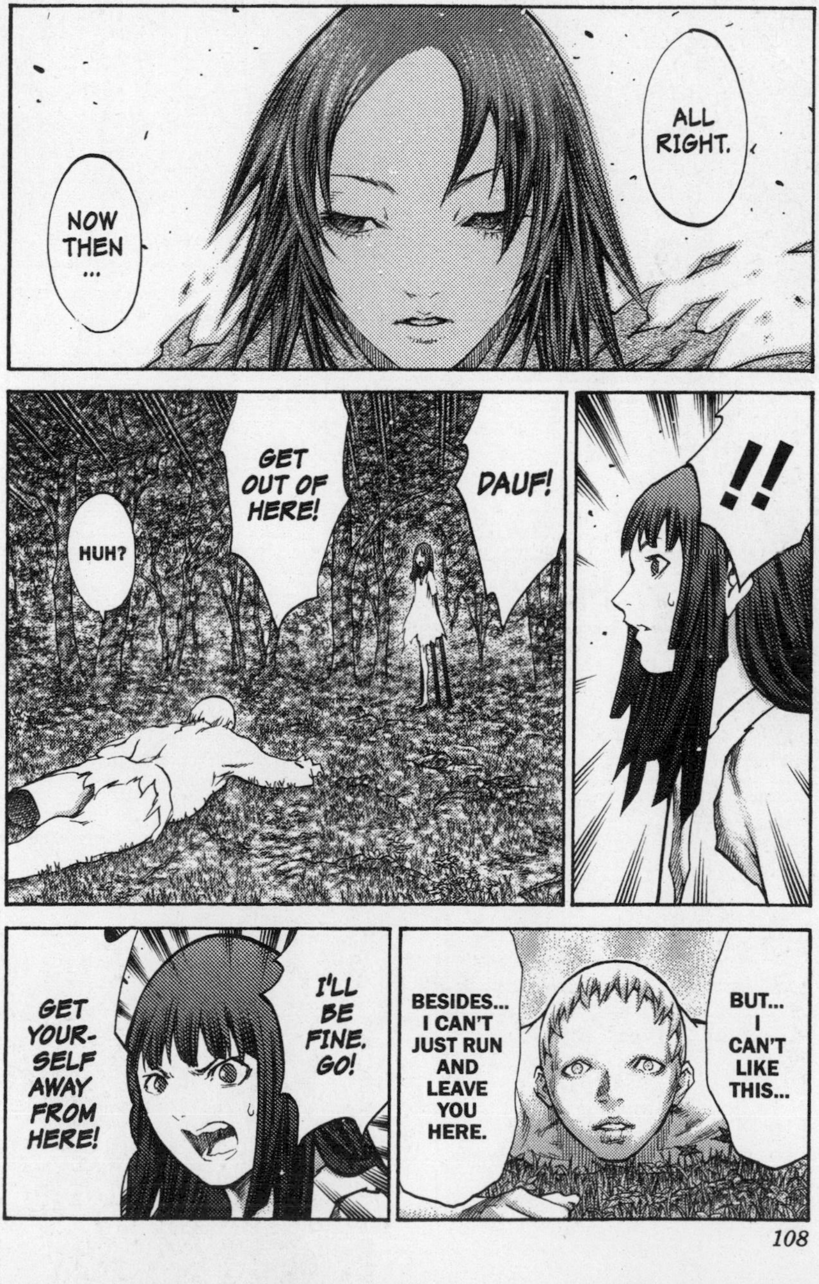
ALL RIGHT.
NOW THEN ...
!!
DAUF!
GET OUT OF HERE!
HUH?
BUT... I CAN'T LIKE THIS...
BESIDES... I CAN'T JUST RUN AND LEAVE YOU HERE.
I'LL BE FINE. GO!
GET YOURSELF AWAY FROM HERE!

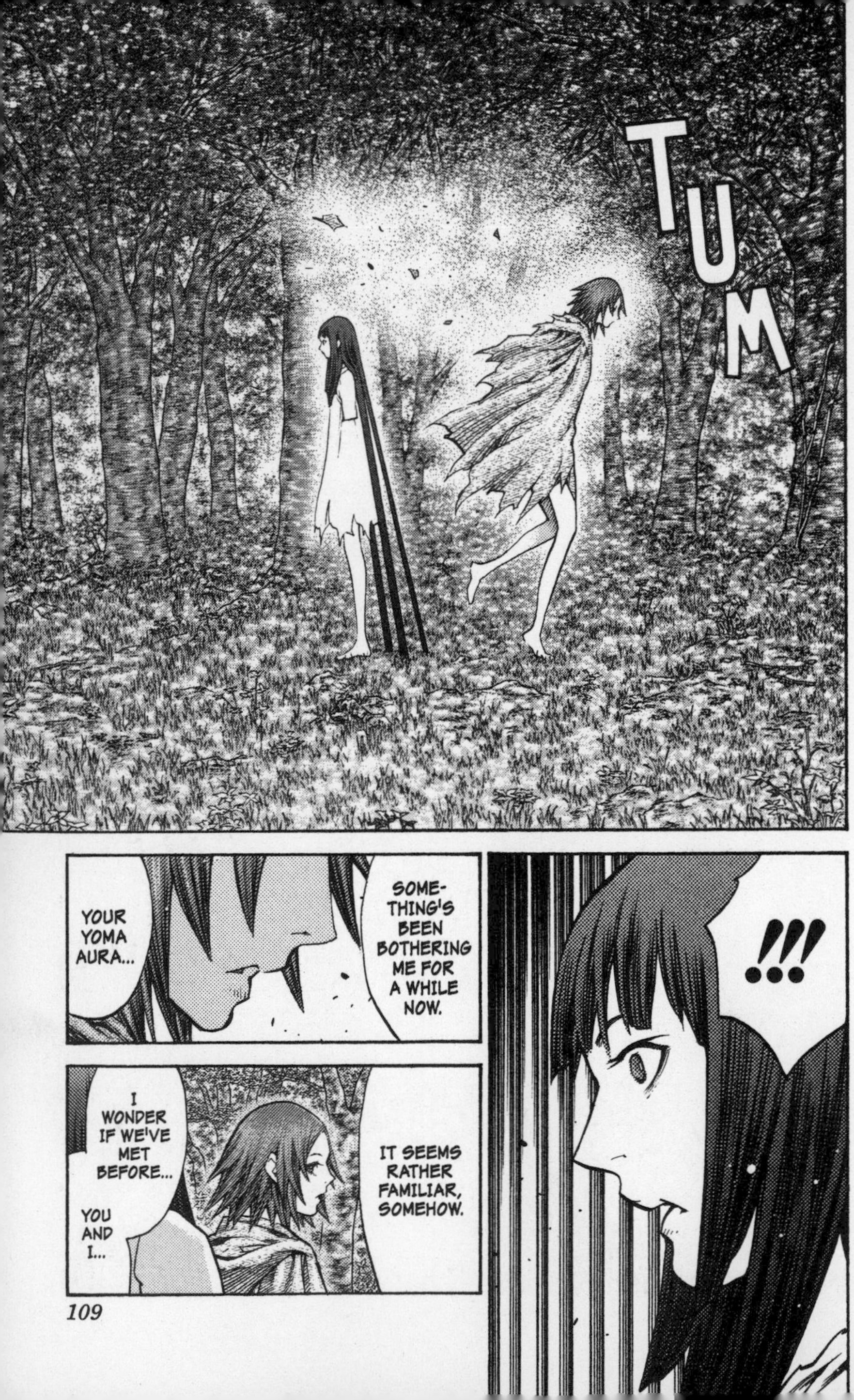
TUM
!!!
SOME-THING'S BEEN BOTHERING ME FOR A WHILE NOW.
YOUR YOMA AURA...
IT SEEMS RATHER FAMILIAR, SOMEHOW.
I WONDER IF WE'VE MET BEFORE...
YOU AND I...

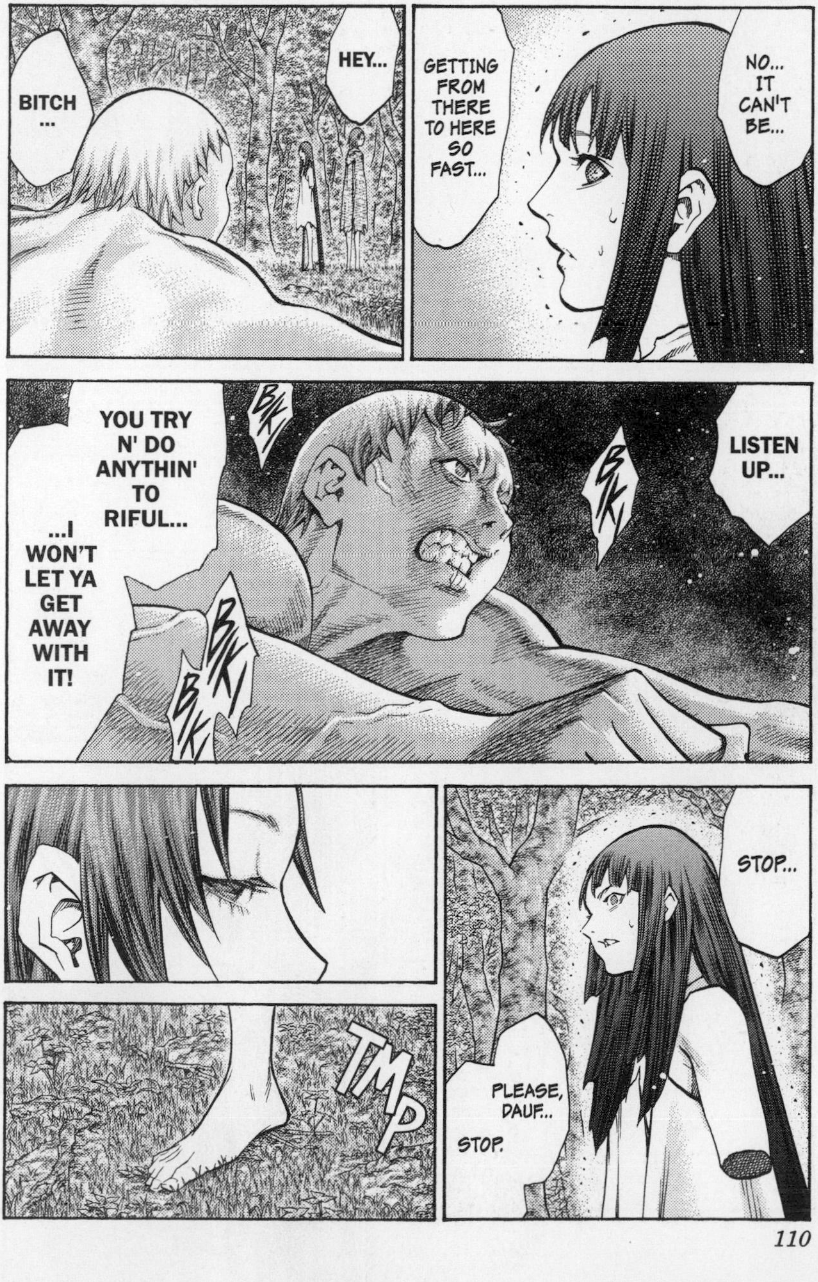
NO... IT CAN'T BE...
GETTING FROM THERE TO HERE SO FAST...
HEY...
BITCH ...
LISTEN UP...
BKI
BKI
YOU TRY N' DO ANYTHIN' TO RIFUL...
...I WON'T LET YA GET AWAY WITH IT!
BKI
BKI
STOP...
PLEASE, DAUF...
STOP.
TMP

READ THIS WAY

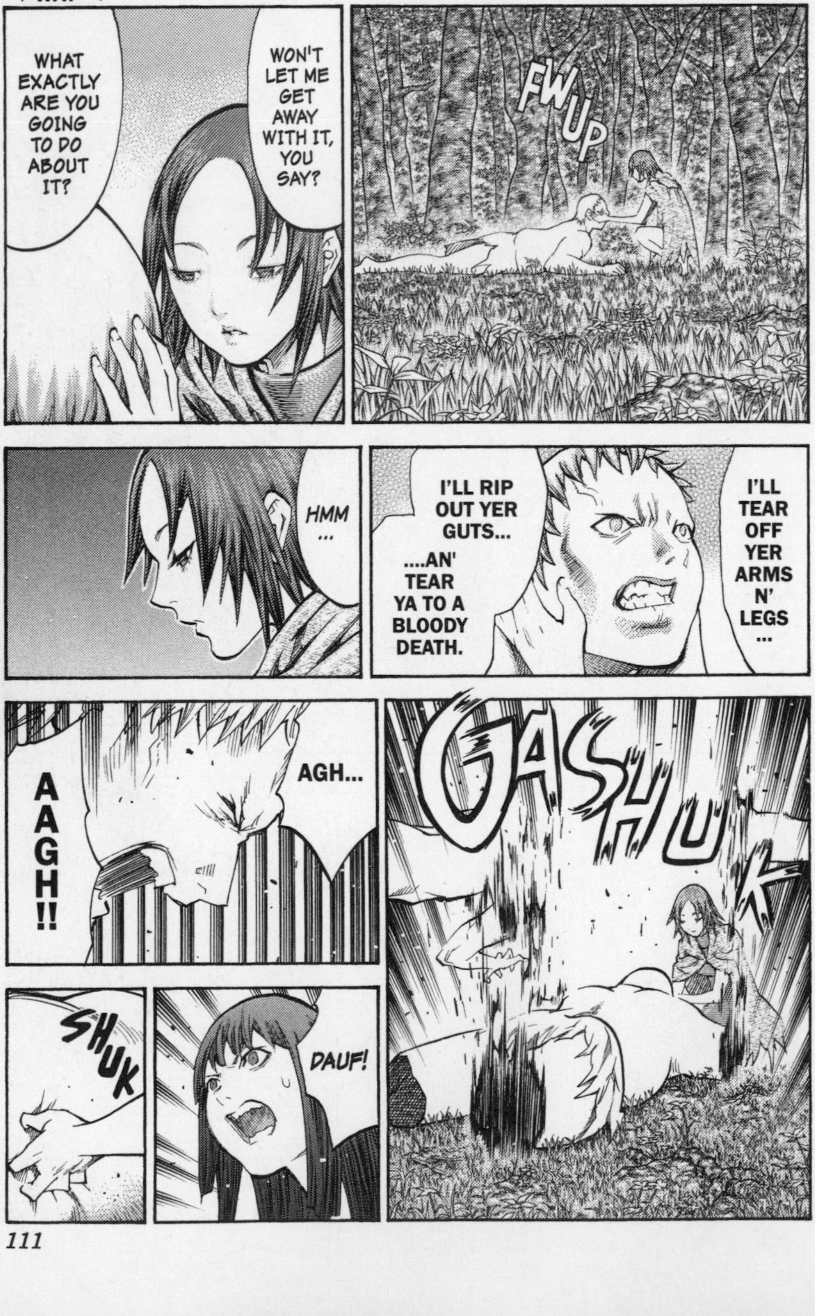
FWUP
WON'T LET ME GET AWAY WITH IT, YOU SAY?
WHAT EXACTLY ARE YOU GOING TO DO ABOUT IT?
I'LL TEAR OFF YER ARMS N' LEGS ...
I'LL RIP OUT YER GUTS...
....AN' TEAR YA TO A BLOODY DEATH.
HMM ...
GASHUK
AGH...
AAGH!!
DAUF!
SHUK

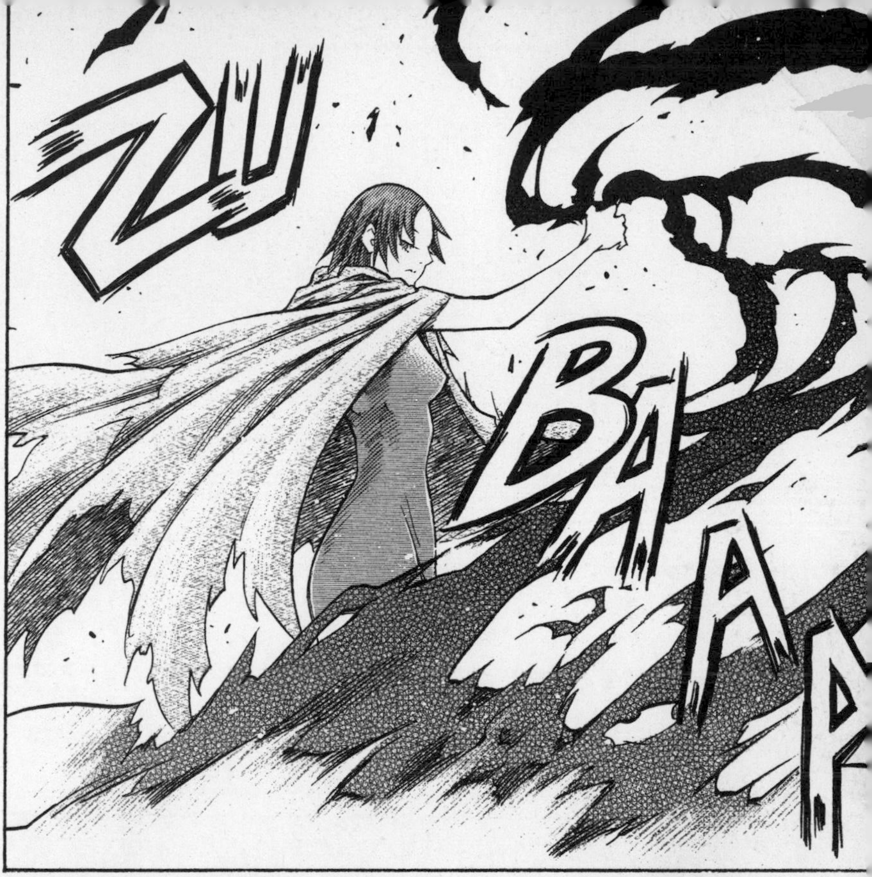
ZU
BAAA
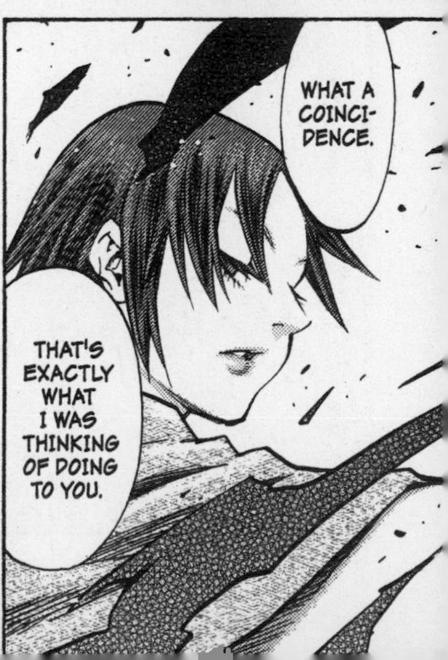
WHAT A COINCIDENCE.
THAT'S EXACTLY WHAT I WAS THINKING OF DOING TO YOU.
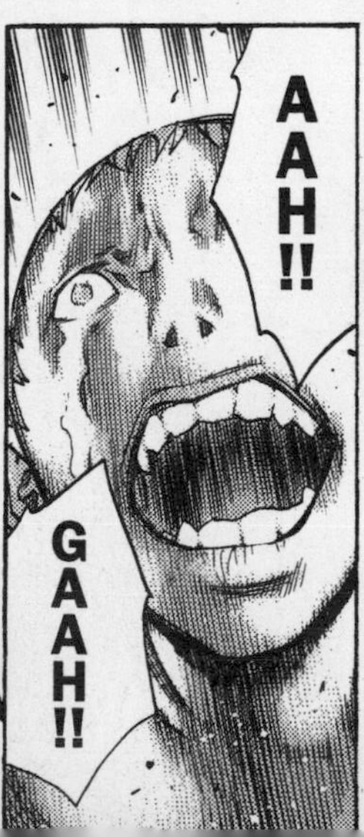
AAH!!
GAAH!!
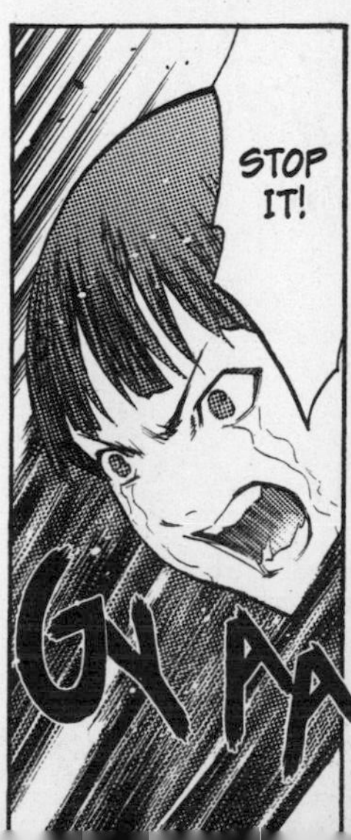
STOP IT!
GYAA

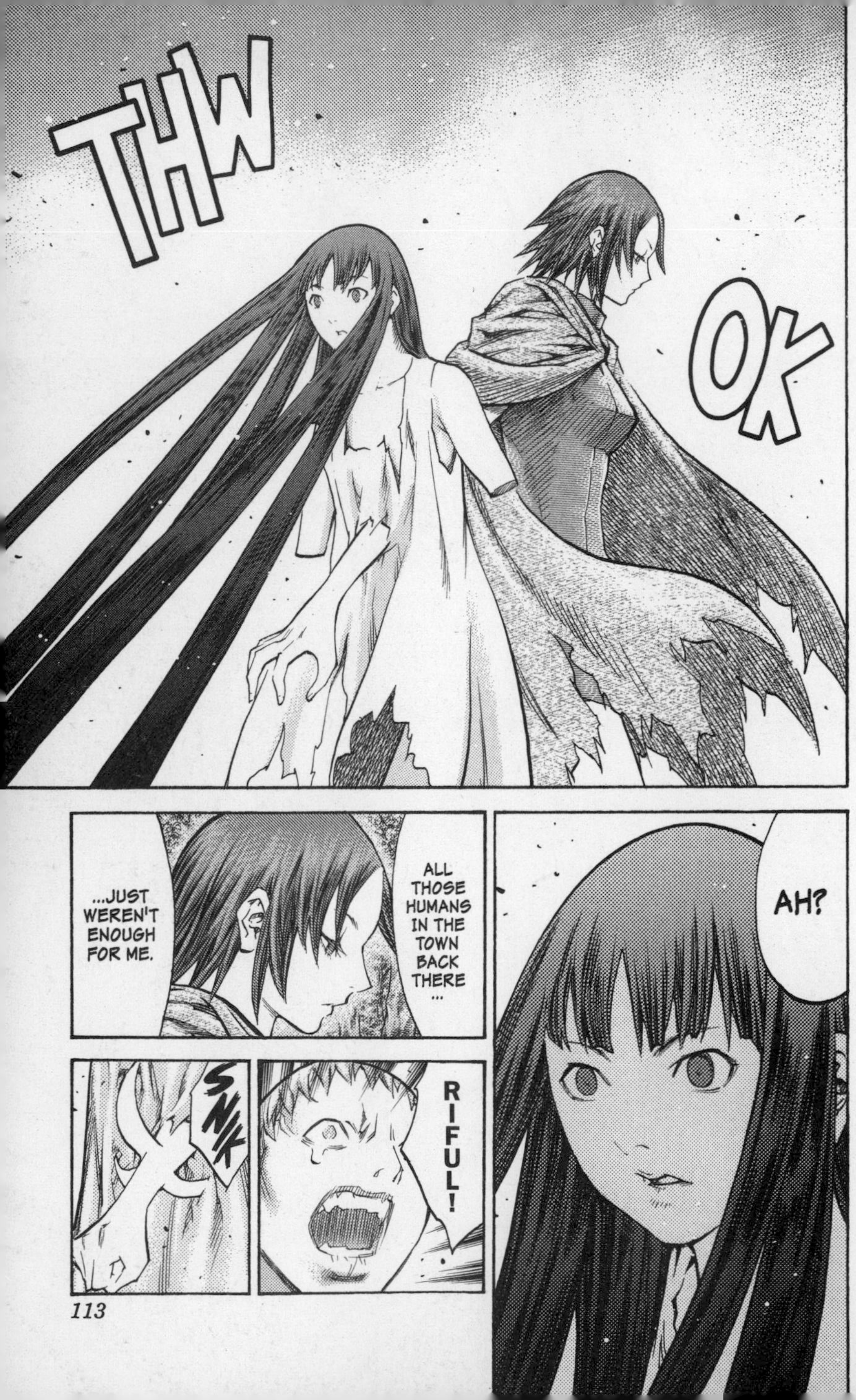
THWOK
AH?
ALL THOSE HUMANS IN THE TOWN BACK THERE...
...JUST WEREN'T ENOUGH FOR ME.
RIFUL!
SNIK

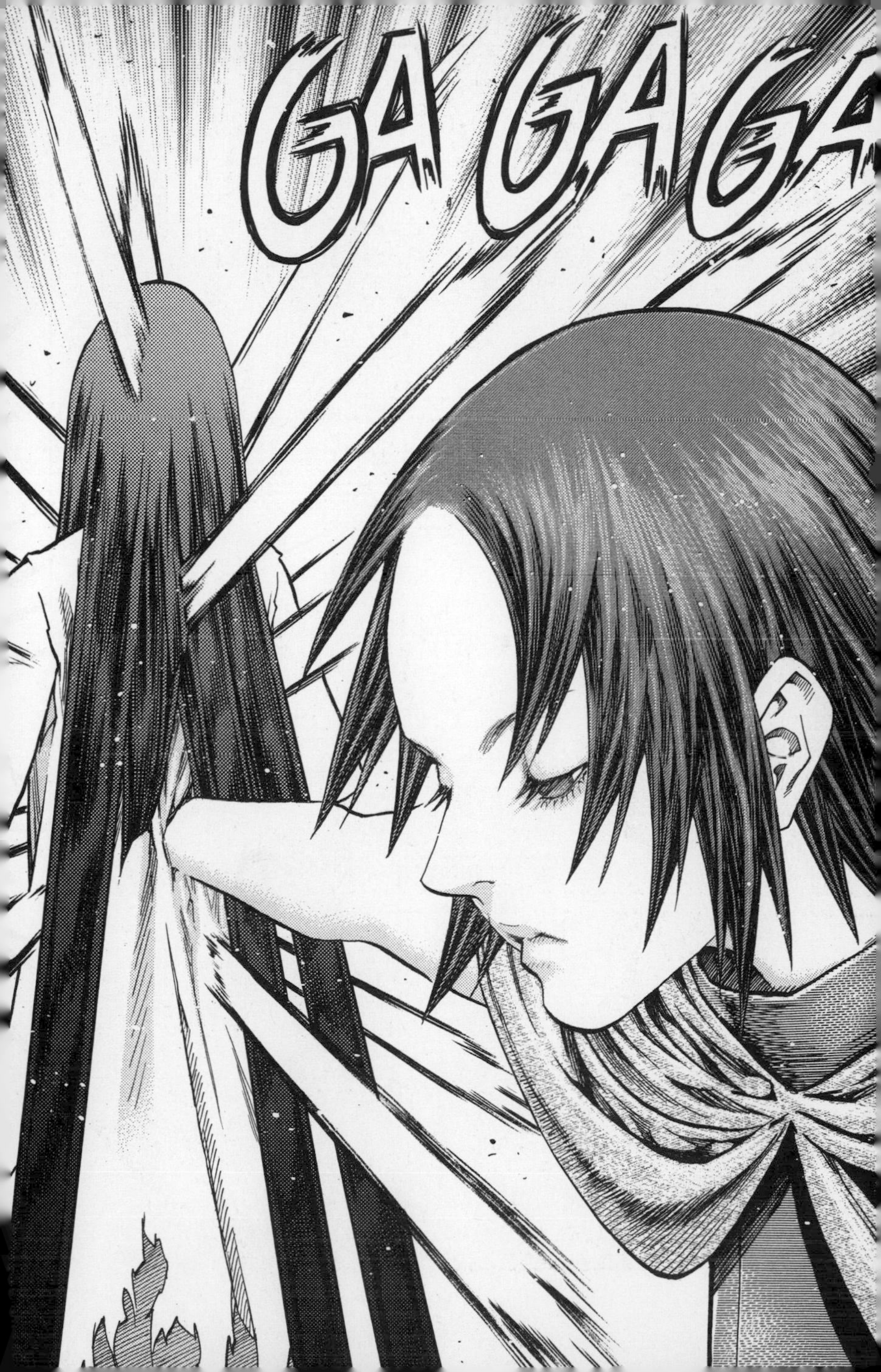
GA GAGA

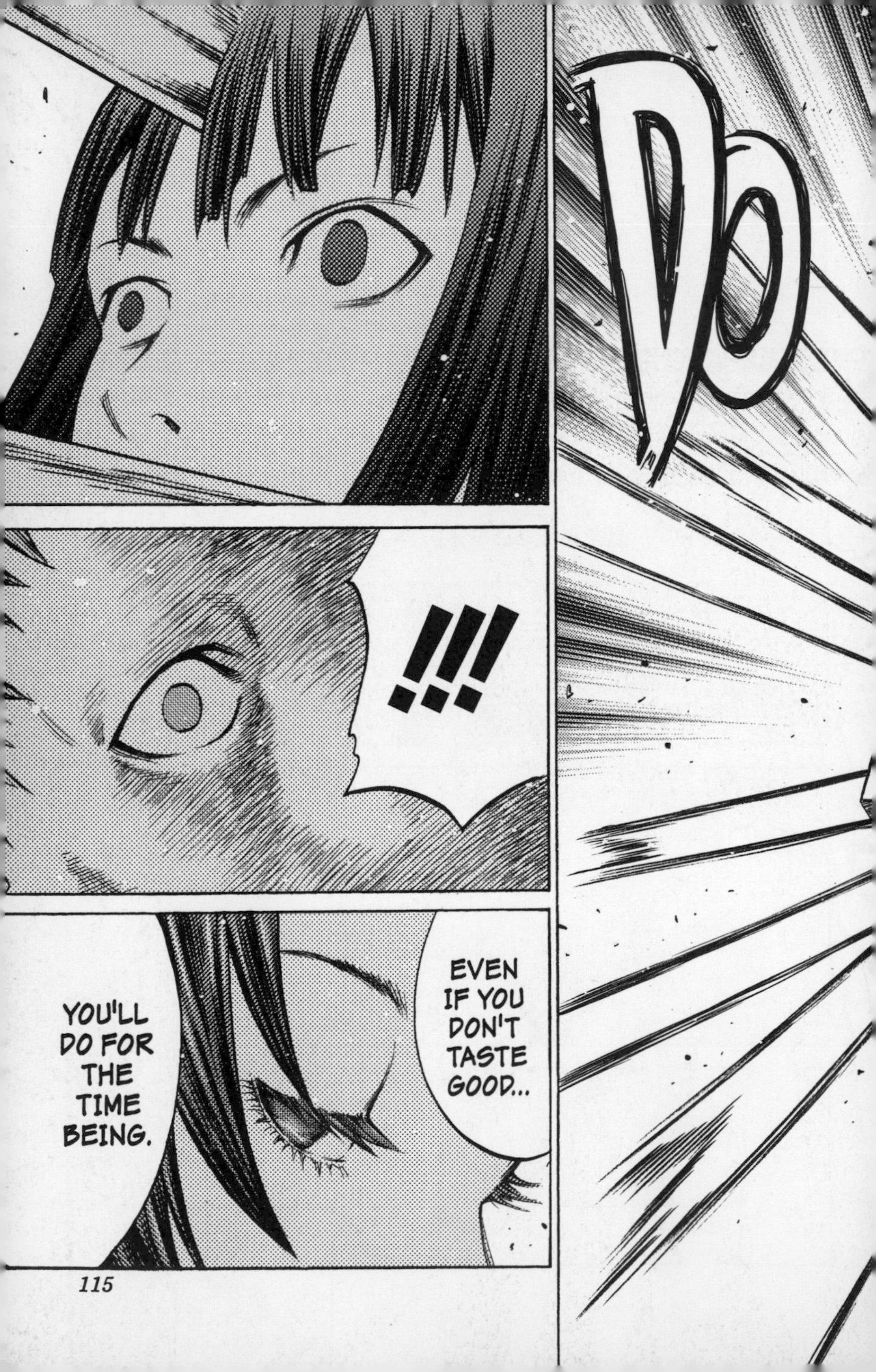
DO
!!!
EVEN IF YOU DON'T TASTE GOOD...
YOU'LL DO FOR THE TIME BEING.

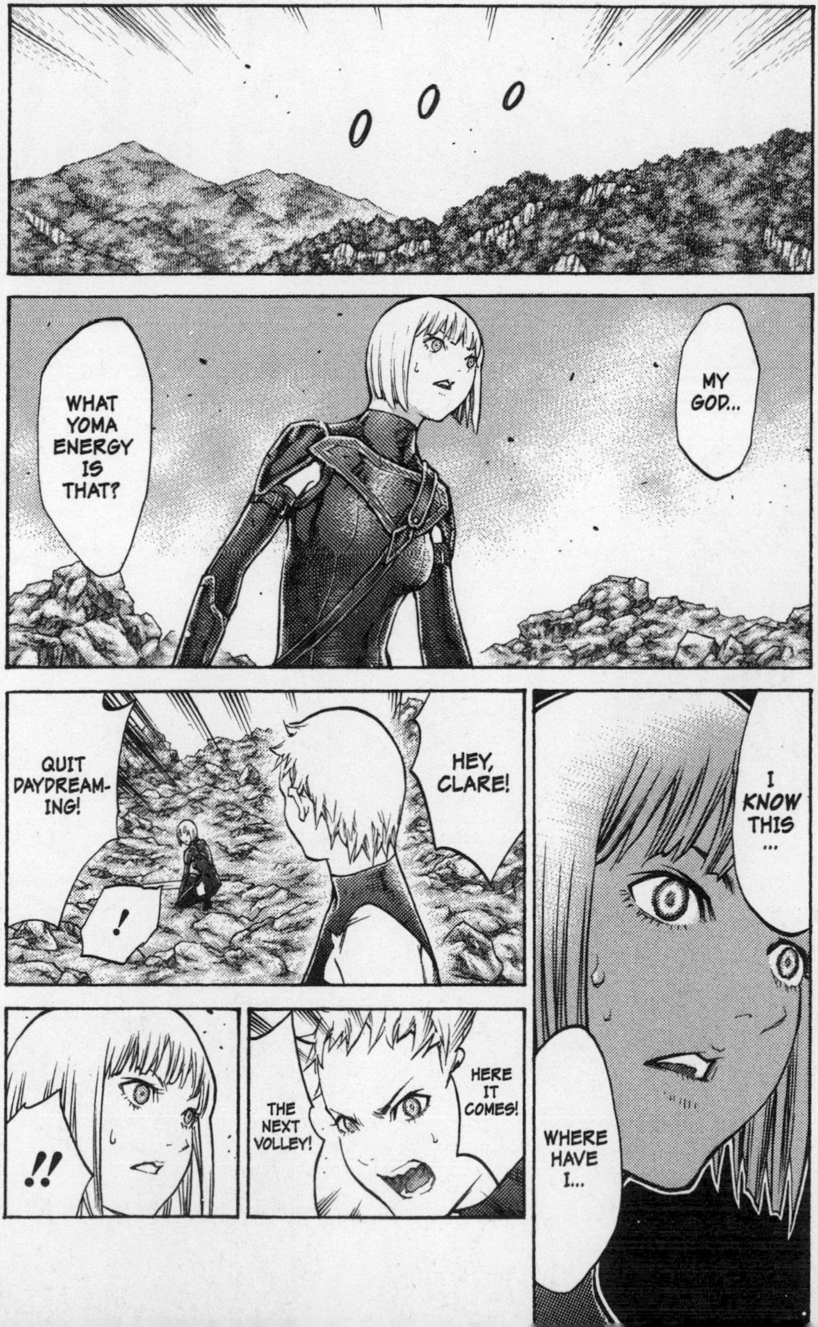

MY GOD...
WHAT YOMA ENERGY IS THAT?
I KNOW THIS ...
WHERE HAVE I...
HEY, CLARE!
QUIT DAYDREAMING!
!
HERE IT COMES!
THE NEXT VOLLEY!
!!

READ THIS WAY

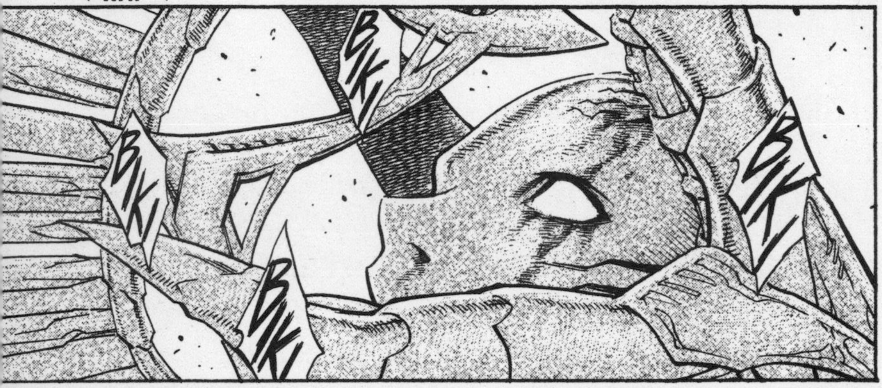
BIKI
BIKI
BIKI
BIKI

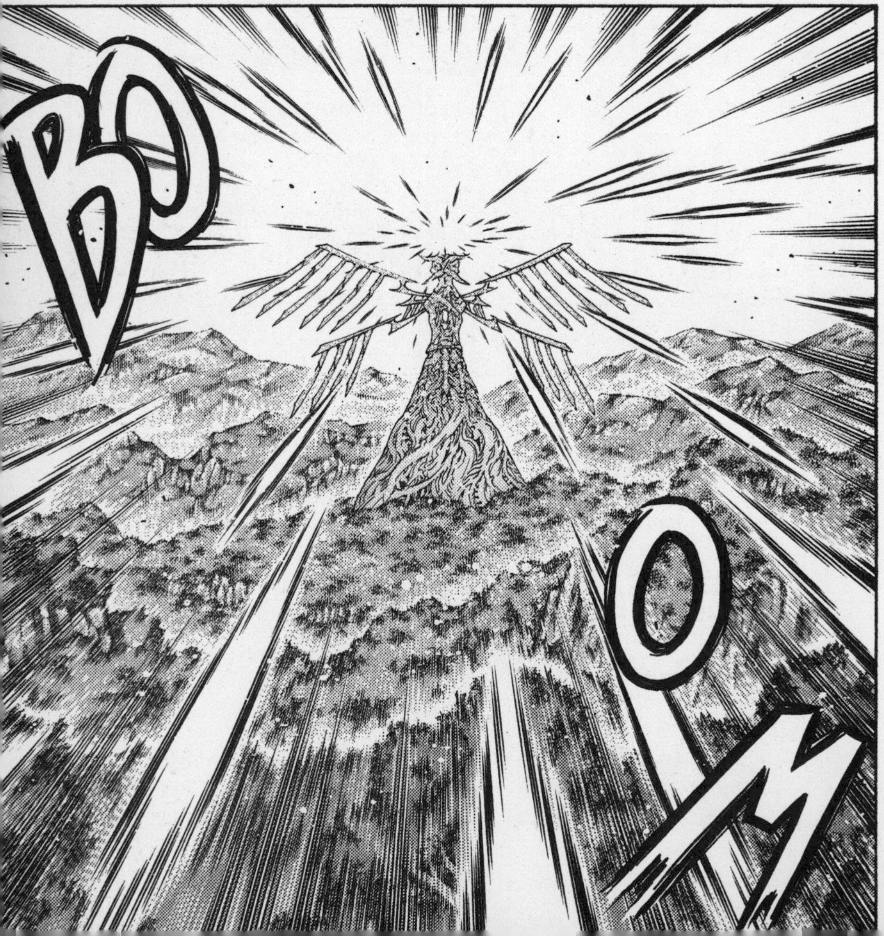
BO
OM

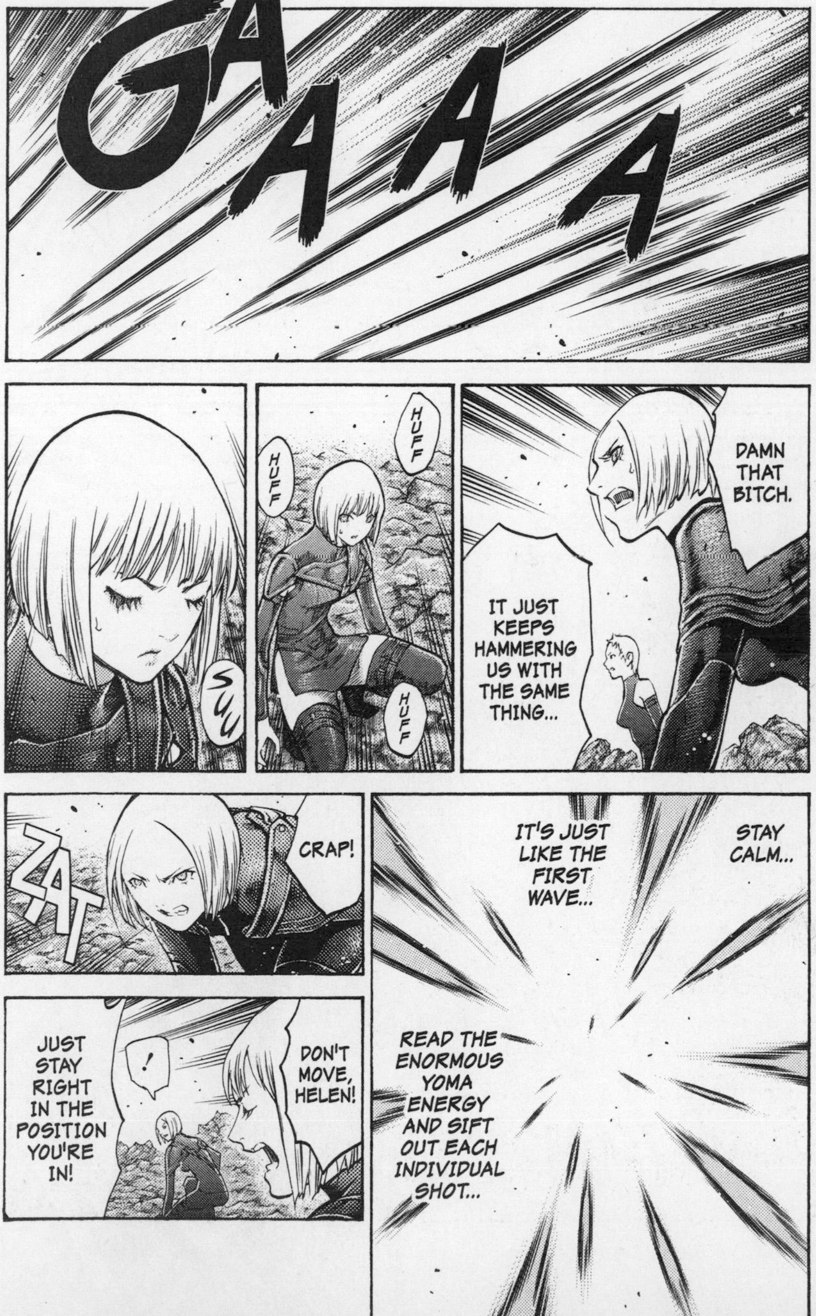
GAAAA
DAMN THAT BITCH.
IT JUST KEEPS HAMMERING US WITH THE SAME THING...
HUFF
HUFF
HUFF
SUUU
STAY CALM...
IT'S JUST LIKE THE FIRST WAVE...
READ THE ENORMOUS YOMA ENERGY AND SIFT OUT EACH INDIVIDUAL SHOT...
CRAP!
ZAT
DON'T MOVE, HELEN!
!
JUST STAY RIGHT IN THE POSITION YOU'RE IN!

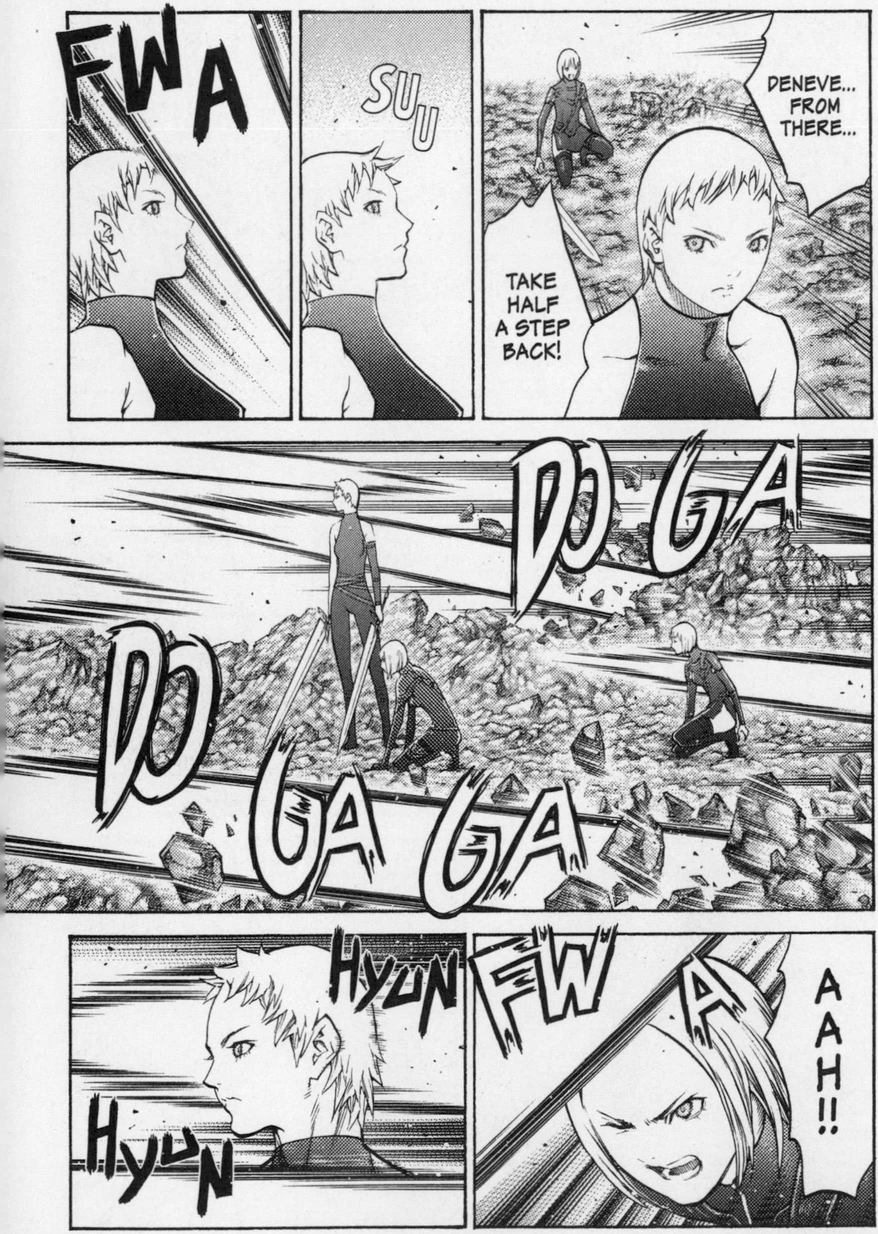
DENEVE... FROM THERE...
TAKE HALF A STEP BACK!
SUU
FWA
DOGA
DOGAGA
FW A
AAH!!
HYUN
HYUN

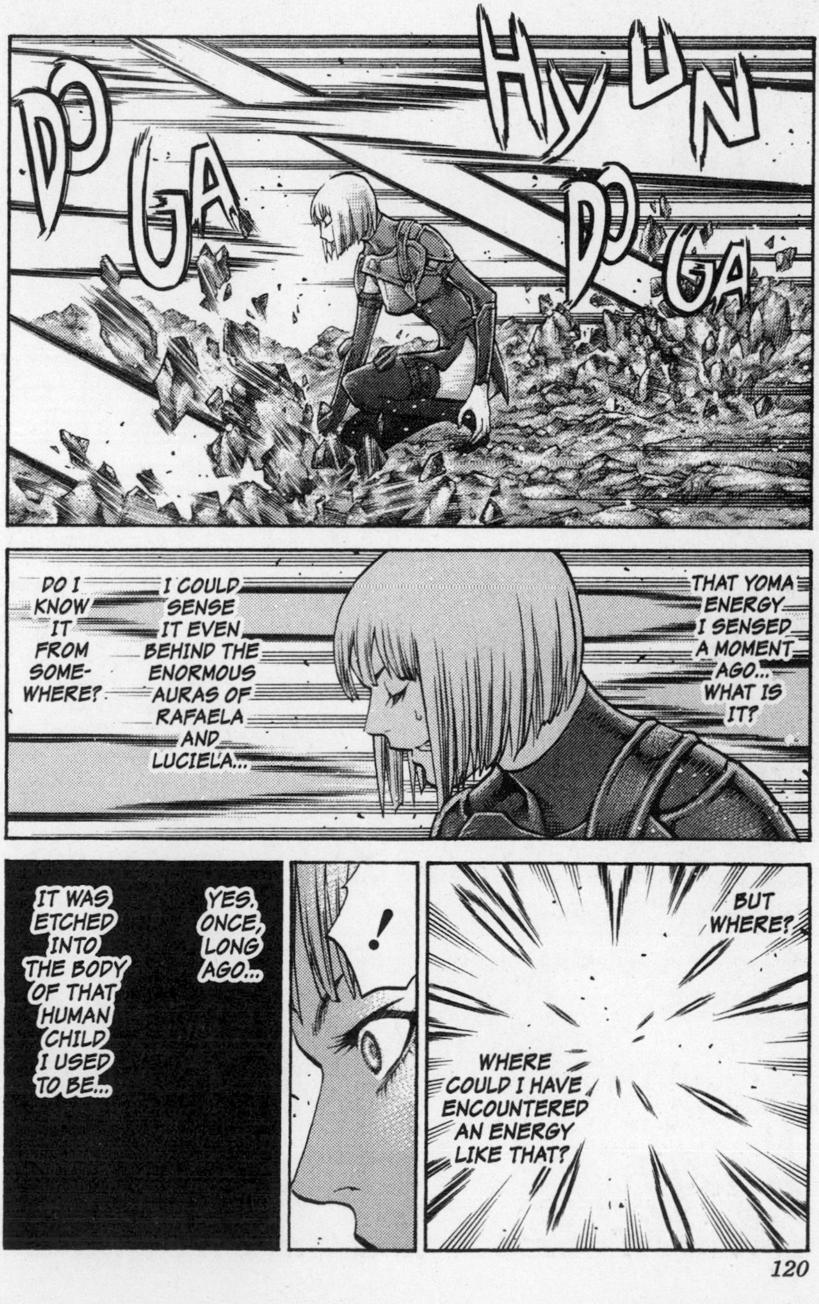
HYUN
DO GA
DO GA
THAT YOMA ENERGY I SENSED A MOMENT AGO... WHAT IS IT?
I COULD SENSE IT EVEN BEHIND THE ENORMOUS AURAS OF RAFAELA AND LUCIELA...
DO I KNOW IT FROM SOME-WHERE?
BUT WHERE?
WHERE COULD I HAVE ENCOUNTERED AN ENERGY LIKE THAT?
!
YES. ONCE, LONG AGO...
IT WAS ETCHED INTO THE BODY OF THAT HUMAN CHILD I USED TO BE...

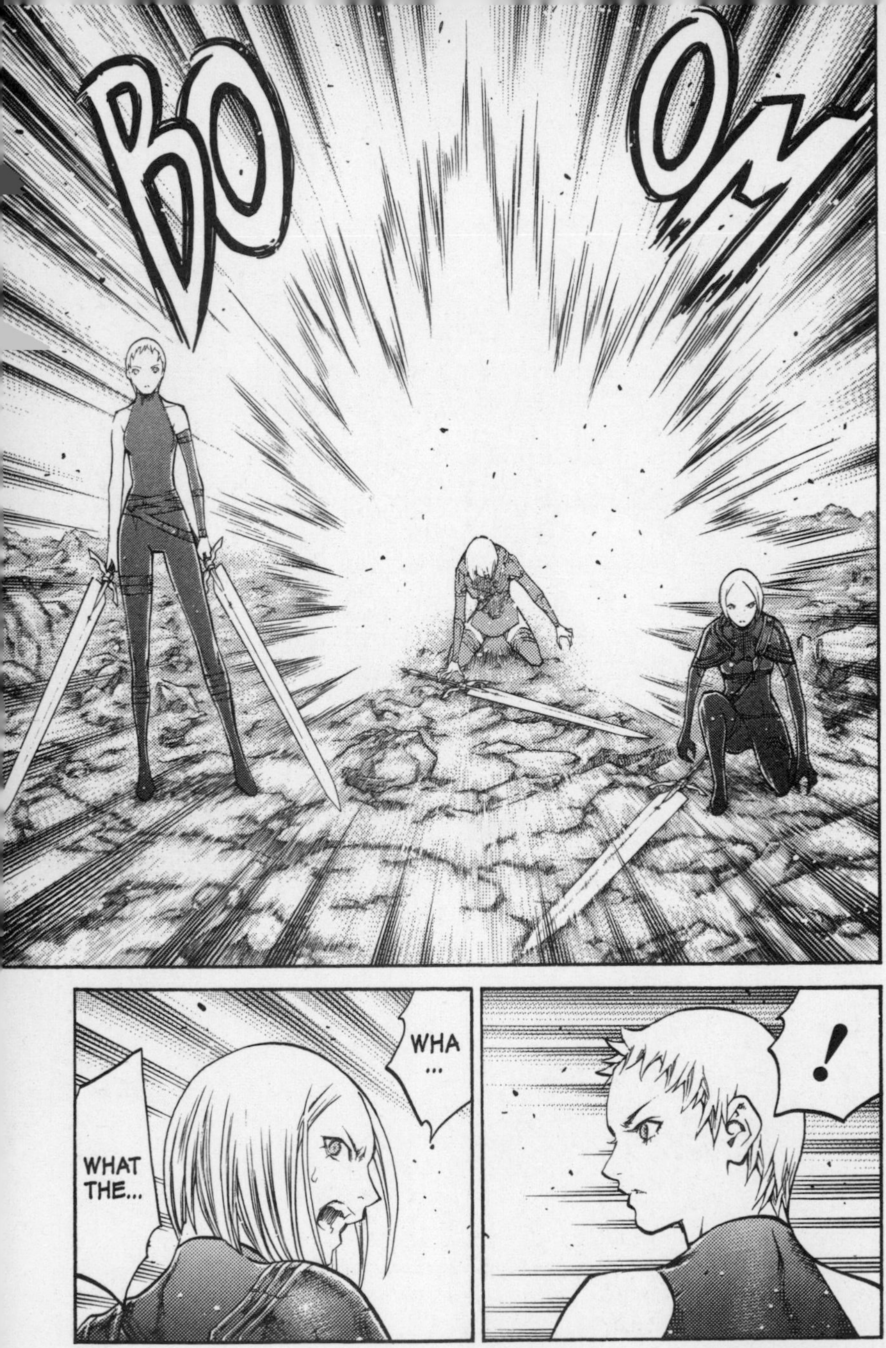
BOOOM
!
WHA...
WHAT THE...

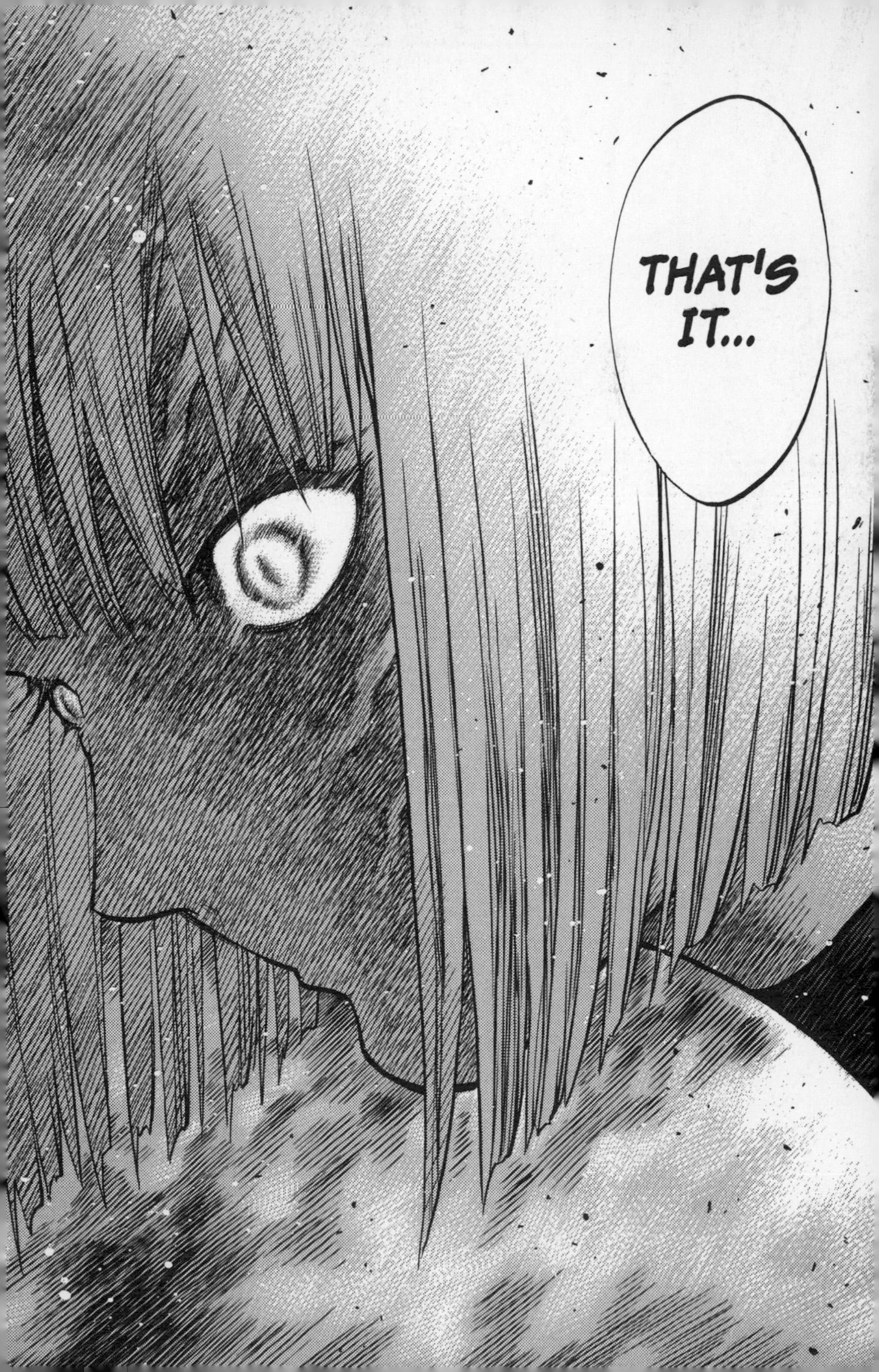
THAT'S IT...

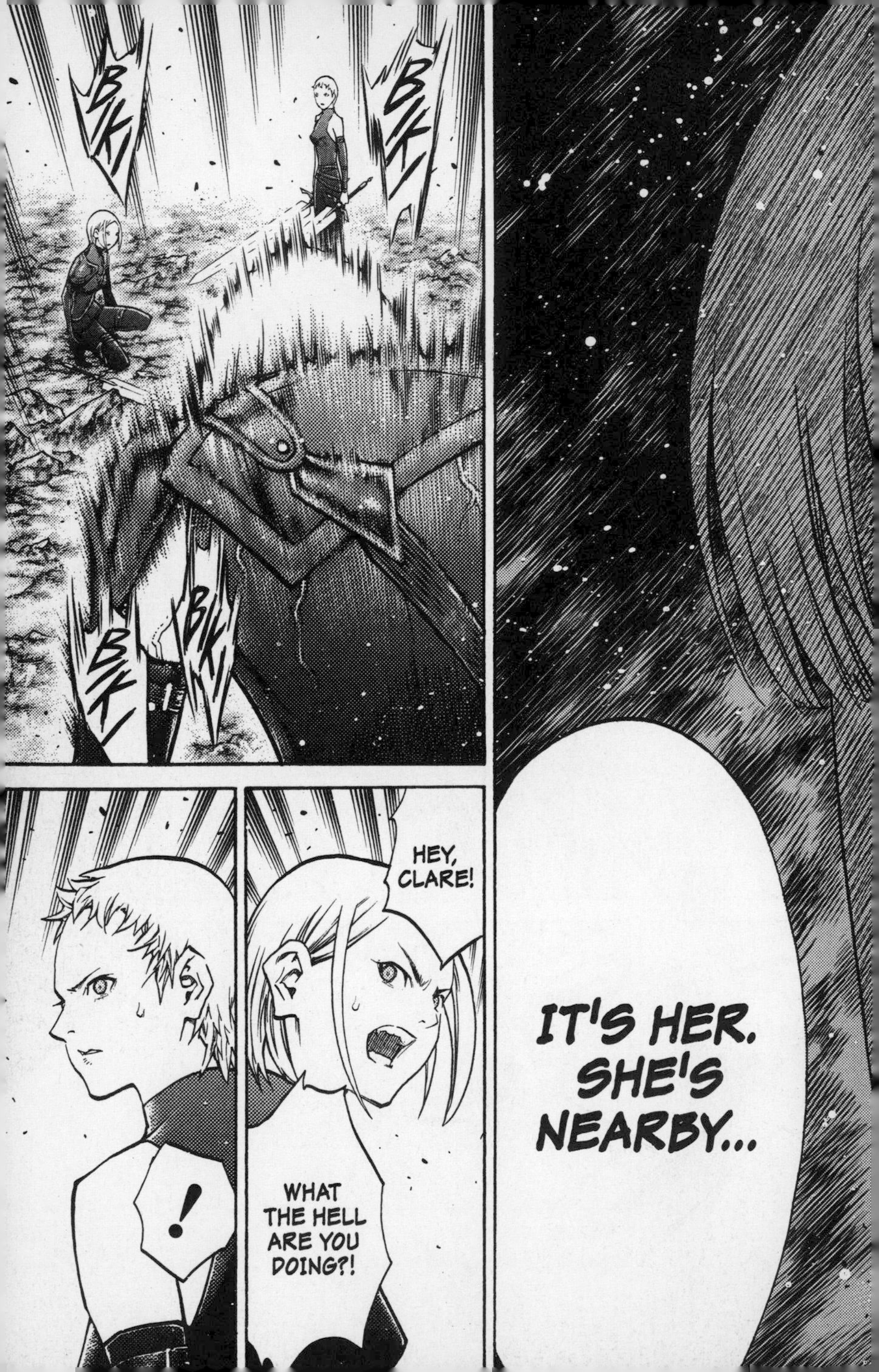
IT'S HER. SHE'S NEARBY...
BIKI
BIKI
BIKI
BIKI
HEY, CLARE!
WHAT THE HELL ARE YOU DOING?!
!

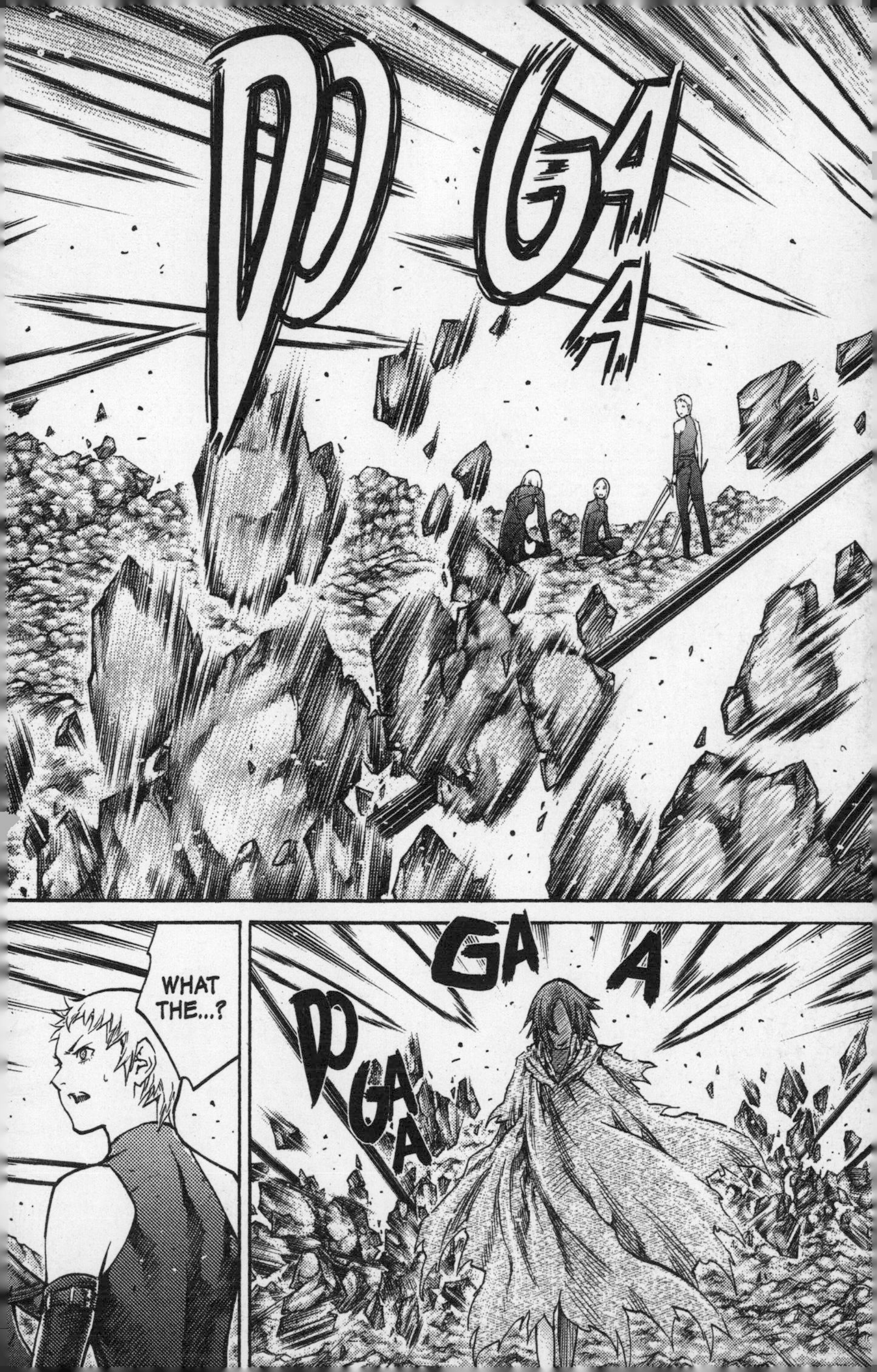
DOGAA
GA A
DOGAA
WHAT THE...?

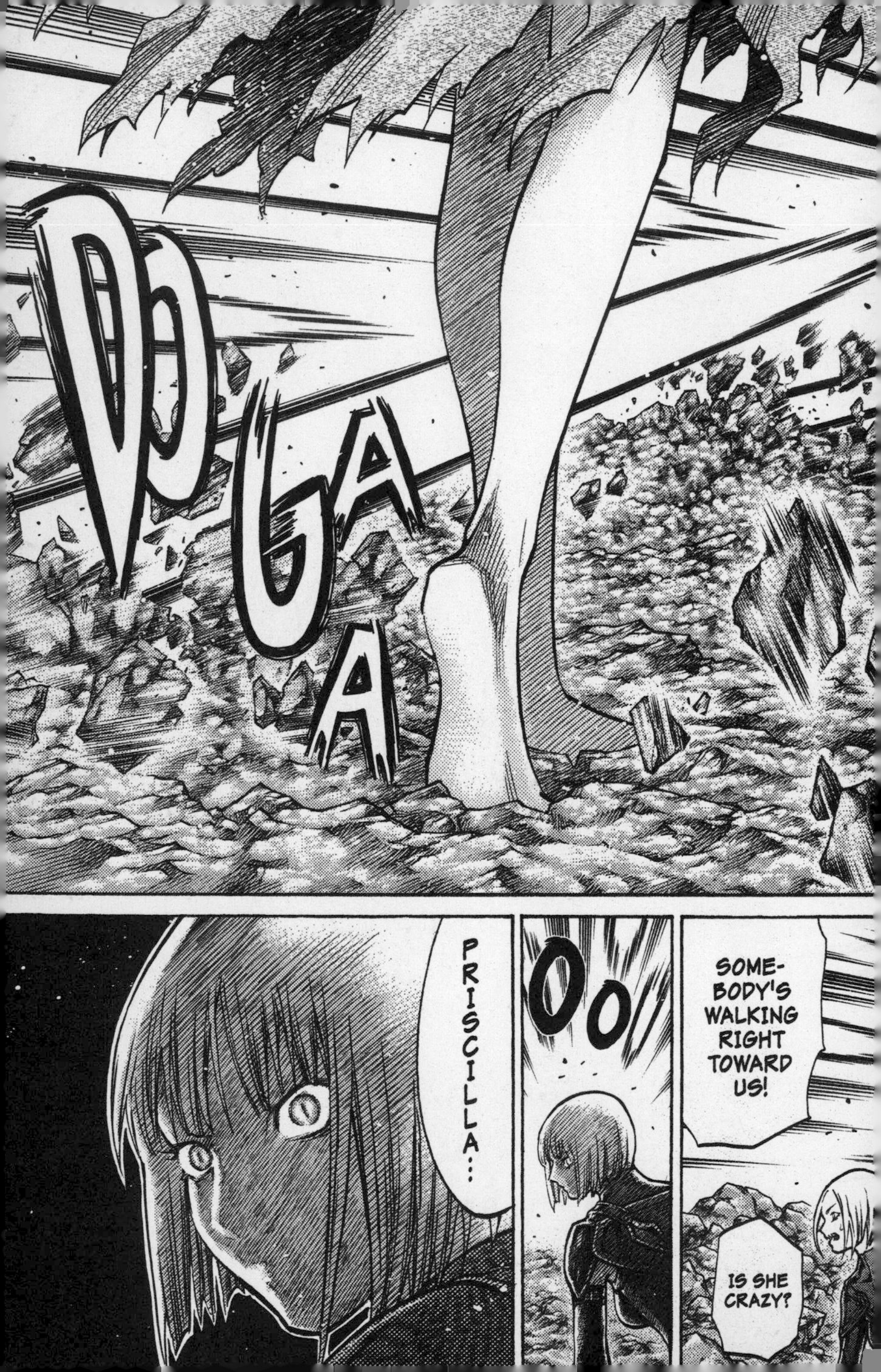
DOGAA
SOME-BODY'S WALKING RIGHT TOWARD US!
IS SHE CRAZY?
OO
PRISCILLA...

クレイモア
Claymore

Scene 100: The Ashes of Lautrec, Part 5

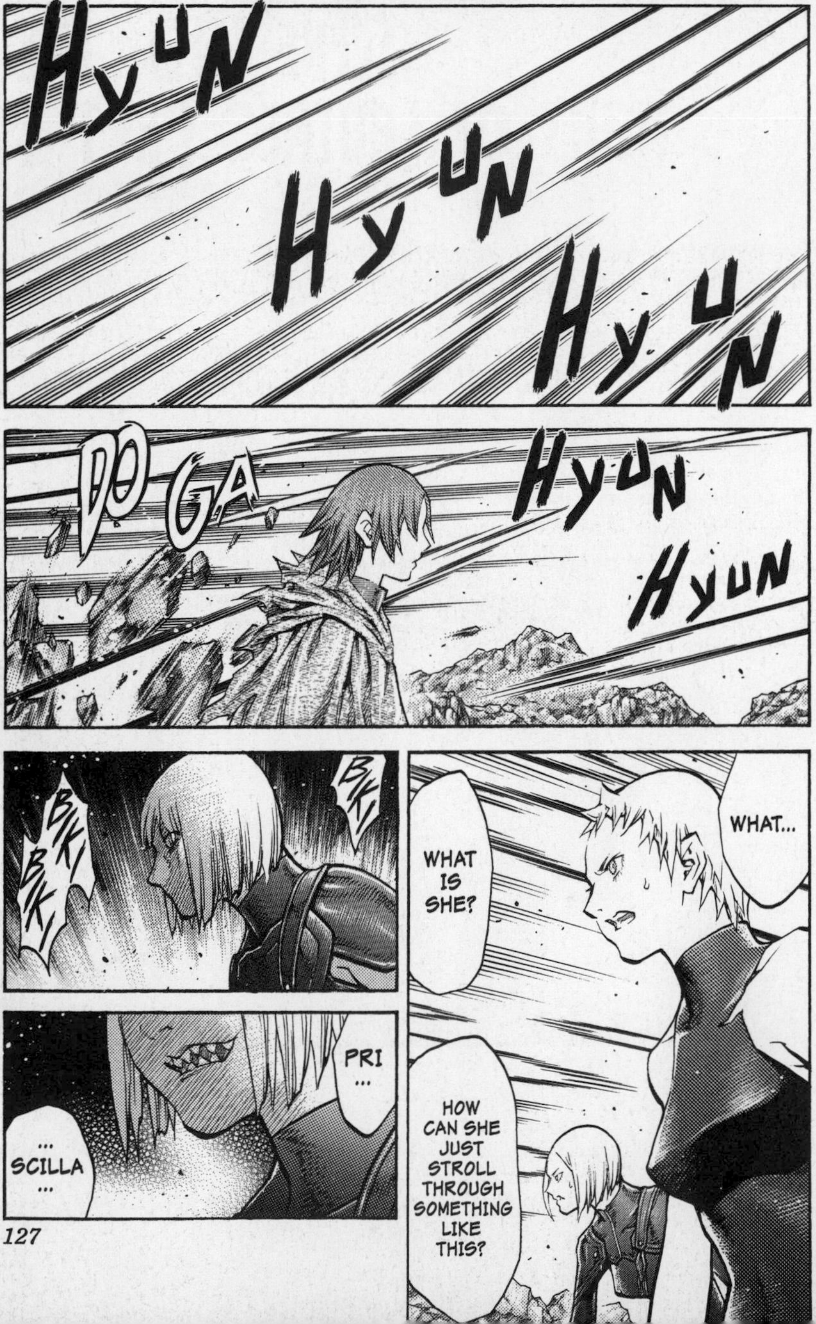
HYUN
HYUN
HYUN
DOGA
HYUN
HYUN
WHAT...
WHAT IS SHE?
HOW CAN SHE JUST STROLL THROUGH SOMETHING LIKE THIS?
BIKI
BIKI BIKI BIKI
PRI...
... SCILLA ...

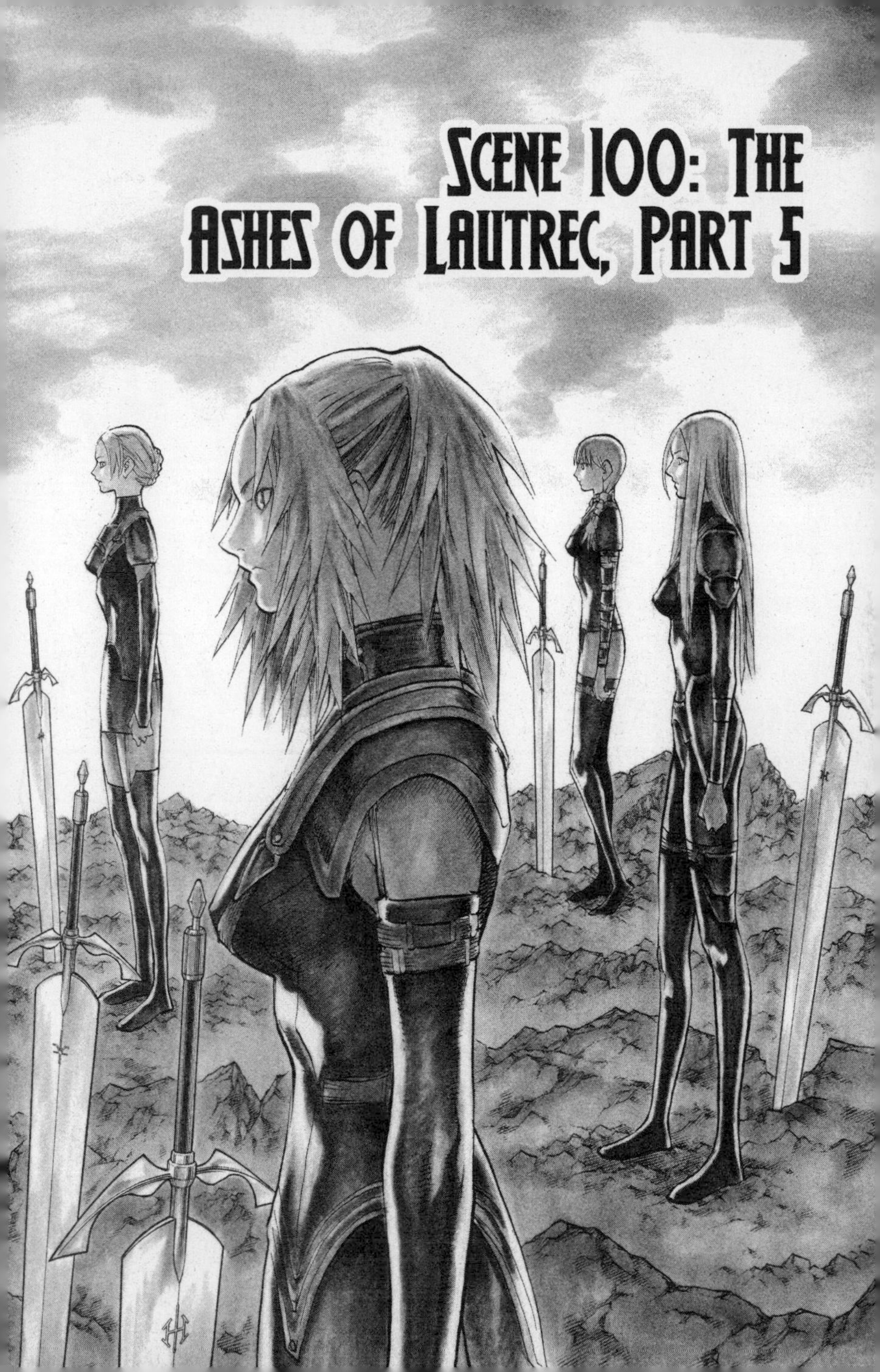
Scene 100: The Ashes of Lautrec, Part 5

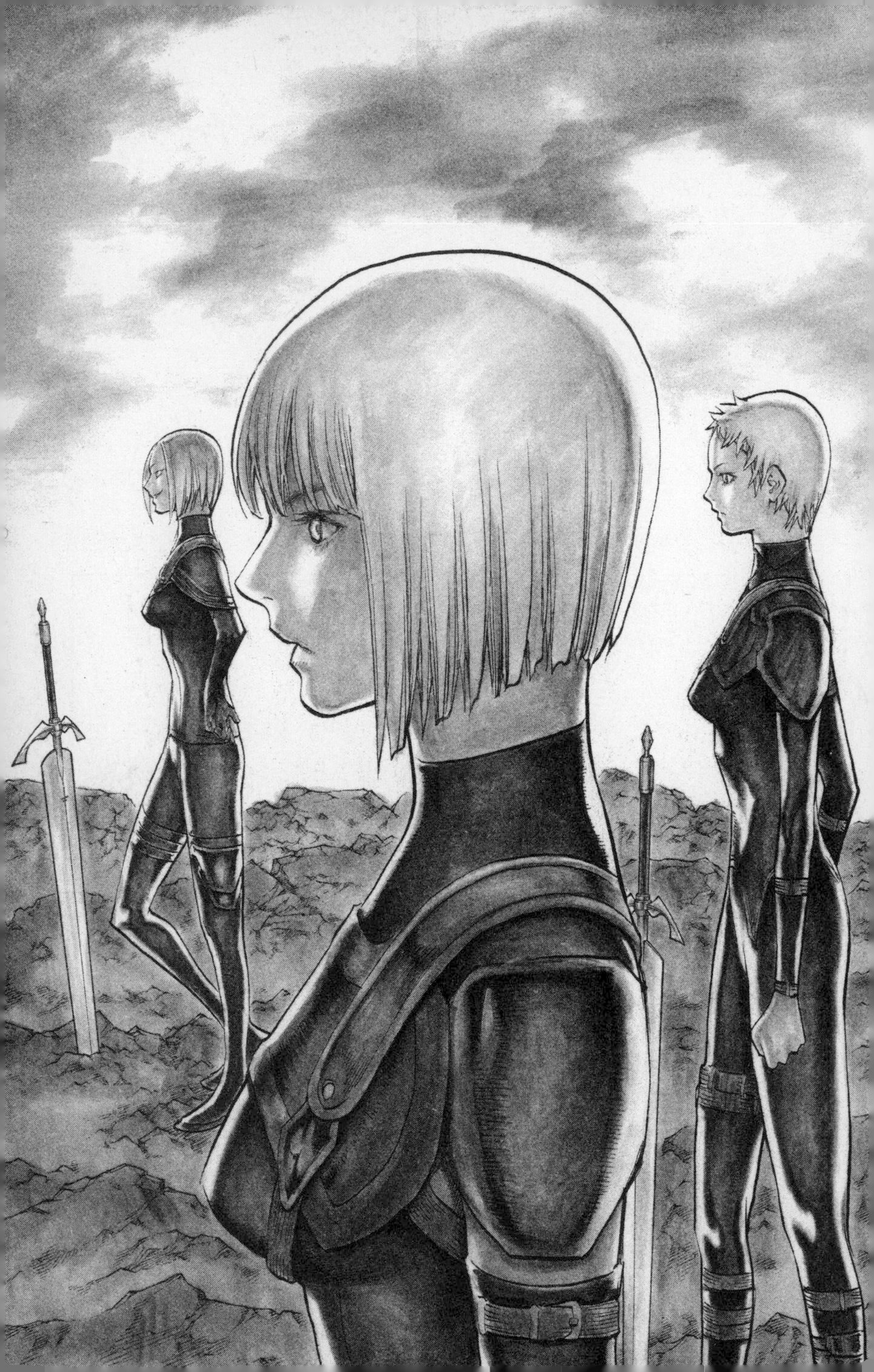

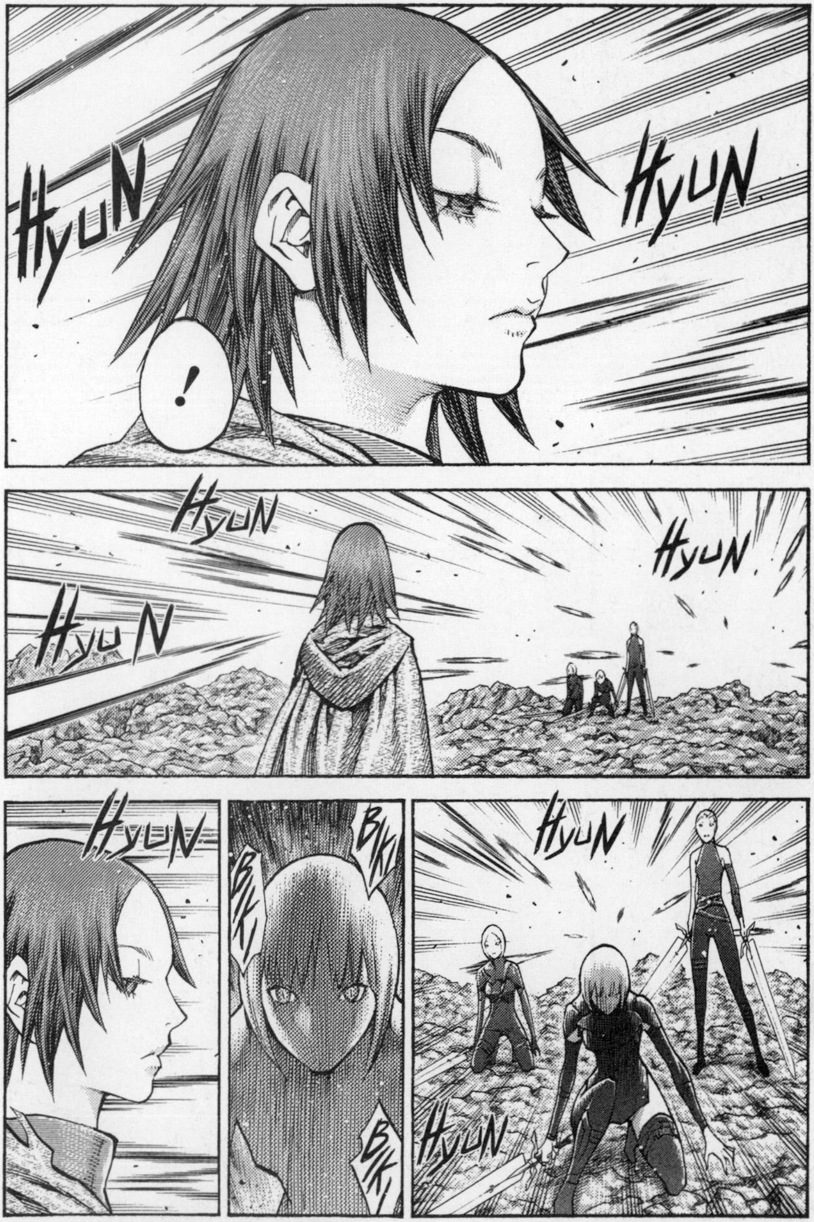
HYUN
HYUN
!
HYUN
HYUN
HYUN
HYUN
HYUN
BKI
BKI
BKI
HYUN

READ THIS WAY

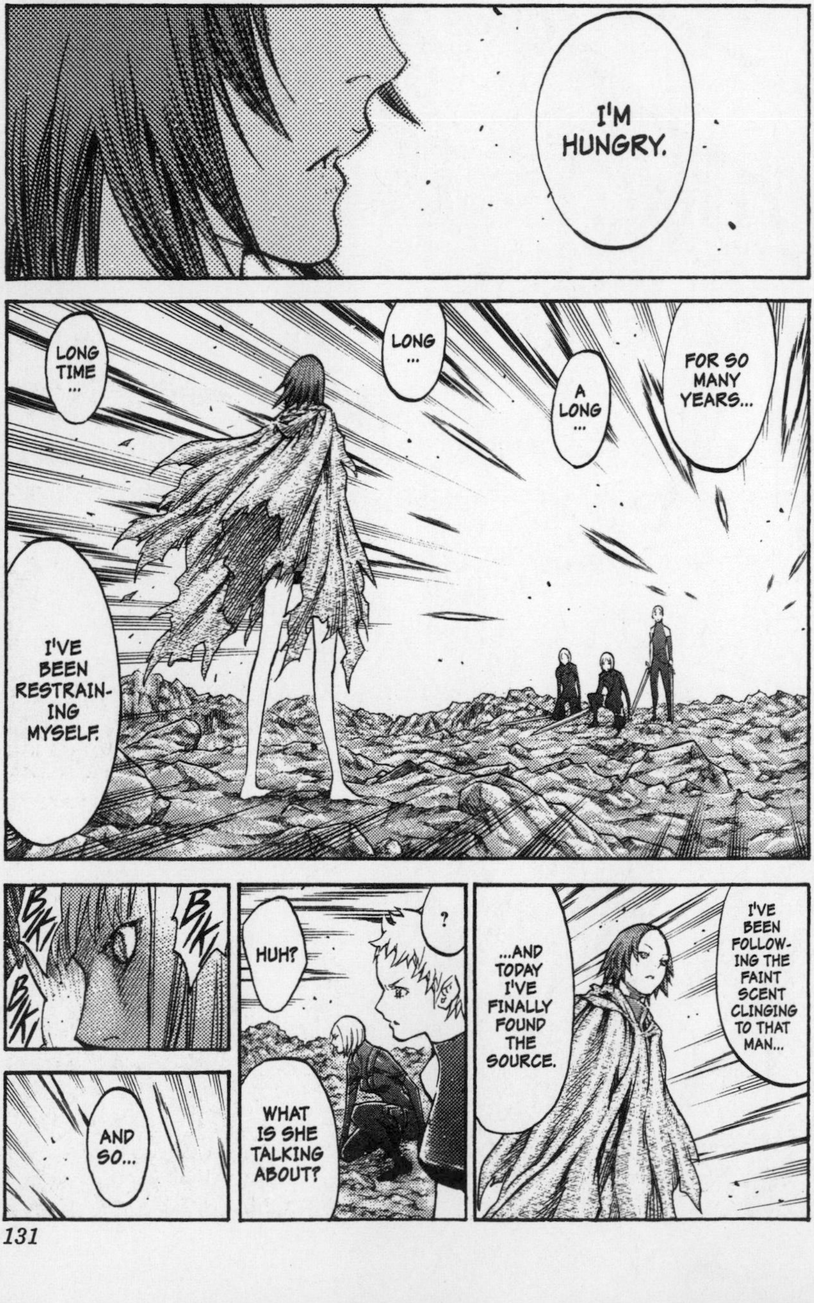
I'M HUNGRY.
FOR SO MANY YEARS...
A LONG ...
LONG ...
LONG TIME ...
I'VE BEEN RESTRAINING MYSELF.
I'VE BEEN FOLLOWING THE FAINT SCENT CLINGING TO THAT MAN...
...AND TODAY I'VE FINALLY FOUND THE SOURCE.
?
HUH?
WHAT IS SHE TALKING ABOUT?
BK BK BK
AND SO...

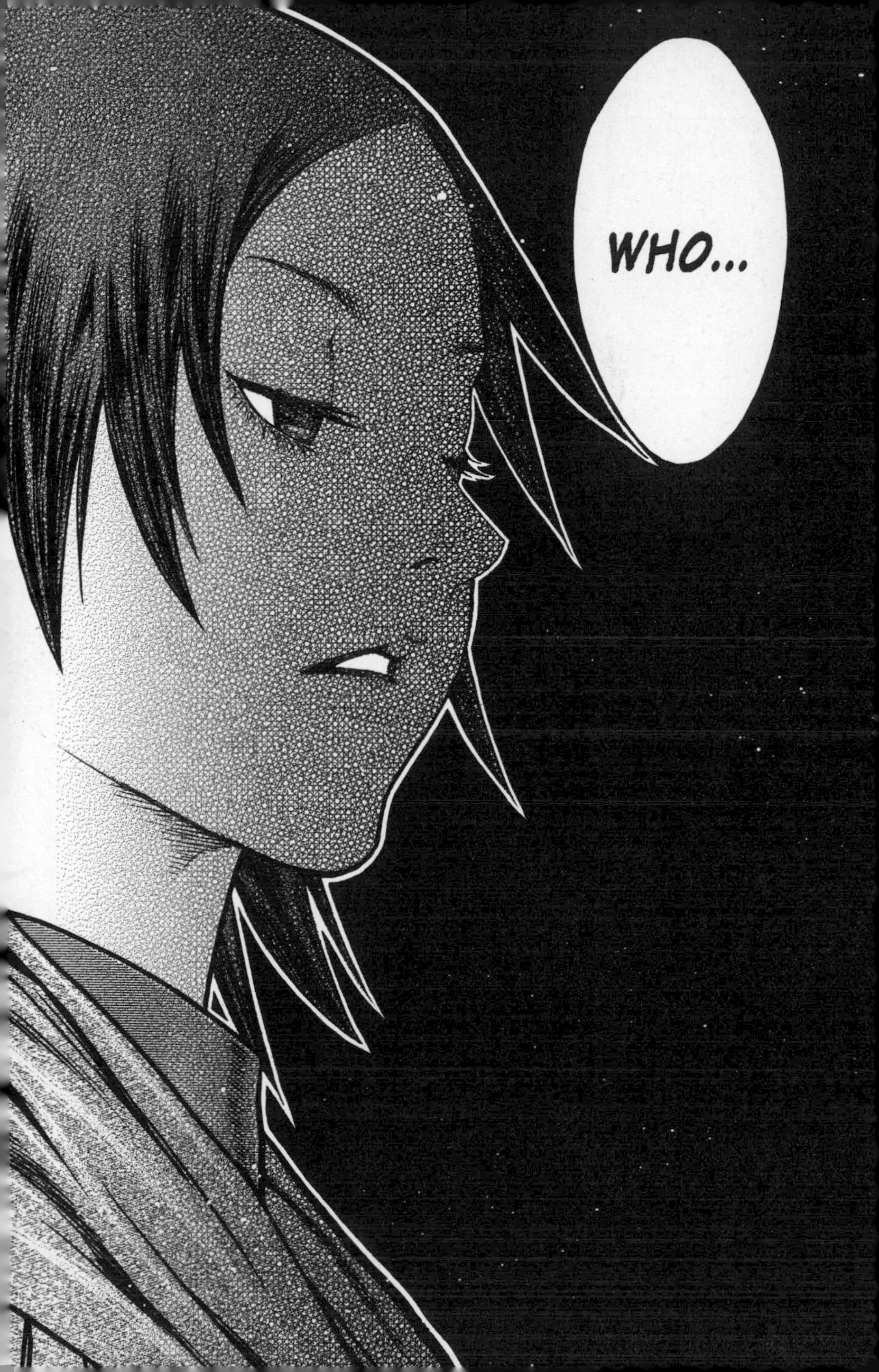
WHO...

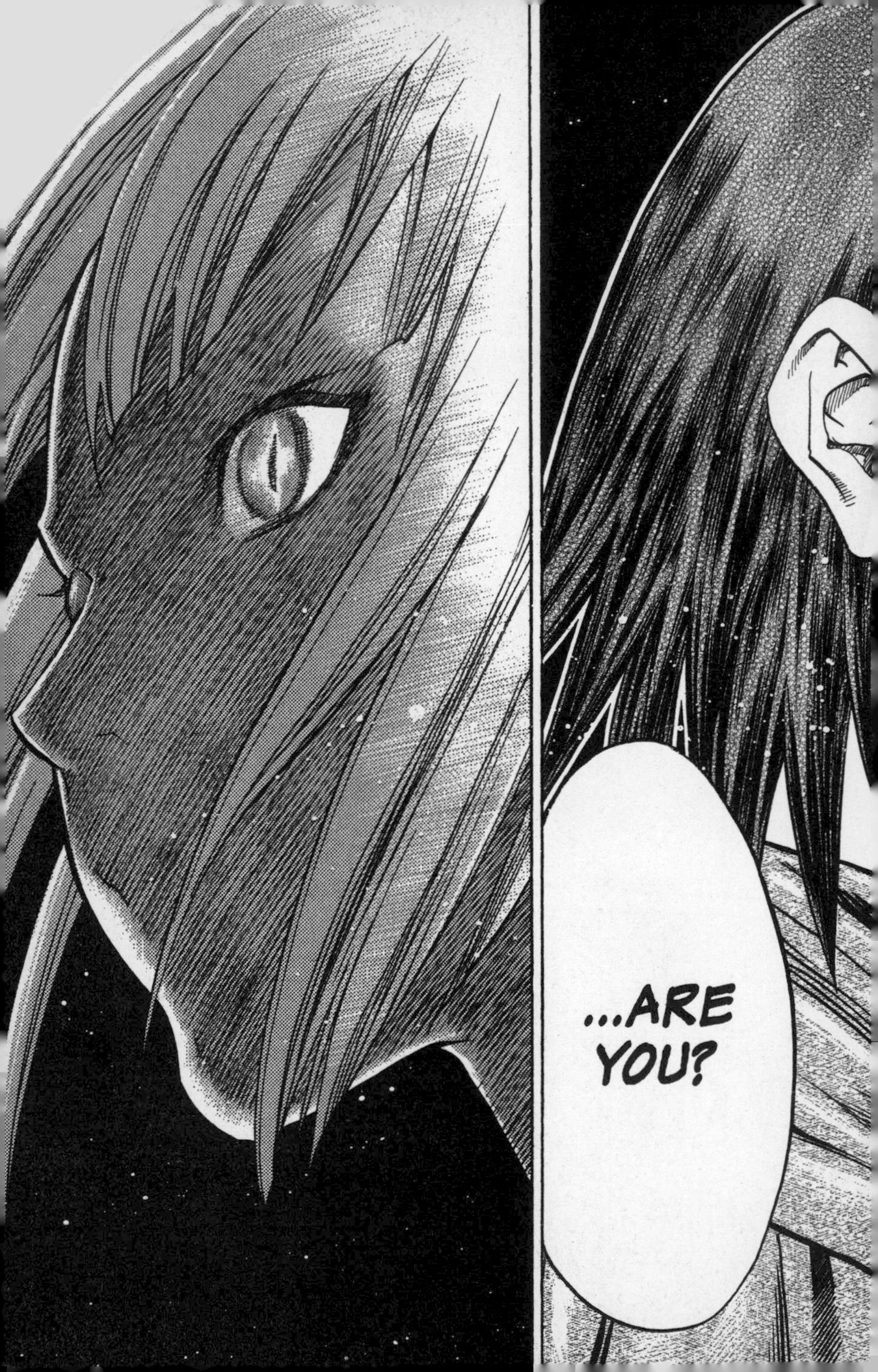
...ARE YOU?

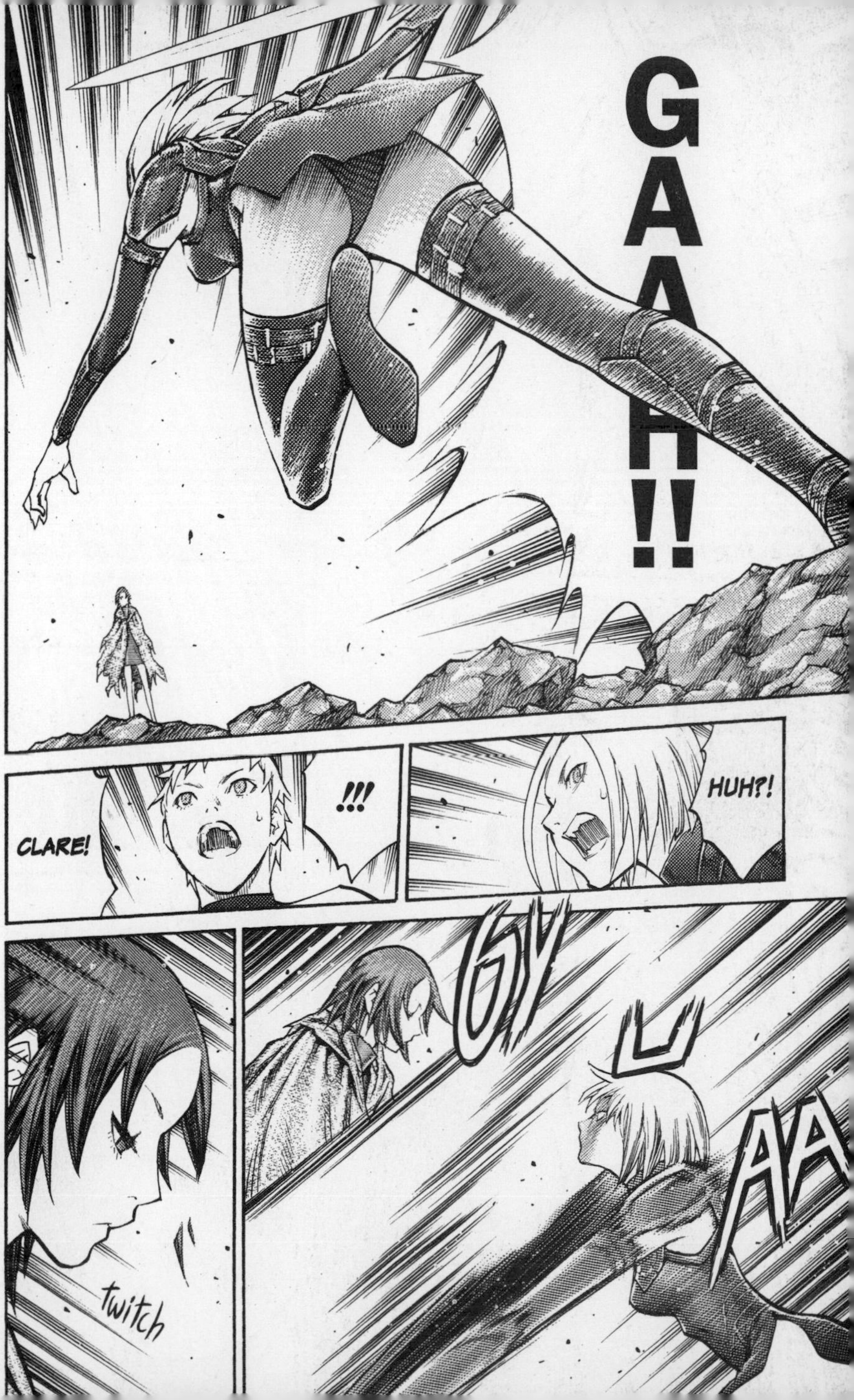
GAAH!!
HUH?!
!!!
CLARE!
GYU
AA
twitch

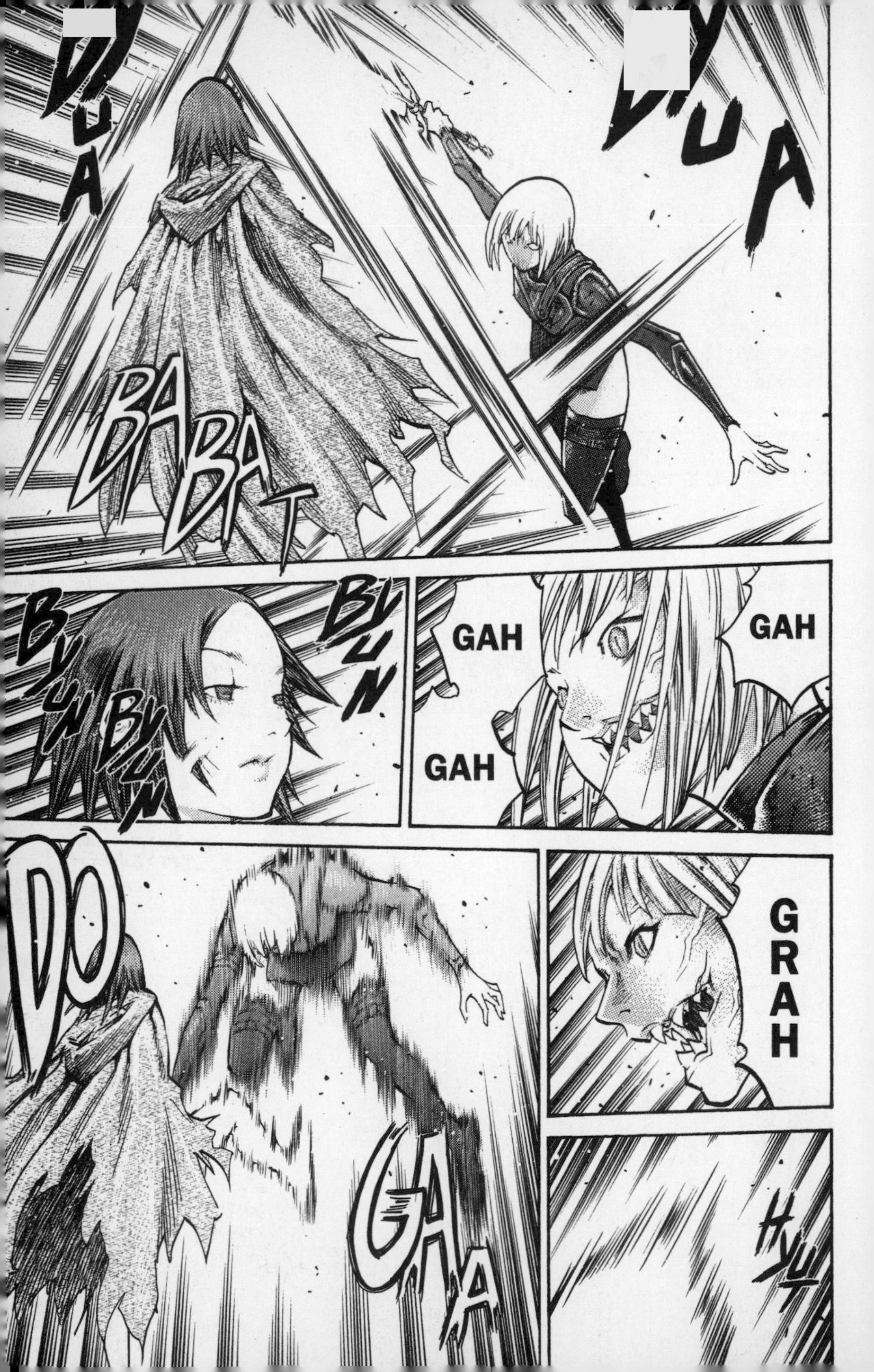
DUA
DUA
BADABADAT
GAH
GAH
GAH
BYUN
BYUN BYUN
GRAH
HYU
DO
GAA

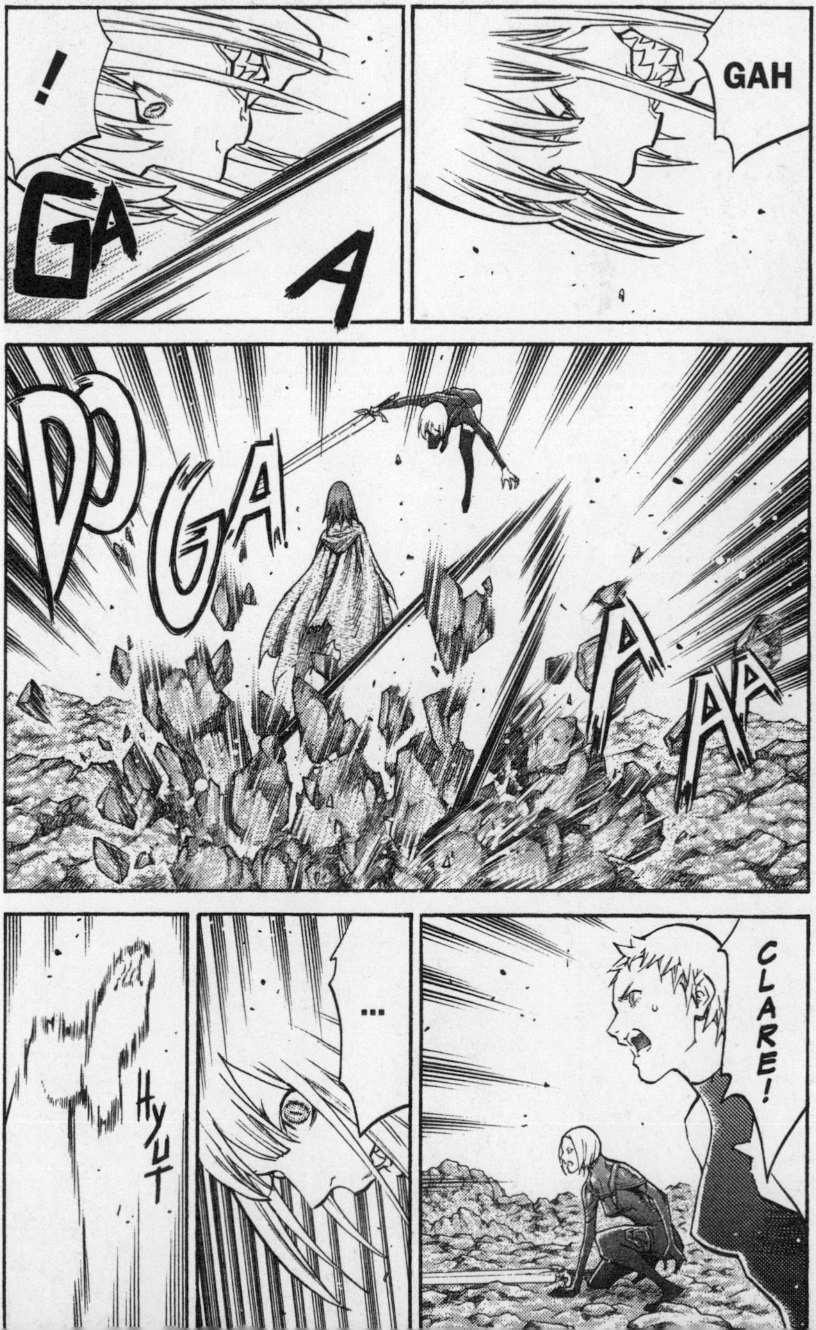
GAH
!
GA
A
DOGA
A
AA
CLARE!
...
HYUT

READ THIS WAY

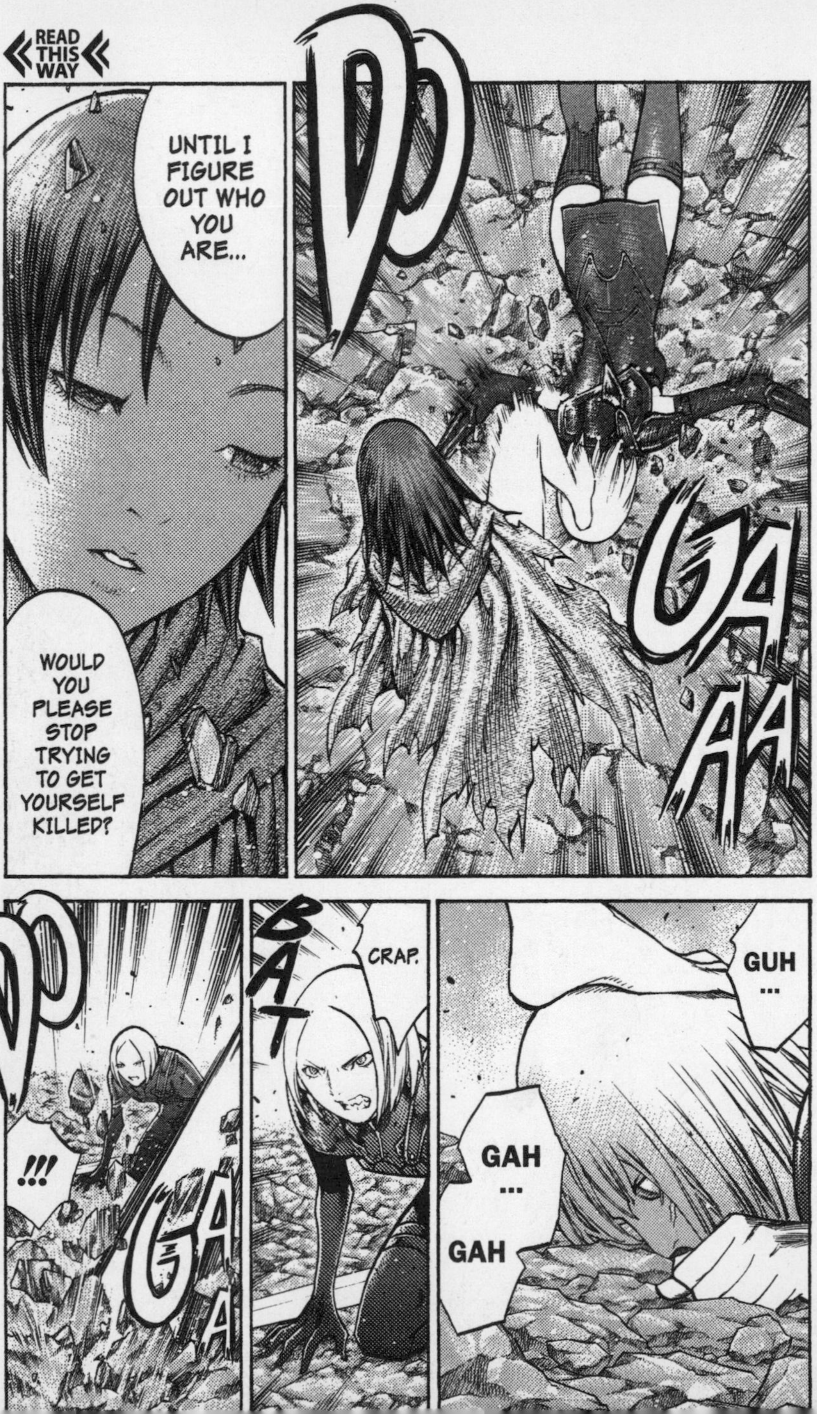
DO
GAAA
UNTIL I FIGURE OUT WHO YOU ARE...
WOULD YOU PLEASE STOP TRYING TO GET YOURSELF KILLED?
GUH ...
GAH ...
GAH
BAT
CRAP.
DO
!!!
GAGA

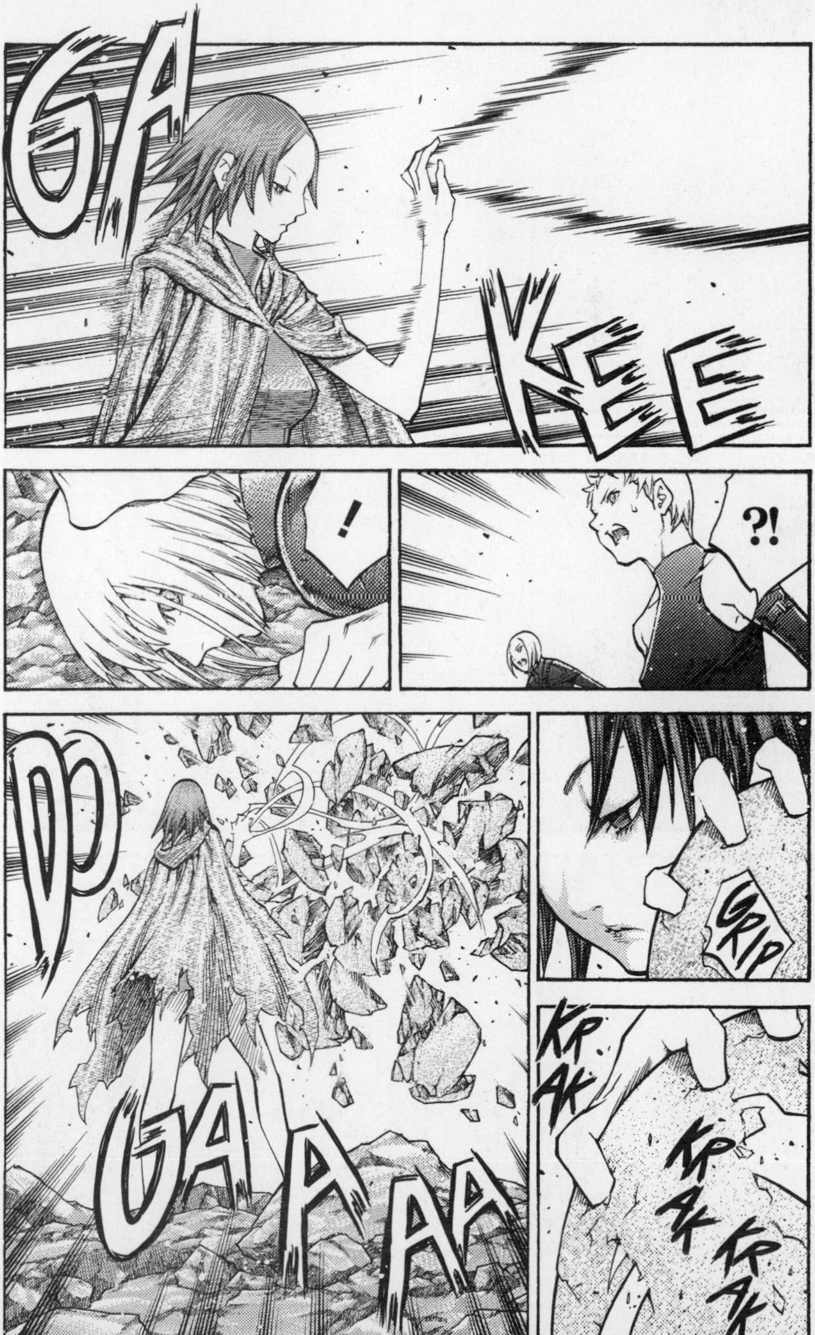
GA
KEE
?!
!
GRIP
KRAK
KRAK
KRAK
DO
GAAA

READ THIS WAY

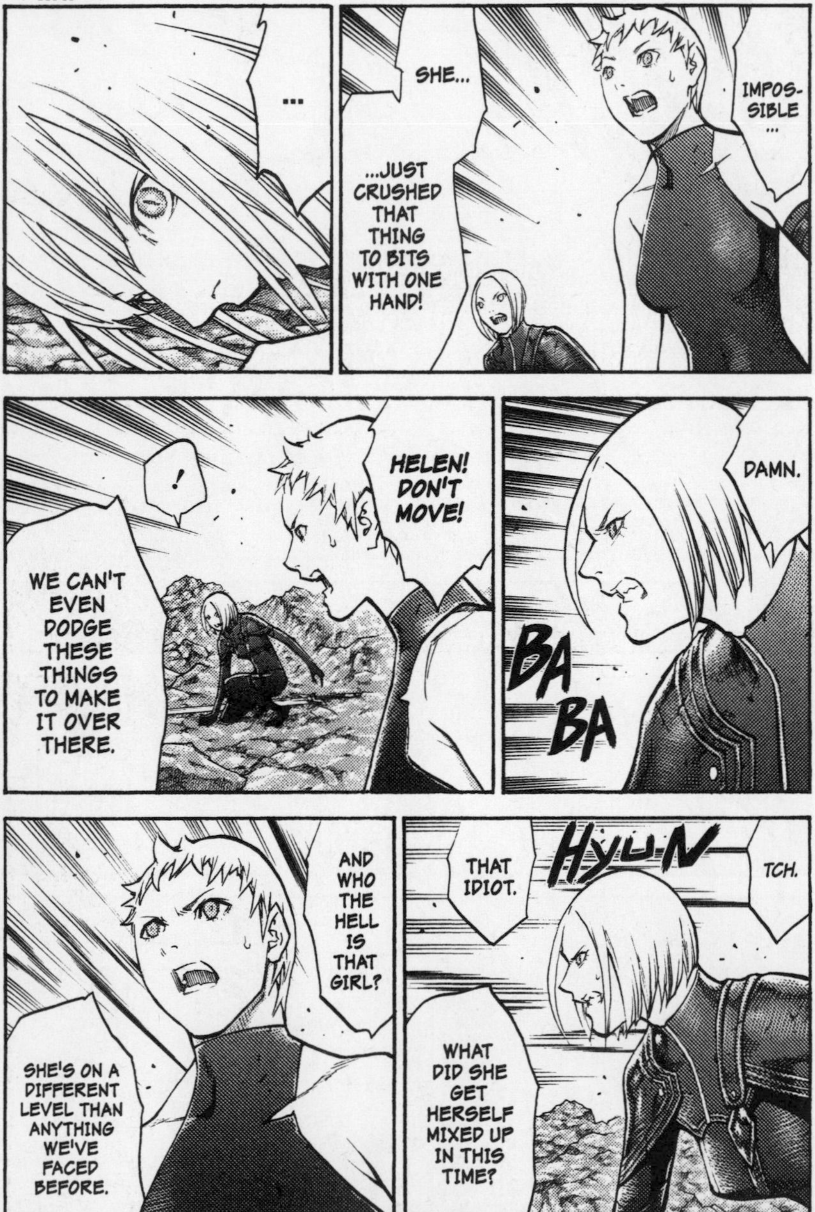

IMPOS-SIBLE...
SHE...
...JUST CRUSHED THAT THING TO BITS WITH ONE HAND!
...
DAMN.
BA BA
HELEN! DON'T MOVE!
!
WE CAN'T EVEN DODGE THESE THINGS TO MAKE IT OVER THERE.
TCH.
HYUN
THAT IDIOT.
WHAT DID SHE GET HERSELF MIXED UP IN THIS TIME?
AND WHO THE HELL IS THAT GIRL?
SHE'S ON A DIFFERENT LEVEL THAN ANYTHING WE'VE FACED BEFORE.

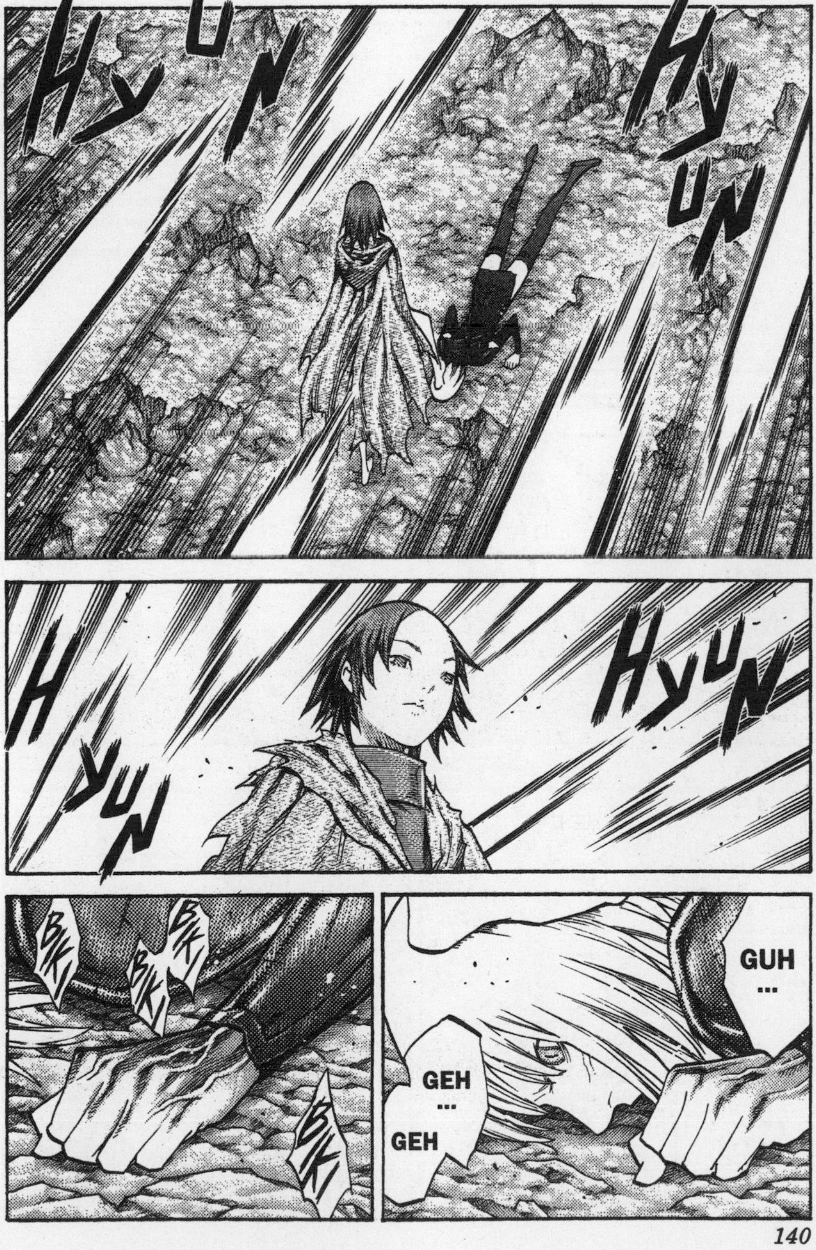
HYUN
HYUN
HYUN
HYUN
GUH ...
GEH ... GEH
BIK
BIK
BIK
BIK

READ THIS WAY

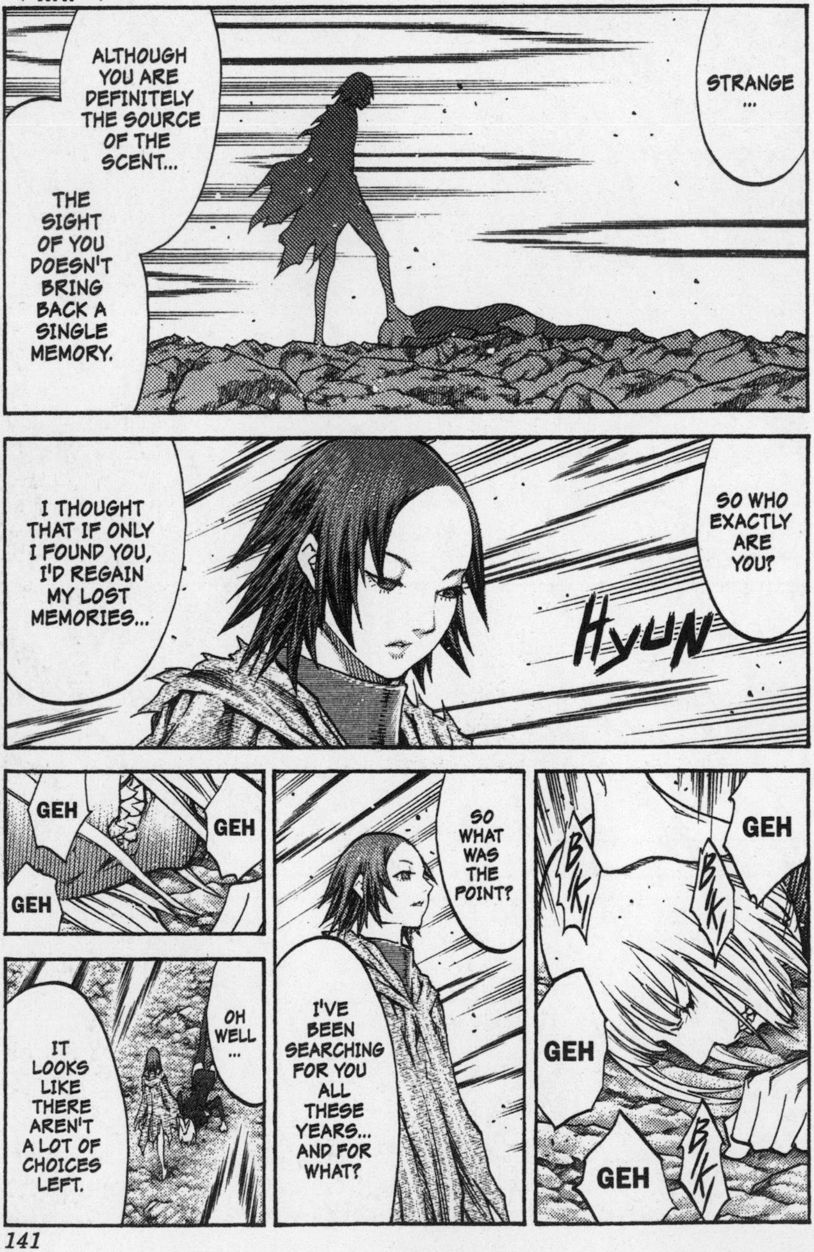
STRANGE ...
ALTHOUGH YOU ARE DEFINITELY THE SOURCE OF THE SCENT...
THE SIGHT OF YOU DOESN'T BRING BACK A SINGLE MEMORY.
I THOUGHT THAT IF ONLY I FOUND YOU, I'D REGAIN MY LOST MEMORIES...
SO WHO EXACTLY ARE YOU?
HYUN
GEH
BIKI
BIKI
GEH
BIKI
GEH
I'VE BEEN SEARCHING FOR YOU ALL THESE YEARS... AND FOR WHAT?
SO WHAT WAS THE POINT?
GEH
GEH
GEH
OH WELL ...
IT LOOKS LIKE THERE AREN'T A LOT OF CHOICES LEFT.

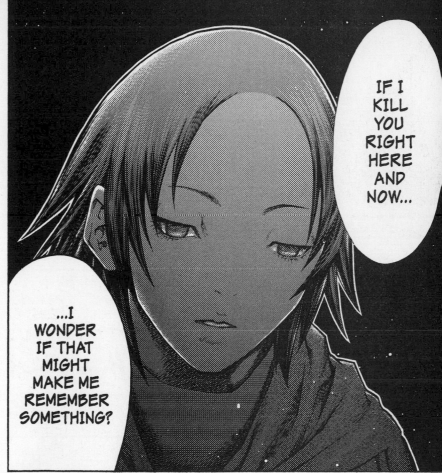

IF I KILL YOU RIGHT HERE AND NOW...

...I WONDER IF THAT MIGHT MAKE ME REMEMBER SOMETHING?

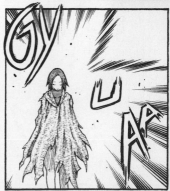

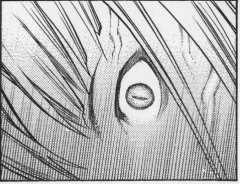

142

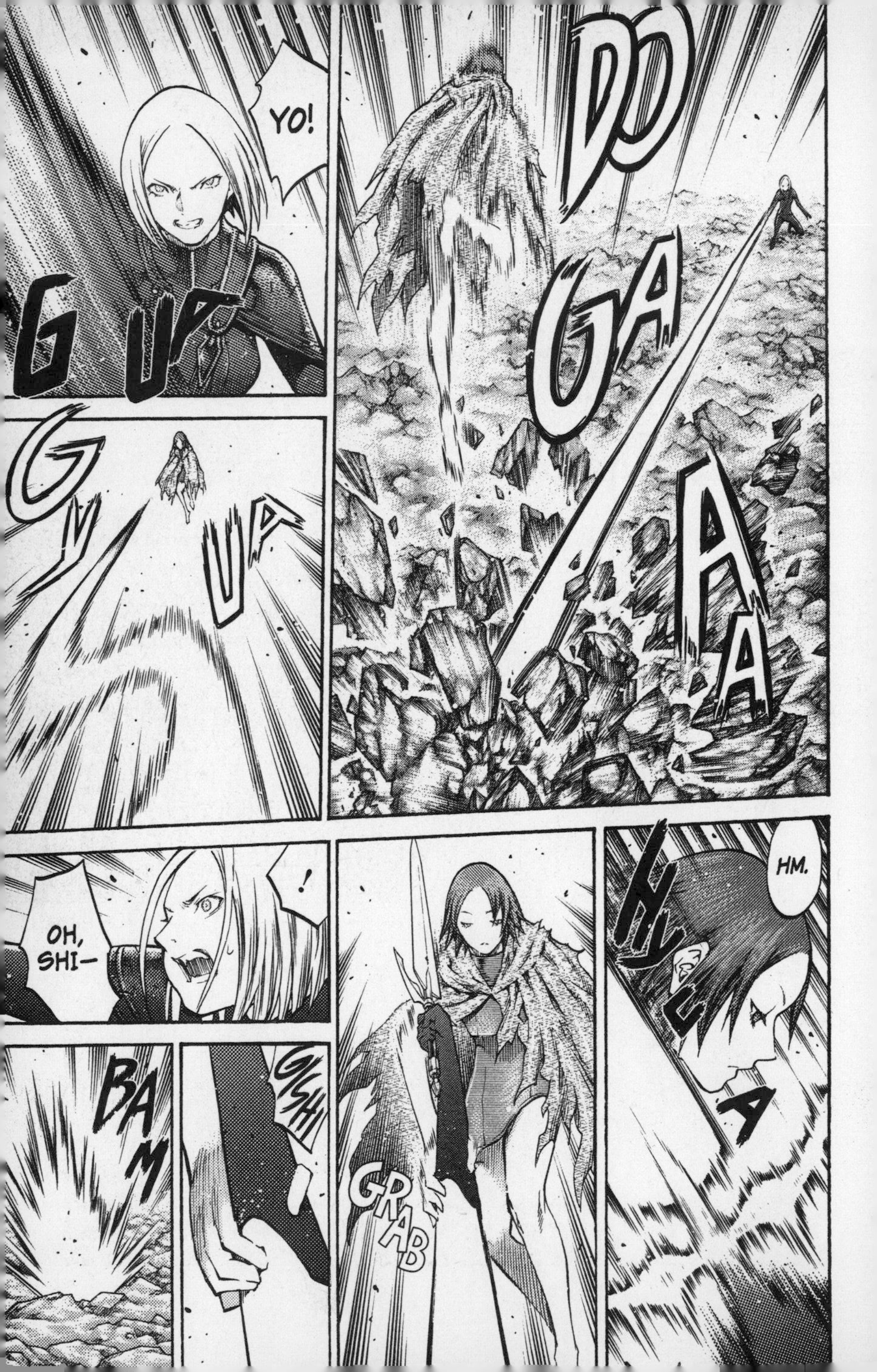
DOGAAA
YO!
GUP
GYUP
HM.
HYUA
GRAB
!
OH, SHI—
GISHI
BAM

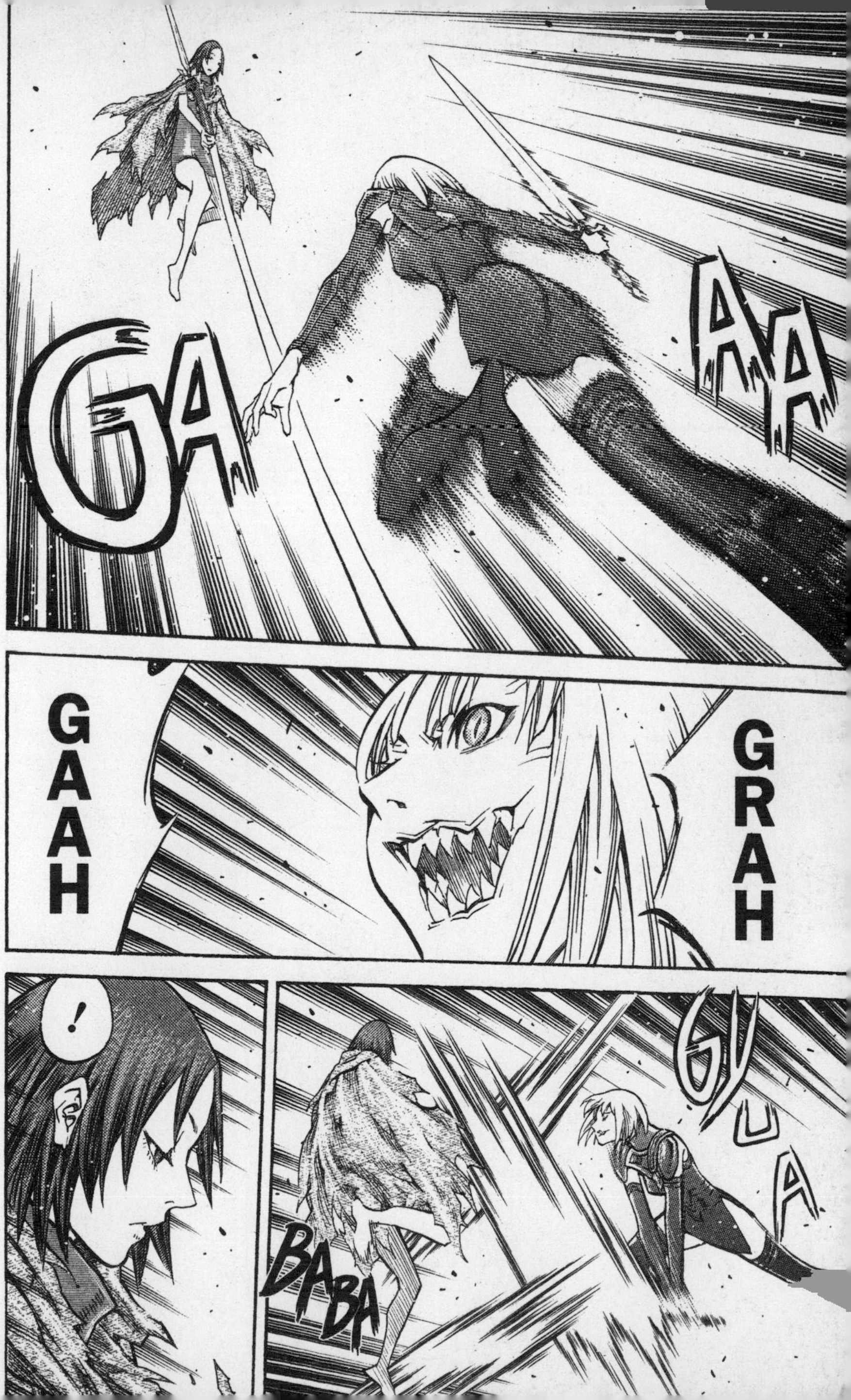
AAA
GA
GRAH
GAAH
GYUA
BABA
!

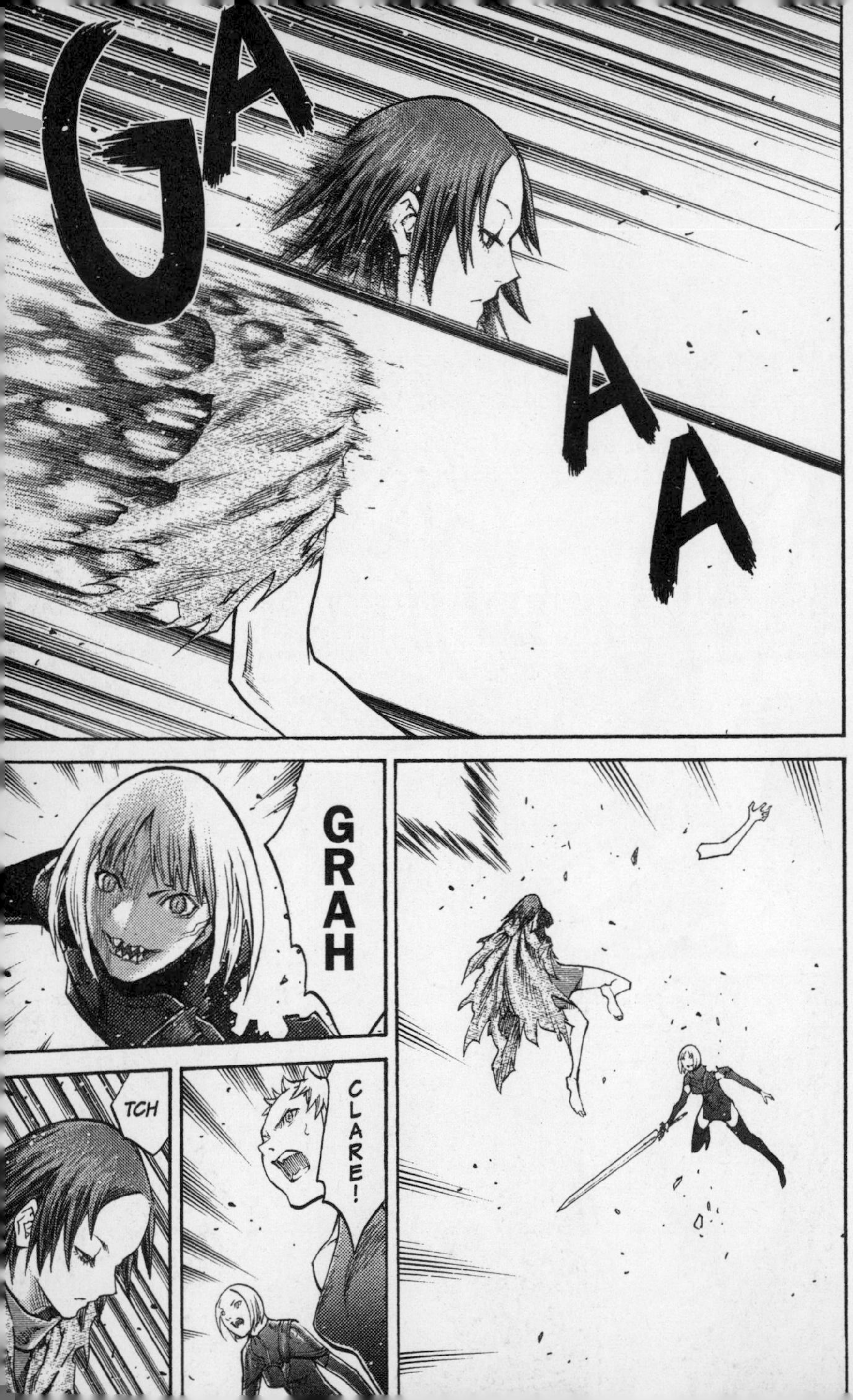
GAAAA
GRAH
CLARE!
TCH

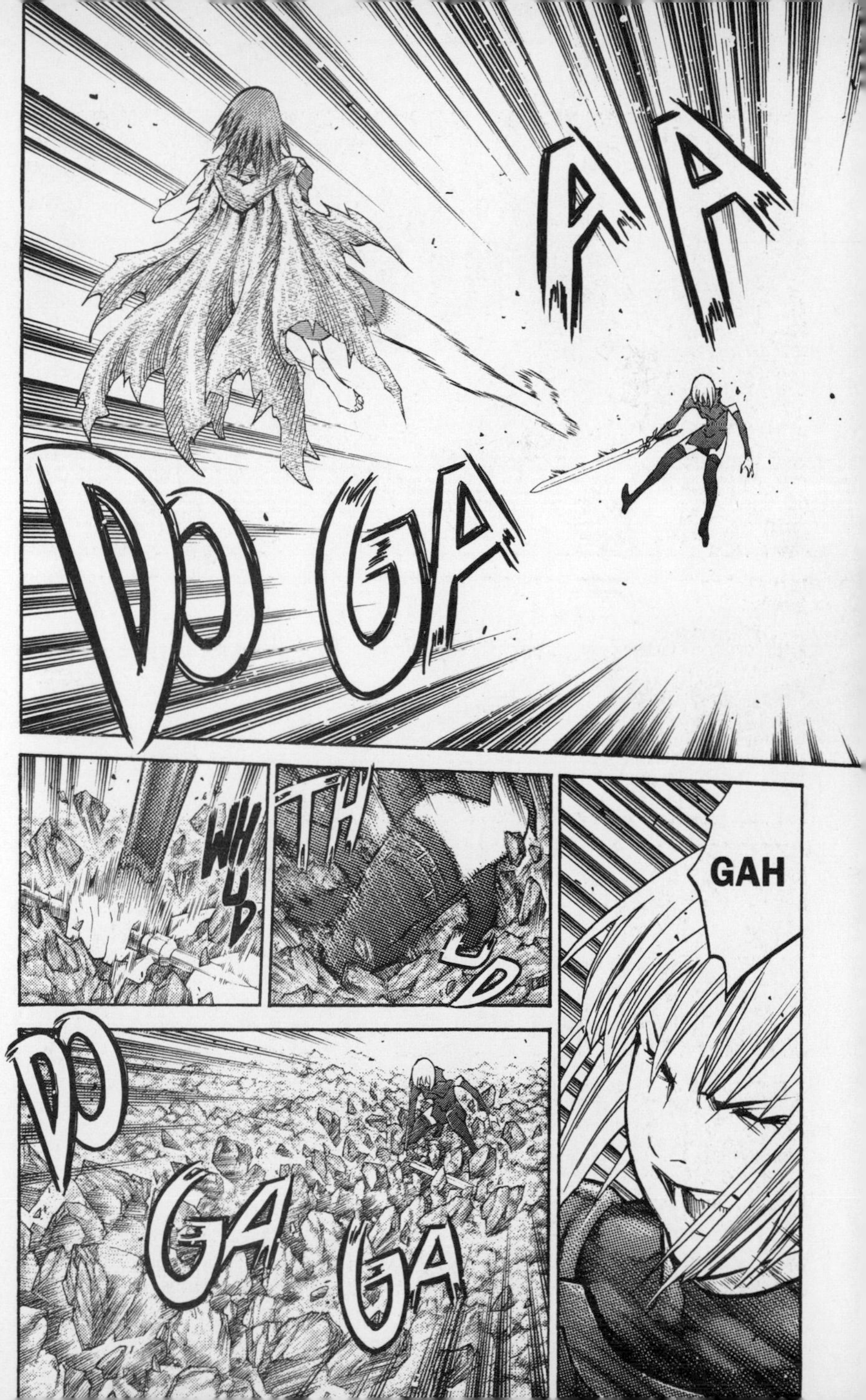
AA
DO GA
GAH
THUD
WHUD
DO GA GA

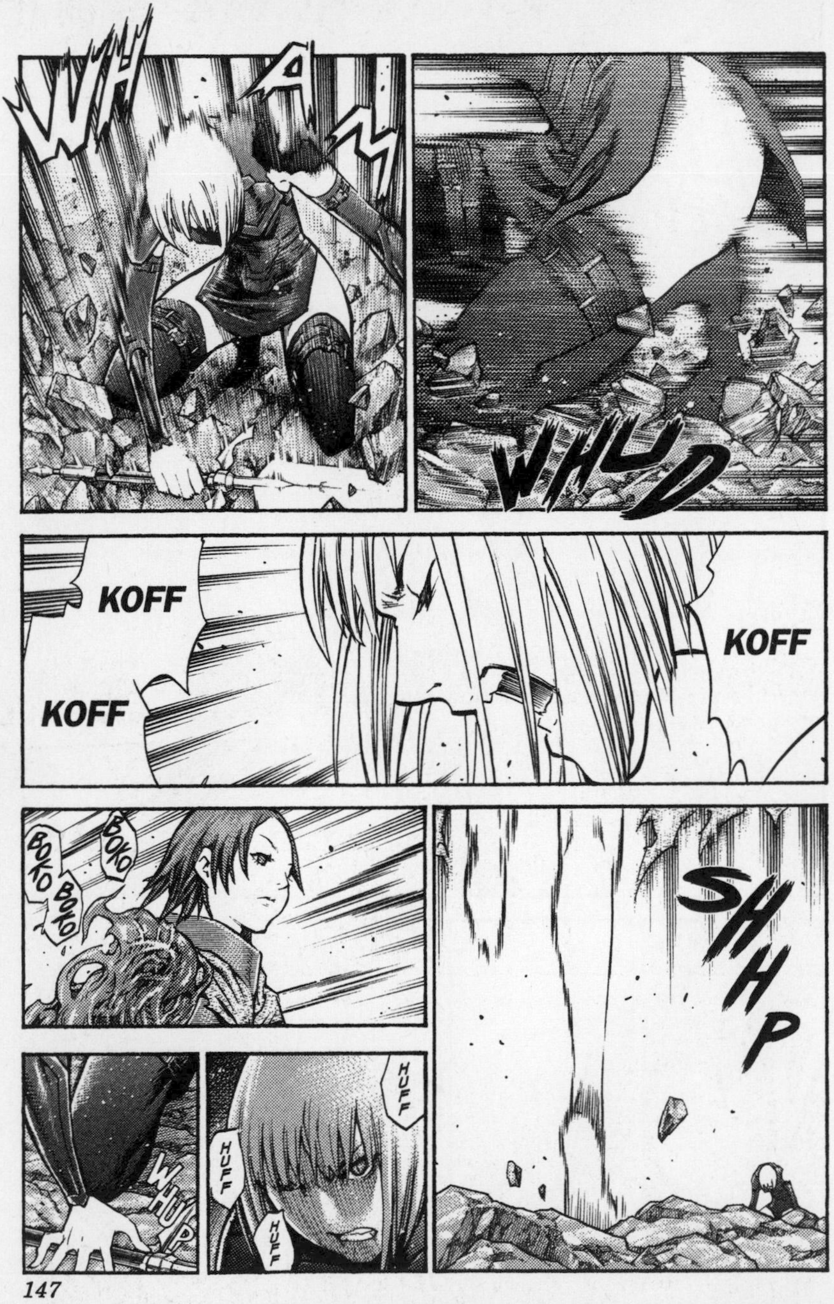
WHUD
WHAM
KOFF
KOFF
KOFF
SHHP
BOKO
BOKO
BOKO
HUFF
HUFF
HUFF
WHUP

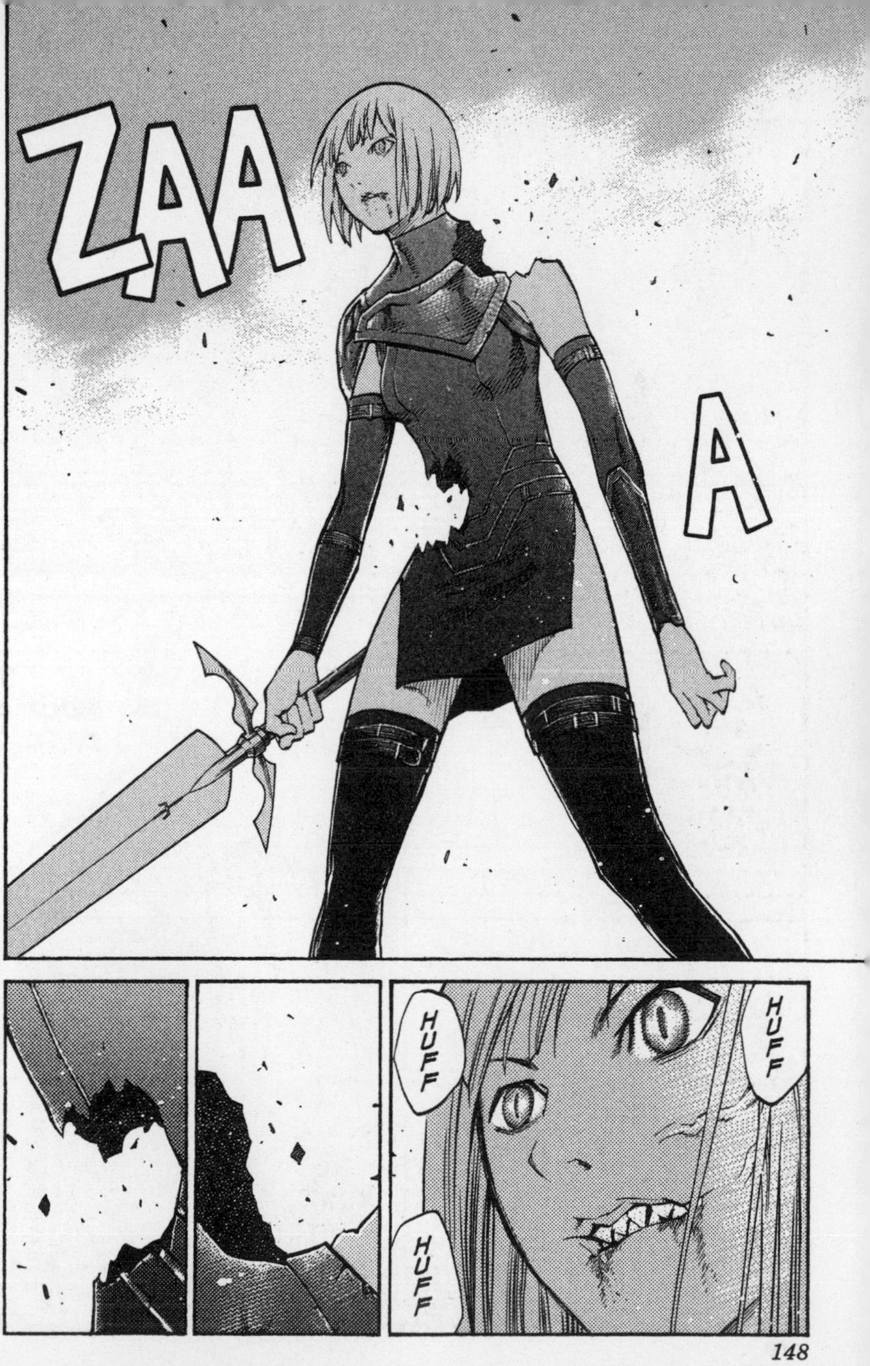
ZAAA
A
HUFF
HUFF
HUFF

READ THIS WAY

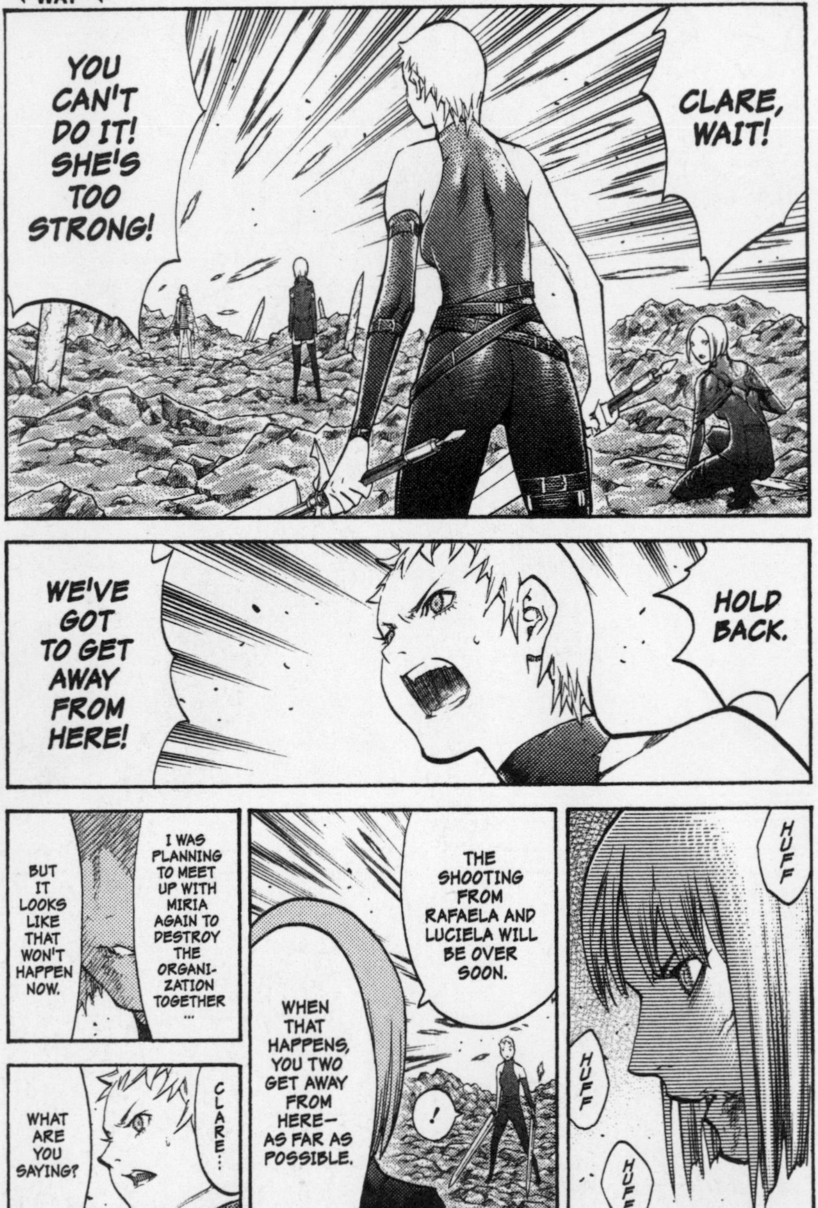
CLARE, WAIT!
YOU CAN'T DO IT! SHE'S TOO STRONG!
HOLD BACK.
WE'VE GOT TO GET AWAY FROM HERE!
HUFF
HUFF
HUFF
THE SHOOTING FROM RAFAELA AND LUCIELA WILL BE OVER SOON.
!
WHEN THAT HAPPENS, YOU TWO GET AWAY FROM HERE—AS FAR AS POSSIBLE.
I WAS PLANNING TO MEET UP WITH MIRIA AGAIN TO DESTROY THE ORGANIZATION TOGETHER...
BUT IT LOOKS LIKE THAT WON'T HAPPEN NOW.
CLARE...
WHAT ARE YOU SAYING?

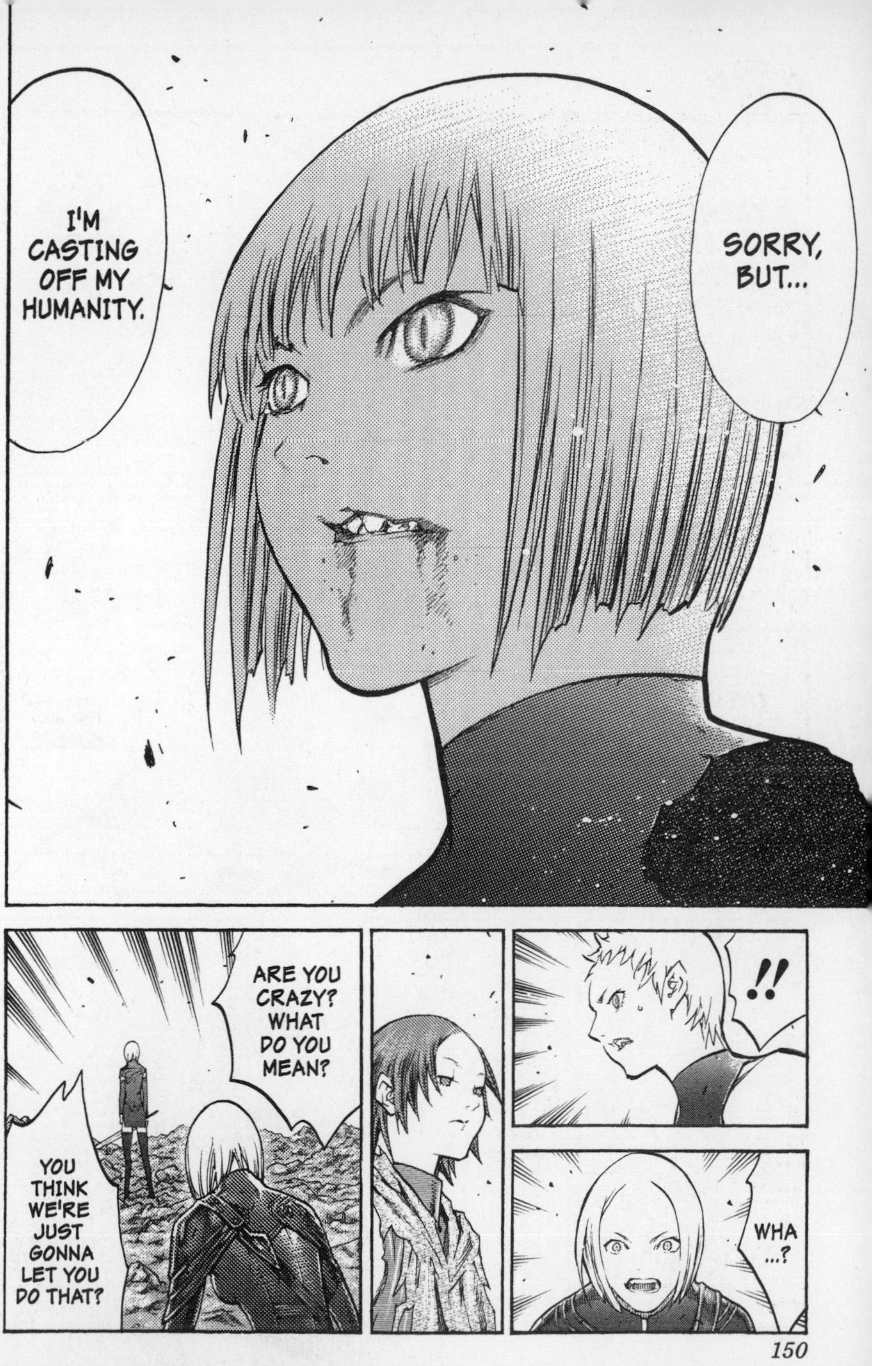

SORRY, BUT...
I'M CASTING OFF MY HUMANITY.
!!
WHA ...?
ARE YOU CRAZY? WHAT DO YOU MEAN?
YOU THINK WE'RE JUST GONNA LET YOU DO THAT?

READ THIS WAY

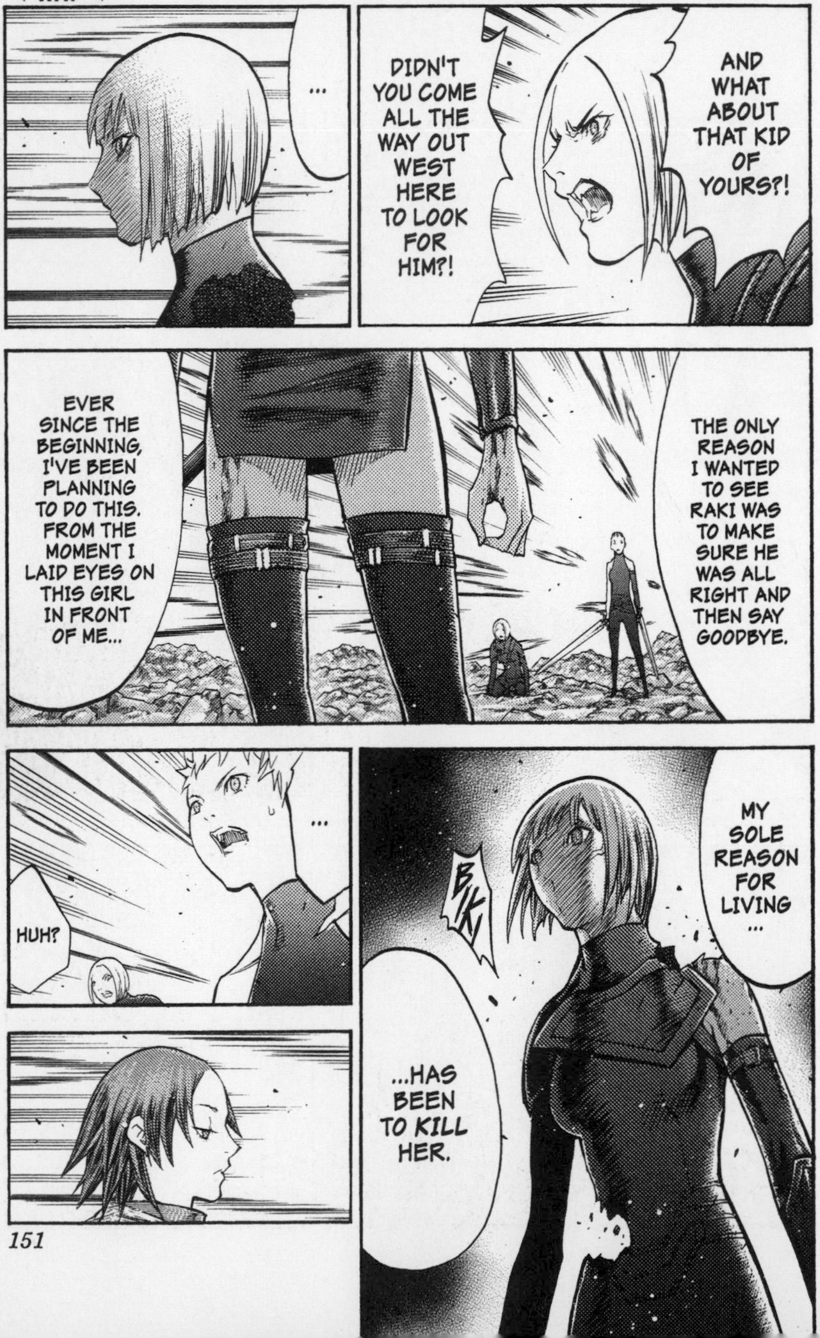
AND WHAT ABOUT THAT KID OF YOURS?!
DIDN'T YOU COME ALL THE WAY OUT WEST HERE TO LOOK FOR HIM?!
...
THE ONLY REASON I WANTED TO SEE RAKI WAS TO MAKE SURE HE WAS ALL RIGHT AND THEN SAY GOODBYE.
EVER SINCE THE BEGINNING, I'VE BEEN PLANNING TO DO THIS. FROM THE MOMENT I LAID EYES ON THIS GIRL IN FRONT OF ME...
MY SOLE REASON FOR LIVING ...
BIKI
...HAS BEEN TO KILL HER.
...
HUH?

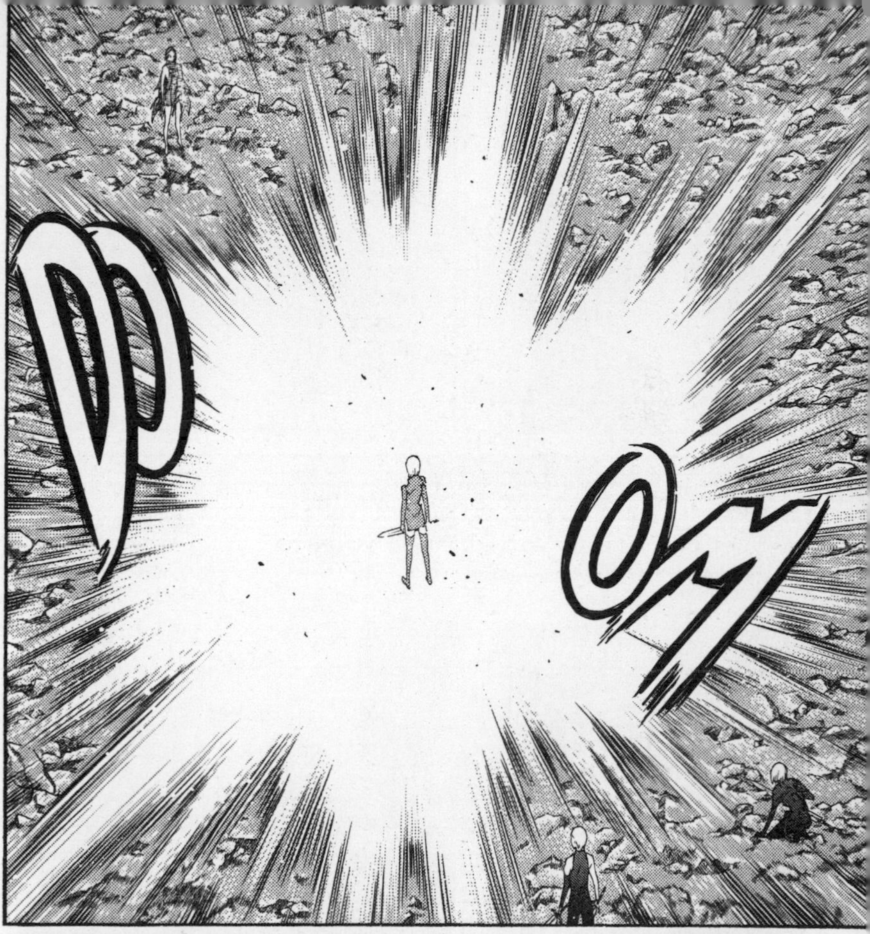
D
OM
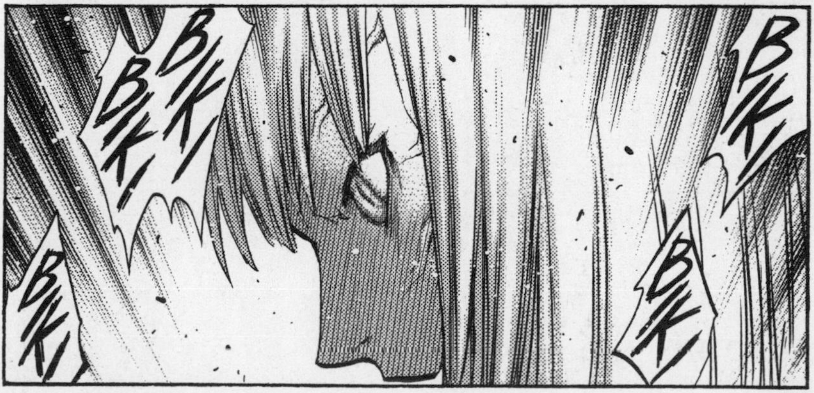
BIK!
BIK
BIK! BIK!
BIK!

READ THIS WAY

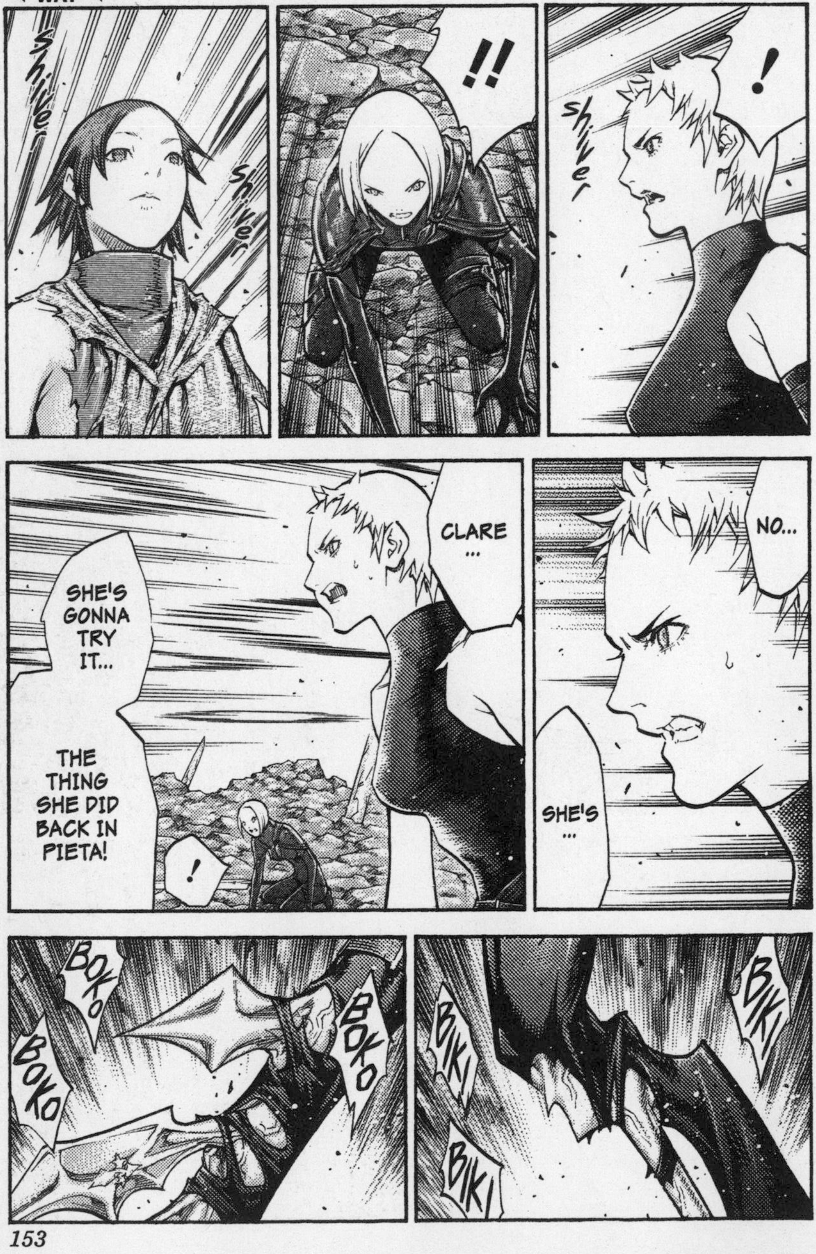
!
shiver
!!
shiver
shiver
NO...
SHE'S ...
CLARE ...
SHE'S GONNA TRY IT...
THE THING SHE DID BACK IN PIETA!
!
BIKI
BIKI
BIKI
BOKO
BOKO
BOKO

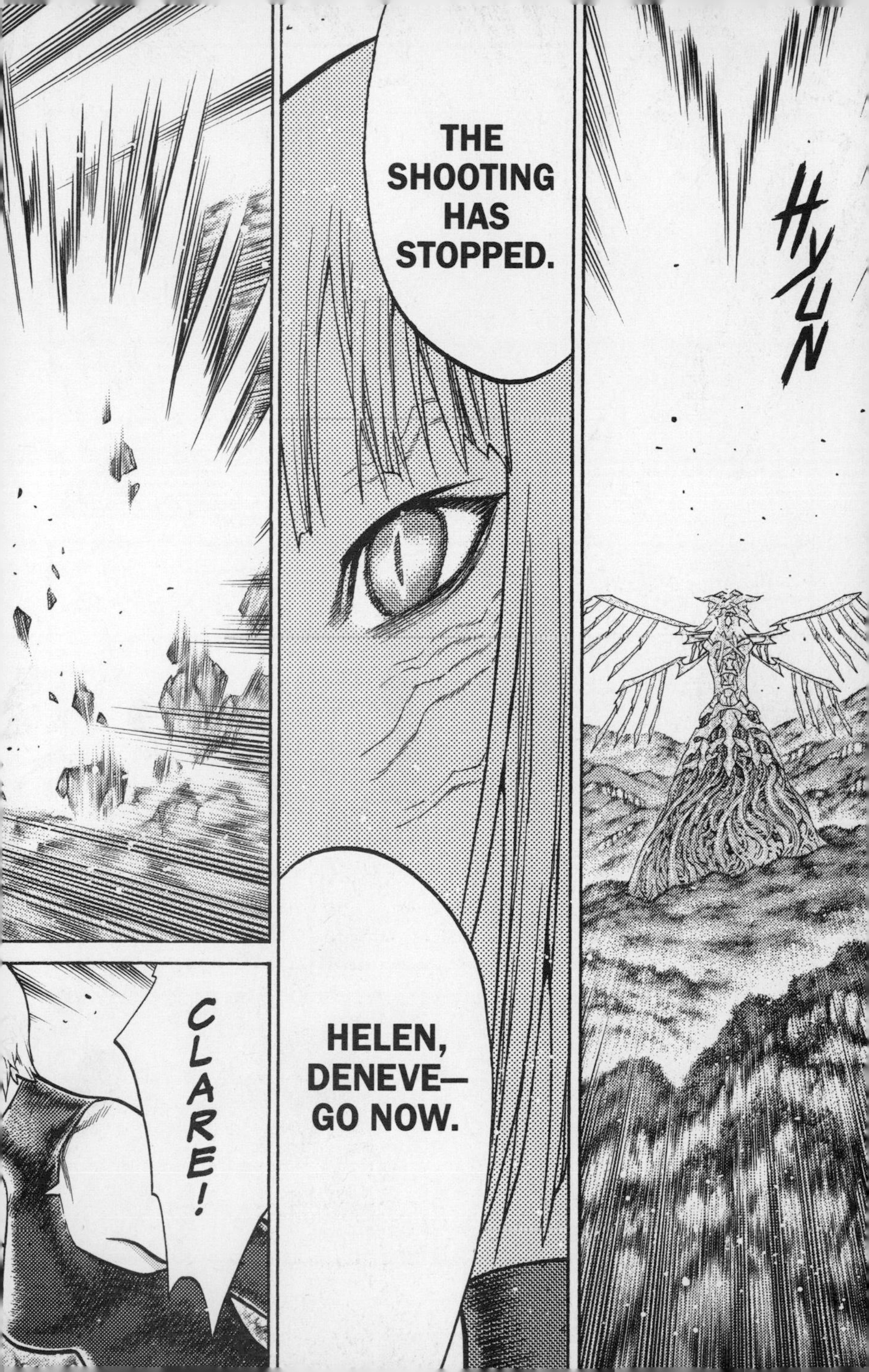
HYUN
THE SHOOTING HAS STOPPED.
HELEN, DENEVE— GO NOW.
CLARE!

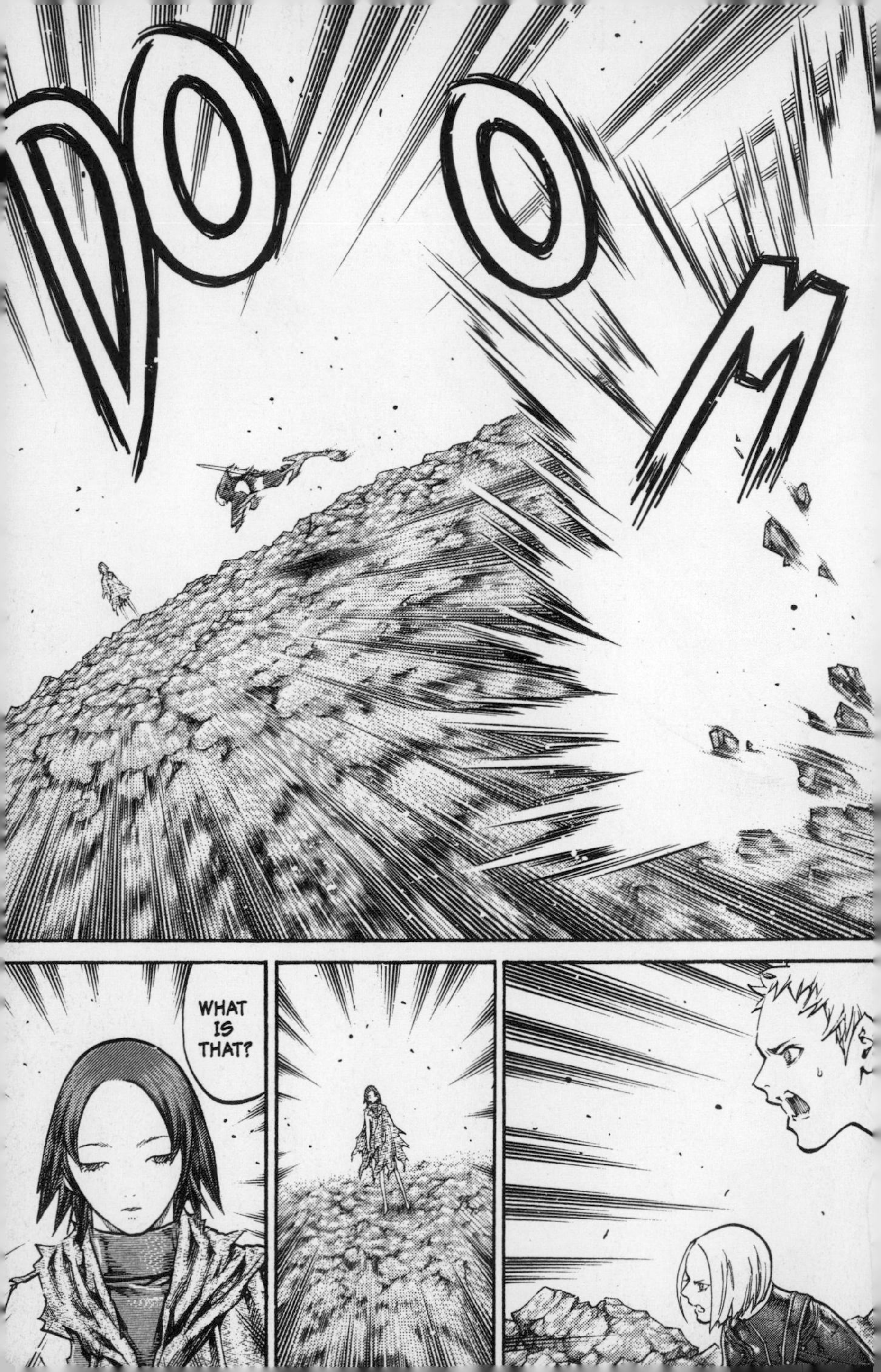
DOOOM
WHAT IS THAT?

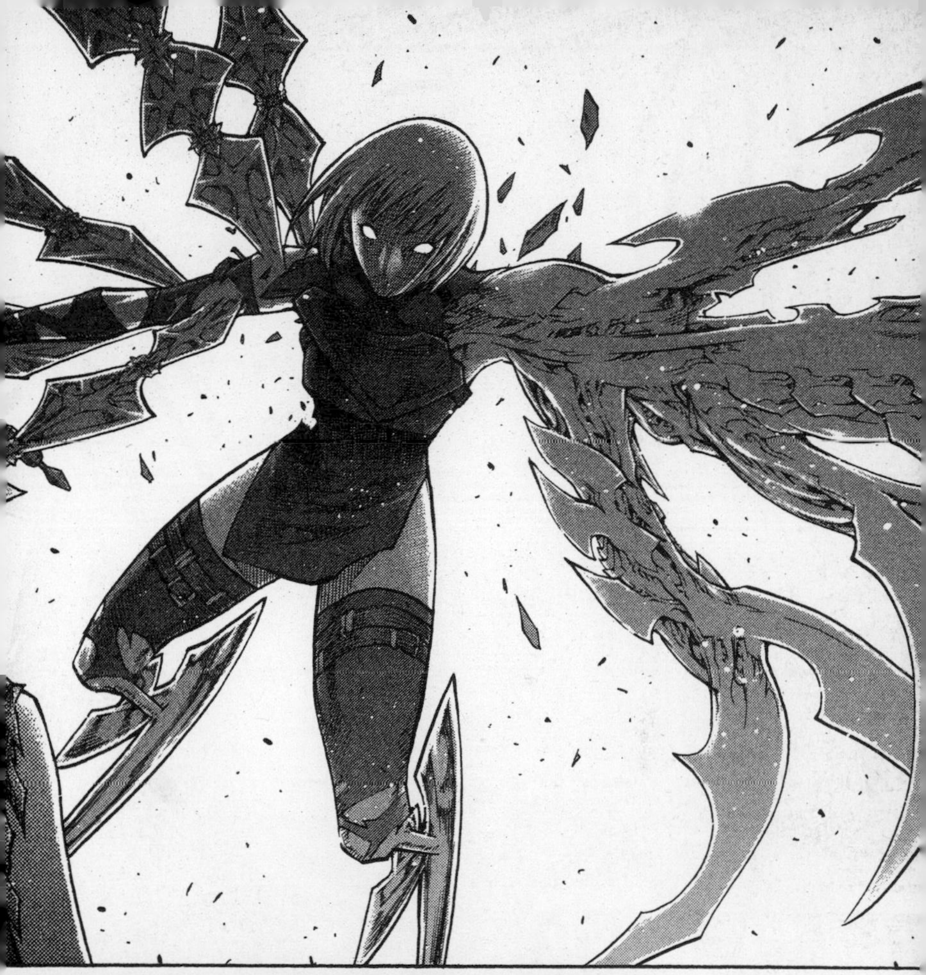
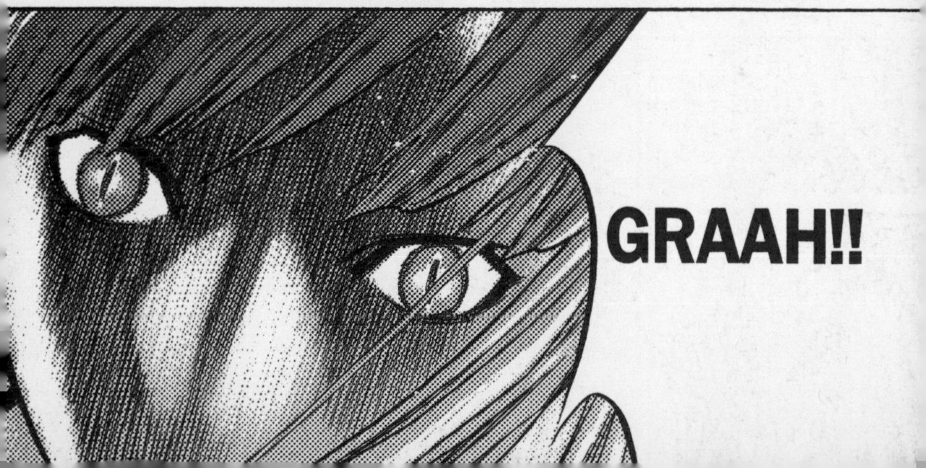
GRAAH!!

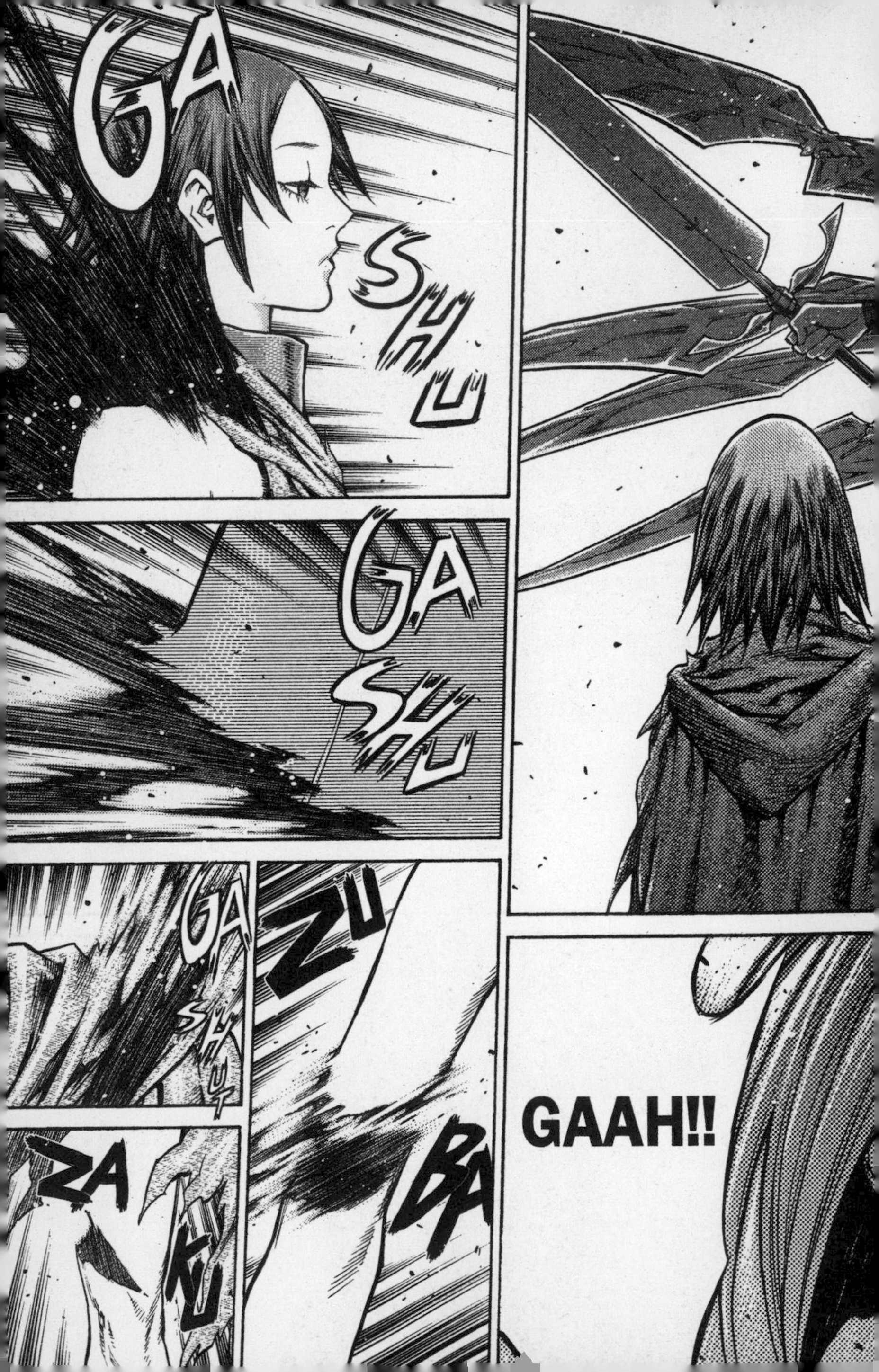
GASHU
GASHU
GAAH!!
ZU
BA
GASHU
ZAKU

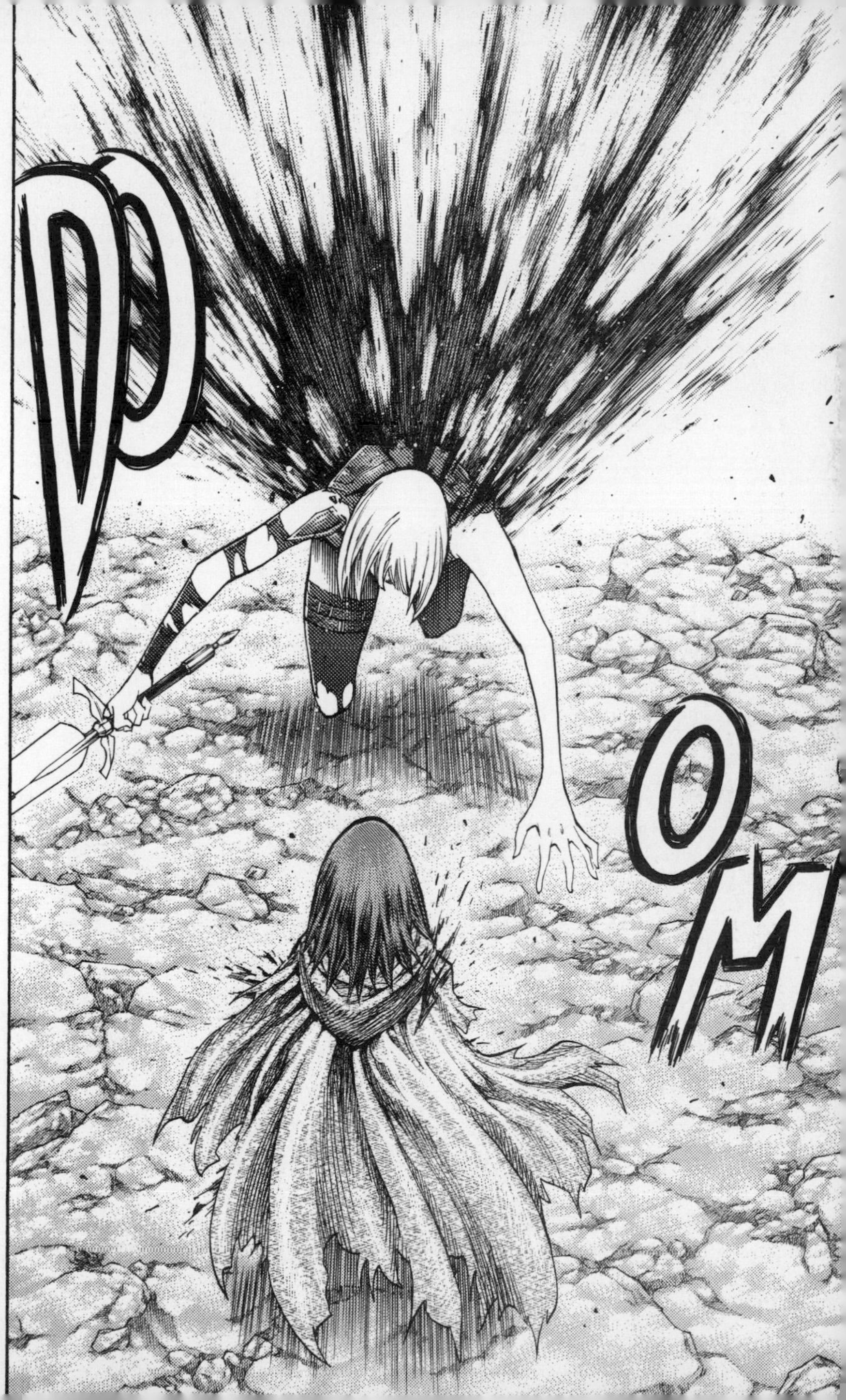
DO
OM

READ THIS WAY

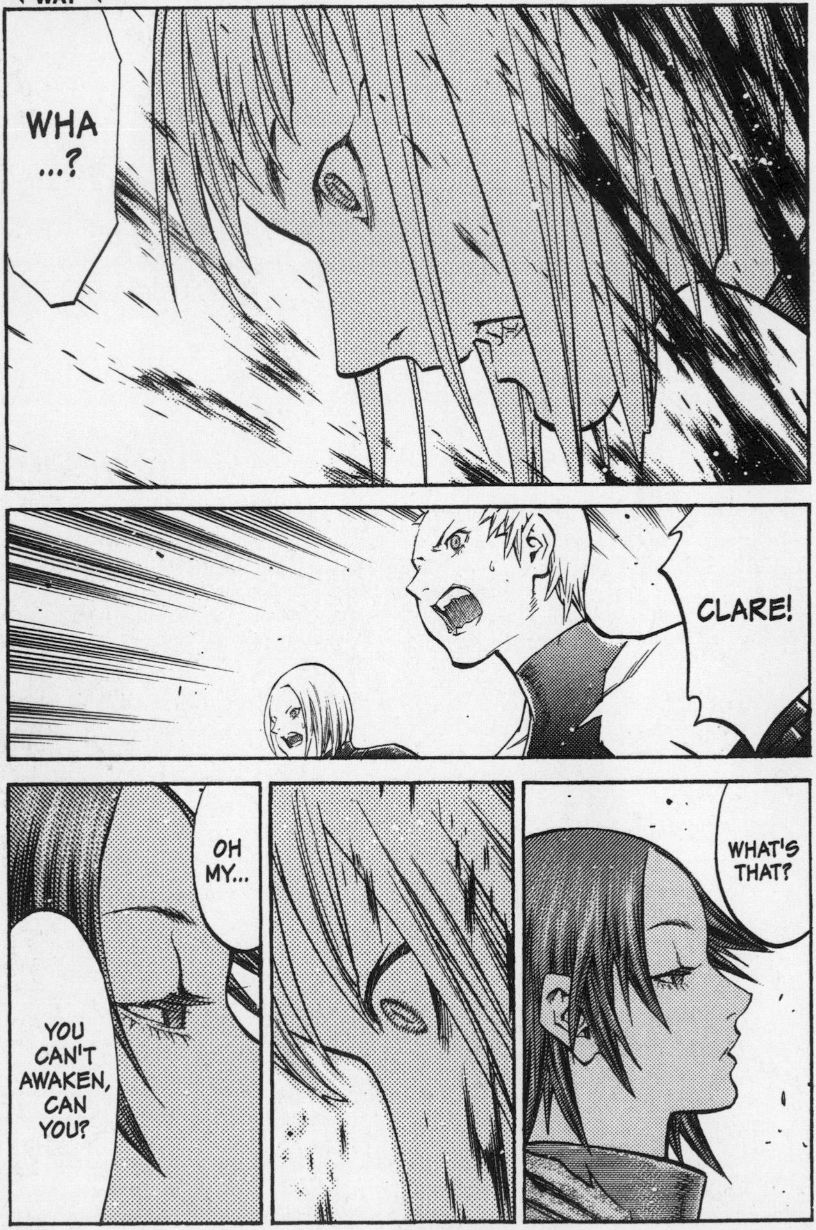
WHA ...?
CLARE!
WHAT'S THAT?
OH MY...
YOU CAN'T AWAKEN, CAN YOU?

クレイモア

Claymore

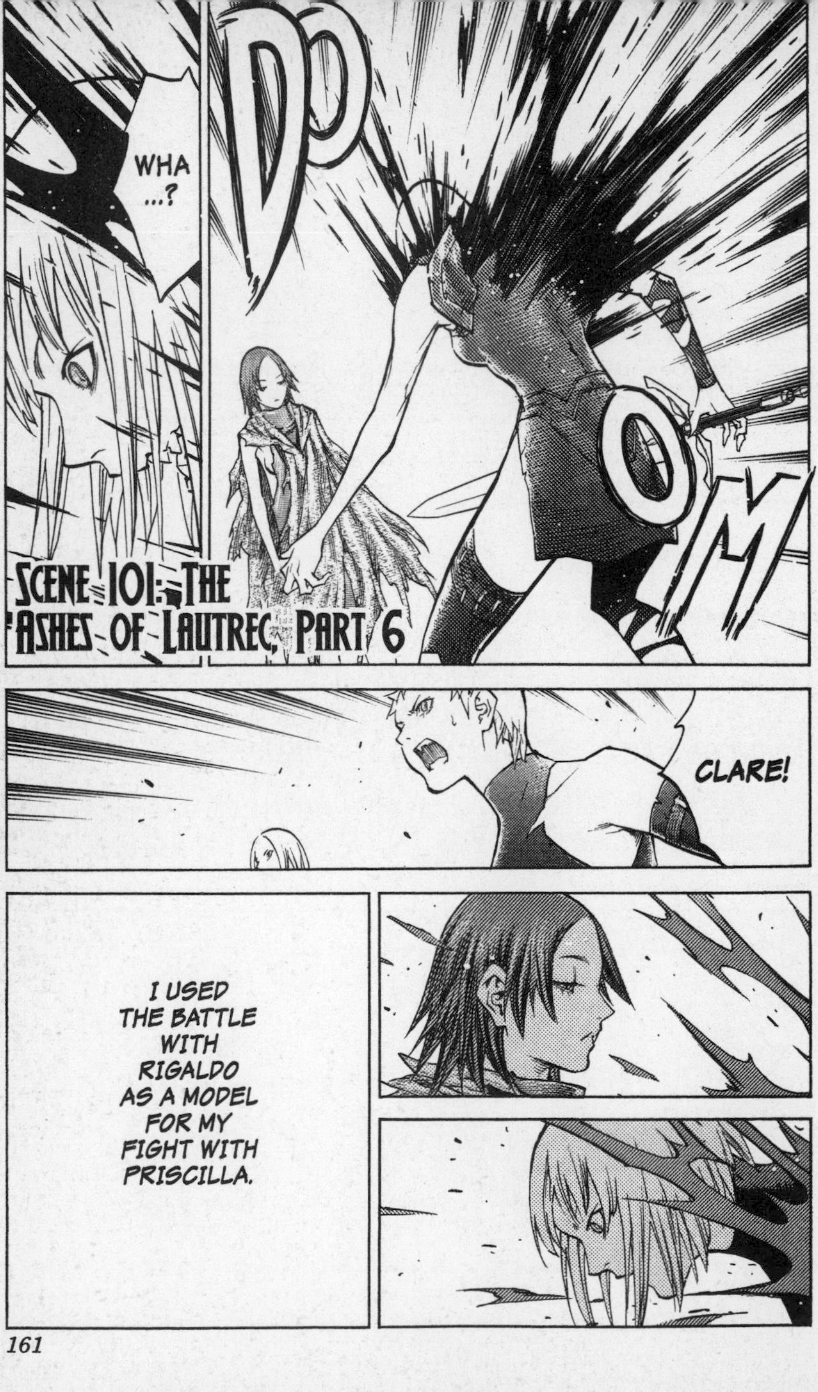
DOOM
SCENE 101: THE ASHES OF LAUTREC, PART 6
WHA ...?
CLARE!
I USED THE BATTLE WITH RIGALDO AS A MODEL FOR MY FIGHT WITH PRISCILLA.

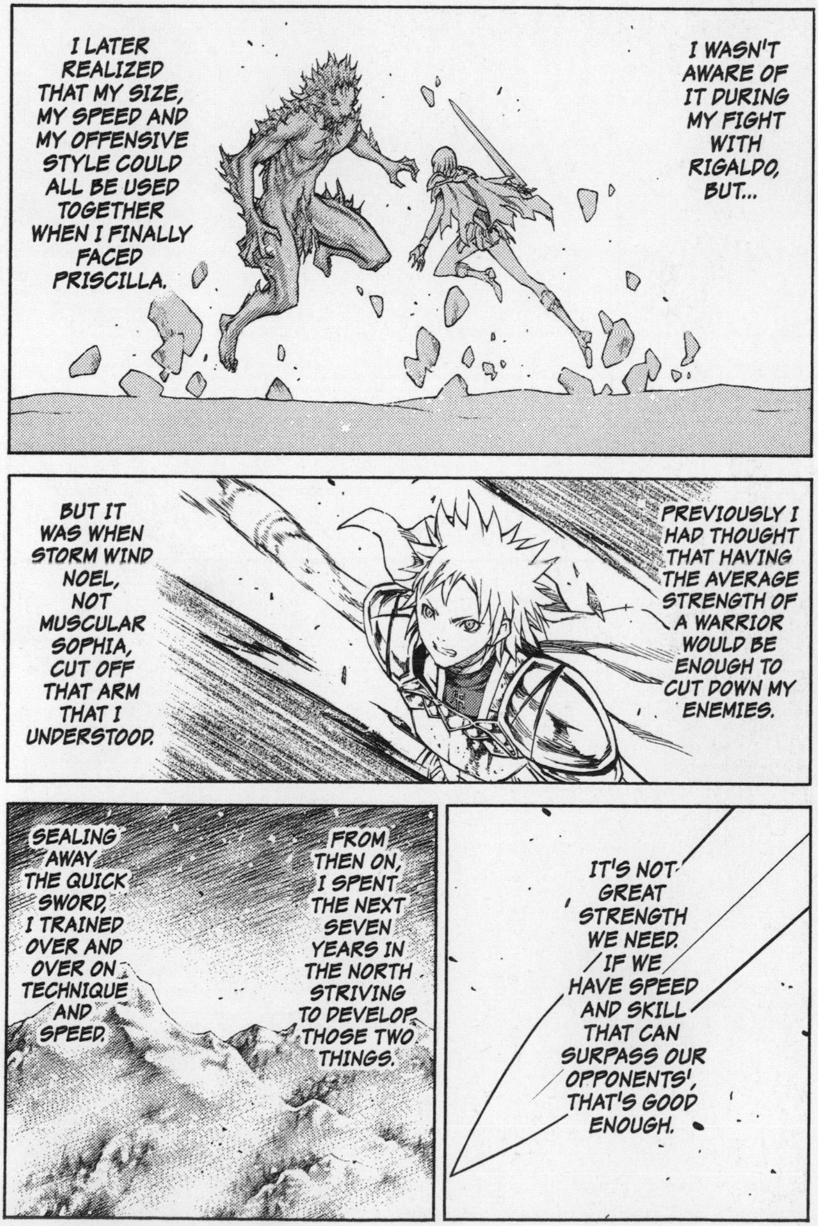
I WASN'T AWARE OF IT DURING MY FIGHT WITH RIGALDO, BUT...
I LATER REALIZED THAT MY SIZE, MY SPEED AND MY OFFENSIVE STYLE COULD ALL BE USED TOGETHER WHEN I FINALLY FACED PRISCILLA.
PREVIOUSLY I HAD THOUGHT THAT HAVING THE AVERAGE STRENGTH OF A WARRIOR WOULD BE ENOUGH TO CUT DOWN MY ENEMIES.
BUT IT WAS WHEN STORM WIND NOEL, NOT MUSCULAR SOPHIA, CUT OFF THAT ARM THAT I UNDERSTOOD.
IT'S NOT GREAT STRENGTH WE NEED. IF WE HAVE SPEED AND SKILL THAT CAN SURPASS OUR OPPONENTS', THAT'S GOOD ENOUGH.
FROM THEN ON, I SPENT THE NEXT SEVEN YEARS IN THE NORTH STRIVING TO DEVELOP THOSE TWO THINGS.
SEALING AWAY THE QUICK SWORD, I TRAINED OVER AND OVER ON TECHNIQUE AND SPEED.

READ THIS WAY

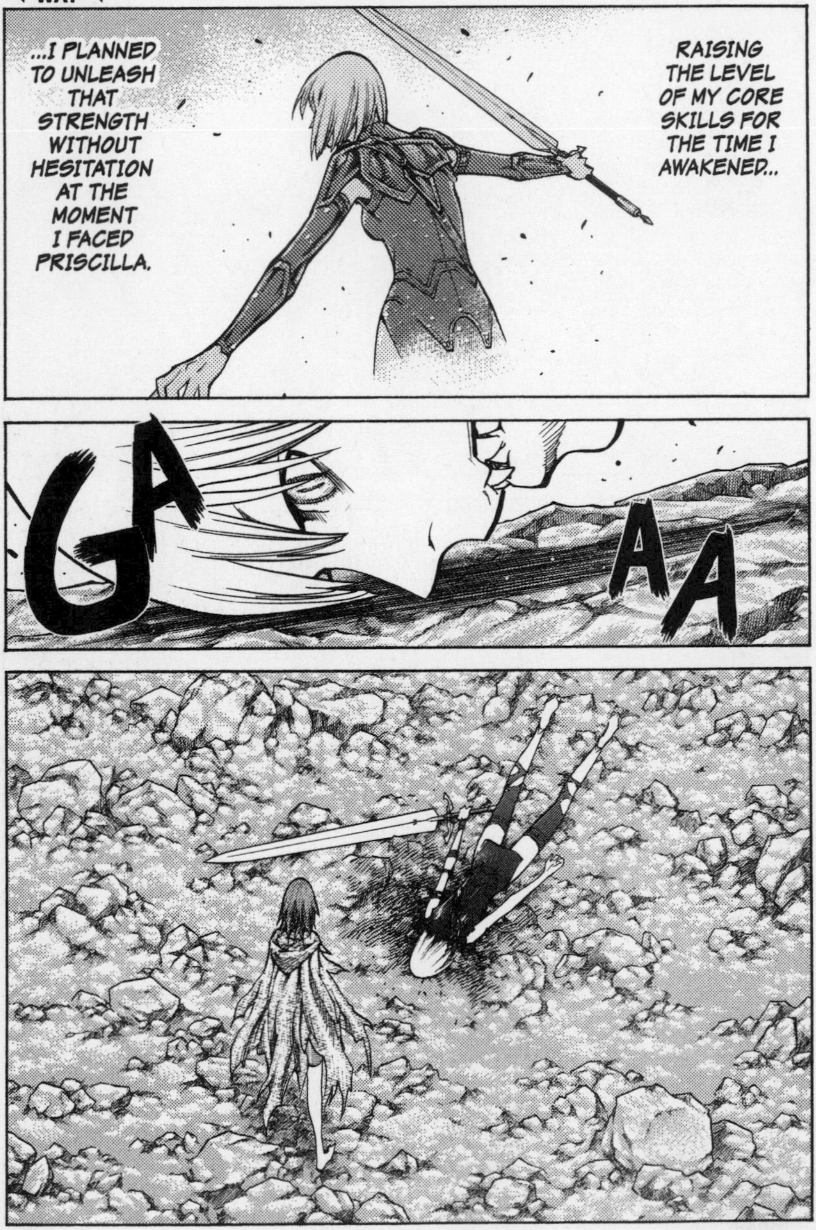
RAISING THE LEVEL OF MY CORE SKILLS FOR THE TIME I AWAKENED...
...I PLANNED TO UNLEASH THAT STRENGTH WITHOUT HESITATION AT THE MOMENT I FACED PRISCILLA.
GAAA

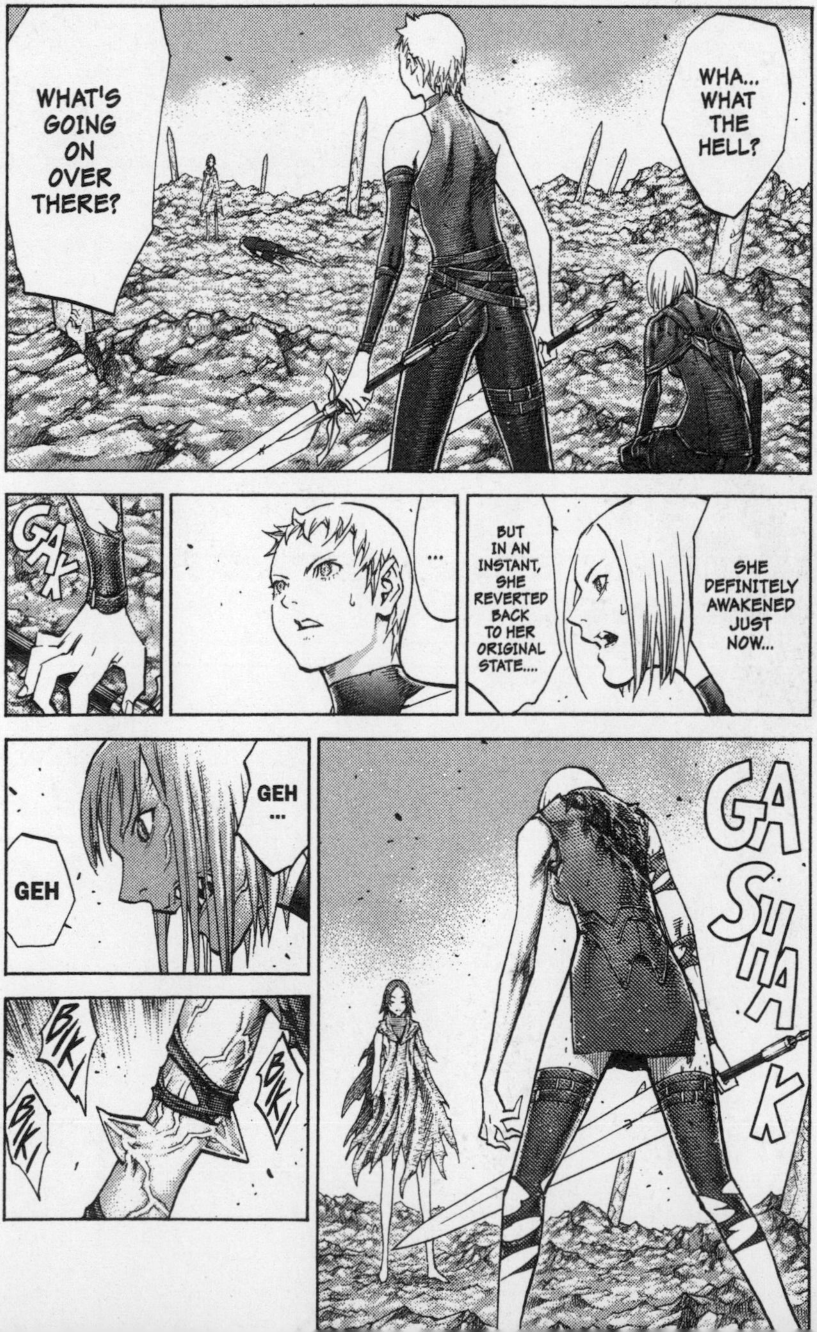
WHA... WHAT THE HELL?
WHAT'S GOING ON OVER THERE?
SHE DEFINITELY AWAKENED JUST NOW...
BUT IN AN INSTANT, SHE REVERTED BACK TO HER ORIGINAL STATE....
...
GAK
GASHAK
GEH ...
GEH
BIKI
BIKI
BIKI

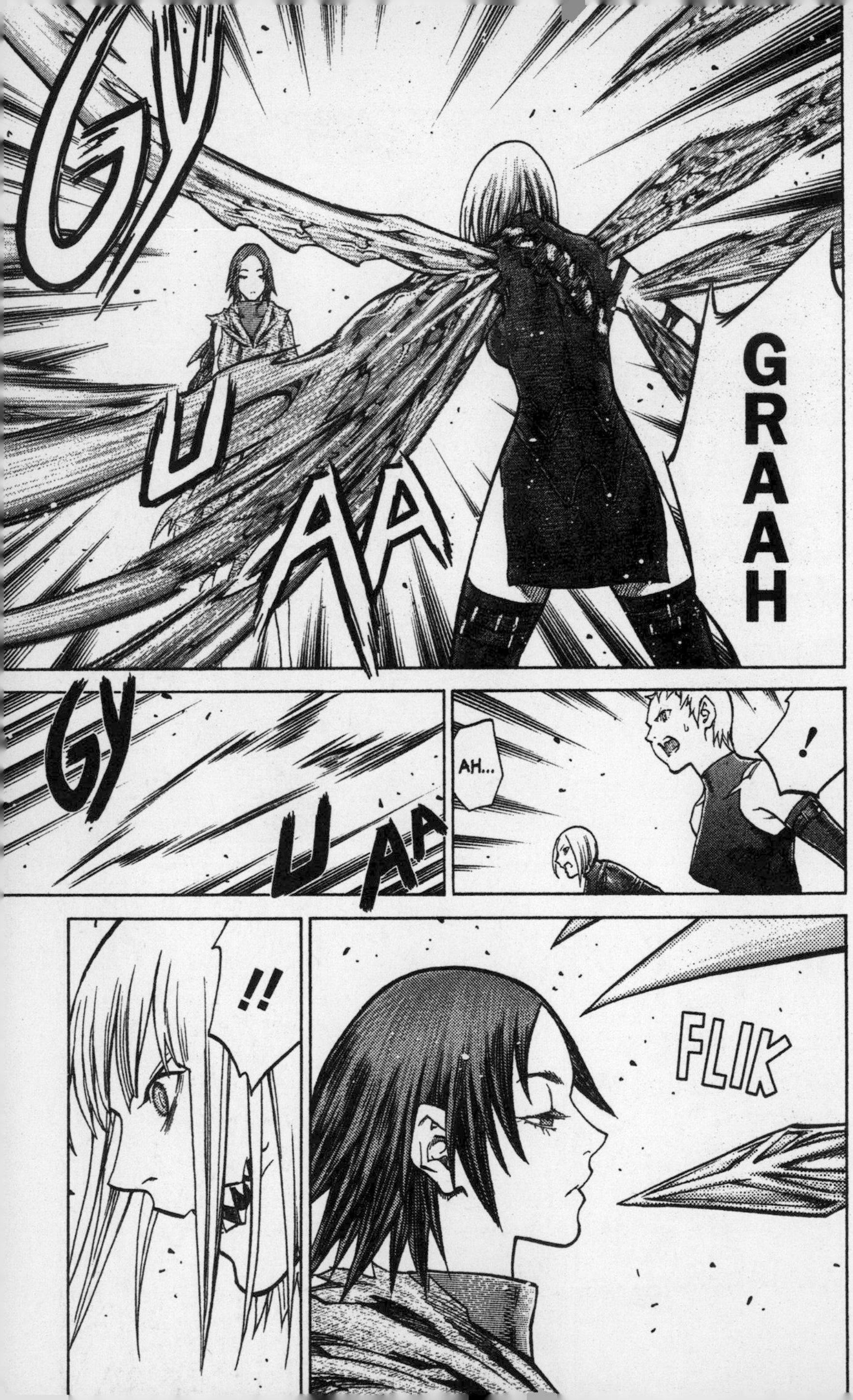
GRAAH
GYUAA
!
AH...
GYUAA
FLIK
!!

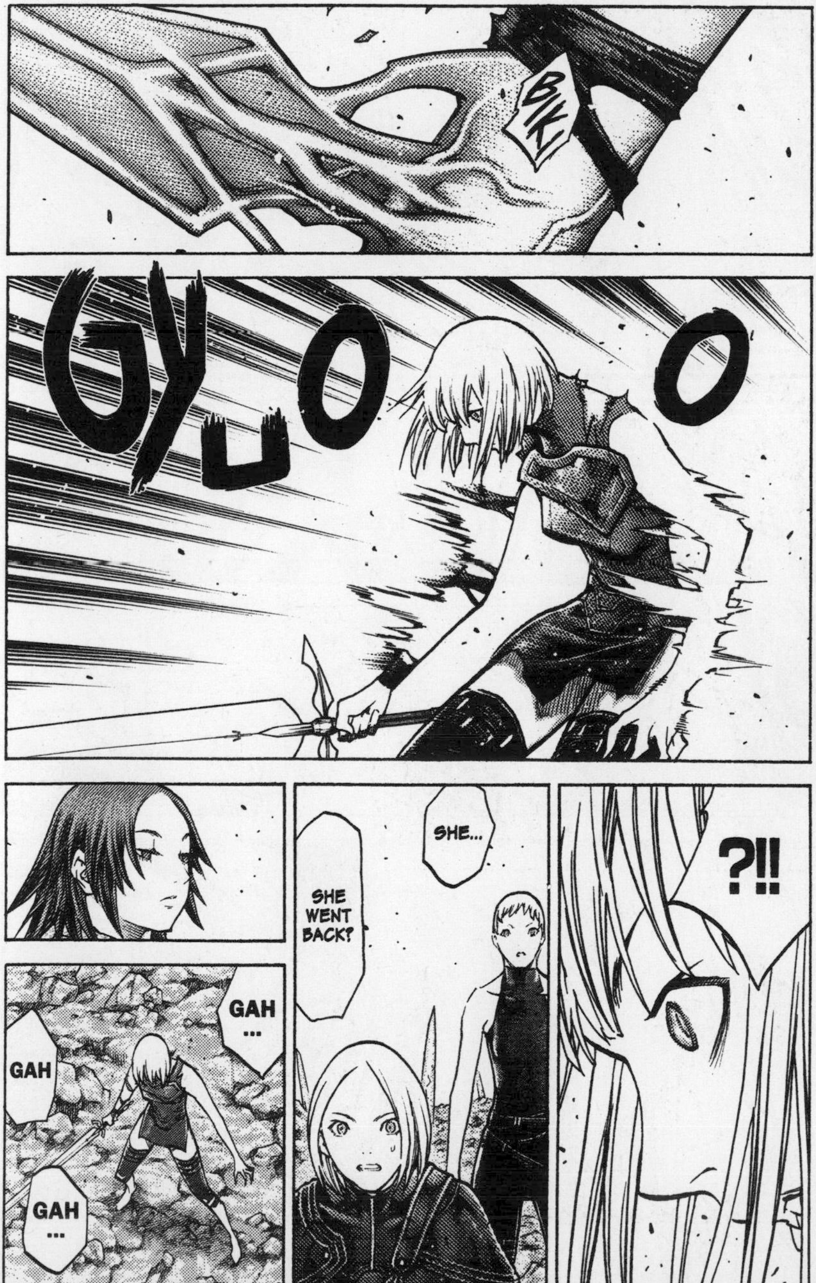
BIKI
GYUOO
?!!
SHE...
SHE WENT BACK?
GAH...
GAH
GAH...

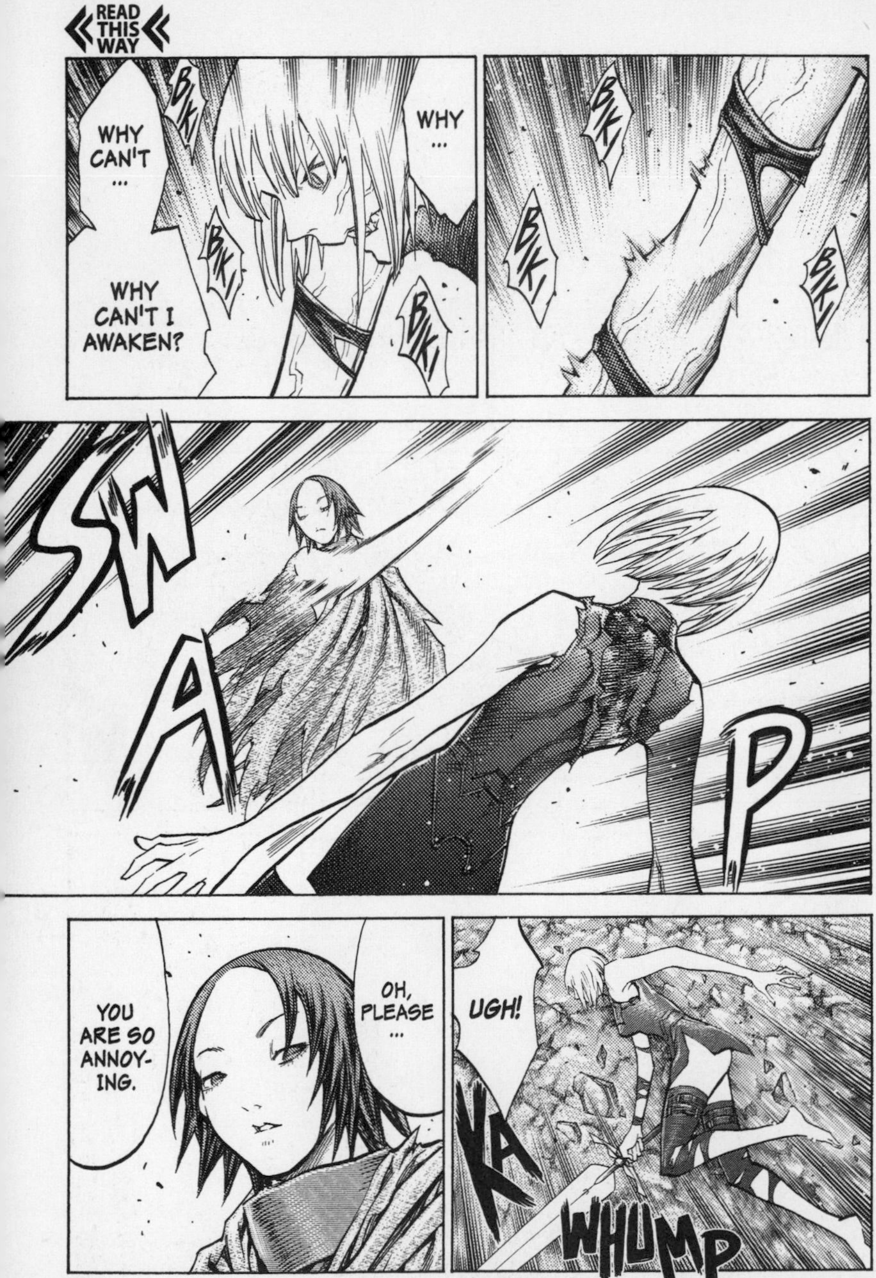
READ THIS WAY
BIKI
BIKI
BIKI
WHY ...
WHY CAN'T ...
BIKI
BIKI
WHY CAN'T I AWAKEN?
SWAP
OH, PLEASE ...
YOU ARE SO ANNOY-ING.
UGH!
KA
WHUMP

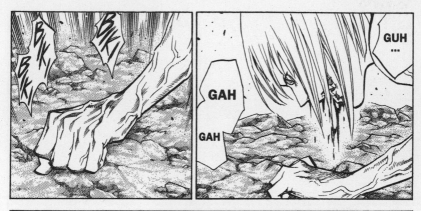

BIKI
BIKI
BIKI
BIKI

GAH

GAH

GUH
...

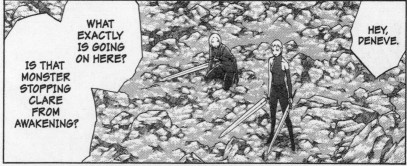

WHAT EXACTLY IS GOING ON HERE?

IS THAT MONSTER STOPPING CLARE FROM AWAKENING?

HEY, DENEVE.

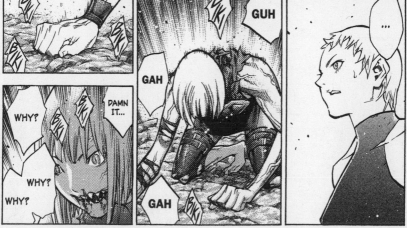

BIKI
BIKI
BIKI

WHY?

WHY?

WHY?

DAMN IT...

BIKI
GUH

GAH

GAH

...

READ THIS WAY

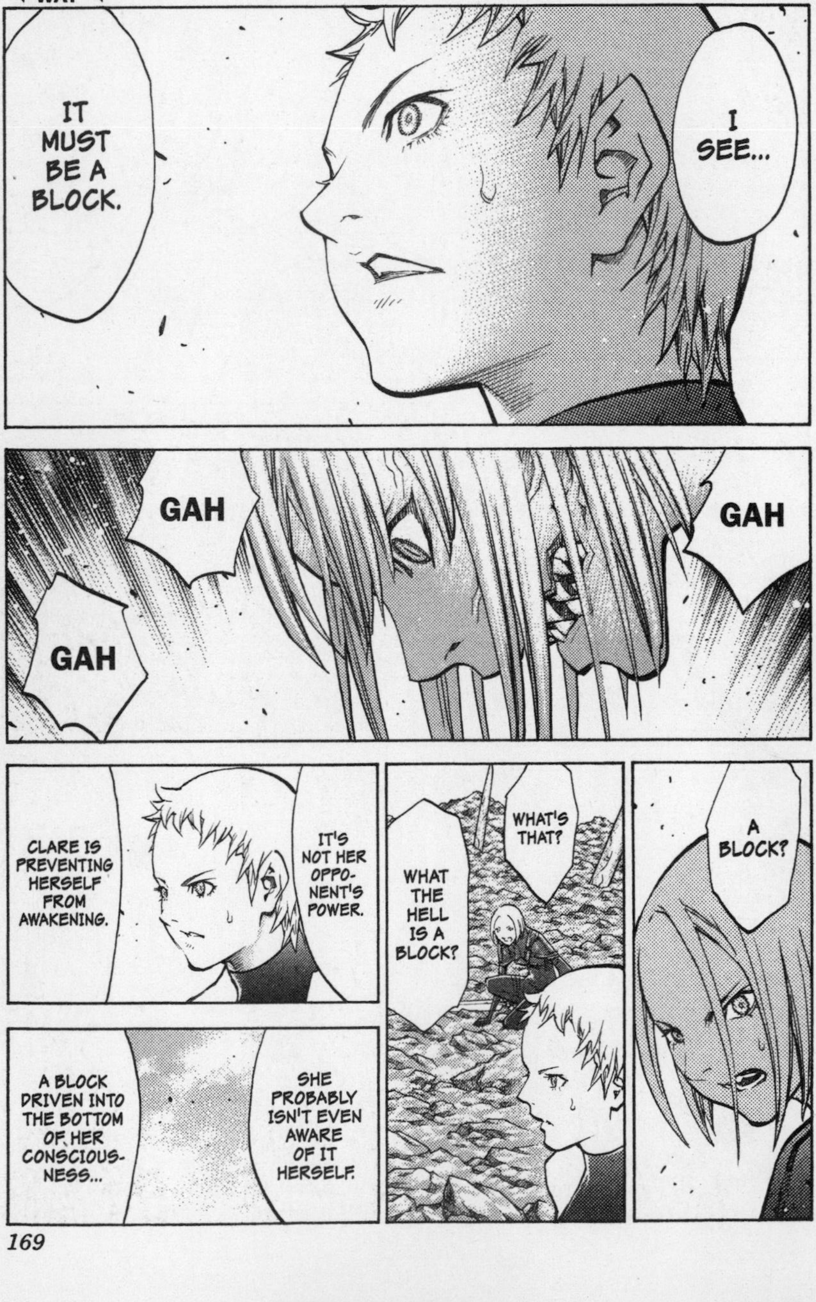
I SEE...
IT MUST BE A BLOCK.
GAH
GAH
GAH
A BLOCK?
WHAT'S THAT?
WHAT THE HELL IS A BLOCK?
IT'S NOT HER OPPO-NENT'S POWER.
CLARE IS PREVENTING HERSELF FROM AWAKENING.
SHE PROBABLY ISN'T EVEN AWARE OF IT HERSELF.
A BLOCK DRIVEN INTO THE BOTTOM OF HER CONSCIOUS-NESS...

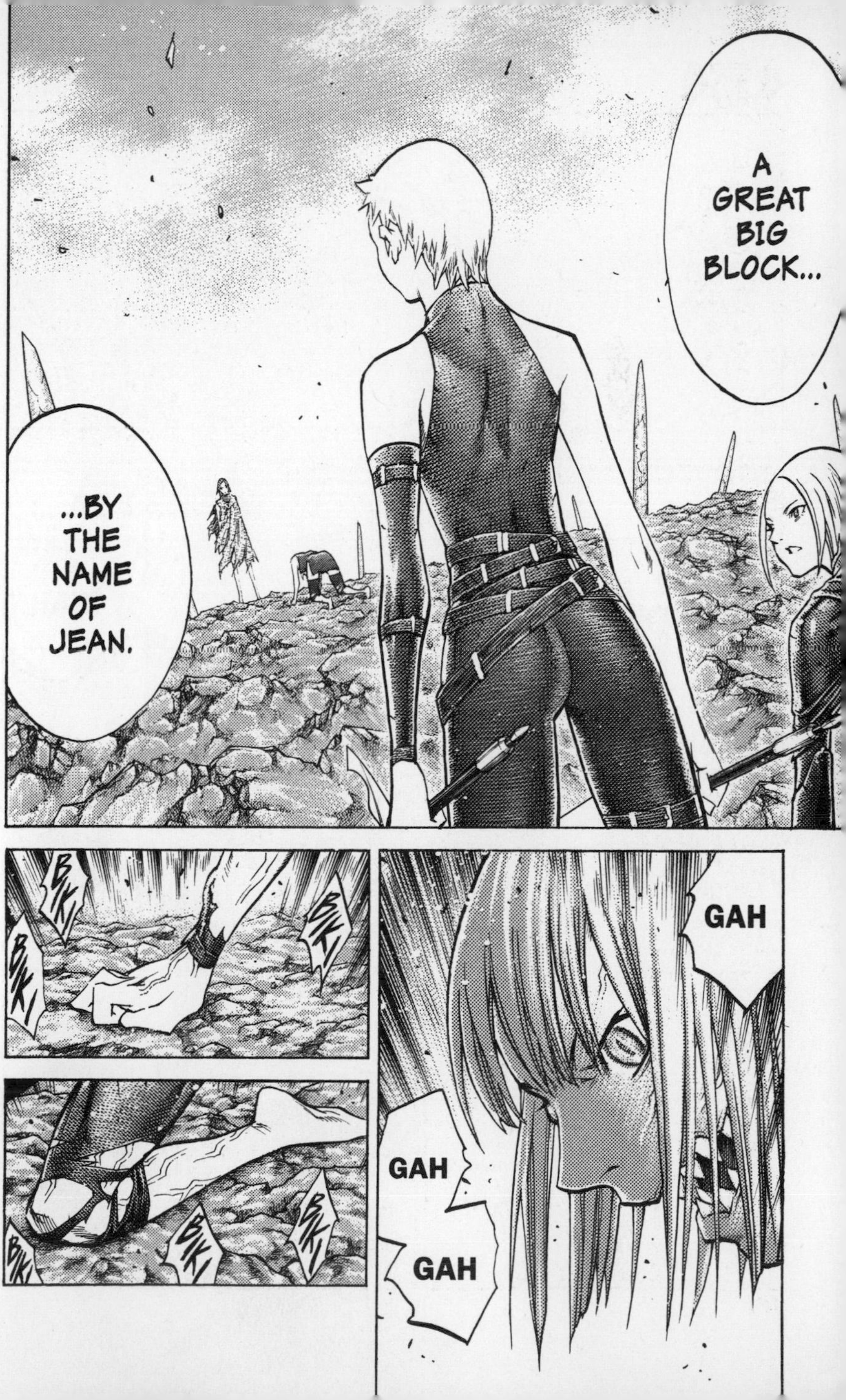
A GREAT BIG BLOCK...
...BY THE NAME OF JEAN.
GAH
GAH
GAH
BIKI
BIKI
BIKI
BIKI
BIKI
BIKI

READ THIS WAY

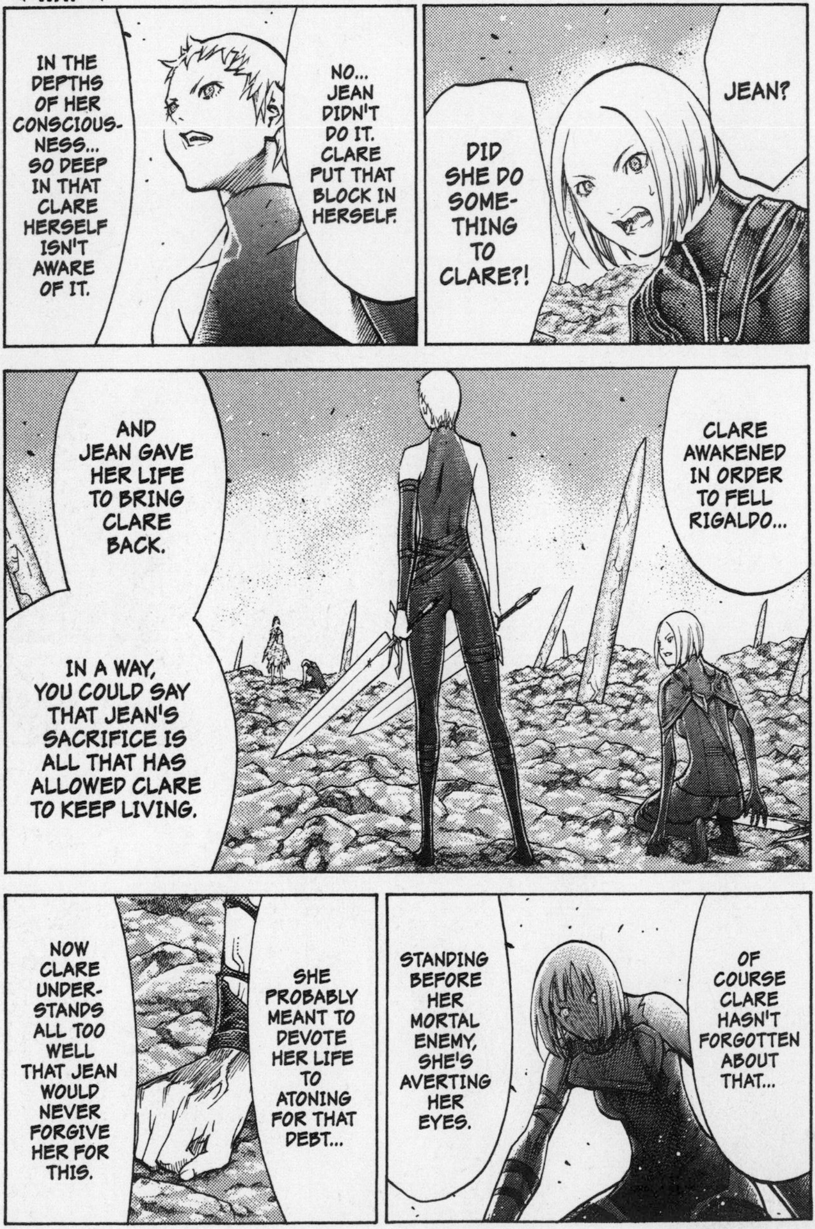
JEAN?
DID SHE DO SOMETHING TO CLARE?!
NO... JEAN DIDN'T DO IT. CLARE PUT THAT BLOCK IN HERSELF.
IN THE DEPTHS OF HER CONSCIOUSNESS... SO DEEP IN THAT CLARE HERSELF ISN'T AWARE OF IT.
CLARE AWAKENED IN ORDER TO FELL RIGALDO...
AND JEAN GAVE HER LIFE TO BRING CLARE BACK.
IN A WAY, YOU COULD SAY THAT JEAN'S SACRIFICE IS ALL THAT HAS ALLOWED CLARE TO KEEP LIVING.
OF COURSE CLARE HASN'T FORGOTTEN ABOUT THAT...
STANDING BEFORE HER MORTAL ENEMY, SHE'S AVERTING HER EYES.
SHE PROBABLY MEANT TO DEVOTE HER LIFE TO ATONING FOR THAT DEBT...
NOW CLARE UNDERSTANDS ALL TOO WELL THAT JEAN WOULD NEVER FORGIVE HER FOR THIS.

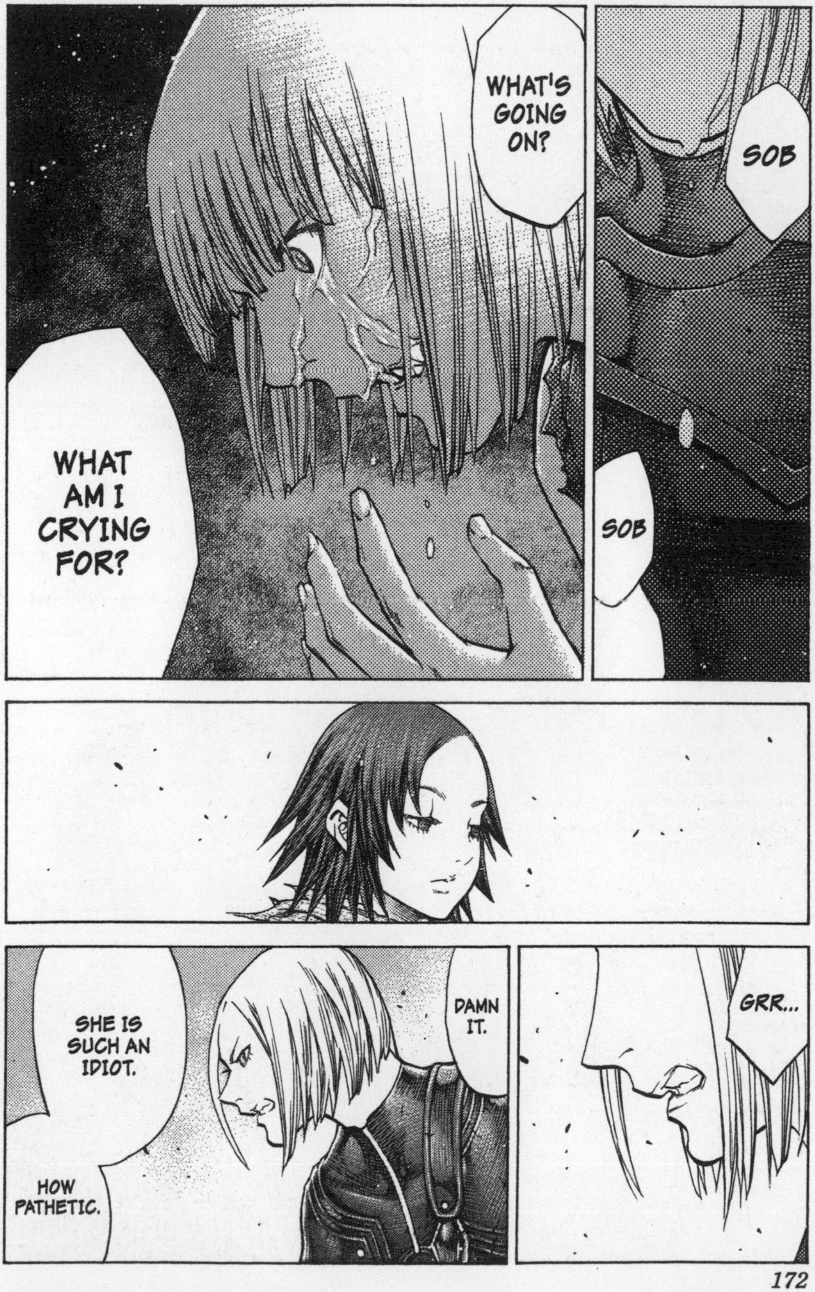
SOB
SOB
WHAT'S GOING ON?
WHAT AM I CRYING FOR?
GRR...
DAMN IT.
SHE IS SUCH AN IDIOT.
HOW PATHETIC.

READ THIS WAY

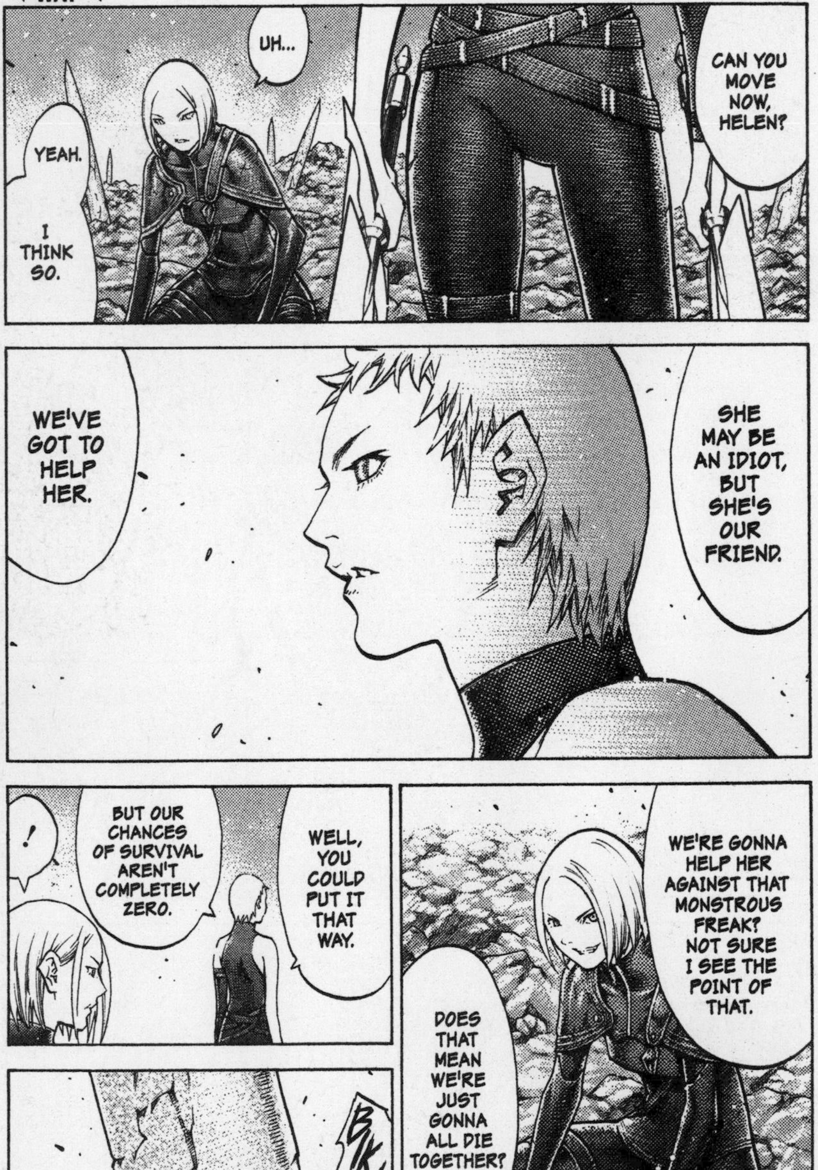
CAN YOU MOVE NOW, HELEN?
UH...
YEAH.
I THINK SO.
SHE MAY BE AN IDIOT, BUT SHE'S OUR FRIEND.
WE'VE GOT TO HELP HER.
WE'RE GONNA HELP HER AGAINST THAT MONSTROUS FREAK? NOT SURE I SEE THE POINT OF THAT.
DOES THAT MEAN WE'RE JUST GONNA ALL DIE TOGETHER?
WELL, YOU COULD PUT IT THAT WAY.
BUT OUR CHANCES OF SURVIVAL AREN'T COMPLETELY ZERO.
!
BKI

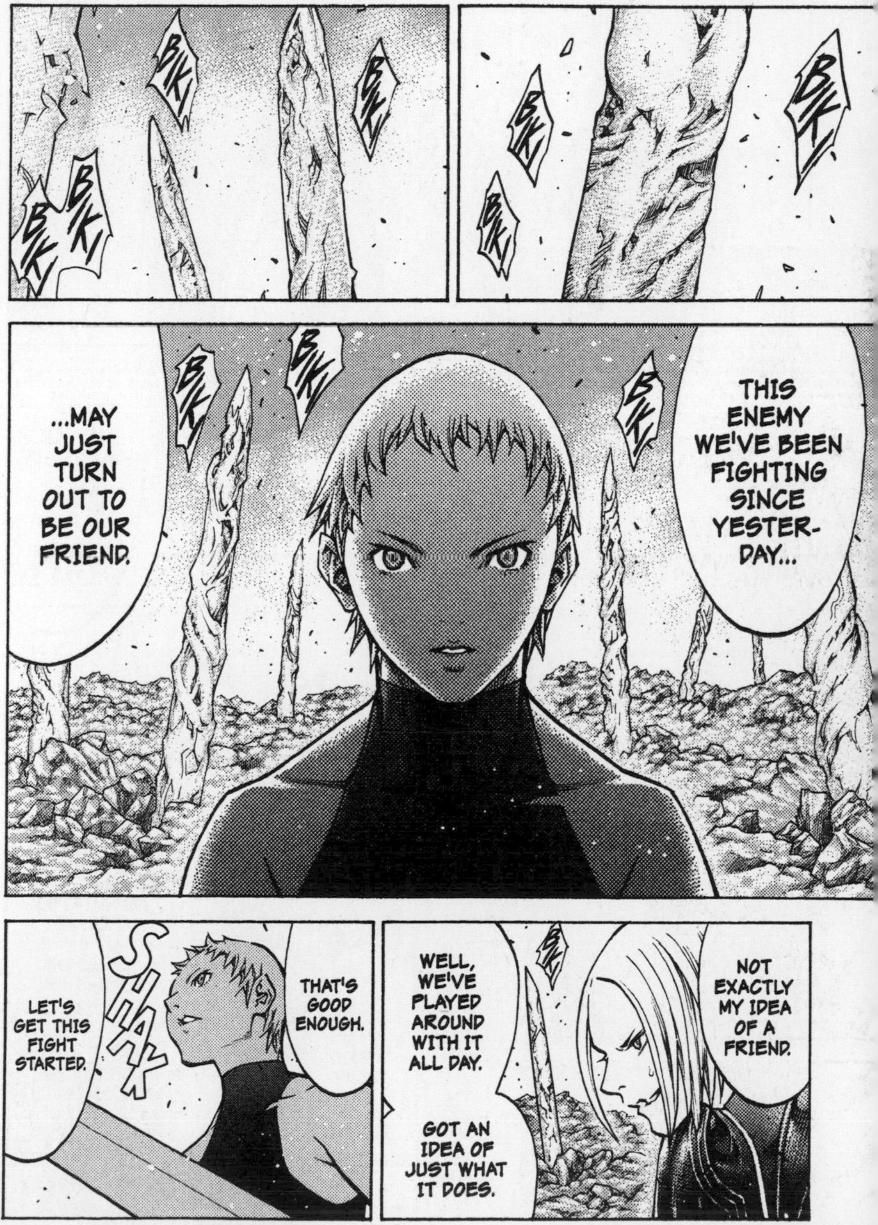
BIKI
BIKI
BIKI
BIKI
BIKI
BIKI
BIKI
THIS ENEMY WE'VE BEEN FIGHTING SINCE YESTER-DAY...
BIKI
...MAY JUST TURN OUT TO BE OUR FRIEND.
BIKI
BIKI
NOT EXACTLY MY IDEA OF A FRIEND.
BIKI
WELL, WE'VE PLAYED AROUND WITH IT ALL DAY.
GOT AN IDEA OF JUST WHAT IT DOES.
THAT'S GOOD ENOUGH.
SHAK
LET'S GET THIS FIGHT STARTED.

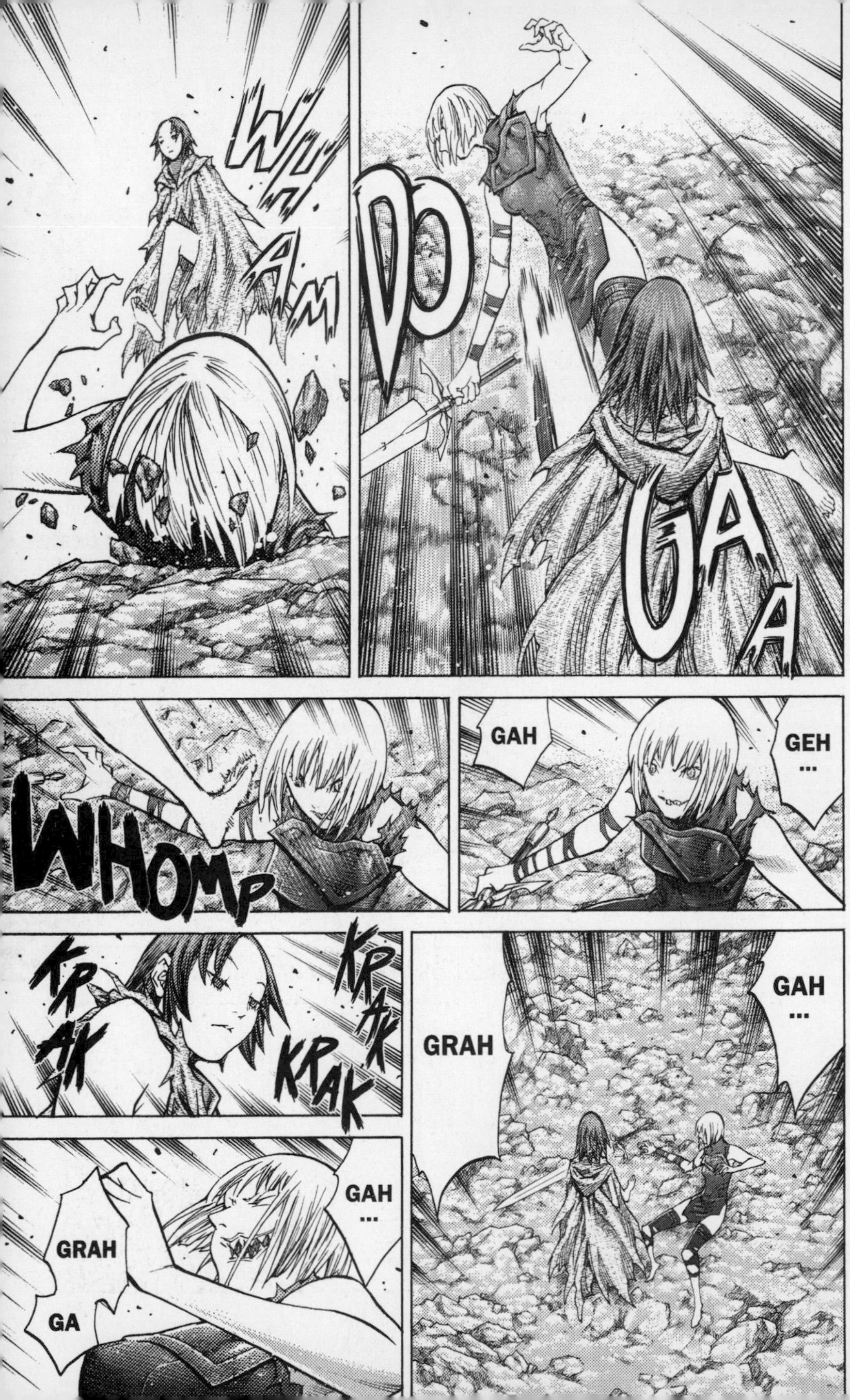

DO
GAA
WHAM
GEH ...
GAH
WHOMP
GAH ...
GRAH
KRAK
KRAK
KRAK
KRAK
GAH ...
GRAH
GA

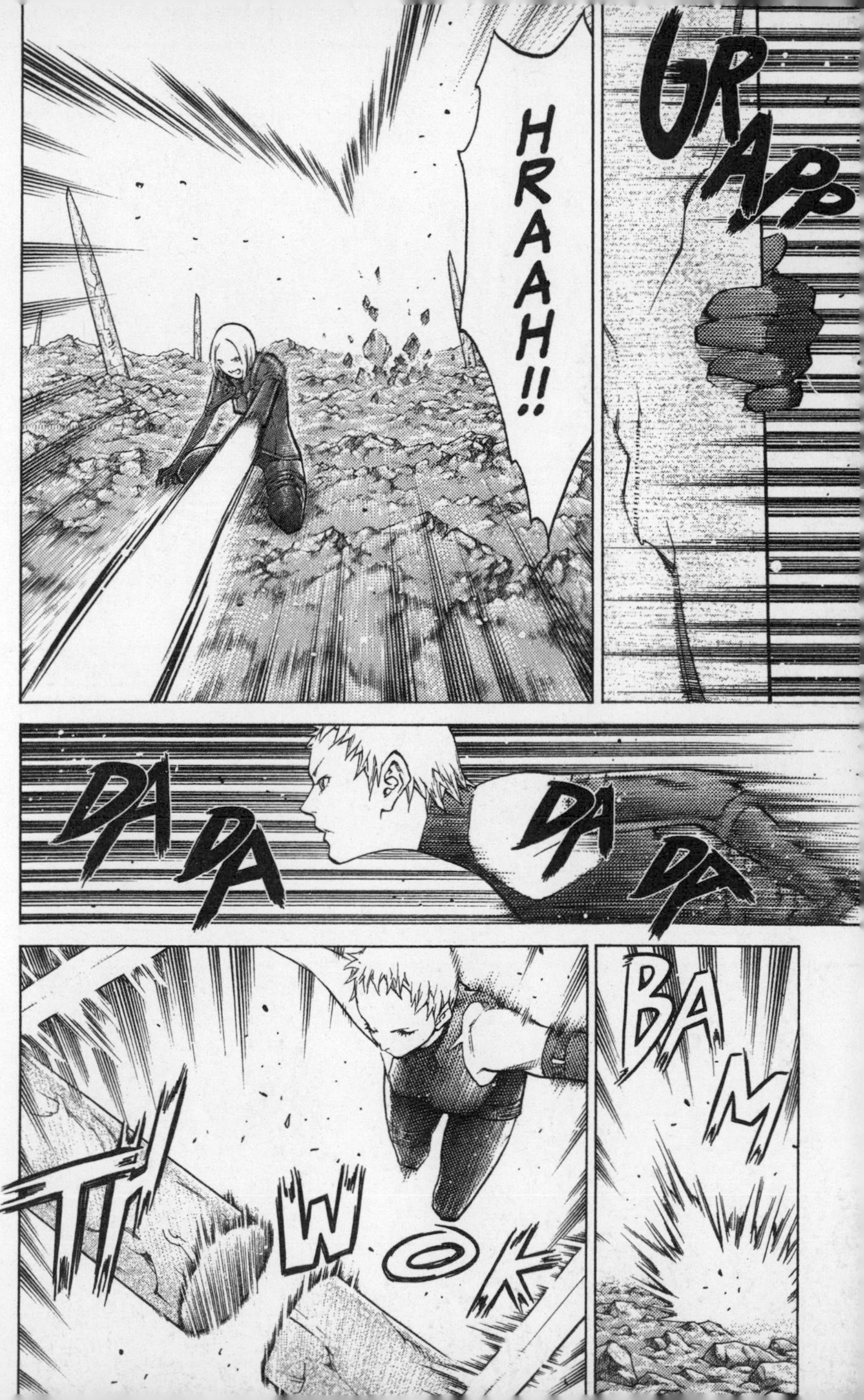
GRAPP
HRAAAH!!
DA DA
DA DA
BAM
THWOK

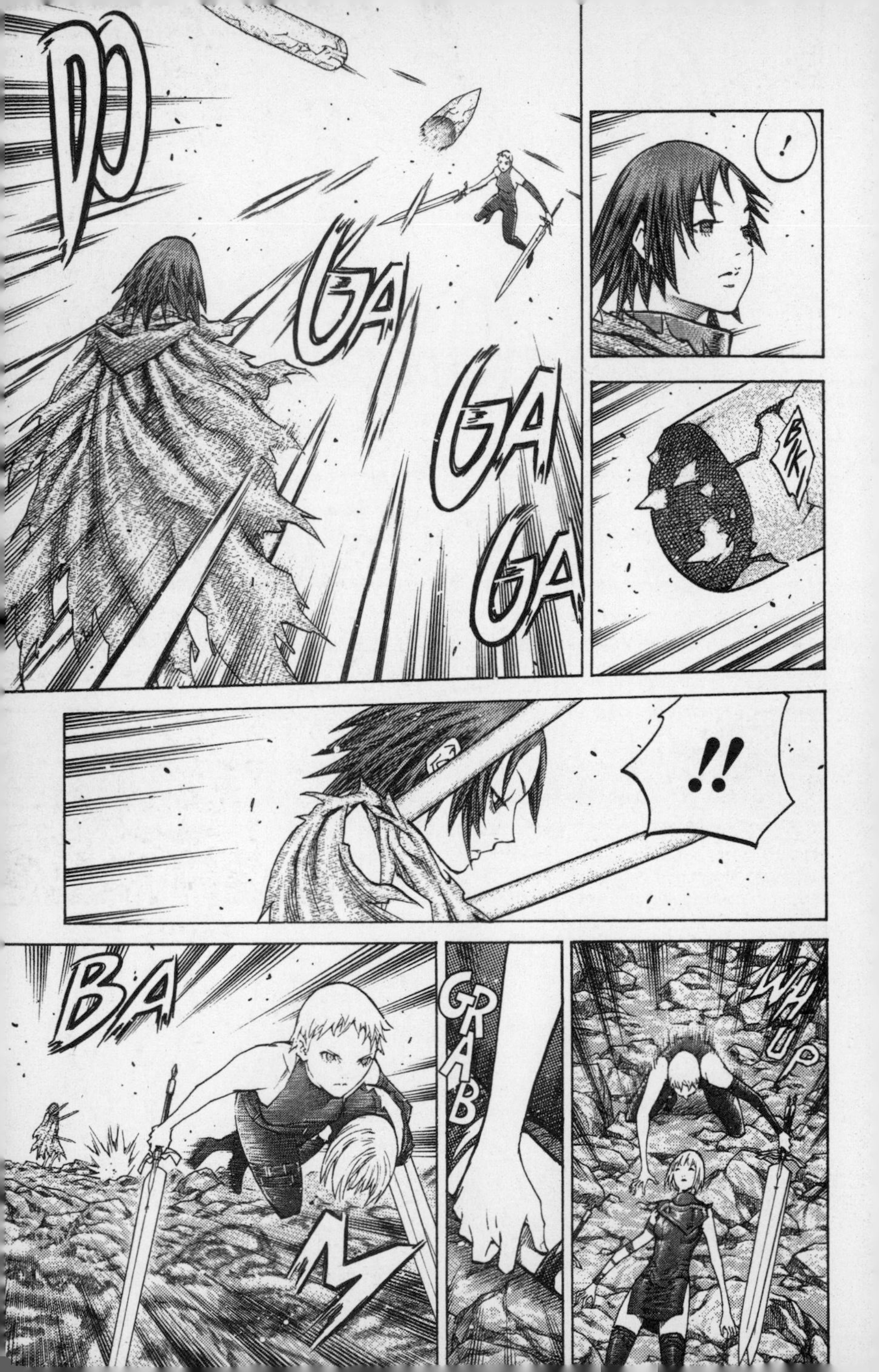
!
BIKI
DO
GA
GA
GA
!!
WHUP
GRAB
BA
M

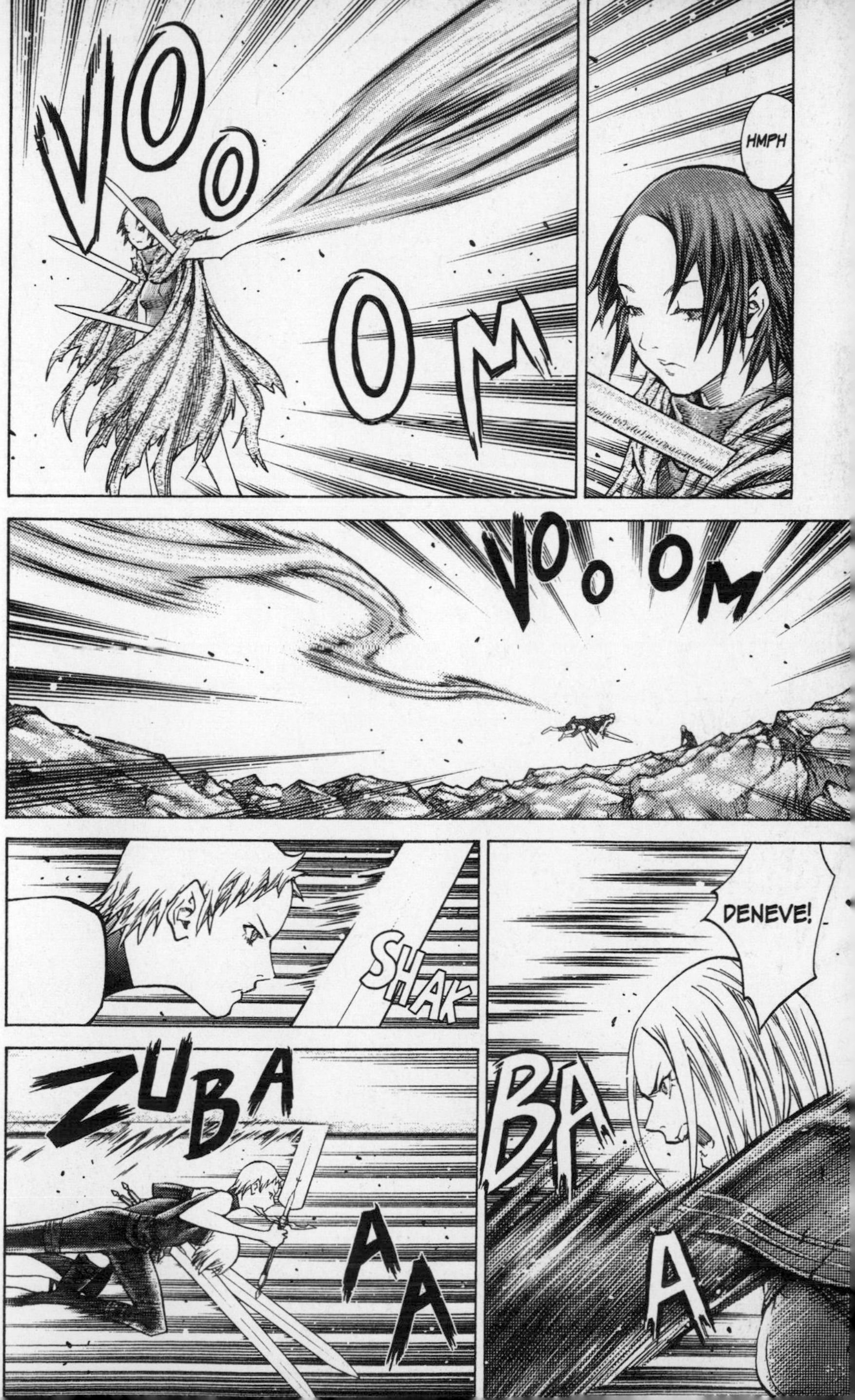
HMPH
VOOOOM
VOOOM
DENEVE!
SHAK
BAAA
ZUBAAA

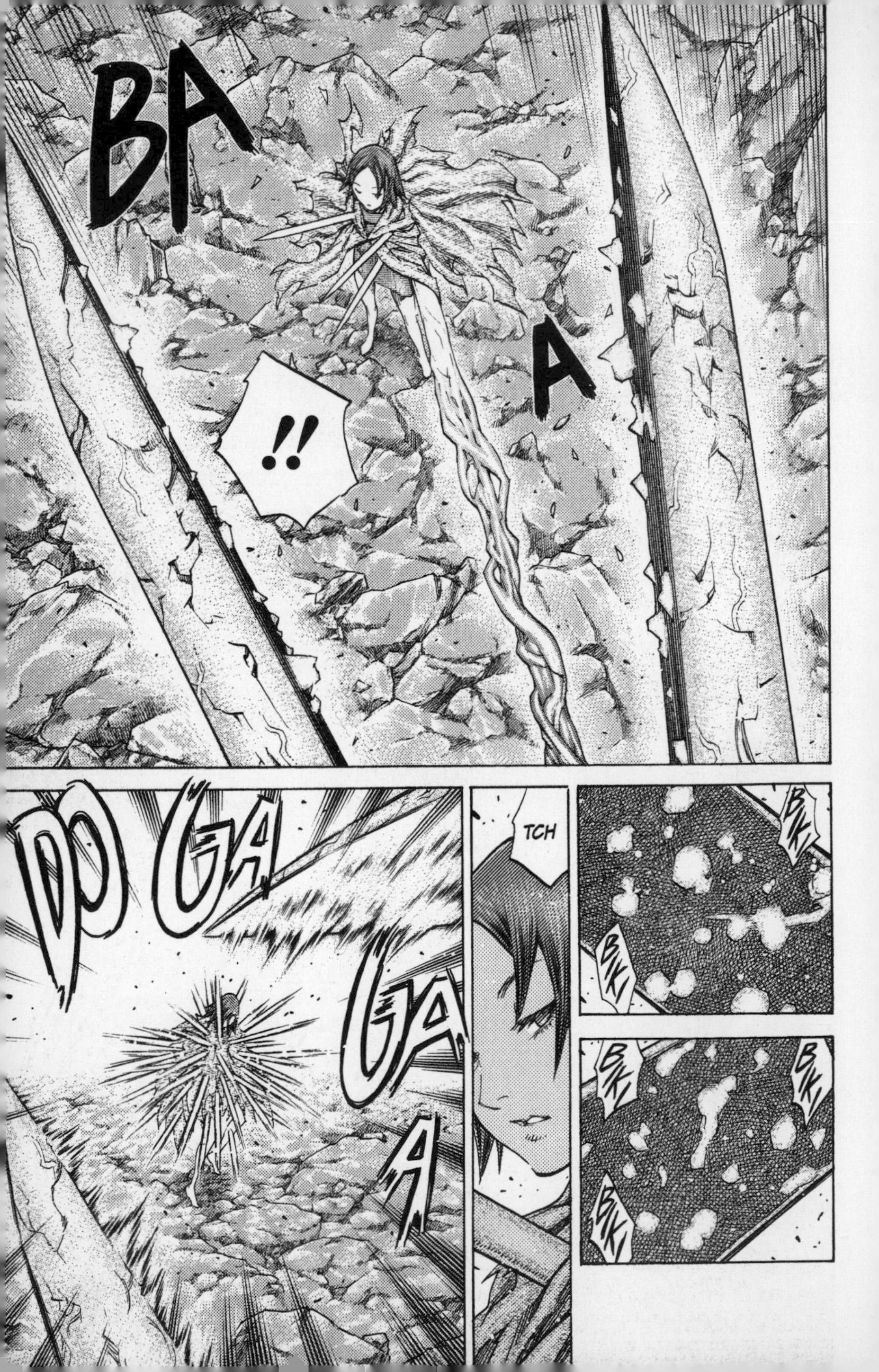
BA
A
!!
BIKI
BIKI
BIKI
BIKI
BIKI
TCH
DO GA
GA
A

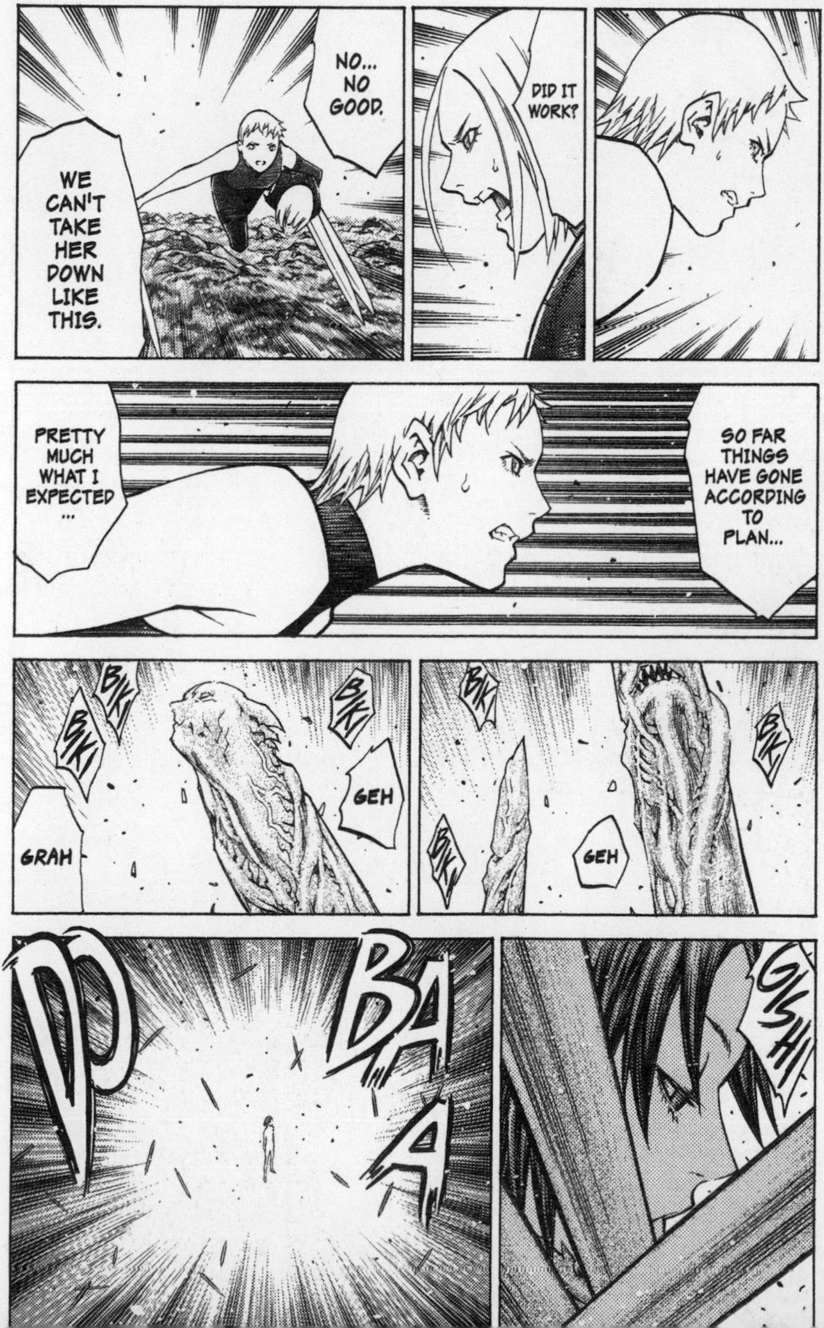
DID IT WORK?
NO... NO GOOD.
WE CAN'T TAKE HER DOWN LIKE THIS.
SO FAR THINGS HAVE GONE ACCORDING TO PLAN...
PRETTY MUCH WHAT I EXPECTED ...
BIKI
BIKI
GEH
BIKI
BIKI
GEH
BIKI
BIKI
GRAH
GISHI
DOBAA

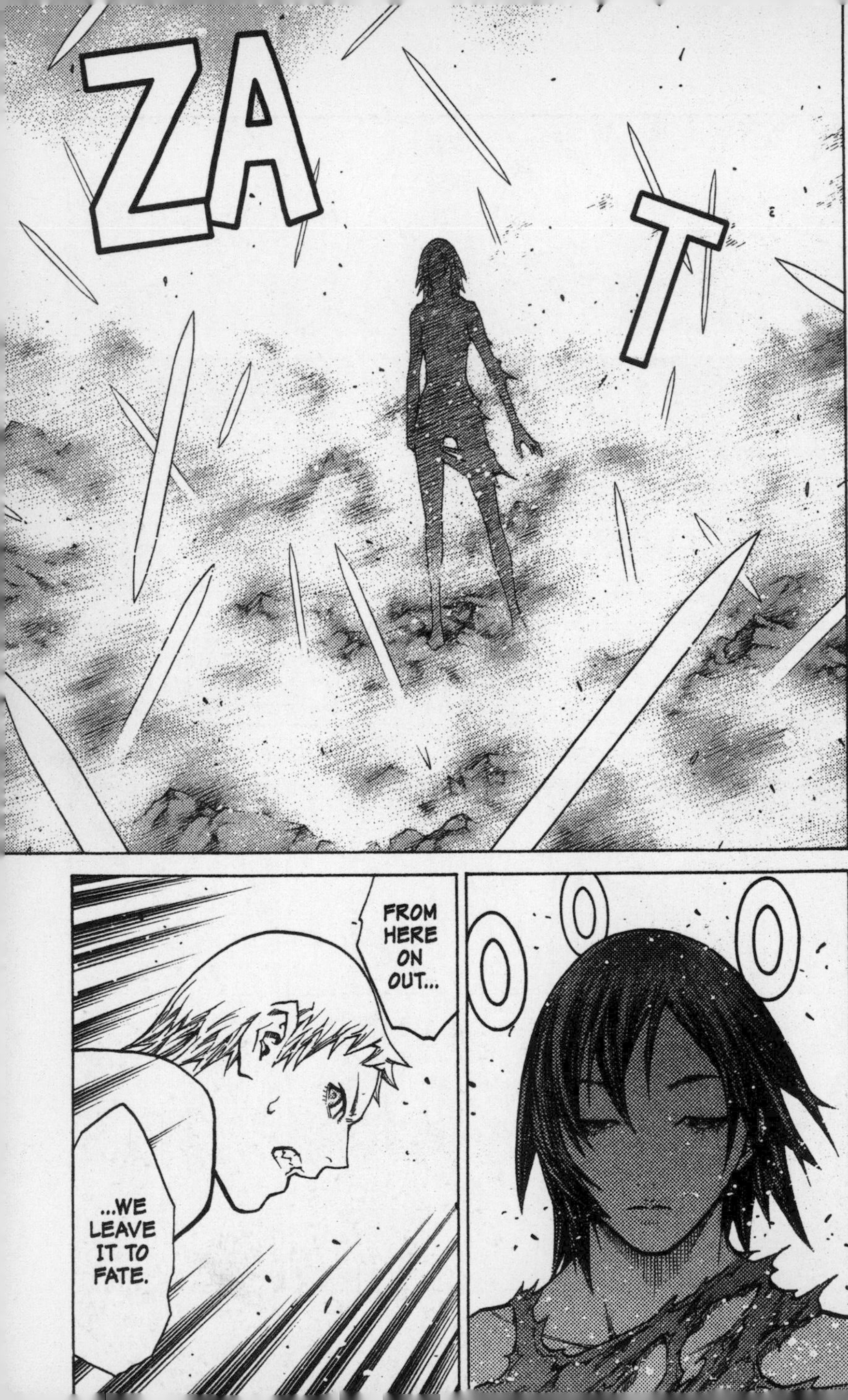
ZAT
FROM HERE ON OUT...
...WE LEAVE IT TO FATE.

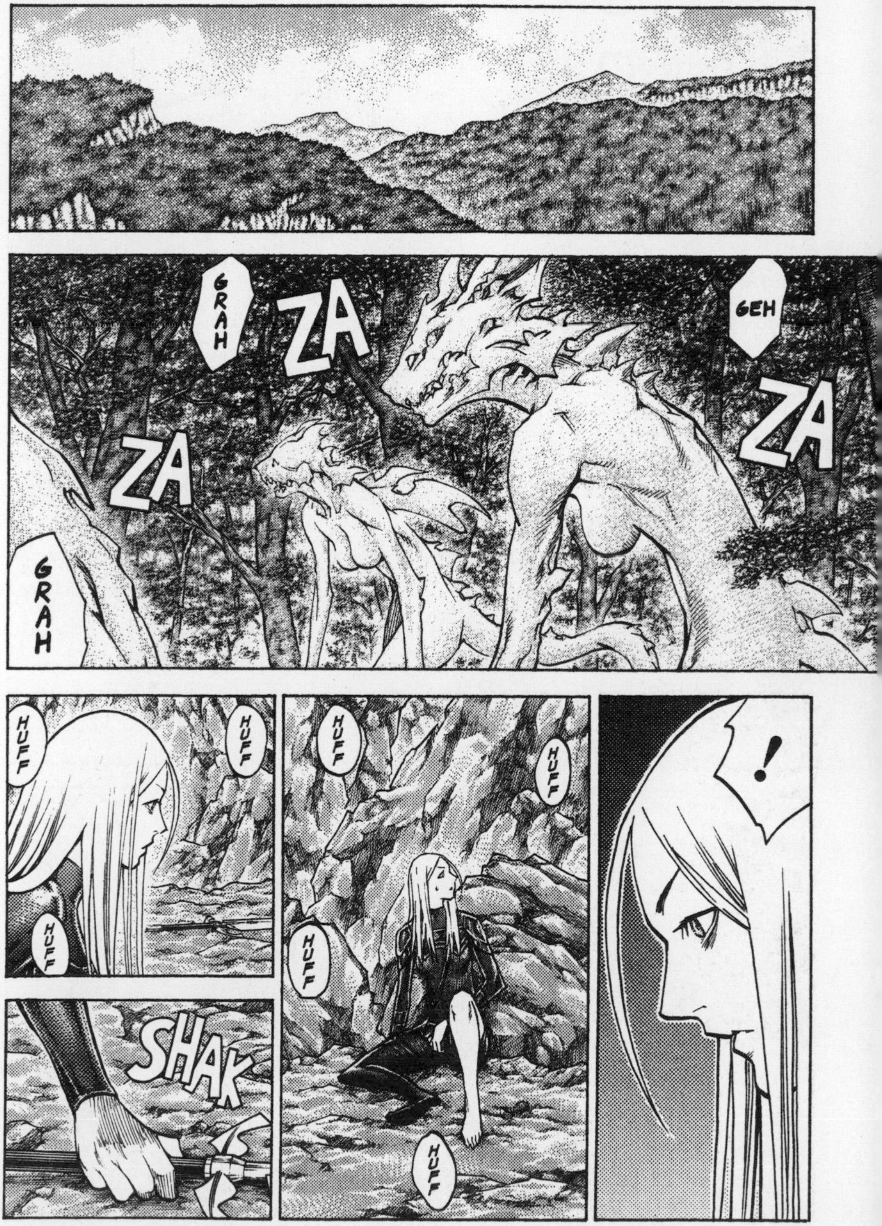
GEH
ZA
GRAH
ZA
ZA
GRAH
!
HUFF
HUFF
HUFF
HUFF
HUFF
HUFF
HUFF
SHAK

READ THIS WAY

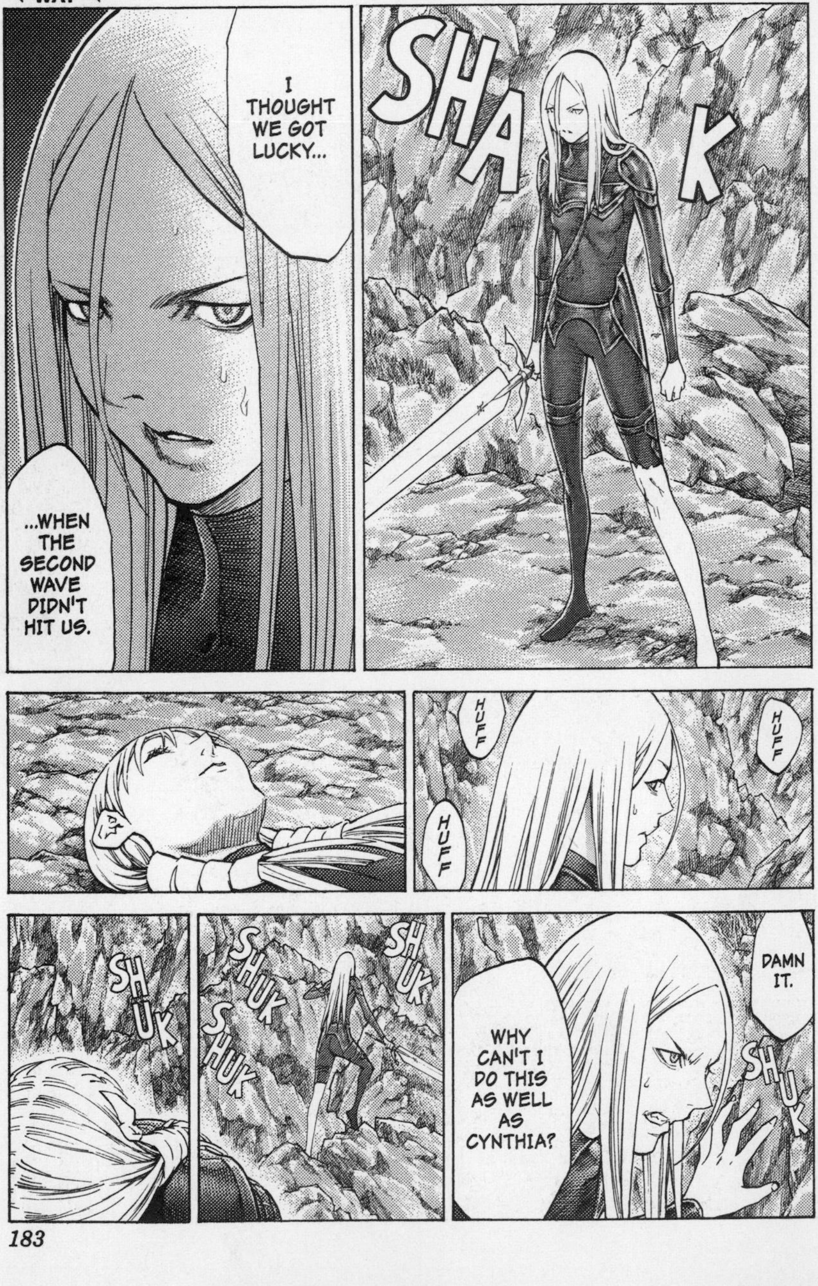
SHAK
I THOUGHT WE GOT LUCKY...
...WHEN THE SECOND WAVE DIDN'T HIT US.
HUFF
HUFF
HUFF
DAMN IT.
WHY CAN'T I DO THIS AS WELL AS CYNTHIA?
SHUK
SHUK
SHUK
SHUK
SHUK

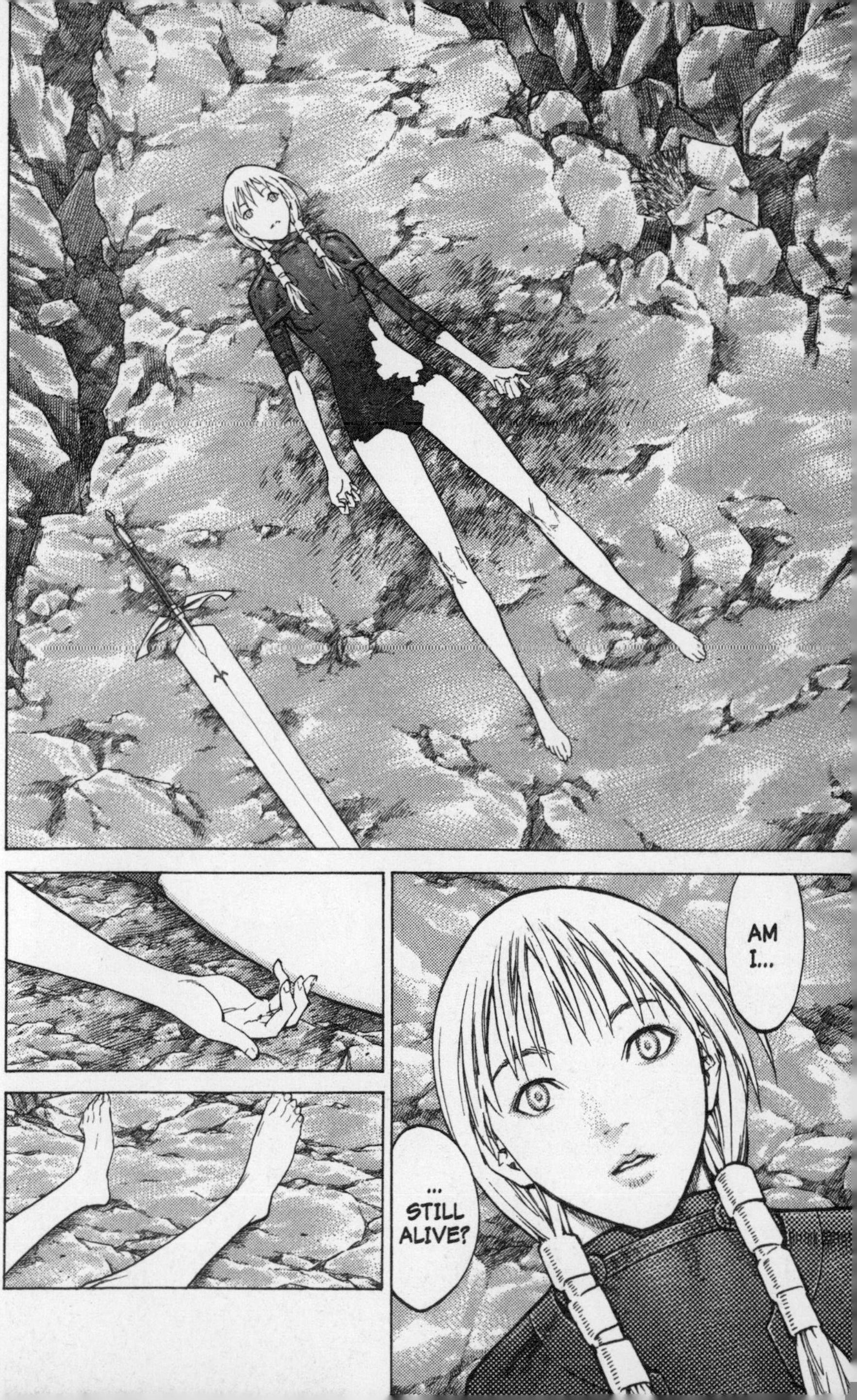
AM I...
... STILL ALIVE?

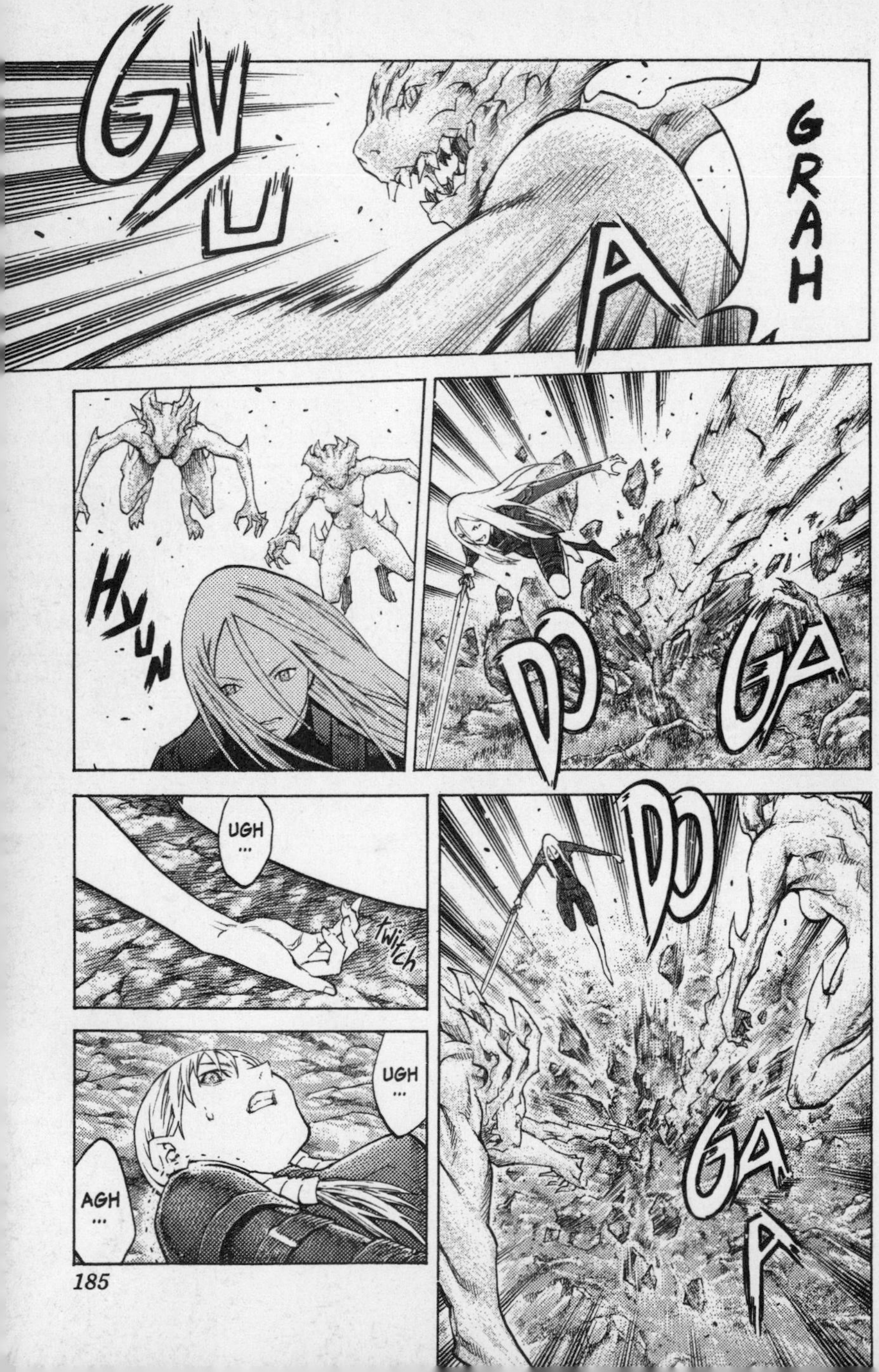
GYU
A
GRAH
DO
GA
HYUN
DO
DO
GA
A
UGH ...
twitch
UGH ...
AGH ...

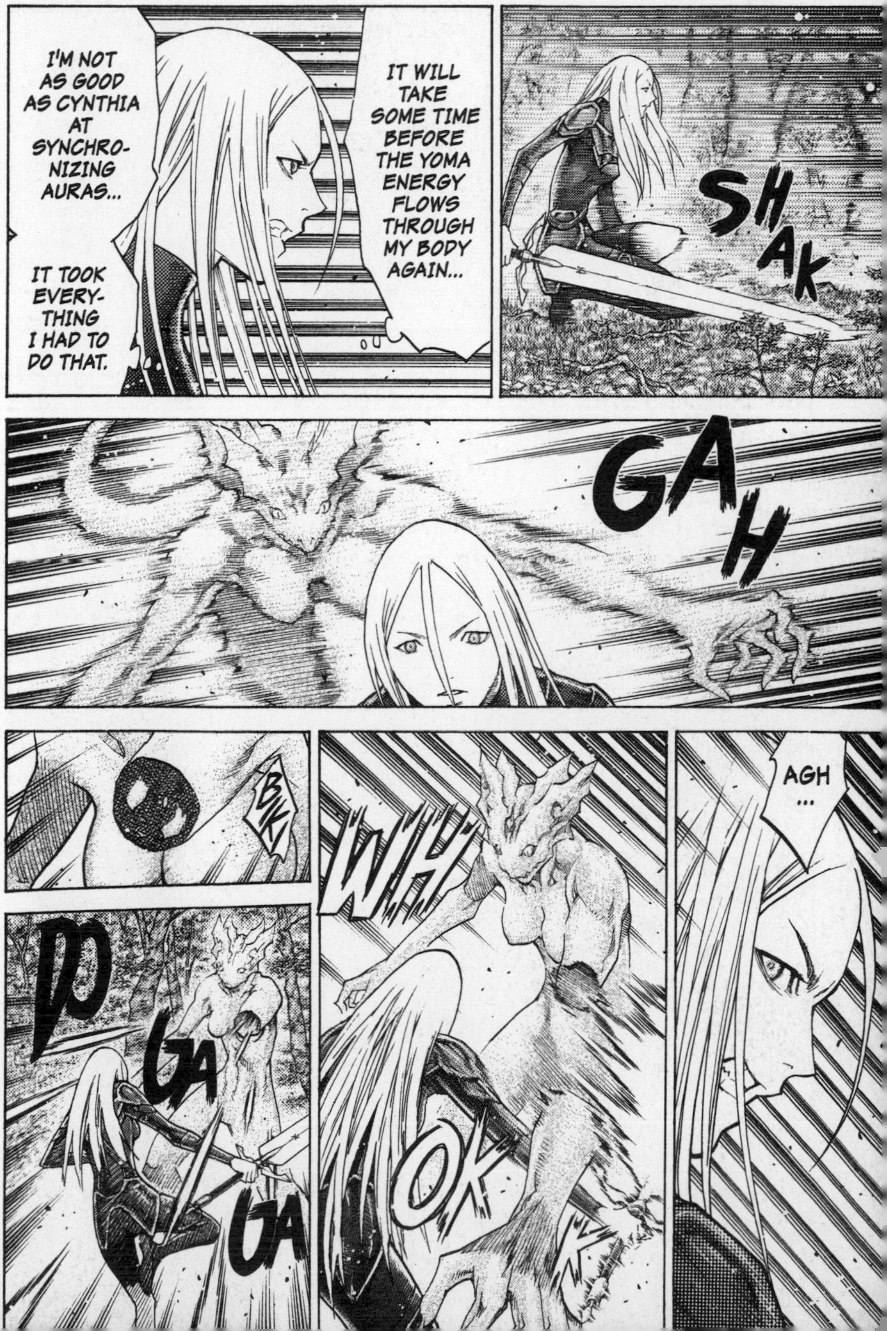
SHAK
IT WILL TAKE SOME TIME BEFORE THE YOMA ENERGY FLOWS THROUGH MY BODY AGAIN...
I'M NOT AS GOOD AS CYNTHIA AT SYNCHRO-NIZING AURAS...
IT TOOK EVERY-THING I HAD TO DO THAT.
GAH
AGH ...
WHA
OK
K
BIKI
DO
GA
GA

READ THIS WAY

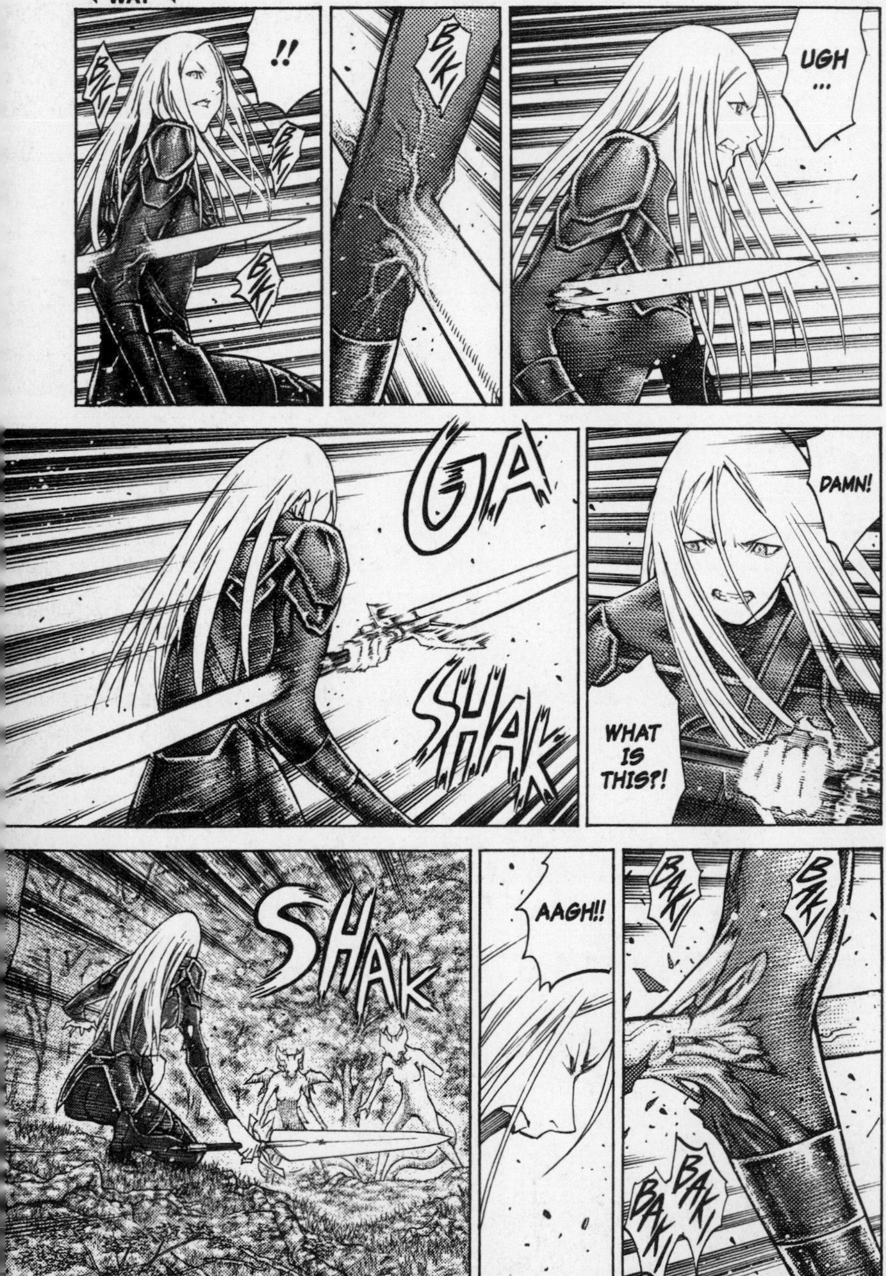
UGH ...
BIKI
!!
BIKI
BIKI
BIKI
DAMN!
WHAT IS THIS?!
GA
SHAK
BAKI
BAKI
BAKI BAKI
AAGH!!
SHAK

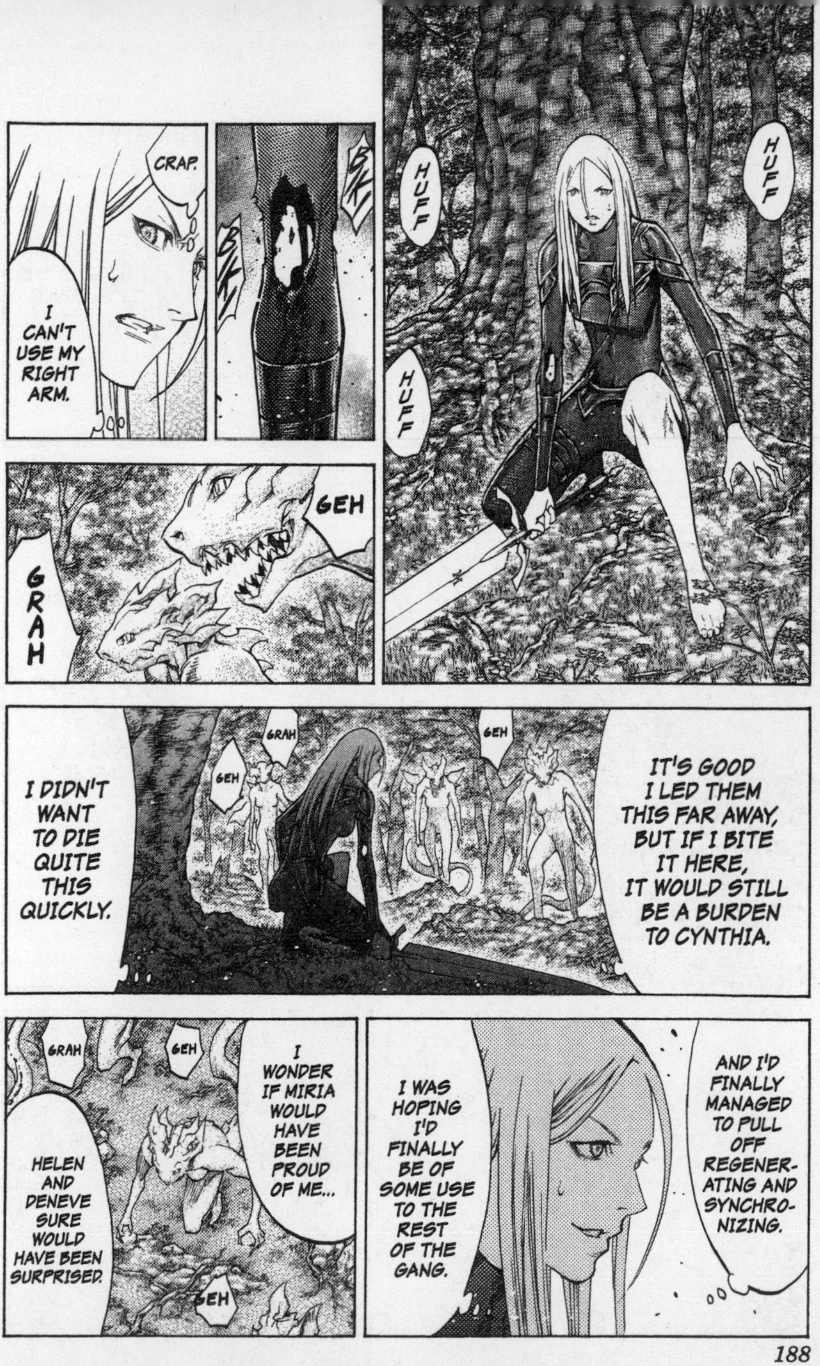
HUFF
HUFF
HUFF
BIKI
BIKI
CRAP.
I CAN'T USE MY RIGHT ARM.
GEH
GRAH
IT'S GOOD I LED THEM THIS FAR AWAY, BUT IF I BITE IT HERE, IT WOULD STILL BE A BURDEN TO CYNTHIA.
GEH
GRAH
GEH
I DIDN'T WANT TO DIE QUITE THIS QUICKLY.
AND I'D FINALLY MANAGED TO PULL OFF REGENERATING AND SYNCHRONIZING.
I WAS HOPING I'D FINALLY BE OF SOME USE TO THE REST OF THE GANG.
I WONDER IF MIRIA WOULD HAVE BEEN PROUD OF ME...
GEH
GRAH
HELEN AND DENEVE SURE WOULD HAVE BEEN SURPRISED.
GEH

READ THIS WAY

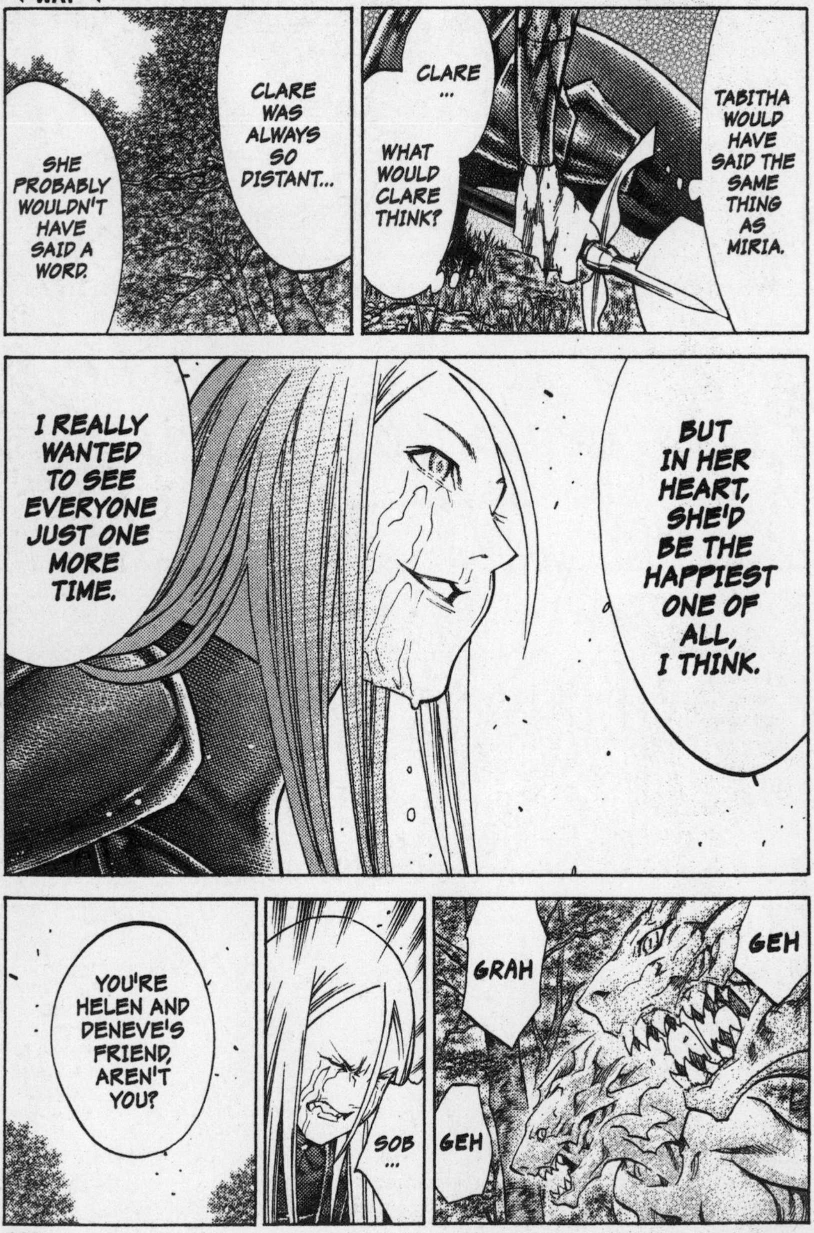
TABITHA WOULD HAVE SAID THE SAME THING AS MIRIA.
CLARE ... WHAT WOULD CLARE THINK?
CLARE WAS ALWAYS SO DISTANT...
SHE PROBABLY WOULDN'T HAVE SAID A WORD.
BUT IN HER HEART, SHE'D BE THE HAPPIEST ONE OF ALL, I THINK.
I REALLY WANTED TO SEE EVERYONE JUST ONE MORE TIME.
GEH
GRAH
GEH
SOB ...
YOU'RE HELEN AND DENEVE'S FRIEND, AREN'T YOU?

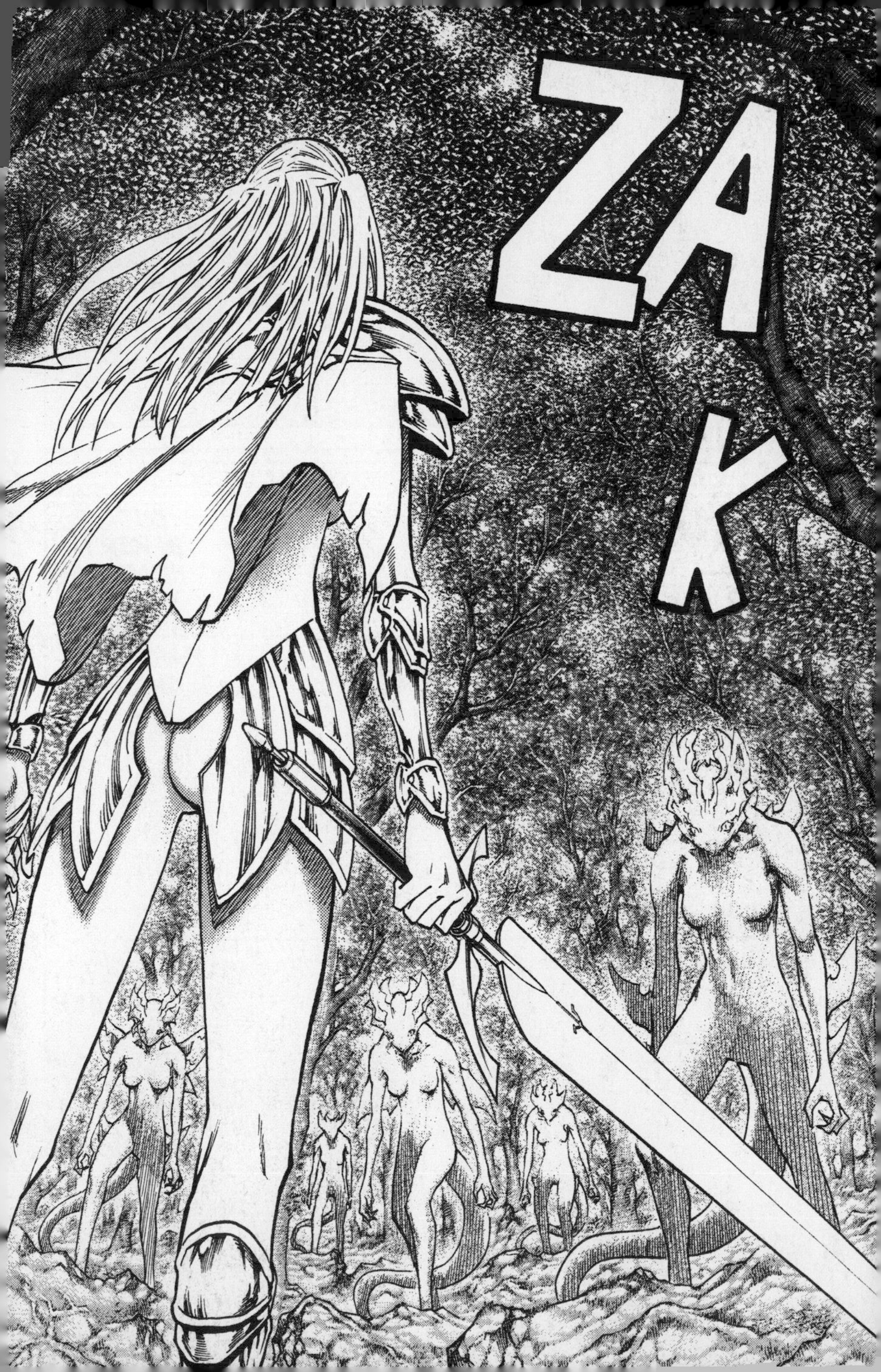
ZAK

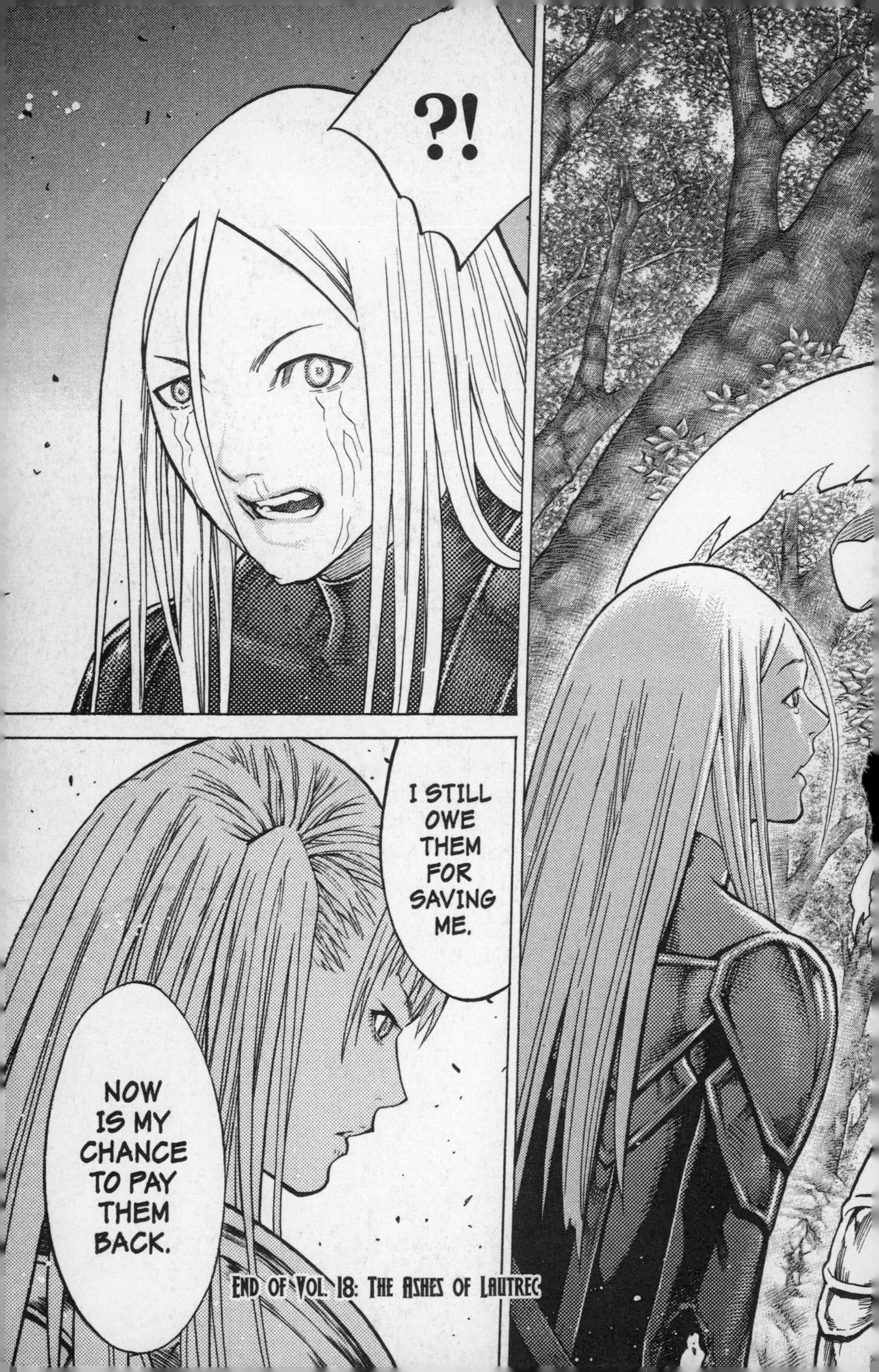
?!
I STILL OWE THEM FOR SAVING ME.
NOW IS MY CHANCE TO PAY THEM BACK.
END OF VOL. 18: THE ASHES OF LAUTREC

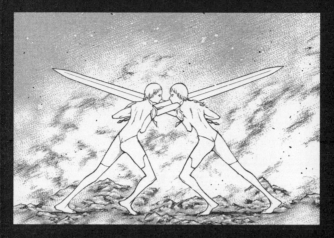

IN THE NEXT VOLUME

Priscilla relentlessly pursues Clare's destruction, while Deneve and Helen remain just as determined to protect her. But when the combined form of Luciela and Rafaela attacks, Clare and her cohorts are pulled into the twisting mass. Meanwhile, in Ribona, Miria heads east to destroy the Organization. She encounters Rubel and his "secret weapons": mysterious warrior twins who may be Alicia and Beth's successors, as well as the Organization's number 10—a deadly fighter who can read Miria's mind...

Available September 2011